Historical Dictionary
of
Mongolia

ASIAN HISTORICAL DICTIONARIES
Edited by Jon Woronoff

Historical Dictionary of Mongolia

ALAN J. K. SANDERS

Asian Historical Dictionaries, No. 19

The Scarecrow Press, Inc.
Lanham, Md., & London

SCARECROW PRESS, INC.

Published in the United States of America
by Scarecrow Press, Inc.
4720 Boston Way
Lanham, Maryland 20706

4 Pleydell Gardens, Folkestone
Kent CT20 2DN, England

British Cataloguing-in-Publication Information Available

Library of Congress Cataloging-in-Publication Data

Sanders, Alan J.K.
Historical dictionary of Mongolia / Alan J. K. Sanders.
p.   cm.—(Asian historical dictionaries : no. 19)
Contents: Includes bibliographical references.
1. Mongolia—History—Dictionaries.   2. Mongols—History—
Dictionaries.   I. Title.   II. Series.
DS798.5.S36   1996   951'.7'003—dc20   95-37202

ISBN 0-8108-3077-9 (cloth : alk.paper)

Tiinale

Contents

Editor's Foreword

Although no longer burdened by the adjective "outer," Mongolia still seems terribly remote to most of us. This is not just a matter of distance, for we hear much more about other places far away. The problem is more a lack of interest and lack of knowledge. The lack of interest should decrease now that Mongolia is truly independent and can tighten its relations with other parts of the world. The lack of knowledge is reduced by this latest historical dictionary, which is the first book to inform us about the momentous changes that have occurred over recent years and also uncover some of the facts hidden in the past while correcting some of the errors arising out of the paucity of information and relative abundance of misinformation during the communist period.

This *Historical Dictionary of Mongolia* focuses on the new Mongolia that is still emerging, providing entries on persons, institutions, places, and events that have become important in the 1990s. It also reviews the communist period, including similar entries, and sometimes takes a look further back, especially in the chronology. Helpfully, it even considers the Mongols beyond Mongolia's borders. Again, to enable scholars to know present-day Mongolia better, appendixes include the new constitution and investment law and lists of members of key government and other bodies. For those who want to find additional material, there is a comprehensive bibliography, which includes much of the unfortunately still limited literature on the modern Mongolian state.

There are not many authorities on modern Mongolia, but this book was written by one of the best, Alan J. K. Sanders. He has long covered Mongolia for the *Far Eastern Economic Review* and was also an editor with the British Broadcasting Corporation. In addition, he has written longer pieces for various yearbooks and journals as well as a book, *Mongolia—Politics, Economics and Society*. At present Sanders is Lecturer in Mongolian Studies at the School of Oriental and African Studies, University of London.

Jon Woronoff
Series Editor

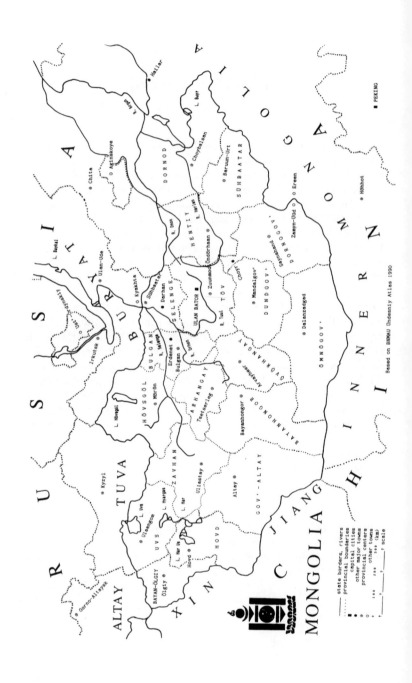

MONGOLIA

state borders, rivers
provincial boundaries
capital cities
other major towns
provincial centers
other towns
scale

Based on BNMAU Undseniy Atlas 1990

Conventions and Spellings

There is no universally agreed system for the spelling of Mongol names. Many have come down to us from the times of the Empire in several variants, derived from the languages of the sources cited (e.g., Persian or Chinese) and according to the methods of transliteration of the original or translation (e.g., English, German, or Russian). For transliterating Mongol into English alone there are several systems with wide variations (e.g., *x* may equal *sh* or *kh,* or not be used at all). For historical figures some writers adopt classical Mongol forms, where they can be established (although they may not be transliterated or even rendered consistently). Mostly I have opted for the spellings of historical persons and place-names that seem to be the widest accepted in the current literature: Genghis Khan, then, rather than Chinggis Khan, Chinges Han, or a host of other doubles. The variants of some names differ greatly, so in the Chronology, I have given those, too, together with modern Cyrillic spellings. The latter have also been used for the rather obscure figures of the period after the collapse of the Empire.

With the exception of some established forms (Ulan Bator, Bogd Khan), names from the modern period are also transliterated from Mongol Cyrillic, the script currently in widest use in Mongolia. Variants, either developed in Mongolia itself or influenced by transliteration from Russian, may be found in other literature about Mongolia. Although Mongolians and Russians now use the same alphabet, a system of Mongolian-Russian transliteration was developed in Moscow and the letters are not completely interchangeable. Moreover, the Mongolian Cyrillic alphabet has two more letters than the Russian alphabet, for the front vowel sounds ö and ü (see Transliteration). In the Dictionary, ö follows o and ü follows u in the otherwise English alphabetical order of entries and of letters within words.

The transliterations used for Mongol (and Russian) are based on the BGN/PCGN systems for maps. Although the Mongol and Russian conventions are different for book titles, generally I have followed the English practice of using capital initial letters for organizations and place-names. Chinese names are rendered in simplified Wade-Giles for older names and Pinyin for modern ones, except that Peking is treated as an established English form. Gazetteers of Inner Mongolia published in

China have their own system of spelling based on Pinyin. A brief glossary of geographical features is to be found at the beginning of the Administrative Gazetteer (Appendix 6).

Mongols have a given name (*ner*) and patronymic (*ovog*), but no inherited family name or shared surname acquired through marriage. They are therefore known by their given name (or a contraction or familiar form of it), which in full also functions as a surname in official documents, and so on. For example, Sühbaatar, perhaps familiarly called Sühee, is also Mr. Sühbaatar. The patronymic consists of the father's given name (in a few cases the mother's) plus the appropriate genitive case ending. In the Dictionary the given name appears first in the entry, followed by the patronymic and title if any. The patronymic or its initial letter helps to distinguish between one Sühbaatar and another: Damdiny (D.) Sühbaatar. The Buryat and Kalmyk Mongols have been obliged to adopt the Russian style of name, patronymic and inherited surname. Mongol given names are drawn from a great variety of sources, Mongolian, Tibetan, Russian, and Chinese, the names of deities, planets, or days of the week, flowers, desirable personal qualities and features, and so on, while superstitious parents may name their child "fierce dog" (Muunohoy) or "not this one" (Enebish).

Within entries, the English names of political parties are often reduced to initial letters (see Abbreviations). Mongolian abbreviations have been avoided, although they are commonplace in texts written in the Mongolian Cyrillic script, e.g., BNMAU—Bügd Nayramdah Mongol Ard Uls (MPR—Mongolian People's Republic). The equivalent in the classical Mongolian script is BüNaMoAU—Bügüde Nayiramdaqu Monggol Arad Ulus. True acronyms are rare; perhaps the best known is Montsame. Lists of Mongolian abbreviations may be found in Sanders, *People's Republic of Mongolia,* the JPRS *Abbreviations in the Mongolian Press,* and Hangin, *Modern Mongolian-English Dictionary.* Many of these are still in use, but a host of new abbreviations has appeared amid the political changes and transition to a market economy, ousting those from the communist vocabulary.

Where Mongol entries appear with alternative spellings in brackets, the latter reflect variants from other scripts or languages. For example, Tayj (taiji, t'ai-tzu): tayj is the Mongol Cyrillic spelling, taiji is derived from the classical Mongolian script, and t'ai-tzu is the Wade-Giles transcription of the Chinese equivalent. The spellings of Buriad (Buryad, Buryaad, Buryat) are derived from the Mongolian Cyrillic, a variant, the Buriad Cyrillic and English via Russian, respectively.

Dates are according to the Gregorian calendar, as supplied in source material. Where other calendars have been converted to this, however, a degree of imprecision may have been introduced; for example, by Russian use of the Julian calendar, or by the Chinese practice in recording dynasties (reigns beginning in the first half-year are dated from that year, whereas reigns beginning in the second half-year are dated from the following year). The dates of some events recorded in the Chronology are disputed because of the difficulty in establishing from the written evidence to which cycle a particular animal year belonged.

Abbreviations

CCP	Chinese Communist Party
CIS	Commonwealth of Independent States (association of former republics of the USSR, not including the Baltic states)
CMEA	Council for Mutual Economic Assistance
Comecon	See CMEA
CPSU	Communist Party of the Soviet Union
EU	European Union
GDR	German Democratic Republic (DDR, East Germany)
IAMS	International Association for Mongol Studies
IMF	International Monetary Fund
KGB	Soviet State Security Committee
KMT	Kuomintang (Guomindang), Chinese National Party
Komsomol	Soviet Communist Youth League
MBDP	Mongolian Believers' Democratic Party
MDA	Mongolian Democratic Association
MDP	Mongolian Democratic Party
MFLP	Mongolian Free Labor Party
MGH	Mongolian Great Hural
MGP	Mongolian Green Party
MIP	Mongolian Independence Party
MNDP	Mongolian National Democratic Party
MNPA	Mongolian New Progress Association
MNPP	Mongolian National Progress Party
Montsame	Mongolian Telegraph (News) Agency
MPP	Mongolian People's Party
MPR	Mongolian People's Republic
MPRA	Mongolian People's Revolutionary Army
MPRP	Mongolian People's Revolutionary Party
MRP	Mongolian Renewal Party
MRYL	Mongolian Revolutionary Youth League
MSDM	Mongolian Social Democratic Movement
MSDP	Mongolian Social Democratic Party
MUHFP	Mongolian United Herdsmen's and Farmers' Party
MUHP	Mongolian United Heritage Party

MUPOP	Mongolian United Private Owners' Party
NKVD	People's Commissariat for Internal Affairs (precursor of the KGB)
PGH	People's Great Hural
PLA	(Chinese) People's Liberation Army
PLC	(MPRP) Party Leadership Council
PRC	People's Republic of China
RSFSR	Russian Soviet Federative Socialist Republic
SLH	State Little Hural
TACIS	Technical Assistance to CIS Countries
TUC	Trade Union Congress
UK	United Kingdom
UN	United Nations
UP	(Mongolian) United Party
USSR	Union of Soviet Socialist Republics
WCP	World Congress of Peace

Transliteration

Names transliterated from the Mongolian Cyrillic alphabet are rendered in the Dictionary in accordance with the following table:

Transliteration	Mongolian Cyrillic	Variants	Transliteration	Mongolian Cyrillic	Variants
a	а		s	с	
b	б		sh	ш	
ch	ч	tch	t	т	
d	д		ts	ц	z
e	э		u	у	
f	ф		ü	ү	u, ue
g	г		v	в	w
h	х	kh, x	y (lone vowel)	ы	i
i	и		y (in diphthong)	й	i
j	ж	dzh, zh, dsh	ya	я	
k	к		ye	е	e
l	л		yo	ё	ë
m	м		yö (before ö)	е	
n	н		yu (before u)	ю	
o	о		yü (before ü)	ю	
ö	ө	o, oe	z	з	dz, ds
p	п		'(not initial)	ь	ĭ(omit)
r	р		"(not initial)	ъ	(omit)

Letters not used: q, w, x in English, and щ (shch) in Mongolian.

RUSSIA

Naushki
o Kyakhta
Sühbaatar
o Altanbulag
SELENGE
R. Selenge
ORHON
R. Orhon
Erdenet
Bulgan ⊕
Darhan
DARHAN-UUL
Selbi
o Sharyngol
BULGAN
Züünharaa
T Ö V
R. Onon
R. Tuul
ULAN BATOR
HENTIY
Zuunmod ⊕
o Nalayh
Baganuur o
Bagahangay
T Ö V
R. Herlen
Öndörhaan ⊕
GOV'SÜMBER
DUNDGOV'
Choyr
o Bor-Öndör
⊕ Mandalgov'
Ayrag
DORNOGOV'

MONGOLIA
central
zone
1994

Saynshand

Züünbayan o

C H I N A

state borders, rivers
...... provincial boundaries
⊞⊞⊞ railroads
⊕ provincial centers
o other towns
⁰ ⁵⁰ ¹⁰⁰ (km)
⌐_____⌐_____⌐ scale

Zamyn-Üüd
o Ereen

Chronology

alliance on the river Kalka (Don valley); Volga Bolgars also defeated. Genghis Khan set off back to Mongolia.

1225   Genghis Khan reached Tuul valley in Mongolia and prepared to resume campaigning against the Tangut (Xixia).

1227   Death of Jochi, ruler of the Kipchak Khanate (southern Russia). Genghis Khan captured the Tangut capital Xingqing (present-day Yingchuan, Ningxia). Genghis Khan died and was taken back to Mongolia for burial; Tolui became regent.

1229   Ögedei, Genghis Khan's third son, proclaimed second Great Khan [later known as Yuan Emperor Tai Zong] (-1241).

1231   Mongol troops invaded Korea.

1233   Death of Tolui, ruler of the "hearth" (Mongol heartland).

1234   General Muqali's defeat of Jürchen (Jin) and capture of Kaifeng.

1235   Ögedei Khan built walls of Mongol capital Karakorum (Qaraqorum, Harherem, Harhorin).

1236   Batu (Bat) Khan, Jochi's son, began campaign in Russia.

1239   Mongol troops conquered Crimea.

1240   Godan, Ögedei's son, ordered invasion of Tibet. Fall of Kiev to Mongol forces.

1241   Great Khan Ögedei died, regency by Ögedei's widow Töregene (Dörgönö or Naymaljin). German and Polish knights defeated at Battle of Liegnitz. Defeat of Hungarian King Andrew's army.

1242   Death of Chaghatai, ruler of the Chaghatai Khanate (Khitan lands).

1243   Batu Khan's Kipchak Khanate styled the Golden Horde.

1246   Despite Batu Khan's opposition, Güyük (Güyug), Ögedei's eldest son (b. 1207), proclaimed third Great Khan [later known as Yuan Emperor Ding Zong] (-1248). Fr. John of Plano Carpini, Pope Innocent IV's envoy, reached Mongolia.

1248   Great Khan Güyük died, regency by Güyük's widow Oghul Ghaimish (Ogul Gaymish hatan).

1251   With Batu Khan's support, Möngke (Mönh), Tolui's eldest son (b. 1209), proclaimed fourth Great Khan [later known as Yuan Emperor Xian Zong] (-1258).

1252   Conquest of Southern Song empire begun.

1253   Hülegü (Hulgu), Tolui's son (b. 1217), began conquest of Iran.

1254   Frère Guillaume of Rubrouck, Franciscan envoy of King Louis IX of France, arrived in Karakorum.

1255   Batu Khan of the Golden Horde died. Sartaq (Sartag), Batu Khan's son, became Khan of the Golden Horde.

1256   Hülegü captured castles of the Assassins.

1257   Mongol troops invaded Annam (Vietnam). Ulaghchi, Sartaq's son, became Khan of the Golden Horde. Berke (Berh), Batu

Khan's brother (b. 1206), became Khan of the Golden Horde (1267); Horde's conversion to Islam begun.

1258 Hülegü entered Baghdad. Great Khan Möngke died.

1260 Kublai (Hubilay), Tolui's son (b. 1215), proclaimed Great Khan [reign title Zhong Tong] at Kaiping (-1294). Ariq-böke (Arig-böh), Kublai's brother, proclaimed Great Khan at Karakorum: civil war ensued. Hülegü invaded Syria.

1263 Hülegü became Ilkhan (Khan of Iran) (-1265). Kaiping renamed Shangdu (upper capital, near present-day Duolun).

1264 Kublai's victory over Ariq-böke confirmed him fifth Great Khan (Zhi Yuan), also called Yuan Emperor Shi Zu. Capital moved to Yanjing (Peking), renamed Zhongdu (middle capital).

1265 Ilkhan Hülegü died. Abaqa (Abaga), Hülegü's son (b. 1234), became Ilkhan (-1282).

1266 Berke Khan of the Golden Horde died.

1267 Kublai moved to new Mongol capital at Zhongdu (Peking). Möngke Temür (Mönhtömör), Batu Khan's grandson, became Khan of the Golden Horde; return to shamanism followed.

1269 Tibetan-based "square script" devised by 'Phags-pa Lama (Pagva lam Lodoyjaltsan, 1235-80), Kublai's *tishri* (preceptor), put into official use.

1272 Khan's capital (Haanbalgasan) Zhongdu renamed Dadu (great capital).

1274 Kublai Khan's first attempt to invade Japan.

1275 Marco Polo arrived in Shangdu, also called Khan Baliq ("Cambaluc").

1276 Mongols captured Emperor Gong Di at Song capital, Lin'an (Hangzhou).

1277 Mongol troops invaded Burma.

1279 Final defeat of Song in Guangdong.

1280 Töde Möngke, Mönke Temür's brother, became Khan of the Golden Horde (-1287). New Mongol invasion of Burma.

1281 Kublai Khan's second attempt to invade Japan: Mongol fleet dispersed by typhoon (called by Japanese *kamikaze*, "divine wind").

1282 Ilkhan Abaqa died. Tegüder Ahmad, Abaqa's brother, became Ilkhan. Mongol troops invaded Java.

1284 Arghun (Argun), Abaqa's son, became Ilkhan (-1291); attempt to establish Buddhism. Mongols invaded Annam again.

1287 Töle-Buqa, Töde Möngke's nephew, became Khan of Golden Horde (-1290).

1288 Mongol troops invaded India.

1289 Ilkhan Arghun wrote to King Phillip of France.

1290 Ilkhan Arghun wrote to Pope Nicholas IV.

1291 Geikhatu (Gayhatu), Arghun's brother, became Ilkhan (-1295).

Toqta, Möngke Temür's son, became Khan of the Golden Horde (-1312).

1292   Second Mongol invasion of Java.

1294   Kublai, Great Khan and Yuan Khan, died. Temür Öljeitü (Tömör Ölziyt Khan, Timur), son of Kublai's third son Chingem (b. 1265), became Yuan Khan (Emperor Cheng Zong) (Yuan Zhen 1295-96, Da De 1297-1307).

1295   Ghazan (Gazan) (1271-1304) became Ilkhan; converted to Sunni Islam.

1302   Ilkhan Ghazan wrote to Pope Boniface.

1304   Death of Ilkhan Ghazan. Öljeitü (Ölziyt), Ghazan's brother, became Ilkhan; adopted Shi'ism.

1305   Ilkhan Öljeitü wrote to King Phillip of France.

1307   Yuan Khan Temür Öljeitü died. Khaissan (Hülüg, Haysan Hüleg, Hai-shan), Chingem's son Darmabal's son (b. 1281), became Yuan Khan (Emperor Wu Zong) (Zhi Da) (-1311).

1311   Yuan Khan Khaissan killed. Ayurbarwada (Ayuurbarvada Buyant, Ayurbarwada, Ayuurbold, Ayuurbalbad, Ayurbadrabal), Khaissan's brother (b. 1285), became Yuan Khan (Emperor Ren Zong) (Huang Qing 1312-13, Yan Shi 1314-20).

1313   Özbeg, Möngke Temür's grandson, became Khan of the Golden Horde; reversion to Islam.

1316   Abu Sa'id (a Sunni) succeeded Öljeitü as Ilkhan.

1320   Yuan Khan Ayurbarwada died. Shidebela (Shidubala, Gegeen Khan, Shadbal, Shoodbal) (1303-23), son of Ayurbarwada, became Yuan Khan (Emperor Ying Zong) (Zhi Zhi).

1323   Yuan Khan Shidebela killed. Yesün Temür (Yesöntömör, Esentömör) (1293-1328), son of Chingem's brother Gamals's second son, became Yuan Khan (Emperor Tai Ding Di).

1328   Yuan Khan Yesün Temür died. Asuchibu (Ashidhev, Esügeva), Yesün Temür's son (b. 1320), became Yuan Khan (Zhi He) but was overthrown. Hüslen (Hüsele Hutagt, Asugbal, Aragibal) (1300-29), Khaissan's eldest son, became Yuan Khan (Emperor Tian Shun Di) but died. Toq Temür (Tögstömör Zayaat, Tugtömör, Toq Temür, Tugtemur) (1304-32), Khaissan's second son, became Yuan Khan (Emperor Wen Zong) (Tian Li 1329-30).

1329   Qoshila (Hooshal), Toq Temür's brother, became Yuan Khan (Emperor Ming Zong). Toq Temür became Yuan Khan again (Tian Li, Zhi Shun 1330-32).

1332   Yuan Khan Toq Temür died. Renchinbal (Renqinbar) (1325-32), Hüslen's son, became Yuan Khan (Emperor Ning Zong) at age seven but was killed a month or so later.

1333   Toghon Temür (Togoontömör Uhaant, Togontemur) (1320-70),

Renchinbal's brother, became Yuan Khan (Emperor Shun Di) (Yuan Tong 1333-34, Zhi Yuan 1335-40, Zhi Zheng 1341-68).

1335 Abu Sa'id, last Ilkhan of Hülegü's line, died.

1342 Pope's envoy John received by Togoontömör at Shangdu.

1346 Black death among Mongol forces in Crimea spread to Europe.

1355 Red Scarves, anti-Yuan rebels, set up "new Song dynasty" in Anhui.

1360 Tamerlane (Tömör Khan) (b. 1336) came to power in Samarkand; conquest of Iran and Mesopotamia.

1368 Ming dynasty founded by Zhu Yuanzhang, Emperor Tai Zu (Hong Wu) in Yingtian (Nanjing); Ming troops drove Mongols from Dadu, ending Yuan dynasty; Toghon Temür Khan fled to Yingchang, Inner Mongolia.

1370 Last Yuan Khan Toghon Temür died in Yingchang. Ayuushridar (Bilegt Khan), Toghon Temür's eldest son (b. 1338), enthroned Khan of Mongolia in Karakorum.

1376 Tokhtamish united the Golden Horde (-1405).

1378 Ayuushridar Khan died. Tögös Temür (Tögstömör), Ayuushridar's brother (- b. 1342), became Khan of Mongolia (-1388).

1380 Mamay's Golden Horde beaten at Battle of Kulikovo by Dmitriy (named Dmitriy Donskoy in honor of the victory). Chinese troops destroyed Karakorum.

1388 Tögös Temür (Usgal, "The Calm") Khan murdered. Tamerlane conquered Khwarazm. Enh Zorigt, Tögös Temür's eldest son (b. 1359), became Khan of Mongolia.

1391 First Dalai Lama (title accorded posthumously) Gedun Truppa (Gendündüv) born (-1474).

1392 Enh Zorigt Khan died. Elbeg, Enh Zorigt's brother (b. 1361), became Khan of Mongolia.

1399 Reign of Ming Emperor Hui Di (Jian Wen) began (-1402). Elbeg (Nigüülsegch, "The Merciful") Khan killed.

1400 Güntömör, Elbeg's eldest son (b. 1377), became Khan of Mongolia.

1402 Güntömör Khan killed. Ügch Hashha became Khan of Mongolia. Death of Ming Emperor Hui Di. Reign of Ming Emperor Cheng Zu (Yong Le) began (-1424).

1403 Ügch Hashha Khan killed. Ölziytömör, Güntömör's brother (b. 1377), became Khan of Mongolia.

1406 Tamerlane died in Otrar campaigning against the Ming.

1409 Oirat (Oyrd) princes attacked China.

1411 Ölziytömör Khan killed. Buyanshir, Güntömör's brother, became Khan of Mongolia.

1412 Oirats killed Buyanshir and made Delbeg, Ölziytömör's son (b. 1395), Khan of Mongolia.

1414   War between Oirats under Mahamud and Eastern Mongols under Arugtay taysh, Buyanshir's minister.
1415   Dalai Lama Gedun Truppa became disciple of Tsongkhapa Lozang Drakpa (Zonhava Luvsandagva), founder of Ge-lug-pa (Yellow Hat) sect of Tibetan Buddhism (1357-1419). Delbeg Khan died. Eseh became Khan (-1425); Mahamud and Arugtay fought for succession.
1418   Mahamud died; Togoon taysh, Mahamud's son, made peace with Arugtay.
1424   Death of Ming Emperor Cheng Zu. Reign of Ming Emperor Ren Zong (Hong Xi) began (-1425).
1425   Death of Ming Empeor Ren Zong. Reign of Ming Emperor Xuan Zong (Xuan De) began (-1435). Death of Eseh Khan.
1426   Eastern Mongols made Ajay (b. 1400) Khan of Mongolia (-1438).
1434   Arugtay killed by Oirat Togoon taysh (-1440). Oirat Daysun Khan ruled Mongolia.
1435   Death of Ming Emperor Xuan Zong. Reign of Ming Emperor Ying Zong (Zheng Tong) aged nine began (-1449).
1438   Ajay Khan killed by Togoon taysh.
1439   Togtoo Buh (Daysun), Ajay's son (b. 1422), became Khan of Mongolia.
1440   Esen Taysh, Togoon's son (b. 1407), became minister of Mongolia.
1449   Ming Emperor Ying Zong captured by Esen Taysh. Reign of Ming Emperor Jing Di (Jing Tai) began (-1457).
1450   Treaty between Mongols and Ming gave temporary peace and trade.
1451   Togtoo Buh Khan murdered by Esen Taysh. Agvarjin Jonon, Ajay's son (b. 1423), became Khan of Mongolia but was killed.
1453   Esen Taysh proclaimed himself Khan of Mongolia.
1454   Esen Taysh killed. Merküs (Mergürges, Mergen Chingis), Daysun's second son (b. 1446), became Khan of Mongolia.
1457   Death of Ming Emperor Jing Di. Ying Zong (Tian Shun) became Ming Emperor again (-1464).
1464   Death of Ming Emperor Ying Zong. Reign of Ming Emperor Xian Zong (Cheng Hua) began (-1487).
1465   Merküs Khan killed. Molon, Merküs's brother (b. 1437), became Khan of Mongolia.
1466   Molon Khan killed.
1468   Bayanmönh Jonon became Khan of Mongolia (-1472).
1472   Death of Bayanmönh Khan. Manduul, Ajay's son (b. 1425), became Khan of Mongolia (-1479).
1474   First Dalai Lama Gedun Truppa died.

1475   2nd Dalai Lama (title accorded posthumously) Gedun Gyatso (Gendünjamts) born in Tibet (-1542).

1479   Manduul Khan died.

1480   Batmönh, Bayanmönh's son (b. 1460), became Dayan Khan of Mongolia (-1517).

1487   Death of Ming Emperor Xian Zong. Reign of Ming Emperor Xiao Zong (Hong Zhi) began (-1505).

1505   Death of Ming Emperor Xiao Zong. Reign of Ming Emperor Wu Zong (Zheng De) began (-1521).

1517   Death of Batmönh Dayan Khan. Bars Bolod, Batmönh's son (b. 1487), became Sayn Alag Khan of Mongolia.

1519   Bars Bolod Sayn Alag Khan died.

1520   Bod' Alag, son of Batmönh's son Törbolod (b. 1498), became Khan of Mongolia (-1547).

1521   Death of Ming Emperor Wu Zong. Reign of Ming Emperor Shi Zong (Jia Jing) began (-1567).

1542   2nd Dalai Lama Gedun Gyatso died.

1543   3rd Dalai Lama (title accorded in 1578) Sonam Gyatso (Sodnomjamts) born near Lhasa (-1588).

1547   Ivan IV "The Terrible" became Tsar of Russia (-1584). Bod' Alag Khan died.

1548   Daraysun Güden, Bod' Alag's son (b. 1507), became Khan of Mongolia (-1557). Altan Khan of the Tümed (Eastern Mongols) marched on Peking.

1551   Altan Khan and the Ming agreed on peace and border trade.

1552   Altan Khan of the Tümed fought the Four Oirat tribes.

1554   Altan Khan founded Höhhot (Huhehot) in Tsahar.

1557   Daraysun Güden Khan died.

1558   Tümen Zasagt Khan, Daraysun's son (b. 1539), ruled Mongolia (-1592).

1559   Altan Khan of the Tümed fought Kokonor (Höhnuur, Qinghai) Mongols.

1567   Death of Ming Emperor Shi Zong. Reign of Ming Emperor Mu Zong (Long Qing) began (-1572).

1571   Altan Khan of the Tümed established relations with the Ming.

1572   Death of Ming Emperor Mu Zong. Reign of Ming Emperor Shen Zong (Wan Li) began (-1620).

1578   Altan Khan of the Tümed met Tibetan leader Sonam Gyatso (Sodnomjamts) at Höhhot and was converted to Buddhism; Sonam Gyatso given title "Dalai Lama," and Altan "Religious King, Brahma of the Gods." Avtay Khan of the Khalkha (b. 1554) given title "Ochiray Khan."

1582   Cossack Yermak defeated Kuchum Khan and seized Siberian capital Isker. Altan Khan of the Tümed died.

1583   Rise of Nüzhen (Manchu) leader Nurhachi of Aisin Gioro clan.
1586   Erdene Zuu monastery founded by Avtay. Avtay Sayn Khan died.
1587   Siberian town of Tobolsk founded.
1588   3rd Dalai Lama Sonam Gyatso died.
1589   4th Dalai Lama Yonten Gyatso (Iondanjamts), great-grandson of Altan Khan, born in Mongolia (-1617).
1592   Tümen Zasagt Khan died. Buyan Setsen Khan, Tümen Khan's son (b. 1555), became Khan of Mongolia (-1603).
1601   Yonten Gyatso sent to Tibet, enthroned as 4th Dalai Lama; his teacher Lozang Chosgyan was the first Panchen Lama ("Great Scholar").
1603   Buyan Setsen Khan died.
1604   Ligden, son of Buyan Setsen Khan's son Mangus Tayj (b. 1592), became Khan of Mongolia (-1634).
1608   Some Oirat (Western Mongol) tribes negotiated entry into Russia and migrated to the Volga. Altan Khan of the Khalkha (Hotgoyd Sholoy Hungtayj) (1567-1627) received an envoy from Russia.
1613   Russian Emperor Mikhail Romanov's reign began (-1645).
1615   Oirat princes adopted Buddhism.
1616   Manchu leader Nurhachi (1559-1626) proclaimed himself Great Khan of the Great Jin (Tengeriyn Süldet) and established his capital at Hetuala (Xinbin, Liaoning). Altan Khan established relations with Russia.
1617   4th Dalai Lama Yonten Gyatso died. 5th Dalai Lama Ngawang Lozang Gyatso (Luvsanjamts) born at Chongyas (-1682).
1618   Nurhachi captured Fushun. Mongolia sent an envoy to Russia.
1619   Nurhachi defeated Ming army at Sarhu.
1620   Death of Ming Emperor Shen Zong. Reign of Ming Emperor Guang Zong (Tai Chang) began (-1620). Death of Ming Emperor Guang Zong. Reign of Ming Emperor Xi Zong (Tian Qi) began (-1627).
1624   Manchus subjugated Eastern Mongols—Horchin, Jalayd, Gorlos.
1625   Nurhachi moved his capital to Shenyang.
1627   Abakhay (1592-1643) became Khan of the Manchus (Deed Eredemt). Death of Ming Emperor Xi Zong. Reign of Ming Emperor Si Zong (Chong Zhen) began (-1644). Siberian town of Krasnoyarsk founded.
1630   Migrating Oirats reached the Volga.
1632   Tsahars defeated by the Manchu.
1634   Ligden Hutag Khan died. Erhhongor became Khan of the Mongols (-1635).

1635	Baatar Hungtayj became Khan of the Oirats and established Jungarian (Züüngar) Khanate in Western Mongolia.
1636	Manchu dynasty named Qing by Abakhay Khan. West Mongolian Torguud (Torguts) nomadized to the Volga. Inner Mongolia came under Manchu administration.
1639	Zanabazar (b. 1635) proclaimed leader of Mongolian Buddhists with the title Bogd Gegeen (-1723); his "palace," Örgöö (Ih Hüree, now Ulan Bator), founded.
1640	Meeting at Tarvagatay, the Oirat princes proclaimed the "Mongol Oirat Constitution."
1642	Manchu forces cross the Great Wall.
1643	Reign of Qing Emperor Shun Zhi (Eebeer Zasagch) began (-1661). Jungarian envoys sent to Russia.
1644	Suicide of Ming Emperor Chong Zhen in Peking. Peasant leader Li Zicheng, "King of Great Shun," reached Peking but retreated before Qing advance.
1645	Qing army entered Nanjing.
1648	Zayapandita (Luvsanperenlei, Ogtorguyn Dalay) of the Oirat (1599-1662) devised the modified "clear script." Khalkha princes established contact with Russia.
1649	Russian Cossacks built fort at Albazin on border of Qing territory.
1650	Bogd Gegeen Zanabazar adopted title Javzandamba Hutagt.
1653	Russians began trading with Oirats in Tomsk.
1661	Reign of Qing Emperor Kang Xi (Enh Amgalan) began (-1722). Irkutsk fort founded.
1666	Üdiyn Shivee (Ulan-Ude) founded.
1671	Galdan Boshigt (1644-1697) became Jungarian Khan.
1673	Galdan Boshigt attacked Khalkha Mongolia.
1680	Galdan Boshigt captured Hami, Turfan, and Kashgar.
1682	Russian Emperor Peter the Great's reign began (-1725). Troitsk (Troitskosavsk) founded. 5th Dalai Lama Lozang Gyatso died.
1683	6th Dalai Lama Tsangyang Gyatso (Tsan"yanjamts) born in Monyul (-1706).
1685	Russian fort at Albazin destroyed by Qing forces. Hovd town founded by Galdan Boshigt.
1686	Irkutsk gained town status.
1687	Galdan Boshigt attacked Khalkha and destroyed Gandan monastery at Ih Hüree.
1688	Tüsheet Khan and Öndör (Bogd) Gegeen considered seeking Manchu protection.
1689	Treaty of Nerchinsk divided territory between Russian and Manchu empires along Ergun (Argun) and Geerbiqi (Gorbitsa) rivers and the Outer Hinggan mountains.

1690   Galdan Boshigt's army reached Ujumchin lands north of Peking but was defeated by Qing forces at Chifeng.

1691   Halh (Outer Mongolian) princes submitted to Manchus at Dolonnor.

1697   Jungarian army destroyed by Manchu troops; suicide of Galdan Boshigt; his nephew Tseveenravdan became Jungarian Khan (1665-1727).

1706   6th Dalai Lama Tsangyang Gyatso died.

1708   7th Dalai Lama Kelzang Gyatso (Galsanjamts) born in Kham (-1757).

1711   First Buryat Bandid Hambo (Buddhist leader) Zayaatyn Dambadarjai born (-1776).

1715   Manchu troops stationed in Uliastay and Hovd.

1717   Capture of Lhasa by Tseveenravdan (Tsi-wang Arabtan).

1720   Qing army expelled Tseveenravdan from Lhasa.

1722   Death of Qing Emperor Kang Xi. Reign of Qing Emperor Yong Zheng (Nayralt Töv) began (-1735).

1723   First Javzandamba (Öndör Gegeen) died.

1724   2nd Javzandamba Luvsandambiydonmi born (-1757).

1725   Reign of Russian Empress Catherine the Great began (-1796).

1727   Prince Savva Raguzinskiy signed Treaty of Kyakhta and Buur river protocol determining border between Russian and Manchu empires. Kyakhta trading town established by Russians on the border. Galdantseren became Khan of Jungaria (-1745).

1733   Manchu governor installed at Uliastay.

1735   Death of Qing Emperor Yong Zheng. Reign of Qing Emperor Qian Long (Tenger Tetgegch) began (-1796).

1737   Foundation of Amarbayasgalant monastery in northern Khalkha.

1739   Manchu-Jungarian agreement: Altai mountains made the border between Oirats and Mongols.

1741   Foundation of the first Buryat datsan, Hambyn Hüree.

1753   Manchu administration extended to the Dörvöd.

1755   Oirat leader Amarsanaa (1718-57) staged anti-Manchu uprising.

1756   The Hotgoyd Chingünjav (1710-57) of the Khalkha joined the uprising.

1757   2nd Javzandamba Luvsandambiydonmi died. 7th Dalai Lama Kelzang Gyatso died. Uprising of Amarsanaa and Chingünjav suppressed by Manchu troops.

1758   3rd Javzandamba Ishdambiynyam born (-1773). 8th Dalai Lama Jampal Gyatso (Jambaljamts) born in Tsang (-1804).

1771   Some Oirats returned from Russia to settle in Jungaria, Qinghai and Inner Mongolia; those who remained on the Volga called Kalmyk.

1773   3rd Javzandamba Ishdambiynyam died.

1775   4th Javzandamba Luvsantüvdenvanchug born (-1813).
1796   Death of Qing Emperor Qian Long. Reign of Qing Emperor Jia
       Qing (Sayshaalt Yeröölt) began (-1820).
1801   Reign of Russian Emperor Alexander I began (-1825).
1804   8th Dalai Lama Jampal Gyatso died.
1806   9th Dalai Lama Lungtok Gyatso (Lündogjamts) born in Kham
       (-1815).
1813   4th Javzandamba Luvsantüvdenvanchug died.
1815   5th Javzandamba Luvsantsültimjigmed born (-1841). 9th Dalai
       Lama Lungtok Gyatso died.
1816   10th Dalai Lama Tsultrim Gyatso (Tsültimjamts) born in
       Lithang (-1837).
1820   Death of Qing Emperor Jia Qing. Reign of Qing Emperor Dao
       Guang (Tör Gerelt) began (-1850).
1825   Reign of Russian Emperor Nicholas I began (-1855).
1832   First "tsam" religious dances performed at Ih Hüree.
1833   Opening of Russian-Mongol school in Kyakhta.
1837   10th Dalai Lama Tsultrim Gyatso died.
1838   11th Dalai Lama Khedrup Gyatso (Haydüvjamts) born in Kham
       (-1856). Completion in Ih Hüree of Gandantegchinlin (Tushita-
       mahayanavipa) temple (named after Tsongkhapa's monastery
       in Tibet).
1839   Beginning of Opium War in China.
1841   5th Javzandamba Luvsantsültimjigmed died.
1843   6th Javzandamba Luvsantüvdenchoyjijaltsan born (-1848).
1848   6th Javzandamba Luvsantüvdenchoyjijaltsan died.
1849   7th Javzandamba Agvaanchoyjivanchugperenlaijamts born
       (-1868).
1850   Death of Qing Emperor Dao Guang. Reign of Qing Emperor Xi-
       ang Feng (Tügeemel Elbegt) began (-1861).
1851   Taiping peasant rebellion in China aimed to establish Taoist
       "kingdom."
1855   Reign of Russian Emperor Alexander II began (-1881).
1856   11th Dalai Lama Khedrup Gyatso died. 12th Dalai Lama Trin-
       ley Gyatso (Prenlaijamts) born at Olga (-1875). Beginning of
       second Opium War.
1858   Russo-Chinese Treaty of Aigun ceded Amur region to Russia.
1860   Russo-Chinese Treaty of Peking ceded Maritime region to Rus-
       sia.
1861   Russian consul took up residence in Ih Hüree. Death of Qing
       Emperor Xiang Feng. Reign of Qing Emperor Tong Zhi (Bürent
       Zasagch) began (-1875).
1864   Russo-Chinese protocol of Chuguchak ceded territory east of
       Lake Balkhash to Russia.

1865   Yakub Beg's troops from Kokand occupied Kaxgar.
1868   7th Javzandamba Agvaanchoyjivanchugperenlaijamts died.
1869   8th Javzandamba Agvaanluvsanchoyjindanzanvaanchigbal-sambuu born (-1924).
1871   Russian troops occupied the Ili valley.
1872   Hovd town seized in Muslim revolt.
1874   8th Javzandamba took power in Ih Hüree.
1875   12th Dalai Lama Trinley Gyatso died. Death of Qing Emperor Tong Zhi. Reign of Qing Emperor Guang Xu (Badruult Tör) began (-1908).
1876   13th Dalai Lama Thubten Gyatso (Tüvdenjamts) born in Thakpo (-1933).
1880   Anti-Manchu mutiny by Uliastay garrison led by Onolt.
1881   Russo-Chinese Treaty of St. Petersburg: China recovered Ili from Russia but lost more territory west of the Khorgos. Reign of Russian Emperor Alexander III began (-1894).
1892   Construction of Trans-Siberian Railway began.
1894   Reign of Russian Emperor Nicholas II began (-1917).
1895   13th Dalai Lama assumed temporal powers and regent resigned.
1896   China agreed to construction of Russian-Manchurian Railway.
1900   Boxer (Yi He Tuan) rebellion against foreigners in China. Anti-Manchu mutiny by Uliastay garrison led by Enhtayvan. Founding of Mongol Ore goldmining company in Mongolia.
1903   Founding by Ayuush of an anti-Manchu liberation movement in Khalkha.
1904   Beginning of Russo-Japanese War. British expeditionary force under Younghusband reached Lhasa. 13th Dalai Lama left Lhasa and arrived in Urga.
1905   Completion of the Trans-Siberian Railway. Strikes and mutinies in Russia after troops fire on petitioners. Russian consulate opened in Hovd town. Uprising in Gorlos, Inner Mongolia, led by Togtoh Tayj.
1906   Movement against Chinese traders and moneylenders in Ih Hüree. Office opened in Peking for Chinese wishing to settle in Mongolia. 13th Dalai Lama left Mongolia for Kokonor then went to Peking.
1907   Russo-Japanese Treaty signed. Bank of China branches opened in Ih Hüree and Uliastay.
1908   Death of Qing Emperor Guang Xu. Reign of Qing Emperor Xuan Tong (Hevt Yos, Pu Yi) began (-1912). Mongolian newspaper *Mongolyn Sonin Bichig* first published in Harbin.
1910   Clashes in Ih Hüree between Mongols and Manchu troops. Manchu amban Sando forced to leave Ih Hüree.
1911   Russian consulate established in Uliastay. Mongolia declared

independence; Javzandamba proclaimed Bogd Khan (Olnoo Örgögdsön) (December).
1912 Republic of China proclaimed by President Sun Yat-sen (1866-1925). Manchu governor and troops left Hovd town. Russo-Mongolian Treaty signed in Niyslel Hüree (former Ih Hüree). Russo-Japanese Treaty signed in St. Petersburg. Visit to Russia by government members Handdorj, Shirnen, and Damdin.
1913 Russo-Chinese Treaty awarded Mongolia autonomy. Russian school opened in Niyslel Hüree. Mongolian-Tibetan Friendship Treaty concluded. Visit to Russia by Prime Minister Sayn Noyon Khan Namnansüren.
1914 Beginning of First World War. Russo-Mongolian agreement on army training.
1915 Russo-Chinese-Mongolian Treaty of Kyakhta recognized Outer Mongolia's autonomy in internal affairs. Russian bank opened in Niyslel Hüree. Nalayh coal mine went into operation.
1916 American-owned Mongolian Trading Company opened at Kalgan (Chuulalt Haalga) in Inner Mongolia.
1917 Soviet power established in St. Petersburg in "October" Revolution under leadership of Vladimir Ilyich Lenin (Ulyanov) (b. 1870).
1918 Soviet power established in Deed Üd (Ulan-Ude).
1919 Soviet Russian government recognized Bogd Khan Mongolia (August). Chinese General Hsü Shu-cheng captured Niyslel Hüree (November). First secret meetings of two Mongolian revolutionary groups named "Konsulyn Denj" and "Hüree" after their locality. Formation of pro-Japanese "Greater Mongolia" government in Dauria.
1920 Russian communists Burtman, Sorokovikov, and Borisov met Mongolian revolutionaries (March/April). Revolutionary groups united as Mongolian People's Party (MPP) (April). Delegation of revolutionaries reached Verkhneudinsk: Bodoo and Dogsom returned to Niyslel Hüree (July/August). Revolutionaries Danzan, Losol, and Chagdarjav went on to Moscow: requested help from Comintern's Far Eastern Secretariat, met Lenin (August-October). "White" Russian Cossack cavalry under Baron von Ungern-Sternberg entered Mongolia (October). Revolutionaries Sühbaatar and Choybalsan, who had stayed in Irkutsk, went to Troitskosavsk (November).
1921 Baron von Ungern-Sternberg captured Niyslel Hüree (February). First Congress of Mongolian People's Party held in Troitskosavsk (Russia); first party Program adopted; Soliyn Danzan elected Chairman (March). Provisional revolutionary government formed with Ministries of the Army, Internal Affairs, and

Finance (March). Mongolian revolutionaries and Soviet Army took Niyslel Hüree (July). Dogsomyn Bodoo appointed prime minister and foreign minister of first People's Government, Sühbaatar appointed commander-in-chief and minister of war (July). Mongolian Revolutionary Youth League founded (August). Limitation placed on powers of the Bogd Khan (November). Mongolian delegation—Soliyn Danzan, Balingiyn Tserendorj, Damdiny Sühbaatar, Shirnendamdin, and Erdenebathaan (interpreter)—met Vladimir Lenin in Moscow, Mongolian-Soviet Treaty concluded (November).

1922   Delegates to Moscow Congress of Far Eastern People's Revolutionary Organizations—Ajvaagiyn Danzan and Buyannemeh—met Lenin in Moscow (January). Mongolian ambassador Tüshee Gün Davaa presented credentials to Soviet President Kalinin (June). Internal Security Office established (July). Bodoo executed for "counterrevolutionary activity" (August). First census of population and livestock held (October). 4th Comintern Congress: MPP delegate Tseren-Ochiryn Dambadorj (October).

1923   Damdiny Sühbaatar (b. 1893) died (February). 2nd MPP Congress: message of thanks to Lenin for Soviet aid in the revolution; call to strengthen friendship with Soviet Russia; party Program amended; plans to purge party of "oppressor class elements"; Ajvaagiyn Danzan elected Chairman (July/August). Mongolia's provinces (named after their local princes) renamed after local geographical features (October).

1924   Vladimir Ilyich Lenin died (January). Bogd Khan, the 8th Javzandamba, died (May). 5th Comintern Congress: MPP delegate G. Gürsed (June). 3rd MPP Congress: noncapitalist path of development chosen, MPP renamed Mongolian People's Revolutionary Party (MPRP); Tseren-Ochiryn Dambadorj elected chairman; S. Danzan executed for bourgeois tendencies (August/September). First session of Mongolian Great Hural (assembly), adoption of country's first Constitution, proclamation of the Mongolian People's Republic (MPR), Niyslel Hüree renamed Ulan Bator; Genden named president of the Little Hural, Tserendorj prime minister (November).

1925   Notes exchanged on withdrawal of Soviet troops from Mongolia (January). Ih Shav' (Buddhist estates in northern Mongolia) renamed Delger Ih Uul Province (March). Mongolian Pioneers' Organization founded (May). 4th MPRP Congress: 2nd party program adopted; plans to strengthen Youth League and Trade Unions (September/October). New currency (tögrög) put into circulation (December).

1926   Treaty of friendship with People's Republic of Tuva (August). 5th MPRP Congress: called for restriction of private capital and development of national and cooperative property (September/October). Law limiting the powers of religion (September). Suppression of "counterrevolutionary uprising" by Yegzör lamas.

1927   State Supreme Court set up (January). Establishment of Stormong (Soviet-Mongolian trade) company (March). First Congress of Mongolian Trade Unions (August). 6th MPRP Congress: failure of Leftists' attempts to criticize the Rightists' "Get rich!" policy (September/October).

1928   Comintern instructs Leftists on defeating Rightists (January/June). China reunited as Chiang Kai-shek entered Peking. 7th MPRP Congress: "Rightists" defeated, Bat-Ochiryn Eldev-Ochir, Peljidiyn Genden, and Olziytiyn Badrah elected Secretaries (October/December).

1929   Choybalsan appointed president of the Little Hural (January). "Agreement on Basic Principles of USSR-MPR Relations" signed (June). Expropriation of feudal and monastery property (September). League for the Elimination of Illiteracy founded (September). League of Mongolian Dialectical Materialists founded (September). Foundation of Soviet-Mongolian Mongoltrans company (December).

1930   8th MPRP Congress: confiscation of feudalists' property ordered; leaders criticized for "premature" attempts to establish communes and rush into the socialist stage of revolution; Genden, Badrah and Zolbingiyn Shijee elected Secretaries (February/April). "Counterrevolutionary uprising" by Tögsbuyant and Ulaangom lamas suppressed (March). Council of Nationalities and Tribes established (May). Duration of army service fixed at three years (June). Foreign trade made a state monopoly (December). Voluntary Society to Promote State Defense established (December).

1931   Government administration department took over responsibilities of Ministry of Internal Affairs (May). Cultural conference of Mongol peoples in Moscow agreed on Latinization of scripts for Halh, Buryats, and Kalmyks. Japanese troops entered Manchuria following "Mukden incident."

1932   Suppression of "feudal-theocratic counterrevolution" in west (April). Resolution of CPSU and Comintern on "bourgeois-democratic" rather than socialist nature of current Mongolian political situation (June). MPRP Central Committee special meeting: "Leftists" defeated, call for New Turn in policy; Eldev-Ochir, Jambyn Lhümbe, and Dorgijavyn Luvsansharav elected Secretaries (June). People's Government renamed the Council of Ministers (July). Establishment of Manchukuo as Japanese protectorate.

1933   Radio broadcasting began in Ulan Bator (February). Hatgal wool washing mill went into operation (July). 13th Dalai Lama Thubten Gyatso died (December). Japanese occupation of Jehol Province (between Manchukuo and Peking). "Outer" Mongolia claimed by Japan to be part of Manchukuo (December).

1934   Ulan Bator industrial combine opened (April). Trial of leaders of the 1932 "counterrevolution" (April). 9th MPRP Congress: rectified Leftist errors and promoted New Turn policy; called for defense buildup in face of threat from Japan; Eldev-Ochir, Luvsansharav, and Has-Ochiryn Luvsandorj elected Secretaries (September/October). Mongolian-Soviet "verbal agreement" on mutual aid in case of invasion (November). State Security Office established (December). Beginning of Chinese communists' Long March from Hunan to Yenan.

1935   Building of narrow-gauge railway from Ulan Bator to Nalayh begun (January). 14th Dalai Lama Tenzin Gyatso (Danzanjamts) born at Taktser, Kokonor (June). 7th Comintern Congress: MPRP delegates Luvsandorj and Banzarjavyn Baasanjav (July). Mongol-Japanese talks on border incidents (July). Law requiring lamas to engage in "work for society" (December). Clash with troops from Manchukuo in Buyr Nuur border area (December). Some Soviet Army technical units invited into Mongolia.

1936   Internal Security Office renamed Ministry of Internal Affairs (February). MPRP Central Committee meeting "smashed" Genden's "Right opportunism" (March). Soviet-Mongolian mutual assistance protocol signed (March). Chinese government protested that protocol was contrary to Russian recognition of Chinese suzerainty in Mongolia (April). Religious Affairs Office subordinated to Ministry of Internal Affairs.

1937   Large-scale closure of monasteries. Marshal Demid poisoned aboard Trans-Siberian Railway train (August). MPRP Central Committee meeting: Luvsansharav and Eldev-Ochir reelected Secretaries, Baasanjav elected Secretary (October). Ulan Bator-Nalayh narrow-gauge railway went into operation (November). Japanese occupation of eastern Inner Mongolia.

1938   Party and government resolution on national minorities (June).

1939   Mongolian and Soviet forces clashed with Japanese Army at Halhyn Gol (May/August). MPRP Central Committee meeting: Luvsansharav and Baasanjav reelected, Dashiyn Damba elected Secretary (July). Beginning of Second World War (September).

Drafting of new Constitition (October-December). Bayantümen-Ereentsav railway went into operation.

1940   10th MPRP Congress: "Democratic" stage of revolution declared finished and socialist stage about to begin; 3rd party Program adopted; Yumjaagiyn Tsedenbal elected general secretary (March/April). 2nd state Constitution adopted by MPR Great Hural (June). Choybalsan elected prime minister, Gonchigiyn Bumtsend elected chairman, Presidium of Little Hural (head of state) (July). Establishment of Bayan-Ölgiy Province (August).

1941   Party and government decree on adoption of Cyrillic script (March). Russo-Japanese neutrality pact (April). Germany invaded Soviet Russia (June). Border agreement with Manchukuo signed in Harbin (October).

1942   Establishment of industrial production associations (February). Founding of Mongolian ("Choybalsan") State University (October).

1943   "Revolyutsionnaya Mongoliya" tank regiment handed over to Soviet Red Army by visiting delegation in Moscow (January). Little Hural sets aside funds for formation of "Mongol' skiy Arad" fighter squadron for Soviet Red Army (March). Establishment of directorate of state farms (March). MPRP Central Committee meeting resolves to turn the Presidium into the Politburo and establish a Secretariat (December). Border clashes as Kazakhs fleeing from Xinjiang entered Mongolia.

1944   Abolition of limitation on electoral rights (September). Little Hural adopted law on state procurement of private livestock.

1945   Yalta conference attended by Churchill, Stalin, and Roosevelt agreed that USSR would declare war on Japan in exchange for preservation of the status quo in Mongolia and possession of the Kuril islands and southern Sakhalin (February). Second World War defeat of Germany (May). USSR and Mongolia declared war on Japan, Japan surrendered (August). Mongolians voted in UN plebiscite for independence (October).

1946   Republic of China recognized Mongolia (January). Friendship Treaty with China signed in Chongjing (February). Mongolian-Soviet Friendship Treaty signed (February). Mongolia applied for membership of United Nations (June).

1947   Border clashes with Chinese troops at Baytagbogd (Peitashan) (June-September). 11th MPRP Congress: Tsedenbal announced 1st Five-Year Plan (1948-52), calling for the doubling of Mongolia's livestock (December).

1948   Establishment of diplomatic relations with DPRK (North Korea). Mongolia reapplied for UN membership (October).

1949   Establishment of diplomatic relations with People's Republic of

China (October). Opening of railway from Sühbaatar/Naushki on the Russian border to Ulan Bator (November). MPRP Central Committee meeting banned "bourgeois nationalist views" in history and literature (December).

1950   Establishment of diplomatic relations with German Democratic and Hungarian, Polish, and Czechoslovak republics (April). MPRP Central Committee meeting approved new election system (August).

1951   295 deputies directly elected to new Great Hural (June).

1952   Horloogiyn Choybalsan (b. 1895) died of cancer in Moscow (January). Yumjaagiyn Tsedenbal appointed Chairman, Council of Ministers (July). Economic aid treaty concluded with China (December).

1953   Great Hural Presidium's resolution on taxation of livestock (May). Bumtsend, Chairman, Presidium of Great Hural, died (September).

1954   295 deputies elected to Great Hural (June). Sühbaatar's remains brought from Altan-Ölgiy cemetery to mausoleum in central Ulan Bator (June-July). Jamsrangiyn Sambuu elected Chairman, Presidium of Great Hural (July). 12th MPRP Congress: Dashiyn Damba elected First Secretary; 2nd Five-Year Plan (1953-57) announced (November).

1955   Formation of livestock production cooperatives (*negdels*) (March). Opening of railway from Ulan Bator to Zamyn Üüd/ Ereen on the Chinese border (December). Establishment of diplomatic relations with India (December).

1956   Soviet railway lines in Mongolia turned over to joint company (April). Establishment of diplomatic relations with Yugoslavia (November).

1957   Handover to Mongolia of Soviet Mongolneft' oil company (May). 233 deputies elected to new Great Hural (June). Moscow conference of communist and workers' parties issued a declaration on the need for peaceful coexistence during the building of socialism; MPRP leaders attended (November).

1958   13th MPRP Congress: "dogmatism" condemned, Damba reelected First Secretary; Three-Year Plan (1958-60) announced (March). Mongolian delegation attended CMEA Council as observers (May). MPRP Central Committee meeting: Tsedenbal replaced Damba as MPRP First Secretary (November).

1959   MPRP Central Committee meeting: Damba expelled for "ideological-political backwardness, conservatism, and inertia"; Politburo members Damdin, Lamchin, and Sürenjav, candidate members Baldan and Samdan expelled for "not conforming to ideological-political standards" (March). First

International Congress of Mongolists (September). MPRP Central Committee meeting reviewed progress of collectivization of livestock (*negdel* formation) (December).

1960   *Tsagaan Sar* (Buddhist new year) proclaimed annual *Negdel* Members' Day—but no longer a holiday (January). Treaty of Friendship and Mutual Assistance with China (May). 267 deputies elected to new Great Hural (June). Adoption by People's Great Hural of 3rd Constitution (July). Moscow conference of 81 communist and workers' parties restated their unity and loyalty to the declaration of the 1957 Moscow conference; MPRP leaders attended (November).

1961   Mongolian delegation attended Warsaw Treaty Political Advisory Council meeting in Moscow as observers (March). 14th MPRP Congress: attended by CPSU Politburo member Suslov, approved Moscow conference documents; 3rd Five-Year Plan (1961-65) announced (July). Mongolian Academy of Sciences founded (May). Mongolia joined the United Nations (October). Founding of Darhan town (October).

1962   Mongolia joined Comecon (CMEA) (June). MPRP Central Committee meeting: Politburo member Tömör-Ochir expelled for anti-party activities following Soviet criticism of Genghis Khan anniversary celebrations (November).

1963   Conference of MPRP ideologists addressed by CPSU Politburo member Ilyichev (January). Diplomatic relations established with the United Kingdom (January). Border agreement with China (February). 270 deputies elected to new People's Great Hural (June).

1964   MPRP Central Commitee meeting: Loohuuz, Nyambuu, and Surmaajav expelled for anti-party activities (December). Mongolian-Chinese border inspection protocol signed.

1965   Visit to Mongolia by CPSU Politburo member and former KGB chief Shelepin (January). Opening of Sharyn Gol opencast coal mine (March). Establishment of diplomatic relations with France (April). Signing of cultural relations agreement with the UK (September).

1966   Signing of Soviet-Mongolian Treaty of Friendship, Cooperation, and Mutual Assistance during visit by CPSU General Secretary Leonid Brezhnev (January). 15th MPRP Congress: Central Committee of 74 members elected; 4th party Program adopted, 4th Five-Year Plan (1966-70) announced (June). 287 deputies elected to new People's Great Hural (June). Founding of the Mongol-British Society in Ulan Bator (October).

1967   Mongolian-Bulgarian Friendship and Cooperation Treaty (June). Opening of Ulan Bator Television Center (September).

Inner Mongolia Regional Revolutionary Committee denounced Ulanfu (Ulaanhüü, former regional CCP First Secretary) as leader of a "counter-revolutionary revisionist clique" and pledged to build a "great wall" against "the Soviet-Outer Mongolian revisionists."

1968   Mongolian-East German Friendship and Cooperation Treaty (September). Mongolia joined the International Labour Organisation (October).

1969   Moscow conference of 75 communist and workers' parties renewed call for unity of action in anti-imperialist struggle; MPRP leaders attended (June). 297 deputies elected to new People's Great Hural (June).

1970   2nd International Congress of Mongolists (September).

1971   Opening of Orbita satellite ground station in Ulan Bator (January). 16th MPRP Congress: Central Committee of 83 members elected; 5th Five-Year Plan (1971-75) announced (June).

1972   Diplomatic relations established with Japan (February). Death of Jamsrangiyn Sambuu, Chairman, Presidium of Great Hural (May). Extension of 1952 economic aid treaty with China (August). Diplomatic relations established with Australia (September). Gombojavyn Ochirbat elected Chairman of TUC (November). Ministry of Justice established (December).

1973   Mongolian-Czechoslovak Friendship and Cooperation Treaty (June). 336 deputies elected to new People's Great Hural (June). Mongolian-Soviet agreement on building of Erdenet joint copper-mining combine (November). Diplomatic relations established with Canada (November). MPRP called for condemnation of "Mao clique" in China (December).

1974   Tsedenbal elected Chairman, Presidium of People's Great Hural; Jambyn Batmönh elected Chairman, Council of Ministers (July). *Utga Zohiol Urlag (Literature and Art)* issue devoted several pages to details of Peking's anti-Mongolian policies. CPSU General Secretary Leonid Brezhnev, on visit for 50th anniversary of the MPR, made "honorary citizen" of Mongolia (November).

1975   Lodongiyn Tüdev elected First Secretary of Mongolian Revolutionary Youth League (June). CMEA plan for development of Mongolia's mineral resources (June). Mongolian-Polish Friendship and Cooperation Treaty (July). "Maoists" attacked for "making a fetish of Genghis Khan" to justify Chinese territorial claims on Mongolia (October).

1976   17th MPRP Congress: Central Committee of 91 members elected; 6th Five-Year Plan (1976-80) announced (June). 3rd International Congress of Mongolists (August/September).

Tsedenbal awarded his fifth Order of Sühbaatar on his 60th birthday (September). Death of Mao Tse-tung (September). Tsedenbal signed aid and border agreements on visit to USSR (October).

1977 New Mongolian-GDR Friendship and Cooperation Treaty (May). 354 deputies elected to new People's Great Hural (June). Mongolia attacked "annexationist policy" of "Great Han chauvinists." China attacked Soviet "annexation and occupation" of Mongolia (September). Soviet Finance Ministry "representation" installed in Mongolian Finance Ministry (September).

1978 Regulations to control travel and residence introduced (February). MPRP resolution calls for economy, thrift, and safeguarding of public property (April). Restrictions on private ownership of livestock reinforced (April). Mongolian protest to China against call for Soviet withdrawal from Mongolia (April). Tsedenbal inspected Soviet army unit in Mongolia and thanked it for providing protection against "Chinese militarists' threat" (May). CMEA Executive Committee meeting in Ulan Bator agreed on urgent need to speed up Mongolia's rate of economic development (September). 1st stage of Erdenet combine put into operation (December).

1979 Expulsion of Chinese residents for "crimes against the state" (March). Visit to Mongolia by the Dalai Lama (June). Tsedenbal awarded rank of Marshal of the MPR (August). Visit to Mongolia by KGB chief Yuri Andropov (August). *Guangming Daily* description of Genghis Khan as "a national hero of one of China's minorities" caused Mongolian indignation (October).

1980 40th anniversary of Tsedenbal's election to post of MPRP General Secretary: criticism of "cult of personality" and "class and nationalist errors" in history (April). Restoration of "tomb" of Genghis Khan at Ejin Horo in Inner Mongolia, destroyed in Chinese "cultural revolution" (May). Textbooks withdrawn following publication of Politburo resolution on "distortion of historical facts" about Mongolia and China (June). 2nd stage of Erdenet combine put into operation (June). MPRP newspaper accused Peking of using Chinese émigrés in Mongolia in "expansionist plots" (December).

1981 3rd stage of Erdenet combine put into operation (February). Space flight by Mongolian "cosmonaut" Jügderdemidiyn Gürragchaa aboard Soviet spacecraft Soyuz 39 and Salyut 6 (March). 18th MPRP Congress: Central Committee of 91 members elected; Tsedenbal adopted title of General Secretary; 7th Five-Year Plan (1981-85) announced; CPSU Secretary Mikhail Gorbachev was guest (May). 370 deputies elected to new

People's Great Hural (June). Visit by Soviet Defense Minister Marshal Dmitriy Ustinov (June). Tsedenbal accused China of "subversion" and "aggressive intentions" (June). 4th stage of Erdenet combine put into operation (June). 60th anniversary of Mongolian revolution marked by military parade in presence of Soviet First Vice-President Vasiliy Kuznetsov (July). Tsedenbal awarded another Soviet Order of Lenin on 65th birthday (September). Tsedenbal called for "rooting out of weeds" in the party ranks (December).

1982   Shirendev, President of the Academy of Sciences, dismissed (January). Mongolian-Chinese Border Inspection Commission met (February-April). Ochirbat, Chairman of the Trade Union Congress, dismissed (May). Col.-Gen. Viktor Chebrikov, First Deputy Chairman of the KGB, attended Mongolian security service's 60th anniversary celebrations (July). Tsedenbal and Brezhnev discussed relations with China (August). 4th International Congress of Mongolists in Ulan Bator (August). Minister of Public Security Luvsangombo accused UK, USA, and Japan of setting up centers to collect intelligence about Mongolia. More Chinese residents expelled for engaging in subversion, drug-running, and the black market. Death of Brezhnev; Yuriy Andropov became CPSU General Secretary (November). New education law introduced teaching of Russian in kindergartens.

1983   Launching of campaign of "reporting achievements to the dear leader Comrade Marshal Tsedenbal" (March). Mongolia attacked China's call for withdrawal of Soviet troops (April). Asia-Pacific Peace and Security Zone conference in Ulan Bator (April). China protested at Mongolian expulsion of Chinese residents (June). Jalan-Aajav, Politburo member and Deputy Chairman, Presidium, People's Great Hural, dismissed (July). Foreign Minister Dügersüren claimed most of Mongolia's 5,000 Chinese residents were not doing "socially useful work," attacked Peking for deploying half the Chinese PLA on Mongolia's border (August).

1984   Dügersüren and Soviet Foreign Minister Gromyko pledged to restore "good-neighborly" relations with China. Jalan-Aajav's dismissal attributed to "vile intrigues against party unity" (February). Death of Andropov; Konstantin Chernenko became CPSU General Secretary (February). Registration of typewriters, duplicators, and photocopiers ordered (July). Tsedenbal called for the normalization of relations with China (July). Border survey protocol signed in Peking (July). MPRP Central Committee plenum: Tsedenbal removed from posts of MPRP General Secretary and Politburo member on grounds of ill health; Politburo member Jambyn Batmönh appointed General Secretary; Batmönh replaced as Chairman, Council of Ministers, by Dumaagiyn Sodnom (August). Lodongiyn Tüdev appointed editor-in-chief of MPRP paper *Ünen* (October). Puntsagiyn Jasray appointed Chairman of the State Planning Commission (December). Batmönh replaced Tsedenbal as Chairman, Presidium of People's Great Hural (December).

1985   Batmönh appealed for "creative atmosphere" to replace "bureaucratism, formalism, and abstraction" in the MPRP (February). Death of Chernenko; Mikhail Gorbachev became CPSU General Secretary (March). "Food Program" launched to increase per capita consumption (June). Batmönh and Gorbachev signed long-term program for development of economic, scientific, and technical cooperation between Mongolia and the USSR in the period up to the year 2000 (August). Batmönh said at Kremlin meeting with Gorbachev that Mongolia supported normalization of Sino-Soviet relations (August). Article in *Ünen* on PRC's 35th anniversary said Chinese leaders' criticism of "Maoism" did not signify a change of policy (August).

1986   19th MPRP Congress: Central Committee of 85 members elected; Batmönh elected General Secretary; rules on party membership tightened; 8th Five-Year Plan (1986-90) announced—emphasis on intensification rather than expansion of production (May). In MPRP congress speech Minister of Public Security Jamsranjav accused "imperialism" of hostile activity against Mongolia and attempts to undermine Mongolian-Soviet friendship and cooperation (May). 370 deputies elected to new People's Great Hural (June). People's Great Hural confirmed Batmönh as Chairman of Presidium (July). Gorbachev's Vladivostok speech on Asia-Pacific security: agreement that Soviet-Chinese border should run down the main stream of the Amur (Heilongjiang); withdrawal of Soviet troops from Mongolia under discussion with Mongolian leaders (July). Mongolian-Chinese consular agreement concluded in Ulan Bator (August). Batmönh called for "openness" on the economic situation (December).

1987   Diplomatic relations established with US (January). Press "openness" seen by MPRP as essence of party ideology (February). State Security Committee Chairman Tsiyregzen warned against anti-Soviet propaganda, rumormongering, and selling secrets to "enemy special services." Politburo resolution on campaign against drunkenness (May). Batmönh admitted shortages of housing, food, and consumer goods (May). At meeting with Gorbachev in Moscow, Batmönh denied MPRP was "shutting its eyes to difficulties and shortcomings" (June). MPRP

Politburo claimed "perestroika" in Mongolia was "in harmony" with developments in USSR "despite difference of scale" (June). Batmönh told MPRP economic management was over-centralized and the economy "stagnant" (June). One Soviet motorized infantry division withdrawn from Mongolia (June). Mongolian-Chinese agreement on settlement of border disputes (June). Visit to Mongolia by Chinese National People's Congress delegation led by Peng Zhen (June). Conference of Asia-Pacific communist and workers' parties in Ulan Bator, not attended by representatives from China, North Korea, or Japan, called for "zone of peace and progress" (July). 1st Mongolian-British round table in Ulan Bator discussed economic and academic exchanges (September). 5th International Congress of Mongolists in Ulan Bator set up the International Association for Mongolian Studies (September).

1988   Puntsagiyn Jasray appointed head of new State Planning and Economic Committee (January). Visit by President Nicolae Ceauşescu of Romania (April). Tserenpiliyn Gombosüren replaced Mangalyn Dügersüren as Foreign Minister (June). National economic conference called for acceleration of reform (June). In MPRP's *Namyn Am'dral* Kinayatyn Zardyhan attacked the "dogmatic interpretation of socialism" in Mongolia from 1950s-1980s (June). Bureaucracy described as "socialism's chief internal enemy" in revolution anniversary report (July). Visit by North Korean President Kim Il-sung (July). Visit by Indian President Venkataraman (July). Sodnom and Soviet Premier Ryzhkov signed in Moscow plan to develop economic relations in the period up to the year 2005 (July). *Ünen* called for reform in nomination and election of deputies and warned that "authoritarianism and intellectual indolence" were undermining "renewal" (Mongolian "perestroika") (August). People's Great Hural Chairman Rinchin received in Peking by President Yang Shangkun (September). Batmönh speech called for greater openness in political and social affairs; press blamed Tsedenbal and his "administrative command" methods for the country's "stagnation" (December). MPRP Central Committee resolution stated that Tsedenbal was "willful and unprincipled" and "belittled collective leadeship"; after years of condemning national pride as "nationalism," the party was reevaluating the historical role of Genghis Khan and the Mongol empire to protect the national cultural heritage (December).

1989   Law on the State Enterprise, emphasizing financial autonomy, came into force (January). Tsagaan Sar (Buddhist new year) restored as national holiday (February). *Ünen* editorial "Democracy or anarchy?" questioned motives of people taking advantage of reforms to "go against the tide" (February). Defense Minister announced Mongolian army to be halved to two motor-rifle divisions, 12,000 men (March). Visit to Peking by Foreign Minister Gombosüren: agreements on intergovernmental commission on economic cooperation, visits by citizens of the two countries, and the opening of a Mongolian consulate-general in Höhhot (April). *Ünen* editorial "Nationalism or internationalism?" opposed "extreme nationalism" and wanted "patriotism" to be balanced by "internationalism" (loyalty to Moscow) (May). Second stage of Soviet troop withdrawal began (May). Visit by Japanese Foreign Minister Sousuke Uno (May). MPRP announced revision of party rules, Program and procedures for rehabilitation of victims of the Choybalsan "personality cult" in the 1930s-1940s (June). Following Batmönh's visit to Moscow Mongolian press called for an "objective and realistic evaluation" of Mongolian-Soviet cooperation (July). Visit to London by Punsalmaagiyn Ochirbat, Minister of Foreign Economic Relations and Supply (July). Disclosure of secret Soviet "extraterritorial" uranium mine at Marday (Erdes) in eastern Mongolia (November). 2nd Mongolian-British round table held in London (November). Minister of Public Security Jamsranjav confirmed "rumors" about investigation of people distributing pamphlets: they were not "anti-state groups undermining the socialist system" but "promoters of the acceleration of restructuring" (perestroika). Kinayatyn Zardyhan called for legalization of "healthy" informal organizations (December).

1990 Anti-MPRP demonstrations by the Mongolian Democractic Union, Social Democratic Movement, New Progress Association and Union of Students (January). Law on Cooperatives turned the *negdel* into cooperatives (January). MPRP Politburo resolution on removal of statue of Stalin from in front of the State Library in Ulan Bator (February). MPRP Central Committee meeting: resignation of all Politburo members and Secretaries; Gombojavyn Ochirbat elected General Secretary, Nyamyn Mishigdorj and Tserenpiliyn Gombosüren Politburo members and Secretaries, Tseveenjavyn Ööld and Lodongiyn Tüdev Politburo members; rehabilitation of Tömör-Ochir, Loohuuz, Nyambuu, and Surmaajav (expelled in 1962 and 1964) (March). Extraordinary MPRP Congress: new party Rules adopted; Politburo renamed Presidium; Ochirbat elected Chairman; Gombosüren gave up post as Secretary, Budyn Sum"yaa, Minister of Culture, appointed member of Presidium and Secretary (April). People's Great Hural amended MPR

Constitution to delete references to MPRP's "leading role" and adopted Law on Elections; Batmönh resigned and Punsalmaagiyn Ochirbat was made Chairman of the Presidium in his place; Sodnom resigned and Sharavyn Gungaadorj (Minister of Agriculture and Food since 1987) was made Chairman of the Council of Ministers in his place; Dashiyn Byambasüren was appointed First Deputy Chairman of the Council of Ministers and Chairman of the State Committee for Socio-Economic Development; the Ministry of Public Security was abolished and the state militia and state security directorates were placed under government control (April). President Ochirbat paid visits to Peking and (with Gombojavyn Ochirbat) to Moscow (May). People's Great Hural adopted law legalizing political parties and amended the Constitution to institute the post of President and create a standing legislature called the Little Hural of 50 members with proportional representation of elected political parties (May). Registration of political parties: Mongolian Democratic Party (MDP), Mongolian Social Democratic Party (MSDP), Mongolian National Progress Party (MNPP), Mongolian Free Labor Party (MFLP), Mongolian Green Party (MGP), and Mongolian Democratic Believers' (Buddhist) Party (MDBP). MPRP Central Committee meeting: Mishigdorj resigned from Presidium; Tsedenbal expelled from the party (June). Elections to the 430-seat People's Great Hural: MPRP with 61.7% of the vote won 357 seats (84.6%), MDP with 24.3% won 16 seats (3.8%), the pro-MPRP Revolutionary Youth League 9 seats, the MNPP 6, the MSDP 4, and independents 39 seats (July). Visit by US Secretary of State James Baker cut short because of Iraqi invasion of Kuwait (August). First session of the new People's Great Hural: Punsalmaagiyn Ochirbat elected President of Mongolia; Radnaasümbereliyn Gonchigdorj elected Chairman of the Little Hural and Vice-President; Kinayatyn Zardyhan elected Vice-Chairman of the Little Hural; seats in the Little Hural distributed as follows: MPRP (MRYL) 31, MDP 13, MNPP and MSDP 3 each; Dashiyn Byambasüren (MPRP) appointed Prime Minister, Davaadorjiyn Ganbold (MNPP) Chief Deputy (September). Mishigdorj appointed ambassador to the Soviet Union (September). Prime Minister Byambasüren called for recalculation of Mongolia's R9.7 billion debt to the USSR (September). President Ochirbat visited Tokyo, returning via Peking (November). Little Hural adopted resolution on principles of transition to market economy; rationing of basic foodstuffs and consumer goods introduced (December).

1991   Trade settlements switched to hard currency (January). Privatization Commission set up with Ganbold as Chairman (January). President Ochirbat had talks with President Bush in Washington, UN Secretary General Pérez de Cuéllar in New York, and President Gorbachev in Mosow (January). Gombojavyn Ochirbat met CCP General Secretary Jiang Zemin in Peking (February). 20th MPRP congress: Central Committee of 99 members elected; Büdragchaagiyn Dash-Yondon (Ulan Bator MPRP leader) elected Chairman, Choyjilsürengiyn Pürevdorj (Deputy Prime Minister) and Büdsürengiyn Tümen (presidential aide) Presidium members (February). Prime Minister Byambasüren had meetings with Soviet and Russian premiers (February). Yumjaagiyn Tsedenbal died in Moscow, funeral in Ulan Bator (April). Defense Minister Lt. Gen. Jadambaa visited Peking and met Premier Li Peng (April). Publication of draft of new Constitution (May). Meat rationing introduced (May). Sanjaasürengiyn Zorig elected President of Mongolian Democratic Union (June). Vice-President Gonchigdorj visited Peking, signed agreement on the opening of eight new border crossing points (June). Prime Minister Byambasüren visited the USA, Mongolia granted "most favored nation" status (June). "Little" privatization (shops and services) began with issue of vouchers (June). US Secretary of State James Baker visited Mongolia again (July). 70th anniversary of Mongolian revolution marked with military parade in Ulan Bator but no "popular demonstration" held (July). Foundation stone laid of memorial to "victims of oppression" (July). State of emergency declared in the USSR by plotters of attempted coup; statements by Soviet coup plotters published in Mongolian press; Zorig expressed concern at "conservative attempt to halt perestroika"; President Ochirbat appealed for national unity. Banning of the Soviet Communist Party; Ulan Bator demonstrators demand the banning of the MPRP (August). Procurator General announced that MPRP Politburo members who resigned in March 1990 would be tried for corruption and abuse of office (August). Mongolia recognized the independence of Estonia, Latvia, and Lithuania (August). State visit to Mongolia by Chinese President Yang Shangkun (August). Presidential decree banned top political and military leaders and judiciary from membership of political parties (September). Visit to Mongolia by the Dalai Lama (September). Agreement with Kazakhstan on employment of Mongolia's Kazakhs (September). Tokyo aid donors' conference granted Mongolia US$155 million (September). Revised draft Constitution debated in Little Hural (October). Zorig founded

Mongolian Republican Party (October). Discovery at Mörön of mass grave of lamas executed in the 1930s (October). Students picketed Chinese embassy following publication of Chinese document on repression of Mongols in Inner Mongolia (October). 3rd Mongolian-British round table held in Ulan Bator (October). Mongolian People's Party founded by Lama Baasan (November). Prime Minister Byambasüren paid official visit to South Korea (November). Revised draft Constitition debated in People's Great Hural (November-December). MPRP radicals headed by Kinayatyn Zardyhan form Mongolian Renewal Party (December). Mongolian United Herdsmen's and Farmers' Party established (December). Soviet troop withdrawal continued; garrison town of Choyr handed over.

1992 New 4th Constitution adopted by People's Great Hural (January). Prime Minister Byambasüren offered to resign over failure of the government's economic policy but was persuaded by the MPRP to stay on (January). 4th Constitution came into force: country's official name changed from Mongolian People's Republic to Mongolia; People's Great Hural and Little Hural replaced by single-chamber National Great Hural; direct election of President; establishment of Constitutional Court (February). Zorig's Mongolian Republican Party merged with the Mongolian Free Labor Party and part of the Mongolian Democratic Party to form the United Party (February). 21st MPRP Congress: Central Committee of 147 members elected chairman (Dash-Yondon) and three vice-chairman (February/March). Mongolian Independence Party formed by MPRP splinter group (March). Mongolian Capitalists' Party and Mongolian United Private Owners' Party set up (March). Leaked Inner Mongolia State Security Bureau document claimed USA was planning to create a "Greater Mongolia" uniting Mongolia, Inner Mongolia, and Buryat Republic, which belonged to China (April). New economic agreement with China concluded in Peking (May). 2nd Tokyo aid donors' conference granted Mongolia US$320 million (May). Elections to the new 76-seat Great Hural: MPRP with 56.9% of the vote won 71 seats, while the Mongolian Democratic, Social Democratic, and National Progress Parties and the United Party with 40% of the vote won only five (June). Government paper *Ardyn Erh* published article by Lt. Col. S. Bat-Ochir of Border Troops, which included a list of territories Mongolia "lost" to Russia and China between 1915 and 1980 (June). Last trainload of Russian army equipment left Mongolia (June). 1st session of National Great Hural: Natsagiyn Bagabandi elected chairman, Puntsagiyn Jasray appointed prime minister and Choyjilsürengiyn Pürevdorj deputy prime minister (July). Prosecution of former MPRP Politburo members abandoned on grounds that they had acted constitutionally (August). 6th International Congress of Mongolists in Ulan Bator (August). IMF halted disbursement of credit to Mongolia for failing to limit the budget deficit and exceeding bank lending target (August). Presidential aide Ravdangiyn Bataa declared: "Our country has no border disputes with neighboring countries" (September). Last Russian soldier left Mongolia (September). Appointment of Lhamsürengiyn Enebish to post of deputy prime minister and Minister of Administration (October). MPRP Central Committee plenum: enlarged Central Committee (169 members), Presidium, and chairman redesignated Little Hural, Party Leadership Council, and secretary-general, respectively (October). Mongolian National Democratic Party formed with Davaadorjiyn Ganbold as leader on amalgamation of Mongolian Democratic, National Progress, and Renewal Parties and the United Party (October). Treaty of Friendly Relations and Cooperation with Ukraine concluded during President Kravchuk's visit (November).

1993   Government proclaimed 1993 to be "The Year of Food." Devaluation of Mongolian tögrög from US$1 = 40 to 150 (January). Treaty of Friendly Relations and Cooperation with Russia concluded during President Ochirbat's visit to Moscow (January). Demonstration in Ulan Bator marking 3rd anniversary of democracy movement protested against MPRP's "neo-communist" policies (March). Snowstorms in western Mongolia killed 12 people and 1.4 million head of livestock (March). IMF "structural adjustment facility" reopened access to credit closed in August 1992 (April). Law on the Government adopted: Mongolian Radio and Television reverted to government status, Ministry of Administration abolished (May). Planned visit to Mongolia by Chinese Premier Li Peng cancelled because of his "illness" (May). Mongolian tögrög "floated": remained stable at around US$1 = 390 (May). Amendments to the Criminal Code abolished crimes against state security and reduced capital crimes (June). Presidential elections: Lodongiyn Tüdev, nominated by the MPRP (38.7%), was defeated by incumbent President Punsalmaagiyn Ochirbat, nominated by National and Social Democrats (57.8%) (June). President Ochirbat announced in inauguration speech a 10% cut in Mongolia's armed forces (June). Visit to USA by Prime Minister Jasray to meet Secretary of State Warren Christopher, congressmen, and IMF and World Bank officals (June). Mongolian anger at Chinese book claiming

Mongolia to be part of China; Chinese government denied it represented official policy (June). No military parade and demonstration held in Ulan Bator to mark 1921 revolution anniversary (July). Heavy rain flooded northern Mongolia, destroying bridges and halting the Trans-Mongolian Railway (July). New presidential council on law and order issued regulations to reduce public drunkenness (July). Amendments liberalized the 1991 Law on Business Units (July). New Foreign Investment Law came into force (July). 3rd Tokyo aid donors' conference granted Mongolia US$150 million for medium- and long-term projects, including $41 million from Japan for railway improvements (September). Treaty of Friendly Relations and Cooperation with Kazakhstan concluded during President Nazarbayev's visit (October). 4th Mongolian-British round table held in London (October). Prime Minister Jasray paid official visit to Japan (November). Adoption of Law on State-Church Relations (November). Formation of the Mongolian United Heritage Party announced (December).

1994   Intelligence official Sanjaasüren claimed files on "corrupt" officials to be destroyed; Prime Minister Jasray, Hural Speaker Bagabandi, and Deputy Speaker Gombojav declared their innocence (January). Law on State-Church Relations challenged in the Constitutional Court and amended (January). Ministry of Infrastructure Development, Ministry of Power, Geology and Mining Industry, and Central Intelligence Directorate set up. Registration of Mongolian United Heritage Party (January). President Ochirbat toured India, Thailand, Laos, Vietnam (February). EU extended TACIS plan to Mongolia (February). Gonchigdorj replaced Batbayar as Mongolian Social Democratic Party leader (March). Democrats demonstrated for an anticorruption law and access to the official media; working groups agreed (April). Prime Minister took charge of Mongolian Civil Defense (April). Visit by Chinese Premier Li Peng; new agreements signed (April). Byambasüren charged in connection with "gold dealers" affair (May). Mongolian script poll: 87.3% favored retention of Cyrillic and 66.5% said time was "not ripe" for introduction of the classical Mongol script for official use (May). Sanjaasüren charged with disclosure of state secrets (May). Mongolia failed to agree to repayment of R10.3bn debt to Russia (June). Mongolia protested against Chinese nuclear test (June). Formation of three new provinces: Darhan-Uul (center Darhan), Orhon (center Erdenet), and Gov'-Sümber (center Choyr). Byambasüren's Mongolian Democratic Renewal Party registered as 18th Mongolian political party (July). Sanjaasüren tried and given 18-month sentence; protests against illegality of trial in absence of a state secrets law (July). Mongolian Great Hural member Elbegdorj forced to resign seat after state secrets charge (July). Demonstrations banned in Sühbaatar Square and near public buildings. Mongolian Great Hural resolved to promote Cyrillic script and postpone introduction of classical Mongol script for official use; Presidential veto overruled by MGH committee (July).

Introduction

Take a million and a half square kilometers of mountains and plains between the 42nd and 52nd parallels of northern latitude and longitude 90 and 120 degrees east, and you have Mongolia. Move this rough oval of territory around the northern hemisphere to a position between longitude 90 and 120 degrees west, and you cover most of the states of Washington, Oregon, Idaho, Montana, Wyoming, North and South Dakota, and Minnesota, plus part of southwestern Canada. Move it once again, to a position between the Greenwich meridian and longitude 30 degrees east, and its boundary embraces France, Germany, Switzerland, Italy, Austria, Hungary, the Czech and Slovak Republics, Slovenia, Croatia, Bosnia, Serbia, and Romania—a region stretching from the Atlantic Ocean almost to the Black Sea.

Beyond providing a scale of size, however, none of these regions bears close comparison. Mongolia is under the climatic influence of the Inner Asian continent and 700 kilometers from the nearest seaport (Tianjin). Once the heart of a vast Eurasian empire, the independent Mongolian state is landlocked between Russia and China. The two million Mongols who live there have 26 million head of livestock roaming free across the fenceless ranges, but only a few thousand automobiles and 1,500 kilometers of surfaced road.

Mongolia declared its independence in 1911, on the collapse of the Manchu dynasty, which had ruled it for 220 years, but for most of this century the Mongols preserved their statehood only under Soviet domination. They paid the political price of this alternative to seizure by China or Japan, and in return received schools and hospitals, modern housing, factories, and transport. The traditional way of life of the Mongols was altered profoundly, increasing their dependence rather than reducing it.

In 1990 the Mongolian democratic movement overthrew the old communist leadership in a peaceful revolution. This watershed in the country's history is variously described as the "birth of democracy," marking the end of the "socialist" MPR or the "period of Soviet domination" and the beginning of the "transition to a market economy." The Mongols achieved political self-determination, but the collapse of Soviet Russia deprived them of their generous patron and the Mongolian economic

1

structure it had built went into sharp decline. Convertible currency was needed for the transition to a market economy, but Mongolia had few realizable assets. International corporations were attracted by Mongolia's potential mineral wealth, but put off by the country's remoteness and lack of infrastructure. After several generations of urbanization, for most people there was no way back to the countryside and the nomadic idyll. Mongols joked that Mongolia was the world's most independent country—nobody depended on it. In a few years their standard of living plummeted. With an annual GNP per capita estimated at US$100, Mongolia became one of the world's poorest nations.

Fortunately, some of the world's richest nations were prepared to help Mongolia survive the transition period. Japan, the USA, the UK, and other donor countries, the International Monetary Fund, and Asian Development Bank are giving Mongolia the necessary means and guidance. For the time being Mongolia needs some US$150-200 million a year to keep its head above water. Donations have enabled Mongolia to buy foodstuffs and petroleum, while medium- and long-term loans will help rebuild the transport network and boost key industrial projects intended to increase Mongolia's export potential. This is helping to create an atmosphere of confidence for the establishment of small companies and joint ventures, and privatization has gradually moved ahead.

Meanwhile, the Mongols have been engaged in a process of rediscovery. The birth of democracy was accompanied by a wave of nationalistic nostalgia, the release of an aching need for free self-expression. Suddenly, Genghis Khan was everywhere, in picture and song, the symbol of what it meant to be a Mongol, or so at least many people thought. The once centralized press exploded into a hundred fragments, reflecting the new political spectrum. The country's first multiparty government became caught up in the euphoria. There was a wish to do things at last "the Mongolian way." The official titles of the "Soviet" period were abandoned in favor of new (or old) "more Mongol" forms. A campaign was launched for the restoration of classical Mongol in the traditional "Uighur" script for official use. The official archives were opened up, to reveal something of the truth about the purges of the past. Lamaism flourished. Cultural and economic contacts were reestablished with the Mongol communities in Chinese Inner Mongolia and the Russian Federation.

But there was another, darker side to things. The Soviet-trained bureaucracy was unable and unwilling to change its ways. Few people knew anything about banking and the stock market. Economic disruption brought unemployment in its train. Mongols enjoying their new-found freedom to travel to look for jobs abroad, especially in Russia, gained the reputation of "Asian Gypsies." Kazakhs from Bayan-Ölgiy Province in western Mongolia left in tens of thousands to take up herding jobs in northern Kazakhstan. Urban crime, especially murder and robbery with violence, rose sharply, often linked with alcohol or drug abuse. Juveniles quit school for business—the resale of cigarettes, soft drinks, and newspapers. Prostitution was on the increase and there were even fears, for the moment exaggerated, of an AIDS epidemic.

Following the adoption of Mongolia's new Constitution in 1992, new general elections were called. The economy remained in a bad way, affected particularly by shortages of fuel and spare parts. The urban population suffered food rationing and power cuts. The rural population reduced livestock sales because there were no consumer goods to buy with the devalued currency. The democrats were divided in the towns and weak in the countryside. The MPRP was backed by the herdsmen in the more numerous rural constituencies and overwhelmed the opposition in most of the larger urban constituencies. With 56.7 percent of the vote countrywide, the MPRP won 71 of the 76 seats in the new Great Hural or national assembly. Since this "vote of confidence," the MPRP, which claims to have abandoned Marxism-Leninism and reformed itself, has been gradually reverting to a kind of "democratic centralism" and extending its political monopoly once again, down to the lowest levels of administration.

In 1993 the democratic opposition parties had a stroke of luck. In the run-up to the presidential elections, the MPRP made the mistake of abandoning the popular incumbent president, Punsalmaagiyn Ochirbat. A longtime member of the MPRP, Ochirbat had angered the party by nominating the "wrong" candidate for prime minister in 1992 and then on a number of occasions vetoing new legislation adopted by the MPRP majority in the Great Hural. The MPRP expected party discipline to bring the ranks into line behind its nominee, Lodongiyn Tüdev, the editor of the party organ *Ünen* (Truth) and a hard-line ideologist who had once dictated national policy on youth and culture. Ochirbat, however, immediately received the nomination of the democrats and won a resounding victory.

Mongolia entered 1994 with a president strong on democracy and constitutional reform, supported by the opposition democrats, and a government strong on centralization and consolidation, supported by the ex-communists. Needless to say, this is not a formula for speedy success in solving the country's pressing problems in the transition to a market economy. President Ochirbat has expressed the hope that one day Mongolia will become an "Asian tiger," but for the moment it is still dependent on Russian oil and Chinese food and consumer goods, and as before, the country's prosperity requires good relations with and between the two giant neighbors. Wisely, Mongolia has already taken steps to end its geopolitical isolation and safeguard its independence by rooting itself firmly in the world political and economic community of nations.

In concentrating on the period of nascent democracy since 1990, this Dictionary focuses on the people who attended its birth and those who now have the task of nurturing it. Most of the politicians are unknown outside Mongolia, and even inside the country, little has emerged to build a coherent picture of their personalities and capabilities, much less their hopes and fears. Key leaders of the former communist regime are also featured, as are some of their victims, as well as figures from the earlier autonomous period. The establishment of the revolutionary regime in 1921 is described in some detail in the entry on Damdiny Sühbaatar. Many of the organizations of the new and old Mongolia are listed, too, a bewildering variety of words, titles, acronyms, and abbreviations in several different languages. There are entries for various Mongol tribes and Mongol-inhabited territories, languages, and scripts, and the old and new names of towns and provinces.

The Mongol empire and its rulers have been much written about, and the bibliography attests to this. The important events and people in Mongol history from the birth of Genghis Khan to the present are listed in the chronology, together with the contemporary rulers of Russia and China and the Dalai Lamas. The text of the 1992 Constitution appears in the appendix. In other words, within reasonable limits, without rewriting 830-odd years of history, I have tried to foresee a good many of the questions that someone interested in modern Mongolia might ask. The sources of the information are mostly Mongol and recent. The appointments of government officials and political leaders are correct as of early August 1994. Some data on economic and social development relate to 1992 rather than 1993, since the usual annual statistical report had not been published. The Mongolian Directorate of Statistics is being reformed, and it will be required in the future to report on the private sector as well as state industry, commerce, and agriculture. Unofficial reports during the first half of 1994 indicate that an upturn in the economy is developing at last, inflation is at its lowest level for three years, and foreign trade is in balance, although unemployment and poverty have become serious social problems.

The Dictionary

- A -

ACADEMY OF SCIENCES. The academy was founded in November 1921 as the *Sudar Bichgiyn Hüreelen,* that is, the Institute (or Committee) of Scriptures and Manuscripts (Russian: *Knizhnaya palata*), but it is also known as the History Committee or Committee of Letters. Onguudyn Jam"yan was its first head, but the "guiding spirit" was the Buryat scholar Jamsrano (qq.v.). The primary task was to collect material on Mongolian history and philology and ethnographic data and register archaeological discoveries. The national archives, set up in 1927, were placed in its charge. Renamed the *Shinjleh Uhaan Hüreelen* (Committee of Sciences) in 1931, it began to undertake studies in botany, agriculture, geography, geology, and mapmaking; in 1940 agriculture was divided into crop raising and animal husbandry sectors.

However, new research institutes were increasingly linked with government ministries—building, education, health, communications, etc.—or the universities (q.v.)—physics, mathematics, biology, social sciences, etc. Meanwhile, the Institute of Party History supervised the writing of the history of the MPRP (q.v.) and the publication of translations of Marxist-Leninist "classics." There was close cooperation with the USSR Academy of Sciences, whose Mongolian Commission supervised Soviet research on Mongolia.

In 1959 the Committee of Science together with the State University (q.v.) were placed under the Committee of Science and Higher Education, but they separated in 1961 on the establishment of the *Shinjleh Uhaan Akademi,* or Academy of Sciences. The Central Public Library and Botanical Gardens in Ulan Bator (q.v.), Züünharaa research station, and the Gobi zonal research station at Bogd (Bayanhongor) are auxiliary institutions of the Academy. Scientific cooperation and research programs with the USSR and its East European satellites were coordinated by Comecon (q.v.). By 1971 two-thirds of the country's scientists were engaged in agricultural research, and new research stations had been opened at Shaamar, Bulgan (Hovd), and Halhyn Gol.

The Academy has seven departments—agriculture, chemistry and biology, geography and geology, medicine, physics and mathematics, sociology, and technology—and runs some 45 specialized research institutes. The president is elected by the assembly of members or Academicians (see Appendix 3). The Academy publishes a regular Bulletin (*Medee*) and various specialized publications—*Studia Mongolica, Studia Ethnographica, Studia Folclorica, Studia Historica, Studia Archaeologica, Studia Museologica,* etc.

ACADEMY OF STATE AND SOCIAL STUDIES. The academy's origins lie in the short-course school of the Mongolian People's Revolutionary Party (MPRP, q.v.) established in Ulan Bator (q.v.) in 1924 and the Party Central School founded on its basis in the following year. Its name was changed to the Party and State School in 1933, but it was renamed the Party Higher School for New Cadres in 1941. From 1953, as the Party Higher School, it experienced a period of expansion, merging with the Higher School of Economics of the MPRP Central Committee (q.v.) in 1959 and becoming a university faculty in 1963. The democratic political changes of 1990 led to the abandonment of its party title and, after a short period as the Political Higher School, it was taken over in 1991 by the State Little Hural (q.v.). As the Academy of State and Social Studies it underwent a profound change of direction. From 1992 it was under the control of the Seal Office (Secretariat) of the Mongolian Great Hural (q.v.). At the end of January 1994, however, the government amalgamated the Academy of State and Social Studies with the Institute for Management Development and the State Policy and Social Affairs Studies Center to form the Institute of State Administration and Management Development (q.v.).

ADILBISH, YONDONPUNTSAGIYN (1946-). Mongolian politician. Adilbish trained as a teacher. He became a political worker in the MPRP Central Committee (q.v.), then Secretary of the Ulan Bator MPRP Committee 1990, Chairman of Dornogov' MPRP Committee 1992, and a member of the MPRP Central Committee in 1990 and 1992. He was elected a member of the Mongolian Great Hural (q.v.) for the MPRP for a four-year term on June 28, 1992, in constituency 6 (Dornogov'). He is a member of two MGH standing committees: education, science, and culture; and internal affairs.

AGINSKOYE. Center of the Aga (Aginskiy) Buryat Autonomous District (*okrug*), part of Russia's Chita Region, area 19,000 sq km, situated 167 km from Chita town. Formed in September 1937 as the Aga Buryat-Mongol National District, the district has a population of some

90,000, of whom 40,000 are Buryats or Buriad (q.v.), called Chita Buryats in Mongolia. They were from Aga and Ulaan Onon *aymags* of the Buryat (Buryat-Mongol) Republic (q.v.), whose borders had been redrawn. The total Buryat population of Chita Region is about 66,700. The local monastery, famous for an extremely fine model of the Buddhist paradise, was wrecked in the Soviet antireligious campaigns of the 1930s.

AGRICULTURE. For details *see* Cooperative Farms, Private Farming, State Farms, Fodder and Grain, as well as Cattle, Horses, Sheep, etc.

AIRLINES. The Mongolian airline MIAT (q.v.) operates routes to Moscow, Irkutsk, and Ulan-Ude (qq.v.) in Russia and to Peking and Höhhot (Inner Mongolia, q.v.) in China, as well as internal flights to Mongolian provincial centers. There are also regular flights to Ulan Bator (q.v.) by the Russian Aeroflot (from Moscow via Omsk or Novosibirsk and Irkutsk) and by Air China (from Peking and Höhhot in Inner Mongolia). Summer charter flights have been introduced from Nagoya (Japan) to Ulan Bator and from Almaty (Kazakhstan) to Bayan-Ölgiy (q.v.). The international airlines flying the Siberian route from Europe to Peking and the Far East (British Airways, Finnair, etc.) have negotiated the fees for transit clearance through Mongolian airspace (700 flights a week at US$40 per 100 km), providing the country with a new source of much-needed hard currency.

AJILCHIN. Former district (*rayon*) of Ulan Bator (q.v.). "Worker" *rayon,* named in honor of the workers of the local industrial enterprises, was formed in 1965 and abolished in 1992. It consisted of Nos. 1-18 wards (*horoo*) and embraced the southern industrial and residential areas of the capital now incorporated in Han-Uul (q.v.) urban district (*düüreg*).

AJILCHIN. Former ward (*horoo*) of Ulan Bator (q.v.). One of the 10 wards abolished in 1965 on the formation of Ajilchin, Nayramdal, Oktyabr', and Sühbaatar (qq.v.) districts (*rayon*), each with smaller numbered *horoo.*

ALBA. Those subject to *alba* (corvée), the *albat* (serfs), were obliged in Manchu (q.v.) times to provide labor or transport, pay state taxes, perform military service, carry out border protection and *örtöö* (q.v.) duties, farm army land, or tend the emperor's herds. The *alba* could be commuted by taxation or substitution. In 1918 about a quarter of the population were *albat.* Serfdom was abolished in January 1922.

ALGAA, JAM"YANGIYN (1946-   ). Mongolian politician. Algaa trained as an engineer. He became Secretary of the Government Production Technology Council as well as a member of the MPRP Central Committee (q.v.) in 1992. He was elected a member of the Mongolian Great Hural (q.v.) for the MPRP for a four-year term on June 28, 1992, in constituency 26 (Ulan Bator). He is a member of two MGH standing committees: education, science, and culture; and economic policy.

ALTANBULAG. Border town in northern Selenge Province. Altanbulag was the first town on Mongolian soil to be liberated by the MPP (q.v.) revolutionaries in March 1921, and its name ("golden source") reflects this. It was the Manchu (q.v.) *maimaicheng,* or trading town, across the border from the Russian Kyakhta (q.v.) and was called by the Mongols Shivee Hiagt, Övör Hiagt, and Mongol Hiagt. Altanbulag was the center of Gazartarialan Province (q.v.) for a short period after the latter's establishment in 1931.

ALTAY. Center of Gov'-Altay Province (q.v.). Previously known as Zasagt-Hany Hüree, Han-Tayshiryn Hüree (1924-1929), and Yösönbulag, Altay was accorded town status in 1961. It is the highest town in Mongolia, at 2,181 m above sea level. The average January and July temperatures are -18.9 and 14.0 degrees C, and the average annual precipitation is 176.9 mm. The distance from Ulan Bator (q.v.) is 875 km. The population is about 19,000. Local industry produces mainly foodstuffs.

ALTAY. Former province (*aymag*) in western Mongolia. The name is derived from the Mongol Altai Mountains (q.v.). Founded in 1931, center Yösönbulag (present-day Altay, q.v.), this province comprised parts of the present-day Gov'-Altay and Bayanhongor provinces (qq.v.). It was merged with Zavhan Province (q.v.) in 1935 and reestablished in 1940 as Gov'-Altay Province.

ALTAY REPUBLIC. Part of the Russian Federation situated on Mongolia's northern border, area 92,600 sq. km. The capital is Gorno-Altaysk (since 1948), previously Ulala (until 1932) and Oyrt-Tura (1932-1948). The territory was originally conquered by Genghis Khan and became part of the Oirat (Oyrd, q.v.) or Jungarian khanate. The "Altaytsy," the native people of the Altay Republic, some 60,000, or one-fourth of the population, are Turkicized Mongol Oirats (Oyrd, q.v.), sometimes called Oirots (q.v.), and possibly related to the Buryad (q.v.). The "Autonomous Oirat *Oblast',*" founded in June 1922 within the Altay *Kray,* was renamed Gornyy Altay Autonomous

Oblast' in January 1948. Like similar territories in the former RSFSR seeking to promote their sovereignty, it opted in the early 1990s to style itself the Altay Republic. Economic and cultural relations with Mongolia are now developing under a bilateral agreement signed in 1992.

AMAR, ANANDYN (1886-1941). Mongolian head of state from 1932-1936, and prime minister 1928-1930 and 1936-1939. Amar was born into the family of a poor noble (*hoh' tayj*) in Daychin Vangiyn Hoshuu of Tüsheet-Han Aymag (present-day Hangal district of Bulgan Province, q.v.). He is also known as Gongor, and with the patronymics Agdangiyn or Agdanbuugiyn. Amar found employment in the foreign ministry of Bogd Han (autonomous) Mongolia 1913-1919. He was one of the founders of the Mongolian People's Party (q.v.), a member of the MPRP Central Committee and its Presidium, and member of the 1st to 7th Little Hurals (q.v.), as well as minister of foreign affairs, minister of internal and economic affairs and deputy prime minister 1923-1928; prime minister from February 21, 1928 to April 27, 1930; chairman of the Science Committee 1930-1932 (member of the Presidium until 1937); chairman of the Presidium of the Little Hural from July 2, 1932 to March 22, 1936; then again prime minister and concurrently foreign minister from February 22, 1936 to March 7, 1939. He was elected to the Presidium of the MPRP Central Committee (q.v.) in August 1924 (until 1925), October 1927 (until 1930), October 1934, and October 1937.

Together with Dansrangiyn Dogsom (q.v.), Amar had come under suspicion of counterrevolutionary activity in the "Lhümbe (q.v.) case" in 1936. At a meeting of the Presidium of the MPRP Central Committee on March 7, 1939, Choybalsan (q.v.) charged Amar with counterrevolutionary activity and Amar was expelled from the party and dismissed from the premiership. He was arrested the same day by the Ministry of Internal Affairs. In July 1939 the Amar case was passed to the NKVD (q.v.), and Amar was sent to the Siberian town of Chita and then to Moscow. He was accused of engaging in espionage for Japanese intelligence and sentenced to death by the Military Collegium of the USSR Supreme Court on July 10, 1941; he was executed on July 27. In a review of the Stalin purges 15 years later, the Military Collegium, meeting on December 15, 1956, found no evidence of Amar's guilt. He was rehabilitated by the Presidium of the MPR People's Great Hural (q.v.) on January 25, 1962. Amar's membership of the MPRP was restored by a resolution of the MPRP Party Control Committee on September 26, 1989. Amar was one of the 32 victims of the Mongolian purges of the 1930s and 1940s (q.v.) sent to the USSR for trial and sentence, details of which were released by the

Russian government in 1993. Amar was the author of several books, including *The Tenth Anniversary and Scientific Production* (1931), *On the Development of the Mongolian National Script* (1933), and *Short History of Mongolia* (1934).

AMARSANAA (1718-1757). West Mongolian Oyrd (q.v.) (Oirat, Jungar) prince who with Chingünjav (q.v.) led an uprising against the Manchu (q.v.). Amarsanaa's 2,500-strong rebel force entered a decisive battle against a Manchu army of 10,000 men on June 30, 1757. After 17 days of bitter fighting, Amarsanaa fled with the remnants of his force to Russia, where he died in exile on September 21, 1757.

AMARSANAA, JÜGNEEGIYN (1953-   ). Mongolian politician. Born in Ulan Bator (q.v.), Amarsanaa graduated in 1975 with a degree in law from the Mongolian State University; he then taught law at the state university and the MPRP Central Committee's (q.v.) Higher Political School. From 1981-1990 he was head of a department in the Ministry of Justice (later Ministry of Law and Arbitration). He obtained a higher degree in law in 1988. He is a member of the MPRP (q.v.). From September 1990-1992, he served as Minister of Law in the government of Dashiyn Byambasüren (q.v.). Not having been reappointed in 1992, Amarsanaa became pro-rector (research and training) of the Great Hural's Academy of State and Social Studies (qq.v.).

AMGALAN. Former ward (*horoo*) of Ulan Bator (q.v.). One of the 10 wards abolished in 1965 on the formation of Ajilchin, Nayramdal, Oktyabr', and Sühbaatar (qq.v.) districts (*rayon*), each with smaller numbered *horoo*.

ANIMAL CYCLE. The traditional Mongolian lunar calendar, like similar Chinese and Tibetan calendars, is based on years named after 12 animals: tiger, hare, dragon, snake, horse, sheep, monkey, chicken, dog, pig, mouse, and ox. (Note that in the Chinese calendar, rat is often used for mouse, rabbit for hare, goat for sheep, and rooster for chicken.) The years are alternately male and female so that six animals are male—tiger, dragon, horse, monkey, dog, and mouse—and six female—hare, snake, sheep (ewe), chicken (hen), pig (sow), and ox (cow). The animal names are combined with five elements—wood, fire, earth, iron, and water—matching the colors blue, red, yellow, white, and black, each element and color applying to a two-year period. The names of the animals alone, in the same fixed order, can also be used for months, or for the 12 "hours" of the day.

Animal	Mongol Name	Hour of Day	Month	Year	Color and Element	New Moon*
tiger	bar	3-5 (4)	1	1998	yellow earth	Jan. 28
hare	tuulay	5-7 (6)	2	1987	red fire	Jan. 29
dragon	luu	7-9 (8)	3	1988	yellow earth	Feb. 17
snake	mogoy	9-11 (10)	4	1989	yellow earth	Feb. 6
horse	mor'	11-13 (12)	5	1990	white iron	Jan. 27
sheep	hon'	13-15 (14)	6	1991	white iron	Feb. 15
monkey	mich	15-17 (16)	7	1992	black water	Feb. 4
chicken	tahia	17-19 (18)	8	1993	black water	Jan. 23
dog	nohoy	19-21 (20)	9	1994	blue wood	Feb. 10
pig	gahay	21-23 (22)	10	1995	blue wood	Jan. 31
mouse	hulgana	23-01 (24)	11	1996	red fire	Feb. 19
ox	üher	1-3 (2)	12	1997	red fire	Feb. 7

* Note that the first day of the new year holiday is the following day.

The lunar new year begins in January or February with the new moon or *tsagaan sar* (white moon). When a leap month is inserted, the Mongolian and Chinese new years may be a month apart. The combination of animals and elements produces 60 uniquely named years, a cycle called a *jaran* from the Mongol word for 60 (also sometimes called a "Buddhist century"). The traditional Mongolian calendar's current *jaran* began in 1984 with the year of the mouse. According to the Mongolian-Tibetan calendar, the first *jaran* began in the year 1027 with the year of the hare, and the current one, the 17th, in 1987.

ANIMAL HERDING. The Mongolians traditionally distinguish five kinds of animals (*tavan hoshuu mal*), which are important to the herding economy: sheep, goats, horses, cattle, and camels (qq.v.). They were all depicted in the coat of arms of the MPR from 1940 to 1960. For numbers, *see* Livestock.

ARD. A commoner or working man in the communist sense, usually a herdsman (Russian rendering: *arat*), and in the plural "the people," as used for the name of the Mongolian People's Republic and People's Great Hural (q.v.).

ARDYN ERH (PEOPLE'S POWER). Mongolian government newspaper. The birth of democracy and onset of multiparty politics, with the ensuing separation of government from the policies of the one constitutional ruling party, brought about in 1990 the rebirth of the newspaper *Ardyn Erh*, a title that had previously existed for a short while in the 1920s. As the government newspaper (four four-page issues a week), *Ardyn Erh* publishes proceedings of the Mongolian Great Hural (q.v.) and the cabinet, presidential decrees and Mongolian laws on adoption, and reports other official statements and business. The biggest-selling newspaper in Mongolia with a circulation of some 60,000 copies, it has essentially surplanted the MPRP organ *Ünen* (Truth) (q.v.).

ARGAL. The dried dung of cattle and other animals collected and burned in *ger* (q.v.) stoves in regions lacking local resources of coal or firewood.

ARGAL'. The wild mountain sheep, much prized for its large horns, hunted in the Gobi Altai Mountains (q.v.).

ARHANGAY. Province (*aymag*) in central Mongolia. Formed in 1931, the province is situated on the northern slopes of the Hangay Mountains (q.v.). With a territory of 55,000 sq km and population of 89,159 (1991), it has 17 rural districts (*sum*); the provincial center is Tsetser-leg (q.v.). There are deposits of coal (Tsaydam nuur), iron ore (Ögiynuur), and precious stones (Shavaryn tsaram). Livestock numbers reached 1,495,900 head (1992) and arable land 47,100 hectares (1989).

ARMY. The Mongolian army has had several different names since it was founded in 1921 as the Mongol Ardyn Juramt Tsereg, a partisan or guerrilla force mainly consisting of cavalry, whose *janjin* (commander) was Damdiny Sühbaatar (q.v.). In the postrevolutionary years, with Soviet technical aid and training, the army received motor vehicles, communications equipment and a few aircraft, and was re-named the Mongol Ardyn Huv'sgalt Tsereg, or People's Revolutionary Troops. The word *armi* (from the Russian *armiya*), replacing *tsereg,* was adopted at the time of the Second World War. After 1945 the army became the Mongolyn Ardyn Armi, or People's Army. Subsequently, with the growth of sophistication, power, and mechanization of the People's Army, it was once again renamed the Mongolyn Zevsegt Hüch, the Mongolian Armed Forces. Throughout their history they were fully equipped and trained by the USSR, and the uniforms and badges of rank worn at various periods were closely similar to their Soviet counterparts.

The president is commander-in-chief. The Ministry of Defense deals with administration and defense policy, while operational matters including mobilization are handled by the General Staff. The main commands are artillery, communications, rear services, and construction troops (engineers). The Ministry of Defense and chief of staff do not command the Mongolian Border Troops and Internal Troops, which were previously under the Ministry of Public Security (abolished 1990), then the Chief Directorate of State Security; the Border Troops have had their own directorate since late 1993. Mongolia has military helicopters, transport aircraft, and jet fighters, but no separate air force. Military air transport used to run the civil airline MIAT (q.v.).

ARTEL'. A craftsmen's association (Russian: *artel'*), of which there were 14 on the formation in 1933 of the Union of Mongolian Handicrafts Producers' Cooperatives (also known by the Russian acronym Kustpromsoyuz). They produced traditional clothing and footwear, *ger* (q.v.) parts and furniture, saddles, harnesses, etc. By 1951 they numbered 152 and their membership had reached 10,000. As clocks, watches, sewing machines, and wireless sets from the USSR became commonplace, new *artel'* were set up to provide repair services. Under the administration of the Central Industrial Cooperative Council, the production of the *artel'* grew to some 20 percent of gross industrial output by 1960. They were placed under the Ministry of Communal Economy and Services established in 1972.

ARVAN. Derived from *arvan,* meaning 10, an administrative unit of 10 households, subdivision of a *bag* (q.v.).

ARVAYHEER. Center of Övörhangay Province (q.v.). Previously known as Sayn-Noyon-Hany Hüree, Arvayheer ("barley fields") was accorded town status in 1963. Its height above sea level is 1,913 m, the average January and July temperatures are − 15.5 and 15.4 deg C, and the average annual precipitation is 254.2 mm. The distance from Ulan Bator (q.v.) is 355 km. The population is about 17,000. Local industries produce bricks and foodstuffs.

AR'SIMPEKS. Foreign trade company exporting hides, skins, furs, and leather goods and importing machinery for the associated industries.

ASRALT HAYRHAN. Mountain in Mongolia. This 2,800 m peak is the highest in the Hentey Mountains (q.v.) and is situated in Töv Province (q.v.), 60 km north of Ulan Bator (q.v.); it is sometimes called Zaluuchuud (youth) peak.

AVTONEFT'IMPORT. Foreign trade company set up by the former Ministry of Foreign Trade to import motor vehicles, aircraft, railway rolling stock, spare parts, petrol, oil, and tires.

AYMAG. Mongolian administrative division. Mongolia's territory is divided administratively into the capital and 21 *aymag,* or provinces (q.v.). The 21 *aymag* are divided into rural districts, or *sum* (q.v.). The *aymag* of Inner Mongolia (q.v.) are usually called leagues. The word *aymag* can also mean a tribe.

AYRAG. Mongolian name for fermented mare's milk or koumiss (q.v.).

AYUUSH, ALDARJAVYN (ARD AYUUSH) (1859-1939). Rebel leader. Ayuush was one of 13 rebels elected by a protest meeting of local herders in Yundendorj Hoshuu of Zasagt-Han Aymag (present-day Tsetseg district of Hovd Province, q.v.) in 1903 to present a petition (*zargyn bichig*) against the excesses of Hoshuu Prince Manibazar; they were arrested, tortured, and fined. On the collapse of Manchu power in 1911, local officials, fearing the renewed spread of rebellion, arrested and imprisoned Ayuush and his friends, but they were freed by supporters on February 29, 1912, and Ayuush took shelter at Höndiyn Am in the nearby hills. He then formed a popular assembly, the Tsetsegnuur *duguylan* (q.v.), and organized a new petition demanding the lightening of the *örtöö* (q.v.) service, abolition of taxes and the writing off of debts, as well as the punishment of Manibazar. The petition received 165 signatures, written in a circle like the spokes of a wheel to conceal the leader's identity. The movement was again suppressed, but fearing the spread of protest to the army, the local court released them on payment of a fine. Ayuush was imprisoned once again in 1915 on the orders of the Uliastay (q.v.) governor and Zasagt-Han Aymag assembly. In 1917 Ayuush arrived in the capital Ih Hüree (q.v.) to protest to the Ministry of Justice, but was sent back empty-handed. Meanwhile, Prince Manibazar died. Ayuush was depicted as a symbol of the liberation struggle after the 1921 revolution, when he filled minor administrative posts.

- B -

BAASANJAV, BANZARJAVYN (1906-1940). Mongolian party leader. Born in the present-day Myangad district of Hovd Province (q.v.), Baasanjav joined the Mongolian Revolutionary Youth League in 1923 and the MPRP (qq.v.) in 1930. From 1927-1928 he was a schoolteacher in the Ulaangom area, but went over to full-time MRYL work as head of a department and secretary of his district committee. In 1931 he became head of a department in the Hovd Provincial MPRP Committee. He was sent to Ulan Bator (q.v.) to be an MPRP Central Committee (q.v.) instructor shortly before his appointment to the post of Chairman of Hovd Provincial MPRP Committee 1932-1936. In October 1936 he was elected a member of the Presidium and Secretary of the MPRP Central Committee and appointed Chairman of the Mongolian Trade Unions, but in February 1940 he was arrested on charges of counterrevolution and executed. He was rehabilitated in 1957.

BAATAR. Derived from *baatar,* meaning hero, a title awarded for military or labor heroism in the communist period. Heroes of the MPR and Heroes of Labor of the MPR receive the Order of Sühbaatar (q.v.), the highest government award, instituted in 1941. The Russian form *bogatyr'* (also meaning a knight) dates back to the times of the Golden Horde (*see* Chronology) and reflects the classical Mongolian spelling.

BAATAR, DUMAAJAVYN (1941-). President of the Mongolian Academy of Sciences (q.v.). Baatar was sent to Moscow in 1959 to study medical applications of nuclear physics at the Medical Institute, but became a physics student at Moscow State University, graduating in biophysics in 1965. On return to Mongolia he specialized in the selective breeding of astrakhan (karakul) lambs. He is the author of numerous monographs and research papers, and was awarded a doctorate in 1982; he is a member (Academician) of the Mongolian Academy of Sciences. At the time of his appointment to the post of president of the Academy on February 25, 1991, he was the director of the Institute of Advanced Technology.

BADAMDORJ, CHIN VAN. A *shanzav,* or administrator, of the Bogd Gegeen's (q.v.) estates, Badamdorj was appointed Minister of Religion and State in 1912, his "ministry" being an extra-governmental office mainly intended to offset the powers of the new post of prime minister. Both posts were abolished in 1915, and Badamdorj became Minister of Internal Affairs. He was prime minister briefly in 1919-1920.

BADRAH, ÖLZIYTIYN (1895-1941). Mongolian party leader. Born in the Dörvöd Dalay Khan's territory (the present-day Davst district of Uvs Province, q.v.), Badrah was Minister of Finance 1924-1925, head of an MPRP Central Committee (q.v.) department 1926-1928, Secretary of the MPRP Central Committee from December 11, 1928 to June 30, 1932, and Minister of Health 1932-1934. He was elected to the Presidium of the MPRP Central Committee in March 1925, and re-elected 1925-1928 and in March 1930. He was expelled from the Central Committee for Left Deviation (q.v.) in 1932 and apparently exiled in Moscow. Badrah was arrested in 1937 on charges of counterrevolutionary activity. He was sentenced to death by the Military Collegium of the USSR Supreme Court in Moscow on July 7, 1941, and executed on July 30. He was rehabilitated by the Mongolian authorities in 1963. Badrah was one of the 32 victims of the Mongolian purges of the 1930s and 1940s (q.v.) sent to the USSR for trial and sentence, details of which were released by the Russian government in 1993.

BAG. A neighborhood, administrative division of a rural district or *sum* (q.v.). The *bag* was abolished in 1927 and reestablished in 1932, then abolished again in the 1950s when the *sum* were reorganized as *sum-negdel* (q.v.). They numbered some 2,500 at that time. The *bag* was made the basic-level administrative unit once again under the 1992 Constitution (q.v.).

BAGABANDI, NATSAGIYN (1950-   ). Mongolian politician. Born in Yaruu district of Zavhan Province (q.v.), Bagabandi went to school in Uliastay (q.v.) and graduated from Leningrad refrigeration engineering school in 1972. He first worked as a repair mechanic and engineer at Ulan Bator (q.v.) distillery and brewery from 1972-1975. He then studied at the Higher School of Food Technology in Odessa (Ukraine), graduating in 1980. From 1980-1984 he was head of the ideological department of the Töv MPRP Committee. He then went back to the USSR to study at the CPSU Central Committee's Academy of Social Sciences in Moscow from 1984-1987, obtaining the higher degree of Candidate of Philosophy. On return to Ulan Bator, his appointments included lector, section head, and departmental aide of the MPRP Central Committee (q.v.) from 1987-1990. Elected a member of the MPRP Central Committee in April 1990 and reelected in 1991 and 1992, he became a member of the Presidium and secretary of the MPRP Central Committee (1990), then vice-chairman (1992). Bagabandi was elected a member of the Mongolian Great Hural (q.v.) for the MPRP for a four-year term on June 28, 1992, in constituency 9 (Zavhan). At the opening session of the MGH in July 1992, he was elected chairman of the MGH. Under the 1992 Constitution (q.v.), the chairman may act as head of state in the event of the president's absence.

BAGAHANGAY. District (*düüreg*) of Ulan Bator (q.v.). Established in 1992, this urban district of some 860 households (1992) consists of two wards (*horoo*), incorporating the railway station and Öndörtolgoy areas of Bagahangay, a junction some 100 km southeast of the capital in Bayan rural district (*sum*) where the branch line to Baganuur (q.v.) joins the Trans-Mongolian Railway. Previously Bagahangay was itself a ward (*horoo*) of the capital.

BAGANUUR. District (*düüreg*) of Ulan Bator (q.v.). Established in 1992, this urban district of some 2,500 households (1992) consists of three wards (*horoo*) incorporating three residential areas, one of *gers* and two of apartments of Baganuur town. The district also includes the former Soviet Army cantonment of 149 buildings handed over to the Mongolian authorities. Before 1992, Baganuur was a *horoo*, then a *rayon* of the capital. The town is situated near opencast lignite mines in Bayandelger *sum* some 90 km east of the capital, and is linked by a branch line from Bagahangay (q.v.) to the Trans-Mongolian Railway.

BAHDAL, GOMBODORJIYN (1954-   ). Mongolian Procurator General 1990-1993. Born in Bayan Uul district, Dornod Province (q.v.), Bahdal studied in Ulan Bator (q.v.) and graduated from the law department of Irkutsk (q.v.) State University. In 1978 he was appointed special cases investigator at the Mongolian State Procurator's Office and later was promoted head of a department. He was appointed Deputy Procurator of Selenge Province (q.v.) in 1979, then Procurator of Ömnögov' Province (q.v.). On return to the State Procurator's Office he became head of the inspection and monitoring department. In September 1990, the People's Great Hural (q.v.) appointed him procurator general, and he held this post until his resignation in June 1993.

BALJINNYAM, BALJIDMAAGIYN (1898-1941). Commander of Border Troops, Ministry of Internal Affairs. One of the 32 victims of the Mongolian purges of the 1930s and 1940s (q.v.) sent to the USSR for trial and sentence, details of which were released by the Russian government in 1993. Sentenced to death by the Military Collegium of the USSR Supreme Court in Moscow on July 5, 1941 (date of execution not known).

BANKS, COMMERCIAL. Banking in Mongolia is supervised by the Mongolbank (q.v.), the former State Bank and Trade and Industry Bank. The following commercial banks were operating in Mongolia at the end of 1993:

Ardyn (People's) Bank: founded in 1991, capital 514.7 m tögrög; Director General A. Tserendorj.

Avtozam (Motor Roads) Bank: founded in 1990, capital 60.5 m tögrög; Director General Ts. Sangidorj.

Bayan Bogd Bank: founded in 1993, capital 82.2 m tögrög; owner D. Ad"yaa.

Ediyn Tenger Bank: founded in 1993, capital 68.7 m tögrög; Director V. Baatar.

Hödöö Aj Ahuyn (Agricultural) Bank: founded in 1991; capital 270.9 m tögrög; Director General Ch. Chuluunbaatar.

Höröngö Oruulalt Tyehnologiyn Shinechleltiyn (Capital Investment and Technological Innovation) Bank: founded in 1990, capital 668.3 m tögrög; Director N. Chuluunbaatar.

Hudaldaa Högjliyn (Trade and Development) Bank: founded in 1991 to manage the foreign transactions of Mongolbank, capital 101 m tögrög; Director General E. Sandagdorj.

Mongol Biznes (Business) Bank: founded in 1993, capital 50.2 m tögrög; Director General A. Davaanyam.

Mongol Daatgal (Insurance) Bank: founded in 1990, capital 295.3 m tögrög; Chairman Sh. Goohüü.

Mongol Horshoo (Cooperative) Bank: founded in 1990, capital 143.4 m tögrög; Chairman Mijidiyn Terbish.

Mongol Shuudan (Post) Bank: founded in 1993, capital 148.4 m tögrög; Director General D. Bayar.

Selenge Bank: A Mongol-Buryat joint venture (named after a local river) founded in 1992, capital 107.9 m tögrög; Director O. Tseveljav.

Töv Azi (Central Asia) Bank: founded in 1992, capital 74.6 m tögrög; Director General D. Süh-Erdene.

Ulaanbaatar (Ulan Bator) Bank: founded in 1993, capital 84.3 m tögrög; Director General A. Myagmar.

Uyldveriyn Huv' Niylüülsen (Industrial Shares) Bank: founded in 1990, capital 411.3 m tögrög; Director General Gendendorjiyn Yansanjav.

BARGA. Mongol ethnic group. The Barga, an East Mongol group, accounted for 0.1 percent (2,100) of the population of Mongolia, according to the 1989 census. The Barga, concentrated mostly in the northern and western districts of Dornod Province (q.v.), speak a dialect of Buryat (q.v.). Barga is also the name given to the territory that the Barga inhabited. *See also* China: Mongol Ethnic Groups.

BARUUN-URT. Center of Sühbaatar Province (q.v.). Accorded town status in 1965. Baruun-Urt's height above sea level is 981 m, the average January and July temperatures are −21.5 and 19.9 deg C, and the average annual precipitation is 191.7 mm. The distance from Ulan Bator (q.v.) is 530 km. The population is about 16,500. Local industry produces mainly foodstuffs.

BATBAATAR, DAADANHÜÜGIYN (1964-   ). Mongolian politician. Batbaatar trained as a lawyer and later became an adviser to a standing committee of the State Little Hural (q.v.) 1990-1992. He was elected a member of the Mongolian Great Hural (q.v.) for the MPRP (q.v.) for a four-year term on June 28, 1992, in constituency 22 (Ulan Bator). He is a member of two MGH standing committees: foreign policy and security, and assemblies and administration.

BATBAYAR, BAT-ERDENIYN ("BAABAR") (1954-   ). Mongolian politician. Born on October 26, 1954, in Tsetserleg, Arhangay Province (qq.v.), Batbayar graduated from the Mongolian State University in 1981 with a degree in biophysics. He was appointed a senior researcher at the Microbiology and Enzymology Science and Production Association. He also spent nine months in the United Kingdom doing research work. Using the pseudonym Baabar, at the beginning of 1990, at the height of the drive for democratic change in Mongolian society, he published two important political booklets. One saw the Soviet period in Mongolian history as one of harmful interference with Mongolian national values and traditions. The other looked ahead to the rebuilding of Mongolia's state structure and its entry into the free community of nations. Batbayar is a founder-member of the Mongolian Social Democratic Party (q.v.), which elected him chairman in March 1990. He was replaced as chairman by Gonchigdorj (q.v.) in March 1994.

BATBAYAR, SHIYLEGIYN (1943-   ). Mongolian politician. Batbayar trained as an economist and worked in the trade unions, becoming a member of the Presidium of the Central Council of the Trade Union Association, then chairman of the Central Council from March 1990-July 1992. He was made a member of the MPRP Central Committee (q.v.) in 1990 and 1992. He was elected a member of the Mongolian Great Hural (q.v.) for the MPRP for a four-year term on June 28, 1992, in constituency 10 (Övörhangay). He is a member of two MGH standing committees: health and social security, and economic policy.

BATJARGAL, ZAMBYN (1945-   ). Minister of the environment 1992-   . Born on February 25, 1945, in Sagil district of Uvs Province (q.v.), Batjargal graduated in 1969 from Leningrad Higher School of Hydrometeorology with a degree in applied mathematics. He first worked as a technician and engineer at the Hydrometeorological Research Institute from 1969-1979, becoming head of its computer center and deputy director from 1979-1982. He was then promoted to deputy director of the Hydrometeorological Service from 1982-1984, and first deputy director from 1984-1987. In 1987 he was appointed director of the information and computer center of the Ministry of Environmental Protection, but transferred to the Secretariat of Comecon (q.v.) from 1988-1990. On the formation of the State Committee for Environmental Control, he was made chairman from October 1990-August 1992. His responsibilities included development of a national policy on mineral extraction. Batjargal was appointed minister of the environment on August 3, 1992, by the first session of the Mongolian Great Hural (q.v.), of which he is not a member.

BATMÖNH, JAMBYN (1926-). Mongolian premier 1974-1984 and president 1984-1990. Born in Hyargas district of Uvs Province on March 10, 1926, Batmönh graduated from the Mongolian State University and the Academy of Social Sciences of the CPSU Central Committee (1958-1961). He was a lecturer at the Mongolian State University and the Higher Teachers' School 1951-1952, lecturer and deputy director of the Higher Party School of the MPRP Central Committee (q.v.) 1952-1958, then head of a department, deputy director, and director of the Higher School of Economics 1962-1967. From 1967 he was deputy director and then director of the Mongolian State University. In 1973 he began work at the MPRP Central Committee, where he became head of the science and education department. In May 1974 he was appointed deputy chairman of the Council of Ministers, and following the general elections Batmönh was appointed chairman of the Council of Ministers (premier) on June 11, 1974. He held this post until Yumjaagiyn Tsedenbal (q.v.) was removed from the party and state leadership in 1984; Batmönh then became general secretary (August) and chairman of the Presidium of the People's Great Hural (q.v.) or head of state (December 12). He resigned these posts on March 14 and 21, 1990, being replaced as MPRP leader by Gombojavyn Ochirbat (q.v.) and as chairman of the PGH Presidium by Punsalmaagiyn Ochirbat (q.v.).

Having joined the MPRP in 1948, Batmönh was elected a candidate member of the MPRP Central Committee in 1971 and a member of the Central Committee and of its Politburo in June 1974, on his appointment to the post of chairman of the Council of Ministers. He was a member of the People's Great Hural 1973-1990. Batmönh was a conventional pro-Soviet communist who made few policy changes after the removal of Tsedenbal. Under the pressure of perestroika in the USSR, toward the end of the 1980s Batmönh inaugurated a policy of economic "renewal" involving the restructuring of government ministries, but the "political openness" he also advocated was quite inadequate, leaving the entrenched party bureaucracy in charge of reform. When the Berlin Wall fell and the proponents of the nascent democracy in Mongolia openly rebelled against "stagnation" and the MPRP in 1990, Batmönh's Politburo, lacking the Kremlin's support, quickly crumpled and collapsed in March 1990. He disappeared from view until January 1994, when he attended a meeting of the Society for Promotion of the Mongol Script (q.v.).

BATMÖNH, OSORHÜÜGIYN (1954-). Mongolian politician. Batmönh trained as a mathematics teacher. He was vice-chairman of Övörhangay (q.v.) MPRP Committee in 1992. He was elected a member of the Mongolian Great Hural (q.v.) for the MPRP (q.v.) for a four-year term on June 28, 1992, in constituency 10 (Övörhangay). He is a member of two MGH standing committees: education, science, and culture, and assemblies and administration.

BATMÖNH, SODNOMYN (1950-   ). Mongolian politician. Batmönh trained as a mathematics teacher. He was secretary of Dornod (q.v.) MPRP Committee 1990, chairman of Dundgov' (q.v.) MPRP Committee from June 1990-1992, a member of the MPRP Central Committee (q.v.) from 1990-1992 and a deputy of the People's Great Hural (q.v.) from 1990-1992. He was elected a member of the Mongolian Great Hural (q.v.) for the MPRP for a four-year term on June 28, 1992, in constituency 8 (Dundgov'). He is a member of two MGH standing committees: education, science, and culture, and assemblies and administration.

BATSUUR', JAM"YANGIYN (1951-   ). Mongolian politician. Born in Harhorin district of Övörhangay Province (q.v.), Batsuur' trained as a physiologist and worked at the Lomonosov State University, Moscow, and the Institute of Genetics and General Biology of the Mongolian Academy of Sciences (q.v.) from 1973-1981. In 1982 he became a postgraduate student of the Vavilov Institute of Genetics, Moscow, gaining a doctorate in biology in 1986. On return to Mongolia he was head of a department at the Institute of Genetics and General Biology and was then appointed director of the Institute of Biotechnology. He was chairman of the State Committee for Technical Progress and Standardization in 1990, minister of national development from August 1990-July 1992, and a member of the MPRP Central Committee (qq.v.) from 1990-1992. He was elected a member of the Mongolian Great Hural (q.v.) for the MPRP for a four-year term on June 28, 1992, in constituency 10 (Övörhangay). He was chairman of the MGH standing committee for education, science, and culture from June 1992 to October 1993 and is a member of the standing committee for foreign policy and security.

BATSÜH, CHOYMBOLYN (1911-1941). Head of special department, Ministry of Internal Affairs. One of the 32 victims of the Mongolian purges of the 1930s and 1940s (q.v.) sent to the USSR for trial and sentence, details of which were released by the Russian government in 1993. Sentenced to death by the Military Collegium of the USSR Supreme Court in Moscow on July 5, 1941, he was executed on July 27.

BATSÜH, DAMDINSÜRENGIYN (1952-1994). Mongolian politician. Born in Hotont district of Arhangay Province (q.v.), Batsüh graduated from the Mongolian State University in 1975 with a degree in engineering. After teaching at the State University and Polytechnic University from 1975-1985, he attended the Belorussian State University, which awarded him a higher degree in economics in 1988. One of the leaders of the Mongolian democratic revolution of 1990, Batsüh helped to found the New Progress Association (q.v.), of which he became president in 1991. He served as a member of the State Little Hural (q.v.) from 1990-1992.

BAT-ÜÜL, ERDENIYN (1956-   ). Mongolian politician. Bat-Üül graduated from the Mongolian State University with a degree in physics and began his working life as a secondary schoolteacher. Later he became a research worker at the astronomical observatory of the Academy of Sciences (q.v.). He was a trailblazer of the democratic movement in Mongolia, founding an informal group called New Times (q.v.) in early 1988, which scattered leaflets and put up posters criticizing the MPRP (q.v.); they were arrested for this, but soon released. Bat-Üül joined the Mongolian Democratic Association (q.v.) on its foundation and was a participant in the hunger strike of March 1990, which helped bring down the Politburo of the MPRP and government. He was elected general coordinator of the Mongolian Democratic Party (q.v.) in April 1990. In October 1992, the Democratic Party became part of the newly formed Mongolian National Democratic Party (q.v.), and Bat-Üül was elected a member of its General Council and became director of the MNDP's Institute of Political Policy. In November 1993, Bat-Üül was elected secretary-general of the MNDP.

BAYAD (BAIT). Mongol ethnic group. The Bayad, a West Mongol Oyrd (q.v.) (Oirat) group speaking the northern dialect, accounted for 1.9 percent (39,200) of the population of Mongolia, according to the 1989 census. The Bayad are concentrated mainly east of Uvs *nuur,* in the eastern districts of Uvs Province (q.v.). They are believed to have inhabited the valley of the Selenge (q.v.) in the twelfth and thirteenth centuries. *See also* China: Mongol Ethnic Groups.

BAYANGOL. District (*düüreg*) of Ulan Bator (q.v.). Established in 1992, this western and southwestern urban district of some 26,800 households (1992) north of the river Selbe consists of 19 wards (*horoo*) incorporating Baruun Hüree residential (*ger*) and Nos. 3, 4, and 10 (apartment) areas (*horoolol*), Naran, Tömör Zam (railway station), and Narlag, Gandan monastery and other northern parts of the former Ajilchin district (q.v.) (*rayon*) of the capital.

BAYANHONGOR. Province (*aymag*) in southwestern Mongolia. The province, formed in 1942, is situated between the Hangay Mountains (q.v.) and the border with China (Alxa League of Inner Mongolia Autonomous Region; during the Chinese "cultural revolution," Bayanhongor bordered on Gansu Province). With a territory of 116,000 sq km and population of 78,641 (1991), it has 19 rural districts (*sum*); the provincial center, after which it is named, is Bayanhongor (q.v.). There are deposits of coal (Bayanbulag), gold (Bayan-Ovoo, Dövönt), and rare metals (Muhar-Ereg). Livestock numbers reached 1,761,900 head (1992) and arable land 7,800 hectares (1989).

BAYANHONGOR. Center of Bayanhongor Province (q.v.). Accorded town status in 1963, Bayanhongor is situated on the Tüyn *gol,* which flows into Lake Orog, and the old *örtöö* (q.v.) road west to Uliastay (q.v.). Its height above sea level is 1,859 m, the average January and June temperatures are − 18.4 and 15.9 deg C, and the average annual precipitation is 216.3 mm. The distance from Ulan Bator (q.v.) is 525 km. The population is about 21,000. Local industries include meat packing and the production of bricks, lime, and foodstuffs.

BAYANJARGAL, CHÜLTEMSÜRENGIYN (1941-). Mongolian politician. Bayanjargal trained as an economist and became a lecturer at the Mongolian State University and chairman of the University MPRP Committee. He was made a member of the MPRP Central Committee (qq.v.) from 1991-1992. He was elected a member of the Mongolian Great Hural (q.v.) for the MPRP for a four-year term on June 28, 1992, in constituency 19 (Darhan). He is a member of two MGH standing committees: budget and finance, and economic policy.

BAYAN-ÖLGIY. Province (*aymag*) in western Mongolia. Formed in 1940, Bayan-Ölgiy ("rich cradle") Province is situated on the borders of Kosh-Agach district of the Altay Republic (q.v.) and Mongun-Tayga district of the Tuva Republic (q.v.) in Russia and Altai Prefecture of Ili Kazakh Autonomous Prefecture, Xinjiang Uighur Autonomous Region in China. With a territory of 46,000 sq km and population of 99,222 (1991), it has 12 rural districts (*sum*); until 1992 there was one ward (*horoo*), Tsagaannuur; the provincial center is Ölgiy (q.v.). The population is mostly Kazakh (q.v.), and the province is sometimes referred to unofficially as a Kazakh "national" province. Large-scale emigration of contracted labor to Kazakhstan in 1991-1992 may have reduced the Kazakh population by as much as 30,000, however. The local minorities include the Dörvöd (q.v.). There is a main road from Tsagaannuur freight transshipping depot into the Altay Republic through the Durbet-Daba pass to Tashanta, providing access to Kosh-Agach (via the Chuya *trakt*), Gorno-Altaysk, Biysk, Bar-

naul, and Novosibirsk in Russia. The designated permanent crossing
points on the border with Russia are Tsagaannuur (for Tashanta) and
Asgatyn Gol (for Aspayty), and a seasonal crossing point at Ulaan-
davaa (for Argamzhi). The designated occasional crossing points on
the border with China are Dayan (for Hungshantzü) and Naransevstey
(for Mazushan). There are deposits of silver (Asgat), wolfram (Ulaan-
Uul), and nonferrous metals (Sagsay). Livestock numbers reached
1,033,900 head (1992) and arable land 5,300 hectares (1989).

BAYAN-ÖLGIY ECONOMIC COOPERATION ZONE. One of six
economic cooperation zones into which Mongolia was divided on the
basis of a government ordinance issued in November 1991 (the others
being the Central, Gov'-Altay, Övörhangay, Sühbaatar, and Ulan Bator economic cooperation zones, qq.v.). It consists of Bayan-Ölgiy,
Hovd, and Uvs Provinces (qq.v.). Each zone has a cooperation office
headed by the secretary of the zonal cooperation council.

BAYANZÜRH-UUL. District (düüreg) of Ulan Bator (q.v.). Established in 1992, this eastern urban district of some 23,400 households
(1992) is named after a local range of hills and consists of 18 wards
(horoo) incorporating Tsagaan Davaa, Ulaanhuaran, Sharhad, Uliastay, Konsulyn Denj, Dar'-Ehiyn Ovoo, Amgalan, and Erdenetolgoy
residential (ger) areas and Nos. 13, 15, and 16 (apartment) areas
(horoolol), Honhor, Sansar, Altan Tevsh, and other parts of the former Nayramdal district (q.v.) (rayon) of the capital.

BAYARBAATAR, SED-OCHIRYN (1956-). Mongolian politician.
Born in Ulan Bator (q.v.), Bayarbaatar graduated from a Soviet university with a degree in automation engineering. He worked for over
10 years at a power station in Ulan Bator. He then joined the Ministry
of Foreign Economic Relations where he was appointed director general of the Mongolimpex Co. His responsibilities included the contracts with foreign firms for the purchase of a mini metallurgical plant
and space communications system. He was then sent to the USSR
Academy of Foreign Trade, where he obtained a higher degree in international economics. He is an MPRP (q.v.) member. From September 1990-1992, he was minister of trade and industry, in which post
he promoted foreign credit and investment in Mongolia and advocated
privatization and currency convertibility.

BAYARTSAYHAN, NADMIDIYN (1962-). Mongolian politician.
Bayartsayhan graduated from Irkutsk Higher School and then taught
in the MPRP's (q.v.) Higher Party School until 1989. From 1989-1992
he studied for a higher degree in economics at the Russian Academy

of Management. He was elected a member of the Mongolian Great
Hural (q.v.) for the MPRP for a four-year term on June 28, 1992, in
constituency 15 (Uvs). In October 1993, he was elected chairman of
the MGH standing committee on food and agriculture, of which he
had been a member; he is also a member of the economic policy standing committee. In November 1993, Bayartsayhan was elected a member of the MPRP's Party Leadership Council (q.v.).

BAYASGALAN, JAMTSYN (1910-1941). Head of the third department, Ministry of Internal Affairs. One of the 32 victims of the Mongolian purges of the 1930s and 1940s (q.v.) sent to the USSR for trial
and sentence, details of which were released by the Russian government in 1993. Sentenced to death by the Military Collegium of the
USSR Supreme Court in Moscow on July 7, 1941, Bayasgalan was
executed on July 29.

BAZARHAND, SANJIYN (1912-1941). Deputy head of counterintelli-
gence department, Ministry of Internal Affairs. One of the 32 victims
of the Mongolian purges of the 1930s and 1940s (q.v.) sent to the
USSR for trial and sentence, details of which were released by the
Russian government in 1993. Sentenced to death by the Military Collegium of the USSR Supreme Court in Moscow on July 6, 1941,
Bazarhand was executed on July 28.

BAZARHÜÜ, AYUURZANYN (1948-   ). Mongolian politician. Born
in Gov'-Altay Province (q.v.), Bazarhüü trained as an accountant and
first worked at the Ministry of Finance. He graduated in 1971 from the
State Institute of International Relations, Moscow, and later was appointed head of the hard currency department of the Ministry of Finance. He was awarded a higher degree of Candidate of Sciences for
a study of Mongolia's financial system. He became chairman of the
State Committee for Prices and Standardization in 1984, then deputy
minister and first deputy minister of finance in 1990. He was appointed minister of finance from August 1990-July 1992 and became
a member of the MPRP Central Committee (qq.v.) from 1991-1992.
He was elected a member of the Mongolian Great Hural (q.v.) for the
MPRP for a four-year term on June 28, 1992, in constituency 5 (Gov'-
Altay). He is chairman of the MGH standing committee for budget
and finance (reelected October 1993), and a member of the standing
committee for economic policy.

BAZARSAD, DASHBALBARYN (1951-   ). Mongolian politician.
Bazarsad became an army officer, later chief of staff of the Border
Troops, chief directorate of State Security, with the rank of colonel

from 1991-1992 and a member of the MPRP Central Committee (qq.v.) from February-September 1991. He was elected a member of the Mongolian Great Hural (q.v.) for the MPRP for a four-year term on June 28, 1992, in constituency 7 (Dornod). He is a member of two MGH standing committees: environmental protection, and foreign policy and security.

BEEL (BEILE). A noble title of the second grade created by the Manchu (q.v.). There were two classes, *beel* (beile) and *bees* (beise).

BILEGSAYHAN, NAMSRAYN (1866-1923). Revolutionary leader. Born in Erdene Vangiyn *hoshuu*, Tüsheet-Han Aymag (present-day Selenge Province, q.v.), Bilegsayhan learned to read and write in Mongol and Manchu and was employed at the *hoshuu* seal office (secretariat) and office of the Kyakhta Minister. He came into contact with Sühbaatar (q.v.) and other revolutionaries in 1920 on their return to Verkhneudinsk from Irkutsk (q.v.) and took up military administration, including recruitment of men from his home *hoshuu* to fight the troops of the Chinese government and of Baron von Ungern-Sternberg (q.v.). He was made a member of the provisional government from March 13 to May 29, 1921, when he returned once again to his *hoshuu* to organize military matters. After the victory of the 1921 revolution he was responsible for provisioning and supplying the army. In September 1921, he was appointed governor of Kyakhta town (Altanbulag, qq.v.) and the border area and helped develop relations with Soviet Russia, but died of illness in 1923.

BOD. Unit for counting livestock (q.v.). At the turn of the nineteenth-twentieth centuries, a *bod* was one horse or five sheep, and a camel was two *bod*; an ox was equal to four sheep, and three goats to two sheep. In the 1960s-1980s a *bod* was one horse or cow, five to seven sheep, or seven to ten goats; a camel was one and a half or two *bod*. This method of counting has survived into the present day, the latest scale being fixed at one *bod* equals one horse or cow, six sheep or eight goats; one camel equals one and a half *bod*. The results of the national census of livestock for 1993, published at the beginning of February 1994, gave the total number of animals as 25,174,688 head, or 8,532,202.8 *bod*.

BODOO, DOGSOMYN (1895-1922). Mongolian prime minister from 1921-1922. Born in the territory of Mandshir *hutagt* (Töv Province, q.v.), Bodoo studied at the Mongolian language and literature school in Niyslel Hüree (q.v.), became a scribe at the Shaviyn Yaam (religious affairs office), then a Mongolian language teacher at the Russian Consul's school of interpreters. He became the Niyslel Hüree representative of the Harbin newspaper *Mongolyn Sonin Bichig* (Mongolian Newspaper) and, using the pseudonym Bold or Bo, correspondent and editor of *Shine Tol'* (New Mirror) and *Niyslel Hüreeniy Sonin Bichig* (Capital's Newspaper). Bodoo was the founder of the secret revolutionary organization set up at Konsulyn Denj (q.v.), which eventually amalgamated with Sühbaatar's Züün Hüree (q.v.) organization to form the Mongolian People's Party (q.v.). He was a member of the MPP delegation, including Chagdarjav, Choybalsan, S. Danzan, Dogsom, Losol, and Sühbaatar (qq.v.), which went to Soviet Russia in 1920 to contact the Bolsheviks. From March 1921, Bodoo served in the provisional revolutionary government as foreign minister, and from April 16, concurrently as prime minister, replacing Chagdarjav. He was confirmed in both posts in July 1921. In view of Soliyn Danzan's visit to Soviet Russia in September 1921, some sources say, Bodoo became chairman of the MPRP Central Committee (qq.v.). He resigned all his posts on January 7, 1922, however, and not long afterward was arrested on charges of treason and executed on August 31, 1922.

BOGD GEGEEN. The "holy enlightened ones," or "high enlightened ones" (Öndör Gegeen), the leaders of Mongolian Lamaism (q.v.), incarnations of Javzandamba Hutagt Zanabazar (qq.v.), especially the eighth and last who became Bogd Khan (q.v.), or head of state, during the period of autonomy from 1911 until his death in 1924. Born in 1869 into the family of an official of the Dalai Lama and named Agvaanluvsanchoyjindanzanvaanchigbalsambuu, he was taken to Mongolia at the age of four.

The communist government disallowed any new incarnations, although there have been several contenders. During the MPR (1924-1992) the role of the country's Buddhist leader was played by the abbot of Gandan monastery (q.v.). In the post-communist period, with the matter of a new incarnation or Bogd Gegeen unresolved, the Gandan abbot's leadership role has been challenged by the abbot of Amarbayasgalant monastery in northern Mongolia, now restored and returned to religious use.

BOGD HAN UUL. Mountain in Mongolia. This mountain in Töv Province lies directly south of Ulan Bator, across the river Tuul (qq.v.); the 2,256 m peak is sometimes called Tsetsee Gün. The government hotel and recreation center of Ih Tenger is situated in a picturesque valley on the northern slope. The Mandshiriyn Hiyd monastery, on the southern slope, is reached by road via Zuunmod (q.v.).

BOGD-HAN-UUL. Former province (*aymag*) in central Mongolia named after Bogd Han Uul Mountain (q.v.). This large province, center Lün (q.v.), was founded in 1923 on the territory of the former Tüsheet-Han (q.v.) *aymag*. In the administrative reforms of 1931 the five large provinces were broken up into 12 (later 18) smaller ones. This province formed parts of the present-day Selenge, Bulgan, Töv, Övörhangay, Ömnögov', Dundgov', and Dornogov' provinces (qq.v.).

BOLAT, AJHANY (1942-   ). Mongolian politician. Born in Bayan-Ölgiy Province (q.v.), Bolat graduated in agricultural economics from the Mongolian Higher School of Economics in 1966. He first worked as an economist on a herding cooperative in Bayan-Ölgiy, but in 1972 was appointed deputy chairman of the planning commission of the Provincial Executive Administration; in 1974 he was elected chairman of Delüün herding cooperative and district executive administration. He joined the Provincial Executive Administration in 1980 as deputy chairman in charge of agriculture; in 1990 he became first deputy chairman. He was elected a deputy of the People's Great Hural (q.v.) in July 1990 and subsequently became a member of the State Little Hural (q.v.) and its legal affairs committee from 1990-1992. Bolat was elected a member of the MPRP Central Committee (qq.v.) in 1992, and a member of the Mongolian Great Hural (q.v.) for the MPRP for a four-year term on June 28, 1992, in constituency 2 (Bayan-Ölgiy). In October 1993, he was elected chairman of the MGH standing committee on assemblies and administration, of which he had been a member; he is also a member of the food and agriculture standing committee.

BOLDBAATAR, JIGJIDIYN (1949-   ). Mongolian politician. Born in Bugat district, Bulgan Province (q.v.), Boldbaatar graduated from the Mongolian State University in 1971 and obtained a Doctorate of History in 1991. He first worked as a teacher at the Mongolian State University from 1971-1976, then as a teacher and department head at the Higher Party School 1979-1990. He was the director of the political studies center of the Higher Political School from June 1990-1991. He also served as a member of the MPRP Central Auditing Commission from 1990-1991, member of the MPRP Central Committee (qq.v.) from 1991-1992, secretary of the Central Committee from 1991-1992, and vice-chairman of the MPRP 1992. He was elected a member of the Mongolian Great Hural (q.v.) for the MPRP for a four-year term on June 28, 1992, in constituency 4 (Bulgan). He is a member of two MGH standing committees: education, science, and culture, and international affairs. He was also the leader of the MPRP party group in the MGH until November 1993, when the post was given to Damdingiyn Demberel (q.v.).

BÖÖRÖGIYN ELS. Sand dunes. The world's northernmost sand dunes, situated at 50 deg 18 min N latitude between Züüngov' and Tes district centers in Uvs Province (q.v.).

BRIGAD. An industrial work team (Russian: *brigada*), or a rural work unit, subdivision of a *negdel*, or state farm (qq.v.), based on a small outlying settlement (usually numbered rather than named) some distance away from the center.

BULGAN. Province (*aymag*) in northern Mongolia. Formed in 1938, the province is situated between the Hangay Mountains (q.v.) and the border with Russia (Zakamensk district of the Buryat Republic, q.v.). From 1956-1960 it included parts of the present-day Selenge Province (q.v.). With a territory of 49,000 sq km and population of 56,670 (1991), it has 15 rural districts (*sum*); the provincial center, after which it is named, is Bulgan (q.v.). The local minorities include the Buryad (q.v.). The designated permanent crossing point on the border with Russia is Egiyn Gol (for Kholtoson). The copper and molybdenum mine at Erdenet (q.v.) is linked by railway to Salhit (Selenge Province) on the Trans-Mongolian Railway. There are deposits of lignite (Sayhan-Ovoo) and gold (Mogod). Livestock numbers reached 1,066,100 head (1992) and arable land 78,100 hectares (1989).

BULGAN. Center of Bulgan Province (q.v.). Previously known as Vangiyn Hüree, and accorded town status in 1961. Bulgan's height above sea level is 1,208 m, the average January and July temperatures are −21.3 and 16.3 deg C, and the average annual precipitation is 324.3 mm. The distance from Ulan Bator (q.v.) is 265 km. Its population is about 14,000. Local industries include flour milling and foodstuffs production.

BUMTSEND, GONCHIGIYN (1881-1953). Politician and statesman. Born into a poor herdsman's family on September 11, 1881, in Züün-bürenhanuul Hoshuu of Tüsheet-Han Aymag (present-day Yöröö district of Selenge Province, q.v.), Bumtsend learned to read and write at the age of thirteen and wrote letters and petitions for the illiterates of his *hoshuu*. By the age of sixteen he had become a skilled woodworker but made his living as a carter at an örtöö (q.v.) station on the road from Kyakhta to Urga (qq.v.). From 1912-1918 Bumtsend was a laborer in Urga, then he returned to his home *hoshuu* to work in the local administration. In 1920 he made contact with the MPP (q.v.)

revolutionaries, for whom he organized the collection of winter clothing and did propaganda work. Following his first meeting with Sühbaatar (q.v.) in 1921, Bumtsend was appointed a unit commander during the assault on Kyakhta and later was engaged in fighting Chinese troops and the forces of Baron von Ungern-Sternberg (q.v.).

Immediately after the victory of the revolution he was sent in pursuit of the Baron's baggage train, which was seized while fleeing eastward at Tsenheriyn Gol in Tsetsen-Han (q.v.) Aymag. As commander of a regiment he was sent to eastern Mongolia, where he destroyed the "counterrevolutionary" forces of Naydan Van and Jambalon at Mogoyt and Matad. He joined the MPRP (q.v.) in 1923. From 1928-1940 Bumtsend was engaged in the strengthening of the revolutionary administration in the countryside and the "elimination of the feudalists as a class" (expropriation of the nobility), as well as the expulsion of foreign "capitalists" (Chinese merchants) from the country. In 1940 the MPRP's 10th Congress elected Bumtsend to the Presidium of the Central Committee (q.v.), and the 8th Great Hural (q.v.) elected him chairman of the Little Hural (q.v.) on July 6, 1940. In 1951 he was elected chairman of the Presidium of the People's Great Hural (q.v.), and he died in office on September 23, 1953. His awards included two Orders of Sühbaatar (q.v.) and the Soviet Order of Lenin.

BURIAD (BURYAD, BURYAAD, BURYAT). Mongol ethnic group. The Buriad, or Buryats, a North Mongol group, accounted for 1.7 percent (35,400) of the population of Mongolia, according to the 1989 census. They are concentrated mostly along Mongolia's northern border and are related to the Buryats of the Buryat (Buryat-Mongol) Republic (q.v.) in Russia. There are two dialects, eastern—Hor', Aga, Barga, and Hudir in the Onon and Ulz valleys, Dornod, and Hentiy provinces—and northern—Tunh, Sanaga, and Tsongool in the Selenge and Üür valleys, Selenge, Bulgan, and Hövsgöl provinces (qq.v.). The Tunh-Sanaga Buryats living in Tsagaan Üür and Hanh districts of Hövsgöl Province and Teshig district of Bulgan Province (now numbering 3,000) claim to have arrived in Mongolia in 1912-1916. Indeed, the Buryats who moved from Russia to Mongolia in the period of Mongolian autonomy formed a small but influential group of skilled craftsmen and civil servants. Both before and after the Mongolian revolution of 1921 the Buryats' ease of communication with the Halh (q.v.) was widely used by the Russians in modernizing the army and strengthening the administration.

BURYAT REPUBLIC. Part of the Russian Federation situated on Mongolia's northern border, area 351,300 sq km. The capital is Ulan-Ude (q.v.). About 300,000 (one-fourth) of the population are Buriad

(Buryat), who, according to some theories, are related to the Oirots (q.v.). *See also* Russia: Mongol Ethnic Groups, and Buriad. The territory was originally conquered by Genghis Khan (q.v.), then colonized by Russia in the seventeenth century. Orthodox Christianity made some headway among the Buryat, although Lamaism (q.v.) became widespread. The Buryat-Mongol "Autonomous Soviet Socialist Republic" (ASSR) was established in February 1923 on the amalgamation of the Buryat-Mongol "Autonomous *Oblast'* " (founded in April 1921 in the RSFSR) and the Mongol-Buryat "Autonomous *Oblast'* " (founded in January 1922 in the Soviet Far Eastern Republic). The borders were adjusted several times, and in 1958 the republic was renamed the Buryat ASSR. Like similar republics in the former RSFSR seeking to promote their sovereignty, it opted in the early 1990s to style itself the Buryat Republic. Economic and cultural relations with Mongolia are now developing under a bilateral agreement signed in 1992.

BUYANNEMEH, SODNOMBALJIRYN (1901-1937). Writer and journalist, victim of the purges. Born in the present-day Delgerhangay district of Dundgov' Province (q.v.), Buyannemeh was educated in the capital Niyslel Hüree (q.v.) in Mongol, Manchu, Chinese, and Russian. He established contact with revolutionaries of the Mongolian People's Party (MPP) (q.v.) in Kyakhta (q.v.) in 1921. He then went to Irkutsk (q.v.) where he helped draft the "MPP Appeal to the People," the first MPRP Program (q.v.), and helped edit the newspaper *Ardyn Ünen* (People's Truth). In January 1922, with S. Danzan (q.v.) and Davaajav, he attended the Moscow Congress of Toilers of the East and met Lenin. In 1922-1923 he was a secretary of the Mongolian Revolutionary Youth League (MRYL) (q.v.) Central Committee and head of a department of the MPP. He was a member of the Presidium of the MPRP Central Committee (qq.v.) from August 1923 until August 1924. From 1924, he worked on the Comintern's (q.v.) instructions in Barga for the Inner Mongolian Party Central Committee and at Ulan-Ude (q.v.) teacher-training school (Buryat Republic, q.v.), advising on the training of literature teachers. In 1926 he became chairman of the Ulan Bator (q.v.) MPRP Committee. From 1929-1936, he worked as editor of *Ardyn Ündesniy Erh* (People's National Power) and in the Bureau of the Literary Association, which he founded in 1928, as well as being chairman of the Arts Council.

Buyannemeh's literary and historical works from 1923-1928 include *Events Linked with the History of the Mongolian Revolutionary Youth League* (with N. Jadambaa), *A Short Modern History* (of Mongolia), poetry and a play, *Baatar Hövgüün Temüüjin*, about Genghis Khan (q.v.). His play, *The Truth*, was performed at the opening of the

Mongolian Revolutionary Theater. Another play, *Dark Rule,* was highly praised at the international theater festival in Moscow in 1933. He also wrote the Mongolian version of *The Internationale,* which was used for a long period as the Mongolian national anthem. At various times he worked on the cultural journal *Ardyn Ündesniy Soyolyn Zam* (People's National Road of Culture) and the newspapers *Ünen* (Truth) and *Ardyn Erh* (People's Power) (qq.v.). He was awarded the title "State Meritorious Literary Worker" by the Presidium of the Little Hural (q.v.) and People's Council of Ministers on September 25, 1935.

Buyannemeh had been linked briefly with the case against S. Danzan (q.v.) in 1924, and in 1932 he was imprisoned for several months, it is said for describing Stalin as a madman. In August 1937, a Soviet NKVD (q.v.) official arrived in Mongolia and drew up a list of 115 "plotters," including Buyannemeh, who were accused of nationalism, right deviation, counterrevolution, and espionage for Japan. Buyannemeh was arrested on September 11, 1937, sentenced to death by the "Special Commission" on October 25, and executed on October 27. The Mongolian Supreme Court published a ruling on November 16, 1962, that the evidence had been falsified.

BUYR. Lake on the Mongolian border. Buyr *nuur,* one of the country's six largest lakes, has a surface area of 615 sq km. This freshwater lake, fed by the river Halh (q.v.) and having an outlet, the river Orshuun, into Dalay Nuur (Hulun Nur) in China's Inner Mongolia (q.v.), is situated at a height of 583 m above sea level on the Inner Mongolian border with the southern part of Dornod Province (q.v.). There is a small fishing industry.

BÜDRAGCHAA, SODNOMBALJIRYN (1933-   ). Mongolian lawyer. Born in March 1933, Büdragchaa worked initially as director of the General Auditing Department of the Procurator General's Office and as procurator of Ulan Bator (q.v.) City. He was appointed first deputy procurator general in July 1979 and procurator general in December 1982. Elected a candidate member of the MPRP Central Committee (qq.v.) in 1976 and 1981, he was promoted to member of the Central Committee in December 1982 and reelected in 1986. He was also elected a deputy of the People's Great Hural (q.v.) in 1977 and reelected in 1986 in an Uvs Province (q.v.) constituency. In June 1988, he was appointed first deputy minister of public security and chairman of the State Militia Directorate and held these posts until the ministry was disbanded in April 1990 and Baastyn Pürev (q.v.) became chief of militia (police). Abolition of the Ministry of Public Security, responsible for crackdowns against dissidents, was one of the demands of the democracy movement of 1989-1990, but the militia generally avoided confrontation with demonstrators. In July 1993, Büdragchaa was appointed chairman of the Council for Organizing and Coordinating Work to Ensure Social Order, set up by President Ochirbat (q.v.) to combat crime.

BYAMBADORJ, JAMSRANGIYN (1954-). Mongolian politician. Byambadorj trained as a lawyer. He was a member of the State Little Hural (q.v.) from January-June 1992. He became a member of the MPRP Central Committee (qq.v.) in 1992. He was elected a member of the Mongolian Great Hural (q.v.) for the MPRP for a four-year term on June 28, 1992, in constituency 16 (Hovd). He is a member of three MGH standing committees: international affairs, assemblies and administration, and health and social security.

BYAMBAJAV, JANLAVYN (1953-). Mongolian politician. Born in Jargalant district, Arhangay Province (q.v.), Byambajav graduated in law in 1977 from Irkutsk (q.v.) State University. In 1977, she became an adviser to the procurator's office in Nayramdal district of Ulan Bator (qq.v.), later working as a procurator and section chief in the State Procurator's Office. She was appointed deputy head of the MPRP's (q.v.) Central Auditing Service in March 1992 and was president of the Mongolian Advocates' Association from 1988-1992. She was not a deputy of the People's Great Hural (q.v.) but was a member of the State Little Hural (q.v.) from 1990-1992 and a member of the SLH committee on women, children, and youth; she became a member of the MPRP Central Committee (q.v.) in 1992. She was elected a member of the Mongolian Great Hural (q.v.) for the MPRP for a four-year term on June 28, 1992, in constituency 22 (Ulan Bator). She is a member of three MGH standing committees: international affairs, legal affairs, and health and social security.

BYAMBAJAV, YADAMSÜRENGIYN (1910-1941). Head of Arhangay Province (q.v.) department, Ministry of Internal Affairs. One of the 32 victims of the Mongolian purges of the 1930s and 1940s (q.v.) sent to the USSR for trial and sentence, details of which were released by the Russian government in 1993. Sentenced to death by the Military Collegium of the USSR Supreme Court in Moscow on July 5, 1941, and executed on July 27.

BYAMBASÜREN, DASHIYN (1942-). Mongolian prime minister from 1990-1992. Born in Binder district of Hentiy Province (q.v.), Byambasüren went to Moscow Higher School of Economics and Statistics in 1960 and graduated in 1964; he also has a higher degree of

Candidate of Economics. He started work in the Central Statistics Directorate in 1965, becoming head of a department, then he was appointed deputy chairman of the State Committee for Prices from 1970-1975, and later chairman of the State Committee for Prices and Standards from 1975-1984. In January 1984, under pressure from Yumjaagiyn Tsedenbal (q.v.), Byambasüren was demoted to the post of manager of a motor transport construction enterprise. In October 1985, after Tsedenbal's removal, Byambasüren was appointed learned secretary, later director, of the Research and Planning Center for Automated Control Systems under the State Committee for Science and Technology. In May 1987, he became director of the Institute for Improving Management Skills under the Council of Ministers. He was appointed deputy chairman of the Council of Ministers in December 1989, then first deputy chairman and concurrently chairman of the State Planning and Economic Committee in March 1990; a week later this committee was renamed the State Committee for Socio-Economic Development.

Byambasüren had joined the MPRP (q.v.) in 1963 and was elected a member of the MPRP Central Auditing Commission in 1976 and a candidate member of the MPRP Central Committee (q.v.) in 1981, but was not reelected in 1986; he was elected a member of the MPRP Central Committee in 1990, 1991, and 1992. He was also a deputy of the People's Great Hural (q.v.) from 1976-1986 and was elected again in July 1990, but surrendered his seat when appointed prime minister on September 10, 1990.

As the leader of the first post-communist government including members of the political opposition, Byambasüren was in charge of the implementation of economic reform, privatization, and the transition to a free market. The country was very soon in deep financial difficulties, having lost most of its small hard currency reserves in speculation on the international money markets and obliged to pay for all its imports in dollars, including those from Russia as of January 1991. During the two years that he was in office, prices and unemployment soared, production fell, the tögrög (q.v.) was devalued, and food rationing was introduced. Increasingly unpopular with the electorate, he considered resigning but was persuaded by the MPRP leadership to stay in office until after the 1992 elections. He resigned on July 20, when a new government was formed by Puntsagiyn Jasray (q.v.).

Byambasüren was elected a member of the Mongolian Great Hural (q.v.) for the MPRP for a four-year term on June 28, 1992, in constituency 18 (Hentiy), and became a member of three MGH standing committees: education, science, and culture, environmental protection, and economic policy. He resigned his MGH seat and MPRP membership in December 1992, however, after repeatedly criticizing the Jasray government and the MPRP for pursuing "Marxist-Leninist" policies. The following January, together with some former government ministers, MGH members, and media leaders, he founded the nonparty Mongolian Development Society (q.v.), of which he became president. A leading promoter of the World Congress of Mongols, held in Mongolia in the autumn of 1993, Byambasüren was elected president of the World Association of Mongols (q.v.) set up by the congress. In June 1994, Byambasüren founded and was elected leader of a new political party, the Mongolian Democratic Renewal Party (q.v.).

- C -

CAMELS. In Mongolia, Bactrian camels are used for riding and as draught animals, carrying up to 200 kg; camel meat is not usually eaten, but the milk is made into curds and cheese. Camels are concentrated in southern and western provinces: Ömnögov' Province (q.v.) has the greatest number—91,253 (1993). There were altogether some 415,000 camels in Mongolia at the end of 1992 and 367,673 at the end of 1993; their number has been in gradual decline for several years. The country produces some 2,500 tons of camel wool, and 25,000-30,000 camel skins a year (1988-1990); production of camel hair blankets averages 90,000 a year (1990-1992). There are a few wild camels (*havtgay*) to be found in Gobi (Gov', q.v.) regions.

CATTLE. In Mongolia, cattle are raised for their meat and milk, mostly on the open range, although mechanized dairy farms relying on supplies of concentrated fodder were set up near large towns when the general introduction of industrialized farming methods became fashionable in the 1970s-1980s. Cattle are concentrated in the central and northern provinces: Hövsgöl and Arhangay (qq.v.) have the greatest numbers—327,458 and 284,126, respectively (1993). There were altogether 2.8 million cattle in Mongolia at the end of 1992 and 2,730,456 in 1993. Yaks (q.v.) and *haynags* (offspring of a Mongolian cow and a yak) are not counted separately. The number of purebred and selected crossbred cattle is small. The average milk yield is low (338 kg a year in 1990). Industrial production of milk fell from 48 million liters in 1990 to 25 million liters in 1992, and butter output also declined, largely because of transport difficulties due to petrol shortages. Live weight on procurement averages 254 kg, and some 500,000 cowhides are procured each year (1988-1990).

CENTRAL ECONOMIC COOPERATION ZONE. One of six economic cooperation zones into which Mongolia was divided on the basis of a government ordinance issued in November 1991 (the others being the Bayan-Ölgiy, Gov'-Altay, Övörhangay, Sühbaatar and Ulan Bator economic cooperation zones, qq.v.). It consists of Darhan and Choyr towns and Selenge, Töv, Dornogov', and Dundgov' provinces (qq.v.). Each zone has a cooperation office headed by the secretary of the zonal cooperation council.

CENTRAL ECONOMIC REGION. One of the three economic regions into which Mongolia was divided in the 1980s (the others being the Eastern and Western Economic Regions, qq.v.). It consisted of the Yöröö-Tuul (river basin) subregion, comprising Ulan Bator and Darhan towns and Töv and Selenge provinces; the Hangay-Hövsgöl (mountain-lake) subregion, comprising Erdenet town and Bulgan, Hövsgöl, and Arhangay provinces; the Ongi-Baydrag (river basin) subregion, comprising Övörhangay and Bayanhongor provinces; and the Gobi (desert) subregion, comprising Dornogov', Dundgov', and Ömnögov' provinces (qq.v.). The region had 70 percent of the country's population, producing 80 percent of the country's gross industrial production and 60 percent of its gross agricultural production, including 80 percent of Mongolia's grain, potatoes, and green vegetables and more than half its meat and milk. While economic regionalization defined the geographical conditions of industrial and agricultural production, it did little to promote regional development. The economic regions were eventually abandoned and superseded by the system of Economic Cooperation Zones (q.v.) introduced in 1991.

CENTRAL GOBI PROVINCE see Dundgov' Province.

CENTRAL PROVINCE see Töv Province.

CHAGDARJAV, DAMBYN (1880-1922). Prime minister in provisional government March-April 1921. Born in the Ih Shav' (q.v.), before the 1921 revolution Chagdarjav was a private trader and in 1916-1917 visited Great Britain, Italy, and Russia. He was a member of the Konsulyn Denj secret revolutionary organization, which amalgamated with the Züün Hüree organization to form the Mongolian People's Party (qq.v.) in 1920. He was also a member of the MPP delegation, including Bodoo, Choybalsan, S. Danzan, Dogsom, Losol, and Sühbaatar (qq.v.), which went to Soviet Russia in 1920 to contact the Bolsheviks. With Danzan he went on to Moscow and was received by Lenin, returning to Irkutsk (q.v.) in November. Chagdarjav was appointed prime minister of the provisional government on March 13, 1921, but on April 16 he was released from his duties and sent as government representative to Urianhay (Tuva, q.v.). In 1922 he was implicated in the charges of counterrevolution against Bodoo (q.v.) and executed.

CHAGDARJAV, TÜSHEET VAN. Member of the General Administration Office in Charge of Halh (q.v.) Affairs set up in November 1911 as a kind of provisional government of Mongolia as Manchu (q.v.) rule collapsed. He was appointed minister of finance in the first government of the Bogd Khan (q.v.), and in 1915 participated in the Mongolian-Russian-Chinese treaty conference in Kyakhta (q.v.), signing the treaty with Shirnendamdin (q.v.). He was succeeded by Beys Luvsanbaldan (1915-1920).

CHANDMAN'-UUL. Former province (*aymag*) in northwestern Mongolia. The large province, center Ulaangom (q.v.), was founded in 1925 on the territory of the former Hovd borderlands (*hyazgaar*) and Dörvöd (qq.v.) *aymags*. In the administrative reforms of 1931, the five large provinces were broken up into 12 (later 18) smaller ones. This province formed parts of the present-day Bayan-Ölgiy, Hovd, and Uvs provinces (qq.v.).

CHIMID, BYARAAGIYN (1934-). Mongolian politician. Born in Shine-Ider district of Hövsgöl Province (q.v.), in 1956 Chimid completed three years of military service during which he was a company instructor at the School for Soldiers and Junior NCOs. He then worked in local government and the Provincial MPRP (q.v.) Committee. From 1962-1966 he studied at the Mongolian State University, graduating in law, in which he also has a higher degree. From 1966-1978, he was a teacher at the Mongolian State University. He served as minister of justice from 1978-1982, chairman of the Supreme Court from 1982-1986, and concurrently chief state arbitrator from 1984-1986, then head of the state organizations department of the Presidium of the People's Great Hural (q.v.) from 1986-1990; in March 1990, he was elected a member of the Presidium. Chimid had been elected a deputy of the People's Great Hural in December 1978, 1981, 1986, and 1990, and was secretary of the standing commission on law drafting and nationality from 1979-1986. He was also secretary of the State Little Hural (q.v.) from 1990-1992. Chimid was elected a candidate member of the MPRP Central Committee (q.v.) in 1981 and 1986, then a member in March 1990 (for a month). Chimid was elected a member of the Mongolian Great Hural (q.v.) for the MPRP for a four-year term on June 28, 1992, in constituency 17 (Hövsgöl). He is a member of two MGH stnading committees: foreign policy and security, and assemblies and administration.

CHIMIDDORJ, NERENDOOGIYN (1914-1941). Head of investigation department, Ministry of Internal Affairs. One of the 32 victims of the Mongolian purges of the 1930s and 1940s (q.v.) sent to the USSR for trial and sentence, details of which were released by the Russian government in 1993. Sentenced to death by the Military Collegium of the USSR Supreme Court in Moscow on July 5, 1941, and executed on July 27.

CHINA: MONGOL ETHNIC GROUPS. In 1990 there were 5,518,800 Mongols living in China, of which about 3 million were in Inner Mongolia (q.v.), 100,000 plus in the Tenger Uul (Tian Shan), Tarvagatayn Nuruu, and Ili valley regions of Xinjiang, as well as small communities in Tibet and Yunnan. The main languages are Inner Mongolian, the dialects of Inner Mongolia, similar to Halh (q.v.); western Mongol or Oirat (Oyrd, q.v.); and Monguor, spoken by isolated communities in Gansu and Qinghai. Many Mongols speak Chinese and some speak other minority languages, and the ethno-linguistic picture is not clear. The main groups inhabit the following administrative areas:

Abag(nar) (Avga): Tsahar (q.v.) of Xilin Gol League, Inner Mongolia.

Ar Horqin: Ju Od League, Inner Mongolia.

Barag (Barga): Hulun Buir League, Inner Mongolia; New and Old (Chipchin) Barga (q.v.) dialects are distinguished, with around 70,000 speakers in 1982.

Bairin: Ju Od League, Inner Mongolia; 317,000 speakers of this dialect in 1982.

Bao'an: Mongol ethnic group in Gansu and Qinghai numbering 12,200 (1990), some of whom are Muslim; their language is spoken by some Monguor (q.v.).

Bayit: Torguud (q.v.), Torgut dialect of Mongols of Bayangol, Xinjiang.

Chahar (Tsahar, q.v.): Ulanqab and Xilin Gol Leagues (former Chahar region), Inner Mongolia; several hundred thousand speakers of this dialect.

Dalad: Ordos of Ih Ju League, Inner Mongolia.

Daur (Dakhur, Dagor, Daguur): Morin Dawa Daur Autonomous Banner and Butha Banner, Hulun Buir League, Inner Mongolia (61,000), and Heilongjiang Province, speaking two main dialects named after the towns of Hailar, to the west of the Da Hinggan Mountains, and Qiqihar (Tsitsihar), to the east, and Butha (35,000). A few live in Xinjiang (they were sent by the Qing, q.v., emperor in 1763 to guard the border). They are a Mongol-speaking Tungus-Manchu people. Their language, which has no written form, preserves many archaic forms from the fourteenth to fifteenth centuries and has assimilated many Manchu-Tungusic words, and is not understood by other Mongols; they numbered 121,400 in 1990.

Dörvöd (q.v.) (Dorbod): Ulanqab League, Inner Mongolia, and one autonomous county in Heilongjiang Province.

Ejine: Ih Ju and Alxa Leagues, Inner Mongolia; speakers of this dialect numbered around 34,000 in 1982.

Gorlos: Jirem League, Inner Mongolia, and one autonomous county in Jilin Province.

Harachin (q.v.) (Harqin): Ju Od League, Inner Mongolia, and one autonomous county in Liaoning Province; 600,000 speakers in 1982.

Horchin (Horqin): Hinggan and Jirem (Cherim) Leagues, Inner Mongolia; 1.3 million speakers of this dialect in 1982.

Jungar (Züüngar, Oyrd): Ih Ju League, Inner Mongolia.

Jürüd (Jarud): Jirem League, Inner Mongolia.

Monguor (Mongor): Linxia County, Gansu, and Qinghai; their language, which has no written form, is full of archaisms and borrowings from Tibetan and Chinese, and is not understood by other Mongols; they number around 100,000, but some Monguor speak Bao'an (*see above*).

Nayman (Naiman): Jirem League, Inner Mongolia.

Oyrd (Oirat): Qinghai (Kok Nur/Höhnuur), Amdo (northern Tibet), Alashan (Alxa, Inner Mongolia), and Tsaidam (Xinjiang); their language is the same as that of the Oyrd of Mongolia and is likewise written in Zayapandita's "clear" script (qq.v.); they numbered around 144,000 in 1990, the main groups being Torguud (Torgut) and Kok Nur (Höh Nuur, Qinghai Mongols).

Onniud (Ognuud): Ju Od League, Inner Mongolia.

Ordos (Urdus): Ih Ju League (former Ordos region), Inner Mongolia; 123,000 speakers of this dialect in 1982.

Sant (Dongxiang) and Sharaygol Mongols: Jishishan County, Gansu, numbering 373,900 in 1990; they are like the Monguor (*see above*) but Muslim.

Shar Uygar (Yellow Uighur): Eastern Yugur, Mongolized Turks in Sunan Yugur Autonomous County, Gansu; they speak Monguor (*see above*) and are Buddhists, and numbered 12,900 in 1990.

Tibet Mongols: Hor Mongols in southwestern Tibet, and Sog Mongols in the Lhasa area.

Torguud (Torgut): Bayangol (Bayingolin) Mongol Autonomous Prefecture and Hoboksar Autonomous County, Xinjiang, on the Kazakhstan border; about 106,000 speakers of this dialect in 1982.

Tsagaan Mongols: "White" Mongols, called Tu by the Chinese, inhabiting the Yellow River (Huang He) basin in Gansu and Huzhu County, Qinghai; they numbered 191,600 in 1990.

Tümd (Tumet): Höhhot and Baotou (Bugat) municipalities and Ju Od League, Inner Mongolia; their language is similar to Harachin (*see above*).

Üzemchin (Ujimqin): Ulanqab and Xilin Gol Leagues, Inner Mongolia.

Urad (Urat): Bayannur League, Inner Mongolia.

Yunnan Mongols: Some 6,000 Mongols live in Yunnan Province, 4,000 in Tonghai county, and another 1,300 in Malipo and Xichou counties. They claim descent from two Mongolian generals, Jantan and Tömör, who invaded the region in 1253.

CHINA-MONGOLIAN BORDER. The border with China extends for 4,676.8 km from Height 4104.0 north of Tavan Bogd in the west to Height 646.7 at Tarvagan Dah (qq.v.) in the east, as does the northern border with Russia (q.v.). Some 210 km of the border is water, 19 rivers flowing into Mongolia and 14 flowing out. The locations of the 639 markers on this border are listed in the Mongolian-Chinese border protocol of 1964: No. 1, on Height 2,760.1, is at a distance of 101.25 km from Height 4104.0, the western terminus; No. 639 is 8.3 m from Height 646.7 at Tarvagan Dah, the eastern terminus. For crossing points, *see* the Mongolian provinces Bayan-Ölgiy, Hovd, Gov'-Altay, Ömnögov', Dornogov', Sühbaatar and Dornod.

CHINA: RESIDENTS IN MONGOLIA. There were around 2,000 ethnic Chinese citizens of Mongolia at the end of 1992. Most had lived in Mongolia for several generations and were engaged in small-scale vegetable farming and marketing or the building industry. At the turn of the century the Chinese community in Outer Mongolia (q.v.) comprised some 75,000 traders, 15,000 workers and craftsmen, and 5,000 agricultural laborers. Their numbers fell from 23,919 in 1926 to 17,496 in 1927. According to the 1956 census, Chinese accounted for 1.9 percent (16,200) of the population, but it was not clear whether all were citizens of Mongolia. The number of Chinese citizens of Mongolia did not include the 13,000 or so contract workers sent by the People's Republic of China to work in Mongolia on construction projects in the 1950s and withdrawn at the time of the Sino-Soviet ideological and territorial disputes in the 1960s. The number of Chinese in Mongolia stood at around 6,000 when the expulsions began in the early 1980s; they were accused by the Mongolian authorities of subversion ("Maoist propaganda"), blackmarketeering or drug peddling, and some 3,000 were obliged to leave for China. With the establishment of new economic links with China and easier cross-border travel following the birth of democracy in Mongolia in the 1990s, Chinese businessmen visited Mongolia in increasing numbers. At the beginning of August 1993, altogether 5,078 Chinese citizens were resident in Mongolia; they were mainly engaged in trade.

CHINGELTEY. Former ward (*horoo*) of Ulan Bator (q.v.). One of the 10 wards abolished in 1965 on the formation of Ajilchin, Nayramdal,

Oktyabr', and Sühbaatar (qq.v.) districts (*rayon*), each with smaller numbered *horoo*.

CHINGELTEY-UUL. District (*düüreg*) of Ulan Bator (q.v.). Established in 1992, this northern urban district of some 23,400 households (1992) is named after a local mountain and consists of 19 wards (*horoo*) incorporating Haylaast, Tasgany Ovoo, Denjiyn 1000, and Chingeltey residential (*ger*) areas and No. 6 (apartment) area (*horoo-lol*), Züün Selbe, the area west of Sühbaatar Square and other northern parts of the former Sühbaatar district (q.v.) (*rayon*) of the capital.

CHINGÜNJAV (1710-1757). North Mongolian (Halh, q.v.) prince who with the Oyrd (Jungar) leader Amarsanaa fought against Manchu (qq.v.) rule. Rallying Mongol deserters from the Manchu army in 1756, Chingünjav attacked the capital Ih Hüree (q.v.). After this and a number of other victories, however, his rebel forces were destroyed, and he and his family were captured by Manchu reinforcements near Hanh, Hövsgöl Province (qq.v.). He was executed in Peking on March 2, 1757.

CHOYBALSAN. Former province (*aymag*) in eastern Mongolia. Choybalsan's name was temporarily given to the present-day Dornod Province (q.v.).

CHOYBALSAN. Center of Dornod Province (q.v.). Previously known as San Beysiyn Hüree and Achit Beysiyn Hüree, after the revolution Bayantümen Hüree and Bayantümen, Choybalsan was renamed after the then prime minister of Mongolia in 1941. It was accorded town status in 1959. Its height above sea level is 747 m, the average January and July temperatures are − 21.3 and 20.6 deg C, and the average annual precipitation is 246.0 mm. The distance from Ulan Bator (q.v.) is 600 km. The population is about 45,000. Local industries include vehicle repairs, woodworking, wool scouring, flour milling, meat packing, and production of concrete, cement, bricks, and foodstuffs.

CHOYBALSAN, HORLOOGIYN (1895-1952). Mongolian prime minister from 1939-1952. Born on February 8, 1895, in Achit Beysiyn *hoshuu* of Tsetsen Han Aymag (present-day Dornod Province, q.v.), at the age of thirteen Choybalsan was sent to the local San Beysiyn *hüree* (monastery) but in 1912 ran away to the capital, Niyslel Hüree (q.v.). After working as a night watchman and delivering meat, Choybalsan attended the Russian School for Translators. From 1914-1918, he attended a gymnasium (high school) in Irkutsk (q.v.). A member of the Konsulyn Denj (q.v.) group of revolutionaries and one of the founders of the Mongolian People's Party (q.v.), he was a member of the delegation including Bodoo, Chagdarjav, S. Danzan, Dogsom, Losol, and Sühbaatar (qq.v.), which went to Soviet Russia in 1920 to contact the Bolsheviks. Remaining in Irkutsk with Sühbaatar, in March 1921 he was elected a member of the provisional revolutionary government and appointed political commissar of the Mongol Ardyn Juramt Tsereg, as the Mongolian People's Army (q.v.) was first called. After the victory of the revolution, he was elected chairman of the Central Committee of the Mongolian Revolutionary Youth League (q.v.) on its formation in August 1921. In 1922 Choybalsan was appointed minister for Eastern Border Affairs, but in 1923 he was sent to a military academy in Moscow. He was elected a member of the MPRP Central Committee (qq.v.) and of its Presidium in August 1924 and reelected from 1925-1940, member of the Presidium of the first Great Hural and commander-in-chief of the renamed Mongol Arydn Huv'sgalt Tsereg, or People's Revolutionary Troops, from 1924-1928. He was then elected chairman of the State Little Hural (q.v.) from January 23, 1929, to April 27, 1930.

Afterward he served as foreign minister from 1930-1931, minister of livestock and agriculture from 1931-1935, deputy chairman of the Council of Ministers from December 1934, first deputy chairman from 1935-1939, minister of internal affairs from 1936-1940, and from September 1937 minister of war and commander-in-chief. He was awarded the rank of marshal in 1936. He became prime minister from March 28, 1939, to January 26, 1952, when he died in Moscow of cancer of the kidney. Choybalsan had many meetings with Stalin and was very close to him, adopting his policies and methods and applying them in Mongolia. Choybalsan used his power to create a system of dictatorship by the ruthless suppression of dissent and opposition, and in the purges of the 1930s and 1940s (q.v.) many tens of thousands of innocent people fell victim to it and lost their lives.

A resolution of the MPRP Central Committee in January 1962 admitted that in 1937-1939 Choybalsan "broke the revolutionary laws and regulations and many hundreds of people suffered without any evidence of guilt. Among those victims were party workers, high officials in the government, high army officers and others. . . The dogmatism of the cult of personality encouraged blind subservience and blocked the people's initiative and understanding." An evaluation of Choybalsan published in Mongolia in 1968 noted that in 1937 he began "to arrest and kill leading workers of the party, government and various social organizations in addition to army officers, intellectuals and other faithful workers." (This evaluation, however, still referred to Prime Minister Genden, q.v., as a "Japanese spy.") While the general picture, if not the details, of Choybalsan's "cult of personality" thus became clearer after 1962, no proper evaluation of the scale and enormity of Choybalsan's crimes was possible before the birth of democracy in the 1990s brought new freedom of expression and opened up the Mongolian and Soviet archives.

CHOYR. Center of Gov'sümber Province (q.v.), population 12,000 (1993). Former Soviet Army No. 10 cantonment of 259 buildings—the largest in the country—handed over to the Mongolian authorities. This "town under national jurisdiction" was established in 1991 within Dornogov' Province (q.v.) on the amalgamation of Choyr, Bayantal, and Shiveegov' wards (*horoo*) and Sümber district (*sum*). In May 1994 these were redesignated to form the new Gov'-Sümber Province. Before the Soviet withdrawal, Choyr and other former Soviet Army cantonments were out-of-bounds to Mongolians and not marked on Mongolian maps. Sümber has a station on the Trans-Mongolian Railway. Local resources include coal (Shivee-Ovoo), tin (Oortsog-Ovoo), fluorspar (Adag, Öndör-Ovoo, Bayan-Ugaal), mineral pigments (Shar shoroo), uranium (Haraat), ornamental stone, and construction materials. There were 105,321 head of livestock in 1993.

CHULUUNBAATAR, SAMDANGIYN (1941-). Mongolian politician. Born in Jargalan district of Gov'-Altay Province (q.v.), Chuluunbaatar graduated in 1962 from the Soviet Komsomol (Communist Youth League) Higher School and in 1973 from the Higher School of the Trade Union Movement (in the former GDR). He worked first as the secretary of a Mongolian Revolutionary Youth League (MRYL) (q.v.) cell in Tayshir district, Gov'-Altay Province, and then at Ulan Bator (qq.v.) industrial combine, later becoming head of a department and lecturer of the Ulan Bator MRYL Committee. After serving as secretary of the Selenge MRYL Committee and then chairman of the Dornod Trade Union Committee, he was appointed head of a department of the MRYL Central Committee and later secretary of the Mongolian Trade Union Central Council. In 1990 he was elected a deputy of the People's Great Hural and of the State Little Hural (qq.v.), and a member of the state organizations standing committee. He became a member of the MPRP Central Committee (qq.v.) in 1992. Chuluunbaatar was elected a member of the Mongolian Great Hural (q.v.) for the MPRP for a four-year term on June 28, 1992, in constituency 21 (Ulan Bator). He is chairman of the MGH standing committee on internal affairs (reelected October 1993) and is a member of the standing committee on health and social security.

CHUNAG, SHARAVYN (1942-). Mongolian politician. Chunag trained as a veterinary surgeon. He served as chairman of the Erdenet (q.v.) MPRP Committee from October 1990-1992 and was elected to the MPRP Central Committee (qq.v.) in 1991 and 1992. Chunag was elected a member of the Mongolian Great Hural (q.v.) for the MPRP for a four-year term on June 28, 1992, in constituency 20 (Erdenet). He is a member of three MGH standing committees: education, science and culture, internal affairs, and health and social security.

COMECON. Acronym for the Council for Mutual Economic Assistance (CMEA), sometimes rendered Council for Economic Mutual Assistance (CEMA), known also by its Russian name, Sovet ekonomicheskoy vzaimopomoshchi (SEV): economic organization of Soviet-bloc countries founded in 1949 with headquarters in Moscow, which coordinated economic development and trade. Mongolia first attended a meeting of the CMEA council in 1958 as an observer and became a member of Comecon in June 1962. Mongolia benefited greatly from membership, receiving large amounts of economic aid through the CMEA from the USSR and Eastern Europe, but was left economically isolated by the collapse of the organization and the regimes supporting it.

COMINTERN. Acronym derived from the Russian acronym Komintern for Kommunisticheskiy Internatsional, Communist International, the Third International. This communist organization was founded by the Bolsheviks in 1919 to further the cause of world revolution and was instrumental in the application of Soviet Russian policies in Mongolia. The Comintern was dissolved in 1943 as a gesture toward Stalin's wartime allies.

CONSTITUTIONS. Since 1924 the Great Hural (q.v.) of the Mongolian People's Republic (Mongolia) has adopted four state Constitutions whose main provisions may be summarized as follows:

First Constitution (adopted by the first Great Hural, q.v., in November 1924): Proclamation of the Mongolian People's Republic, the transfer of political rule to the working people and the elimination of the remnants of despotism; nationalization of land, water, and mineral wealth; declaration of the rights of the people, equality before the law, and suffrage (except for "feudalists" and lamas resident in monasteries) at eighteen; the *soyombo* (q.v.) symbol of Mongolian independence was adopted as the state arms.

Second Constitution (adopted by the eighth Great Hural in June-July 1940, and modeled on the 1936 Soviet Constitution): Proclamation of the state of "herdsmen, workers and intelligentsia" and its aim, to ensure the country's "non-capitalist road of development for the future transition to socialism"; broadening of the range of disenfranchised persons to include "counter-revolutionaries"; declaration of the MPRP (q.v.) as the "vanguard of the working people and core of all their organizations"; new state arms depicting a herdsman on horseback and the heads of a cow, sheep, goat, and camel reflected the predominance of livestock (q.v.) raising in the economy.

Amendments to the Second Constitution (adopted by the ninth Great Hural in February 1949): Introduction of electoral reform, including the secret ballot, universal suffrage, and direct elections. Subsequently the Little Hural (q.v.) was abolished and the Great Hurals were renumbered.

Third Constitution (adopted by the fourth People's Great Hural, q.v., in July 1960): Proclamation of the state of "workers, collectivized herdsmen and working intelligentsia" and its aim, to complete the "building of socialism and in the future build a communist society"; the preamble described the MPRP as the "guiding and directing force of society and the state"; the Great Hural was renamed the People's Great Hural; in new state arms reflecting industrialization the four animal heads were displaced by a cog wheel and ears of wheat.

Amendments to the Third Constitution (adopted by the eleventh People's Great Hural in March and May 1990): The references to the MPRP's "guiding" role were deleted from the preamble; a State Presidency was instituted and the Little Hural (indirectly elected second chamber) reestablished as a standing legislature.

Fourth Constitution (adopted by the twelfth People's Great Hural in January 1992): The first "democratic" constitution in Mongolia's history, establishing the multiparty directly elected single-chamber Mongolian (National) Great Hural and other institutional reforms (for the text of the Fourth Constitution *see* Appendix 4). New state arms embodied a flying horse, a swastika border, and other Buddhist symbols.

COOPERATIVE FARMS. Production associations (*negdel*) run collectively on a cooperative basis to promote livestock (q.v.) raising. In 1985-1990 there were 255 of these, scattered all over Mongolia, supported by 17 inter-farm enterprises and nine inter-farm cooperatives (1990). The range and numbers of livestock differed according to natural conditions—43 percent of *negdel* owned 40,000 to 60,000 head; most were also growing some fodder and some were raising pigs (q.v.). One *negdel* averaged 61,500 head of livestock, 1,200 hectares of arable land, 19 tractors, and 2 grain harvesters, while there were 72 head of jointly owned livestock and 19 head of personal livestock per member. In 1990 the *negdel* owned 58.6 percent of the country's livestock, that is, 15.15 million head, and the 141,100 *negdel* members privately owned 24.7 percent, or 6.39 million head.

The first attempt at the collectivization of livestock herding began under the influence of the Left Deviation (q.v.), and by the end of 1930 nearly 30 percent of all poor and middle herdsmen's households had been forced to join collectives (*hamtral*), or communes. Following widespread uprisings in 1932 and the adoption of the New Turn (q.v.) policy, the collectives were disbanded and replaced by voluntary co-operatives (*nöhörlöl*) and production associations (*negdel*), of which there were 91 in 1940. Collectivization was completed in the 1950s, the number of *negdel* rising from 165 in 1952 to a maximum of 727 in 1958 with 108,200 households, 75 percent of the total. The number of livestock owned by *negdel* rose from 280,500 in 1952 to 16.9 million in 1960, when the *negdel* had been consolidated and their number had dropped to 354. A national Union of Production Associations was established in 1967 to regulate membership. Gradually the *negdel,* which were run by councils of members, were reorganized as centers of local government at a rural district (*sum*) level called *sum-negdel* (q.v.). The country's transition to a free-market economy since 1990 has encouraged the dissolution of the *negdel* and many members have withdrawn their livestock and gone over to private farming (q.v.).

- D -

DAGVASÜREN, DOGDOMYN (1947-). Mongolian politician. Dagvasüren trained as an engineer. He served as chairman of the Dornod Province Hural Executive Administration (qq.v.) from October 1991-July 1992. He was elected a member of the Mongolian Great Hural (q.v.) for the MPRP (q.v.) for a four-year term on June 28, 1992, in constituency 7 (Dornod). He is a member of two MGH standing committees: assemblies and administration, and food and agriculture.

DALANZADGAD. Center of Ömnögov' Province (q.v.). Accorded town status in 1965. Dalanzadgad's height above sea level is 1,465 m, the average January and July temperatures are −15.4 and 21.2 deg C, and the average annual precipitation is 132.5 mm. The distance from Ulan Bator (q.v.) is 520 km. The population is about 14,500. Local industries produce ferroconcrete and foodstuffs. Reflecting the status of Ömnögov' as the country's leading camel-raising province, Dalanzadgad is sometimes called the "camel capital" and has a museum of camel-breeding (*see* Camels).

DALAYHÜÜ, MINJÜÜRIYN (1950-). Mongolian politician. Dalayhüü began his working life as a planner and administrator. He served as chairman of the Arhangay Province Hural Executive Administration (qq.v.) from January 1991-July 1992. He was elected a member of the Mongolian Great Hural (q.v.) for the MPRP (q.v.) for a four-year term on June 28, 1992, in constituency 1 (Arhangay). He is a member of two MGH standing committees: budget and finance, and food and agriculture.

DAMBA, CHIMIDIYN (1900-1941). Head of corrective labor directorate, Ministry of Internal Affairs. One of the 32 victims of the Mongolian purges of the 1930s and 1940s (q.v.) sent to the USSR for trial and sentence, details of which were released by the Russian government in 1993. Sentenced to death by the Military Collegium of the USSR Supreme Court in Moscow on July 5, 1941, and executed on July 30.

DAMBA, DASHIYN (1908-1993?). Mongolian politician. Born on March 29, 1908, in Teshig district of Bulgan Province (q.v.), Damba joined the Mongolian Revolutionary Youth League (q.v.) in 1924 and worked as MRYL secretary at district and provincial levels and on Ulan Bator (q.v.) City MRYL Committee. In 1929-1930 Damba helped "carry out party and government measures linked with the liquidation of the class of feudalists and the transfer of their property to poor herdsmen." He joined the MPRP (q.v.) in 1930 and graduated from the MPRP's Higher Party School. In 1932 he was among MPRP cadres sent to the Mongolian People's Revolutionary Army (MPRA) to improve political work among the soldiers, who were fighting a virtual civil war to impose MPRP policies on a reluctant nation. He held the rank of MPRA commissar at battalion, regiment, and division level. In 1938 he was elected first secretary of the Ömnögov' MPRP Committee. In July 1939 he was elected member of the Presidium (reelected in April 1940) and secretary of the MPRP Central Committee (qq.v.) while working as secretary of the Ulan Bator MPRP Committee. Damba seems to have been involved in Choybalsan's plot to arrest Losol (qq.v.). During the Second World War Damba helped organize Mongolian aid for the Soviet Army and was awarded the Soviet Order of the Red Banner of Labor.

Damba became a candidate member of the MPRP Politburo in 1943, a member of the Politburo in 1947, and was second secretary of the MPRP Central Committee from 1947-1954. In April 1954 he replaced Yumjaagiyn Tsedenbal (q.v.) as first secretary. He was also a member of the Presidium of the People's Great Hural (q.v.). In November 1958, six months after his reelection by the MPRP congress, Damba was "relieved of his duties at his own request"; three other Politburo members also resigned. He was replaced as MPRP leader by Yumjaagiyn Tsedenbal. According to charges against him published in March 1959, he was dismissed from the MPRP for "profound ideological-political backwardness, conservatism and inertia." The manner of Damba's appointment and dismissal, however, temporarily depriving Premier Tsedenbal of the party leadership, reflected the party-state conflict in the post-Stalin Soviet "collective" leadership from 1953-1958, when CPSU First Secretary Nikita Khrushchev engineered the removal of Georgiy Malenkov and Nikolay Bulganin to take over the premiership for himself. Damba has been described by some observers as "pro-Chinese," although there is no evidence for this beyond the fact that Mongolian (and Soviet) relations with China were good in the 1950s. After 1958 Damba worked as director of an animal husbandry machinery station and deputy director of the Higher School of Agriculture. He is believed to have died in 1993.

DAMBADORJ, TSEREN-OCHIRYN (1899-1934). Mongolian party leader. Born in Niyslel Hüree (q.v.), Dambadorj attended the Manchu and Russian interpreters' school in Niyslel Hüree from 1910-1912 and the Russian gymnasium in Troitskosavsk (Kyakhta, q.v.) from 1913-1914, then a secondary school from 1917-1918. He became a revolutionary partisan in 1921, when he joined the Mongolian People's Party (q.v.). According to one source he was acting chairman of the MPP Central Committee when he attended the first meeting of the provisional revolutionary government on March 13, 1921 (*see* Soliyn Danzan). After the revolution he studied at the Plekhanov Higher School of National Economy in Moscow from 1929-1932. He was elected vice chairman of the Central Committee from January-March 1922 and chairman from March 15, 1922 to January 2, 1923, and from August 31, 1924 to October 1928. Dambadorj was elected a member of the Presidium of the MPRP Central Committee (q.v.) in August 1923 and reelected from 1924-1927 until December 1928. The seventh MPRP Congress expelled him from the Central Committee for Right Opportunism (q.v.), and he was sent to work as trade representative at the Mongolian embassy in Moscow, where he died of illness in 1934.

DAMDINBAZAR, (JALHANZ HUTAGT) SODNOMYN (1874-1923). Mongolian prime minister from 1922-1923. Born in present-day Nömrög district of Zavhan Province (q.v.), Damdinbazar was educated in Mongol and Tibetan and from the ages of sixteen to twenty was a novice in a monastery at Ih Hüree (q.v.). He joined the national independence movement in 1911. Sent to the western frontier, he established contact with Hatanbaatar Magsarjav (q.v.) and participated in the liberation of Hovd town (q.v.) in 1912. He was in favor of preserving Urianhay (q.v.) as part of Autonomous Mongolia (q.v.) and opposed Russian expansion there. In 1919 on behalf of the Bogd Khan's (q.v.) government he engaged in efforts to establish contact with the US consul in Kalgan, with a view to the opening of a US consulate in Urga (Niyslel Hüree, q.v.). He was an official under the Chinese Minister Ch'en Yi, during the house arrest of the Bogd Khan. A member of the delegation (with Dashjav and Shirnendamdin, qq.v.) that went to Baron von Ungern-Sternberg (q.v.) in January 1921, to discuss formation of a new government, he was appointed prime minister in the short-lived government of five revived ministries set up by the baron in the name of the Bogd Khan. He ignored approaches made to him by the provisional revolutionary government after the liberation of Mongolian Kyakhta (q.v.) in March 1921. In Zasagt-Han Province (q.v.) in June 1921, he was contacted by Comintern (q.v.) messengers, and at the end of July he informed Soviet representatives accompanying Red Army units of his readiness to oppose the White (Russian Tsarist) forces. He joined Magsarjav in Uliastay (q.v.) and participated in the campaign against the Whites. The abbot of the Jalhanz Hutagtyn *hüree*, Damdinbazar was at his monastery with his 700 lamas when Prime Minister Bodoo (q.v.) was purged. Damdinbazar was appointed prime minister of Mongolia on March 3, 1922, and died in office on June 23, 1923.

DAMDINSÜREN, JAMSRANGIYN JÜN VAN (MANLAYBAA-TAR). (1871-1920?). A Barga Mongol, born in Inner Mongolia (q.v.), Damdinsüren led Mongol troops in the expulsion of the Chinese from southern Mongolia after the formation of the government of the Bogd Khan (q.v.) in 1912. Losol (q.v.) saw action with him. As a Counsellor First Class of the Ministry of the Army, he participated in the Mongolian-Russian-Chinese treaty conference in Kyakhta (q.v.) in 1915. He was imprisoned by the Chinese in 1920 and died in captivity.

DAMDINSÜREN, JANTSANGIYN (1897?-1938?). Mongolian head of state from 1927-1929. Born in 1897 or 1898 in Van Nayantyn *hoshuu* of Tsetserleg-Mandal Province (present-day Ider district of Zavhan Province, q.v.), Damdinsüren studied Tibetan for eight years and then classical Mongolian in a *ger* (q.v.) school from the age of twelve. He was taken on at sixteen as a scribe in the *hoshuu* seal office (local government administration). In 1923 he began work as a scribe in the Javhlant (q.v.) governor's office, then was appointed head of a new rural district administration. Having been elected a local delegate to the fourth Congress of the Mongolian Revolutionary Youth League (q.v.) in 1925, Damdinsüren was elected a member of the MRYL Presidium and administrator of the MRYL Central Committee. In 1926 the fifth MRYL Congress elected him chairman of the MRYL Central Committee, the fifth MPRP Congress elected him a candidate member of the MPRP Central Committee (qq.v.), and the Great Hural elected him a member of the Little Hural (qq.v.). In 1927 he was reelected chairman by the sixth MRYL Congress, the sixth MPRP Congress elected him a member of the MPRP Central Committee, and the Central Committee elected him a member of its Presidium. The fourth Great Hural reelected him to the Little Hural, and the Little Hural elected Damdinsüren chairman of the Presidium of the Little Hural from November 16, 1927 to January 23, 1929.

The fifth Great Hural, held in the period from December 1928-January 1929, appointed him deputy prime minister and minister of agriculture. The seventh MRYL Congress released him from the duties of chairman of the MRYL Central Committee. When his ministry was divided in 1929, he became the country's first minister of livestock. The eighth MPRP Congress in 1930 released him from membership of the Presidium of the MPRP Central Committee, and he became head of the secretariat of the Central Committee's agitation department. In 1930-1931, in the campaign to set up communes, he returned to Zavhan and served as secretary of a commune and then director of a collective farm (*hamtral*). From 1931-1934 he worked in Ulan Bator (q.v.) as secretary general and secretary of the Mongolian Cooperatives, but he returned to Zavhan once again to be head of a department of the local cooperatives. From 1934-1938 he was second deputy head of the Zavhan provincial administration and head of the livestock department. He was arrested on false charges of counterrevolution in 1938.

DAMIRAN, TSERENDASHIYN (1948-). Minister of Construction and Town Planning from 1992-1994. Born on September 15, 1948 in Chandman' district of Hovd Province (q.v.), Damiran graduated in 1971 from the Mongolian State University with a degree in building engineering. He started work as an engineer in an agricultural construction organization in 1971, then became a senior engineer in an electrical and plumbing installation company from 1972-1982, when he was appointed director. On the privatization of the company (called the "Wheel") in 1991, he became the director general. Damiran, who is not a member of the Mongolian Great Hural (q.v.), was appointed minister of construction and town planning on August 5, 1992, by the first session of the MGH. In a reshuffle in January 1994, Damiran's ministry was amalgamated with the Ministry of Roads, Transport and Communications to form the Ministry of Infrastructure Development, of which Damiran was appointed deputy minister.

DANSHIYTSOODOL, GOMPILYN (1905-1941). Minister of justice. One of the 32 victims of the Mongolian purges of the 1930s and 1940s (q.v.) sent to the USSR for trial and sentence, details of which were released by the Russian government in 1993. Sentenced to death by the Military Collegium of the USSR Supreme Court in Moscow on July 5, 1941, and executed on July 30.

DANZAN, AJVAAGIYN (YAPON) (1895-1932). Mongolian party leader from 1923-1924. Born in Tüsheet-Han (q.v.) Province, Danzan joined the Mongolian People's Party (q.v.) in 1921. He was elected vice-chairman of the MPRP Central Committee (qq.v.) from 1922-1923 and chairman (*tergüün darga*) from January 2, 1923, to August 31, 1924. He was a member of the Presidium of the MPRP Central Committee from February 1923 to August 1924, when he became a deputy member until March 1925. After serving as the Mongolian envoy to Soviet Russia in 1924-1925, Danzan was posted to Peking, Shanghai, Tianjin, Nanjing, and Harbin in 1926-1928 to promote Mongolian-Chinese relations. He then worked at the Institute of Manuscripts (*sudar bichgiyn hüreelen*), the future Academy of Sciences (q.v.), from 1929-1931. He was charged with counterrevolution and died in 1932 before going to trial.

DANZAN, DARIYN (1942-   ). Mongolian politician. Danzan trained as an economist. He served as director general of the Bank of Capital Investment and Technological Renewal from January 1991-July 1992. He became a member of the MPRP Central Committee (qq.v.) in 1992. He was elected a member of the Mongolian Great Hural (q.v.) for the MPRP for a four-year term on June 28, 1992, in constituency 17 (Hövsgöl). He is a member of two MGH standing committees: budget and finance, and economic policy.

DANZAN, SOLIYN (1884-1924). Mongolian party leader. Born in Sayn-Noyon-Han (q.v.) Province, Danzan was one of the founders of the Züün Hüree (q.v.) secret revolutionary organization, which merged with the Konsulyn Denj (q.v.) organization to form the Mongolian People's Party (MPP) (q.v.). He was a member of the MPP delegation, including Bodoo, Chagdarjav, Choybalsan, Dogsom, Losol, and Sühbaatar (qq.v.), which visited Soviet Russia in 1920 to contact the Bolsheviks. Danzan went on to Moscow and met Lenin three times, in 1920, in November 1921, when he was the leader of the delegation that signed the Mongolian-Soviet treaty of friendship, and in January 1922, while attending the Moscow Conference of Eastern People's Revolutionary Organizations. He had been elected chairman of the Central Committee at the First Congress of the MPP on March 3, 1921, but he was replaced by Bodoo, according to some sources because of his second visit to Moscow beginning in September. Danzan also served from 1921 as minister of finance, deputy prime minister, then commander in chief (*Büh tsergiyn janjin*) in 1923-1924. He was elected a member of the Presidium of the MPRP Central Committee (qq.v.) in February 1923 and reelected in August 1923. Accused of representing the interests of the bourgeoisie, engaging in business with Chinese firms, and harming Mongolian-Soviet friendship, Danzan was executed during the MPRP's third Congress in 1924.

DARHAD (DARHAT). Mongolized Turkic ethnic group. The Darhad accounted for 0.7 percent (14,300) of the population of Mongolia, according to the 1989 census. The Darhad are concentrated mostly in north-western districts of Hövsgöl Province and speak a dialect of Halh (qq.v.).

DARHAD SHAV'. Former district in northern Mongolia. The Darhad (q.v.) lands west of Lake Hövsgöl in present-day Hövsgöl Province (q.v.) were estates administered by the Javzandamba Hutagt or Bogd Gegeen (qq.v.). The word *shav'* (q.v.) was used for vassals of the Lamaist (q.v.) church.

DARHAN. Center of Darhan-Uul Province (q.v.). Founded in October 1961, Darhan is an industrial town fueled by the coal mines at Sharyn Gol, to which it is linked by a 63 kilometer rail link. The first factories went into operation in 1965. Darhan was a "town under national jurisdiction" comprising four wards (*horoo*), Hongor, Hötöl, Orhon, and Salhit. In May 1994 these were redesignated to form the new Darhan-Uul Province, and the cement production center of Hötöl was transferred to Sayhan *sum* of the surrounding Selenge Province. There are Trans-Mongolian Railway and motor road links with Russia and Ulan Bator (q.v.), and Salhit is a railway (q.v.) junction. Local industries include production of building materials, cement, bricks, ferroconcrete, woolen textiles, carpets, sheepskin coats, clothing, dairy produce, confectionery, and animal feed, as well as woodworking, meat packing, fruit and vegetable canning, flour milling, and vehicle and railway rolling stock repairs. A metallurgical works is under construction to reduce scrap iron and make castings. Livestock numbers reached 145,500 head (1992) and arable land 20,700 hectares (1989). The town's population was around 82,135 in 1991, but with the withdrawal of large numbers of Soviet technicians and their families from Mongolia, it fell to 66,800 in 1993.

DARHAN-UUL. Province (*aymag*) in north-central Mongolia. Established in May 1994, the province consists of six former *horoo* of Selenge Province reorganized into *sum* (qq.v.): Darhan and Nayramdal *horoo* combined as Darhan *sum;* Hongor and Salhit *horoo* combined as Hongor *sum;* and Sharyn Gol and Orhon *horoo* redesignated as *sum;* the provincial center is Darhan (q.v.), a former "town under national jurisdiction."

DARIGANGA. Mongol ethnic group. The Dariganga (Dar'ganga), an East Mongol group, accounted for 1.4 percent (28,600) of the population of Mongolia according to the 1989 census. They are concentrated mostly in the Dariganga district of Sühbaatar Province and speak a dialect of Halh (qq.v.).

DARIGANGA. District in south-eastern Mongolia. The Manchu (q.v.) emperor's herds were pastured in this district named after its distinctive national minority. It acquired separate status in 1760 and remained independent of neighboring *aymags* (q.v.) until its incorporation in Dornod Province (later, Sühbaatar Province, q.v.).

DASHDEMBEREL, CHOVDRONGIYN (1936-   ). Mongolian politician. Born in Öndörshireet district of Töv Province (q.v.), Dashdemberel graduated from the Higher Agricultural School in 1960 as a veterinary surgeon, and also from the CPSU Central Committee's Higher Party School in 1972. After working in Ulan Bator (q.v.) and Töv Province, he was deputy chairman from 1966-1974, then chairman of Töv Executive Administration (q.v.) from 1974-1985. He next served as first secretary of Hentiy (q.v.) MPRP Committee and became a member of the MPRP Central Committee (qq.v.) from 1986-1990. A deputy of the People's Great Hural (q.v.) and secretary of the Presidium, he later became general secretary of the People's Great Hural (q.v.) from 1990-1992 and head of the Presidential Secretariat from 1990-1992. He was elected a member of the Mongolian Great Hural (q.v.) for the MPRP for a four-year term on June 28, 1992, in constituency 14 (Töv). He is a member of two MGH standing committees: internal affairs, and food and agriculture.

DASHJAV, BELIGT GÜN DA LAM (DASHZEGVE). Minister of Internal Affairs after the death of Tserenchimed (q.v.), concurrently a deputy minister of religion and state under Badamdorj (q.v.). He was the leader of the Mongolian delegation at the Mongolian-Russian-Chinese treaty conference in Kyakhta (q.v.) until he was replaced by Shirnendamdin (q.v.). In 1915 he was replaced as minister of internal affairs by Badamdorj (q.v.).

DASHTSEDEN, DASHDONDOGIYN (1943-   ). Mongolian politician. Dashtseden trained as a lawyer and worked at the Legal Studies Research Institute. He was elected a member of the Mongolian Great Hural (q.v.) for the MPRP (q.v.) for a four-year term on June 28, 1992, in constituency 3 (Bayanhongor). He was the chairman of the MGH standing committee for assemblies and administration from June 1992 to October 1993 and is a member of the standing committee for environmental protection.

DASH-YONDON, BÜDRAGCHAAGIYN (1946-   ). Mongolian party leader. Born in Tsetserleg district of Hövsgöl Province (q.v.), Dash-Yondon graduated from the Mongolian State University in 1968 and has the higher degree of Candidate of Philosophy. He first worked as a history teacher at the MSU from 1968-1974. He was appointed an instructor at the MPRP Central Committee (qq.v.) from 1978-1979, then deputy director of the MPRP Higher Party School from 1979-1985. He became deputy head, then head of the party organization department of the MPRP Central Committee from 1985-April 1990, a member of the MPRP Central Auditing Commission from 1986-1990 and a member of the MPRP Central Committee from 1990-1991. He was elected chairman of the Ulan Bator (q.v.) MPRP Committee from April 1990-February 1991 and concurrently a member of the MPRP Presidium from November 1990-February 1991. Chairman of the MPRP from February 1991, he was redesignated secretary general of the MPRP in October 1992.

DAVAASAMBUU, DALRAYN (1951-   ). Minister of finance since 1992. Born on February 2, 1951, in Santmargats district of Zavhan Province (q.v.), Davaasambuu graduated in 1972 from the Ulan Bator Finance and Economics Technical College and in 1979 from the Moscow Higher School of International Relations. He started work in the Ministry of Finance in 1972, moving in 1979 to the convertible currency directorate, where he became head of a department; he was appointed head of the foreign economic relations directorate and deputy minister of finance from 1990-August 1992. Davaasambuu, who is not a member of the Mongolian Great Hural (q.v.), was appointed minister of finance on August 10, 1992, by the first session of the MGH.

DEEL. The Mongolian national dress. A long double-breasted gown of a traditional style worn by men and women. Usually made of delicately patterned silk, and often bright in color, it buttons up on the right side to a high collar and has long sleeves, sometimes covering the hands. A silk sash of contrasting color is worn around the waist, and lambswool or fur lines the gown in winter. The detail of the design varies from tribe to tribe.

DELGER-IH-UUL. Former province (*aymag*) in northern Mongolia. This province, founded in 1925, comprised the Javzandamba Hutagt's (q.v.) estates, the Darhad *Shav'* (q.v.), and Urianhay district of present-day Hövsgöl Province (q.v.).

DELGERTSETSEG, JÜGDERIYN (1946-   ). Mongolian politician. Born in Urgamal district of Zavhan Province (q.v.), Delgertsetseg graduated as a mechanical engineer from Kiev Higher School of Light Industry in 1969 and from 1969-1977 worked in Ulan Bator's (q.v.) carpet industry. From 1977-1980 he was director of Ulan Bator woolen textile mill and from 1980-1992 he was director of Erdenet (q.v.) carpet factory. He became a member of the MPRP Central Committee (qq.v.) in 1992. He was elected a member of the Mongolian Great Hural (q.v.) for the MPRP for a four-year term on June 28, 1992, in constituency 20 (Erdenet). He is a member of three MGH standing committees: budget and finance, food and agriculture, and economic policy.

DEMBEREL, BAZARYN (1934-   ). Mongolian politician. Demberel trained as a physician. He was minister of health in the 1960s-1970s, later appointed head of the department of medicine of the Academy of Sciences (q.v.), of which he is a member. He was elected a member of the Mongolian Great Hural (q.v.) for the MPRP (q.v.) for a four-year term on June 28, 1992, in constituency 13 (Selenge). He was a member of the MGH standing committee for education, science, and culture from 1992-1993 and was elected chairman in October 1993.

DEMBEREL, DAMDINGIYN (1941-   ). Mongolian politician. Born in Manhan district of Hovd Province (q.v.), Demberel graduated from the Higher School of Economics in 1964 and from the CPSU's Higher Party School in 1977. From 1964-1968 he was deputy head of Hovd Provincial Trade and Procurement Directorate, and from 1968-1970 a lecturer at Hovd Provincial MPRP (q.v.) Committee. He then served as first secretary of Hovd Provincial MRYL (q.v.) Committee from 1970-1972, head of a department at the MRYL Central Committee from 1972-1975, an organizer at the MPRP Central Committee from 1977-1990, and first secretary of Zavhan (q.v.) MPRP Committee from 1990-1991. He was also a member of the MPRP Central Committee from 1990-1992. Demberel was elected a deputy of the People's Great Hural (q.v.) from 1990-1992, member of the State Little Hural (q.v.) from January-July 1992, and then elected a member of the Mongolian Great Hural (q.v.) for the MPRP for a four-year term on June 28, 1992, in constituency 16 (Hovd). He is a member of three MGH standing committees: budget and finance, health and social security, and economic policy. In November 1993, Demberel was elected leader of the MPRP party group in the MGH and subsequently secretary of the MPRP Party Leadership Council (q.v.).

DEMBERELTSEREN, DASHDORJIYN (1952-   ). Mongolian chief justice since 1990. Born in Bürd, Övörhangay Province (q.v.), Dembereltseren graduated from Irkutsk (q.v.) State University and began work as an investigator at the Mongolian Supreme Court. Later he was appointed a member, then deputy chairman of Ulan Bator (q.v.) Court. From 1981-1990 he was deputy head, then head of a department of the Presidium of the People's Great Hural (q.v.). The PGH appointed him chairman of the Supreme Court in September 1990. His title became chief justice in accordance with the 1992 Constitution (q.v.). In April 1993 he was elected chairman of the General Council of Courts.

DEMID, GELEGDORJIYN (1900-1937). Mongolian minister of war and army commander from 1930-1937. Born in present-day Ih-Tamir district of Arhangay Province (q.v.), Demid became a partisan and joined the Mongolian People's Party (q.v.) in 1921. He served from 1921-1926 in various units and taught at the General Military School. From 1926-1929 he studied at Tver' cavalry school in the USSR, then returned to the General Military School to become its commandant and commissar. Demid was elected a member of the Presidium of the MPRP Central Committee (qq.v.) in March 1930, June 1932, October 1933, and October 1934, and from 1930 he held the posts of president of the Military Council, minister of war, army commander-in-chief, and second deputy chairman of the Council of Ministers. In 1936 he was awarded the rank of marshal. In circumstances that have not been satisfactorily explained, Demid died from poisoning aboard a Trans-Siberian Railway train at Tayga station (north-east of Novosibirsk) on August 22, 1937. Other members of the Mongolian delegation to Moscow and their wives were also poisoned, and Division Commander Jantsanhorloo also died. For a time, Demid was linked with Genden (q.v.) in accusations of spying for the Japanese.

DINOSAURS. Fossil remains in the Gobi desert, or Gov' (q.v.). Southern Mongolia's eroded hillsides abound in the fossils of predators and herbivores. The discovery of "dragon bones" is recorded in Chinese annals as long as 1,700 years ago. The first important scientific discoveries in Mongolia, including nests of dinosaur eggs, were made in 1922-1925 by the American Museum of Natural History expeditions led by Roy Chapman Andrews. Subsequent Mongolian, Soviet, Polish, and US expeditions have brought many new finds to light. Important finds have been made at Altan Uul and Gurvan Sayhan Uul, as well as Bayanzag, Naran Bulag, Nemegt, and Shavar Us in Ömnögov' Province (q.v.). According to paleontologists, the fossils are mostly from the Cretaceous period (145-65 million years ago), including the herbivore Protoceratops and Hadrosaurus; Velociraptor and the birdlike Oviraptor and Psittacosaurus; Erlikosaurus (found at Bay-shintsav, Hanbogd district); and the predators Segnosaurus (Amtgay, Hanbogd district) and Therizinosaurus (Heremiyn Tsav, Gurvantes district); the armored Saichania dinosaurs, named after the Gurvan Sayhan Mountains; Ornithomimidae, toothless ostrichlike dinosaurs also found in North America; and Deinonychus, Tarbosaurus, Sauro-lophus, Gallimimus, and Avimimus (Udan Sayr, Sevrey district). In Dundgov' (q.v.) Garpimimus, an Ornithomimus with teeth, was found at Hürenduh, Bayanjargalan district, in 1981.

DOGSOM, DANSRANGIYN (DANSRANBILEGIYN) (1884-1941). Mongolian head of state from 1936-1939. Born in present-day Bayan-Ovoo district of Hentiy Province (q.v.), Dogsom was a member of the Züün Hüree revolutionary organization, which amalgamated with the Konsulyn Denj organization to form the Mongolian People's Party (qq.v.). He was also a member of the MPP delegation, including Bodoo, Chagdarjav, Choybalsan, S. Danzan, Losol, and Sühbaatar (qq.v.), which went to Soviet Russia in 1920 to contact the Bolshe-viks. From 1921 he worked in the Ministry of Internal Affairs, Min-istry of War, MPRP Central Committee (qq.v.) and Economic Coun-cil; he was a counselor in the Hovd Border Region and at Altanbulag (q.v.) on the Russian border; and he served as first secretary at the Mongolian representation in Moscow in 1927 and as Mongolian rep-resentative in Tuva (q.v.) in 1933-1934. Dogsom was elected chair-man of the Presidium of the Little Hural (q.v.) from February 22, 1936 to July 9, 1939 and was elected to the Presidium of the MPRP Central Committee in March 1936, October 1937, and July 1939. In 1939 he was arrested on charges of counterrevolution. He was sentenced to death by the Military Collegium of the USSR Supreme Court in Moscow on July 7, 1941 and executed on July 30. He was one of the 32 victims of the Mongolian purges of the 1930s and 1940s (q.v.) sent to the USSR for trial and sentence, details of which were released by the Russian government in 1993. Dogsom was rehabilitated in 1962.

DOLGORJAV, TSEVEGIYN (1913-1941). Head of Övörhangay Prov-ince (q.v.) department, Ministry of Internal Affairs. One of the 32 vic-tims of the Mongolian purges of the 1930s and 1940s (q.v.) sent to the USSR for trial and sentence, details of which were released by the Russian government in 1993. Sentenced to death by the Military Col-legium of the USSR Supreme Court in Moscow on July 5, 1941, and executed on July 27.

DORJ, ERDENIYN (1910-1941). A Buryat (Buryad, q.v.) who worked in the administrative apparatus of the Mongolian Ministry of Internal

Affairs. One of the 32 victims of the Mongolian purges of the 1930s and 1940s (q.v.) sent to the USSR for trial and sentence, details of which were released by the Russian government in 1993. Sentenced by the Military Collegium of the USSR Supreme Court in Moscow on September 28, 1940, to eight years' imprisonment, he died on November 24, 1941, in Ust'vymlag (Soviet Ust'vym Labor Camps Directorate, Komi Republic).

DORJBARGA, SEREETERIYN (1905-?). Procurator general of the Mongolian People's Revolutionary Army. One of the 32 victims of the Mongolian purges of the 1930s and 1940s (q.v.) sent to the USSR for trial and sentence, details of which were released by the Russian government in 1993. Sentenced by the Military Collegium of the USSR Supreme Court in Moscow on July 10, 1941, to five years' imprisonment, he was released from a Krasnoyarsk corrective labor establishment on July 15, 1944.

DORLIGJAV, DAMBIYN (1959-   ). Mongolian government official. Born in Züüngov' district of Uvs Province (q.v.), Dorligjav graduated from the agricultural vocational school in Hovd (q.v.) in 1978 and worked as a veterinary surgeon in Züüngov' until he was called up for army service in 1979. In 1988 he graduated from the Mongolian State University with a law degree and went to work at the Ulan Bator (q.v.) Procurator's Office. Later he became a research worker at an institute run by the Mongolian Revolutionary Youth League (q.v.) Central Committee. One of the founders of the Mongolian Democratic Party (q.v.), Dorligjav was a deputy coordinator of the MDP Political Coordinating Center. He was elected a deputy of the People's Great Hural (q.v.) for the MDP in an Ulan Bator constituency in 1990 but surrendered his seat on appointment as deputy prime minister in charge of social affairs (1990-1992); his responsibilities included education, health, culture, sport, labor, wages, religious affairs, parties, and public organizations. Dorligjav was also chairman of the State Commission for the Introduction of the Mongolian Script for Official Business until his replacement by Lhamsürengiyn Enebish (q.v.) in November 1992, when he became a secretary of the commission. In September 1992, he was appointed legal aide to Prime Minister Puntsagiyn Jasray (q.v.). When the Mongolian National Democratic Party (q.v.) was established in 1992, Dorligjav was elected a member of the General Council.

DORNOD (EASTERN). Province (*aymag*) in eastern Mongolia. Formed in 1931, and initially including Dariganga and other parts of the present-day Sühbaatar Province (q.v.), Dornod Province is situated on the borders of Russia (Kyra, Aksha, and Borzya districts of Chita Region) and China (Hulun Buir, Hinggan, and Xilin Gol Leagues of Inner Mongolia Autonomous Region; during the Chinese "cultural revolution," when Inner Mongolia, q.v., was truncated, Dornod bordered on Heilongjiang and Jilin Provinces). With a territory of 123,500 sq km and population of 76,593 (1991), it has 14 rural districts (*sum*); until 1992 there was one ward (*horoo*), Ereen; the provincial center is Choybalsan (q.v.), the former Bayantümen. The local minorities include the Buryad and Barga (qq.v.). There are deposits of gold (Tsagaan Chuluut), zinc, and lead (Ulaan Tsav), other nonferrous metals (Chuluunhoroot), and salt (Hön Nuur); the oil field (Tamsagbulag) is not currently in production; railway rolling stock repairs are carried out at Bayantümen and woodworking at Ereen. Livestock numbers reached 796,500 head (1992) and arable land 48,100 hectares (1989).

Choybalsan has a railway link with Russia via Chuluunhoroot (Ereentsav) and Solov'yevsk, providing access to Borzya, Aginskoye, and Chita on the Trans-Siberian Railway; branch lines run to the lignite mine at Aduunchuluun and from Chingis Dalan to the uranium mine at Marday, near Dashbalbar. The narrow-gauge line built in the Second World War from Choybalsan to Tamsagbulag is no longer operating. A road from Mangut, opposite Ereen, goes to Chita. The designated permanent crossing points on the border with Russia are Ulhanmayhan (for Deed Ul'han), Yalamhyn gol (for Novyy Durulguy), and Ereentsav (for Solov'yevsk), and seasonal crossing points Shivriyn Am (for Mikhail Pavlovsk), Tsagaan Chuluut Uul (for Türgen), Togtor (for Övörtogtor), Höh Uul (for Buylesen), and Yamalhyn Gol (for Imalka). There is a customs post at Erdes. The designated occasional crossing point on the border with China is Havirga (for Arhashaat).

DORNOGOV' (EAST GOBI). Province (*aymag*) in south-eastern Mongolia. Formed in 1931, the province is situated on the border with China (Xilin Gol, Ulanqab, and Bayannur Leagues of Inner Mongolia Autonomous Region). With a territory of 11,000 sq km and population (including Choyr town) of 57,612 (1991), it has 13 rural districts (*sum*); until 1992 there were four wards (*horoo*), Hajuu-Ulaan, Saynshand, Zamyn-Üüd, and Züünbayan; the provincial center is Saynshand (q.v.). The town of Choyr (q.v.) in the northern part of the province was a Soviet Army cantonment. The Trans-Mongolian Railway, which enters Chinese Inner Mongolia (q.v.) at the designated permanent crossing point of Zamyn-Üüd for Ereen (Erhlien), provides access to Peking as well as Ulan Bator (q.v.), and branch lines run to the oil town of Züünbayan and from Ayrag to the fluorite mines at Bor-Öndör (Hentiy

Province). There are deposits of coal (Saynshand), copper (Tsagaan Suvraga), and fluorite (Har Ayrag, Ih Het, and Züüntsagaandel). The oil fields (Züünbayan and Tsagaan Els) and oil refinery (Züünbayan) are not currently in production. Livestock numbers reached 870,900 head (1992) and arable land 800 hectares (1989).

DÖCHIN. Derived from *döchin,* or forty, an administrative unit of 40 households in use in the period from 1927-1932.

DÖRVÖD (DERBET). Mongol ethnic group. The Dörvöd, a West Mongol Oyrd (q.v.) (Oirat) group speaking the northern dialect, accounted for 2.7 percent (55,200) of the population of Mongolia, according to the 1989 census. The Dörvöd are concentrated mainly west of Uvs *nuur,* in the western districts of Uvs Province and northern district of Bayan-Olgiy Province (qq.v.). *See also* China: Mongol Ethnic Groups.

DÖRVÖD. Former provinces (*aymag*) in western Mongolia. From 1911-1919 the Dörvödiyn Tögs Hölög Dalay Han *aymag,* embracing parts of the present-day Uvs and Bayan-Ölgiy Provinces (qq.v.) north of Lake Uvs, and Dörvödiyn Unen Zorigt Han *aymag,* south of Lake Uvs. This territory was included in Chandman'-Uul (q.v.) *aymag* from 1925. Dörvöd *aymag,* founded in 1931, center Ulaangom, was later renamed Uvs Province (qq.v.).

DUGUYLAN. Derived from *duguylan,* or circle, an anti-Manchu (q.v.) "circle" of *ard* (q.v.) whose members in presenting petitions signed their names in a circle, like the spokes of a wheel, to conceal the identity of their leader.

DUNDGOV' (MIDDLE GOBI). Province (*aymag*) in south-central Mongolia. Formed in 1942 from parts of the former Ömnögov', Dornogov', and Töv provinces (qq.v.), the province has a territory of 78,000 sq km, population of 51,895 (1991), and 15 rural districts (*sum*); the provincial center is Mandalgov' (q.v.). There are deposits of lignite (Tsagaan-Ovoo and Tevshiyn Gov') and iron ore (Bayanjargalan). Livestock numbers reached 1,591,100 head (1992) and arable land 900 hectares (1989).

DUUT. Mongolia's highest district center. Duut in Hovd Province (q.v.) is the highest settlement in Mongolia, situated at an altitude of 2,400 m above sea level.

DÜÜREG. Urban district or borough. New legislation on local government introduced following the adoption of the 1992 Constitution (q.v.) brought about big administrative changes in the Mongolian capital. These included the replacement of the four large urban districts (*rayon*, q.v.) with 12 *düüreg* named after local features in the area of Ulan Bator (q.v.)

- E -

EAST GOBI PROVINCE *see* Dornogov' Province.

EASTERN ECONOMIC REGION. One of the three economic regions into which Mongolia was divided in the 1980s (the others being the Central and Western Economic Regions, qq.v.). It consisted of Choybalsan town and Dornod, Hentiy, and Sühbaatar provinces (qq.v.). The region had 9 percent of the country's population, 20 percent of its cultivable land, and 15 percent of its livestock, producing 13 percent of the country's wool and 15 percent of its meat and obtaining some 90 percent of its agricultural production from grain growing. While economic regionalization defined the geographical conditions of industrial and agricultural production, it did little to promote regional development. The economic regions were eventually abandoned and superseded by the system of Economic Cooperation Zones (q.v.) introduced in 1991.

EASTERN PROVINCE *see* Dornod Province.

ECONOMIC COOPERATION ZONES. On the basis of a government ordinance issued in November 1991, Mongolia was divided into six economic cooperation zones: Bayan-Ölgiy, Central, Gov'-Altay, Övörhangay, Sühbaatar, and Ulan Bator (qq.v.). Each zone has a cooperation office headed by the secretary of the zonal cooperation council. It is intended that zoning will promote medium-term intrazonal economic development, making outlying zones less dependent on the center. In interzonal economic development, however, the great imbalance of potential is likely to continue, since the country's population, transport infrastructure, and industry will remain concentrated in the Central and Ulan Bator zones.

ECONOMIC REGIONS. In the 1980s Mongolia was divided into three economic regions: Central, Eastern, and Western (qq.v.). Economic regionalization defined the geographical conditions of industrial and agricultural production, but did little to promote regional development, largely because they were too large and diverse. They were eventually abandoned and superseded by the system of Economic Cooperation Zones (q.v.) introduced in 1991.

ECONOMY *see* Agriculture, Electricity, Foreign Trade, Industry, Mining, Transport, etc.

EDUCATION. Before the 1921 revolution, religious schools in monasteries taught young lamas to read the scriptures in Tibetan and Mongol, while the few secular schools were for training clerks to work in the local administration. The first government-run primary school was opened in the capital in November 1921, and by 1924 it had 419 pupils studying Mongolian language (q.v.) and arithmetic. The first secondary school, opened in 1923, ran five-year courses in language, mathematics, history, geography, physics, and chemistry. The early development of general education in Mongolia is closely linked with the name of the Buryat intellectual Erdenebathaan (q.v.), minister of education from 1926-1929. The Ministry of Education, established in 1924, devised a 10-year plan for the development of education and teacher training from 1926-1936. A nationwide "cultural offensive" was called in 1930-1931, however, following the government's decision to adopt the Latin script (q.v.) and wipe out adult illiteracy in Mongolia. From 1937, increasing numbers of Mongolian students were sent to the USSR for training in vocational schools. Mongolia's first vocational school for training skilled workers opened in 1938. Higher education in Mongolia became possible with the opening of the university (q.v.) in 1942.

The number of general education schools in Mongolia rose from 331 with 24,000 pupils in 1940 to 359 with 50,000 pupils in 1947, but it was estimated that some 9,000 children aged eight to twelve were still not attending school at that time. The law making universal education of school-age children compulsory was not adopted until 1955 however. In 1980, 113 elementary schools taught grades 1 to 4, 108 complete secondary education schools covered grades 1 to 11, and 150 incomplete secondary education schools 1 to 9 only. By 1990 the number of complete secondary education schools had risen to 267. Statistics indicate the growth of educational facilities from 1950 to 1990 as follows:

	1950	1990
General education day schools	421	634
Number of students attending	68,600	440,900
Vocational training schools	-	44
Number of students attending	-	29,100
Specialized secondary schools	12	31
Number of students attending	3,200	18,500
Higher education establishments	4	9
Number of students attending	1,500	12,700*

*plus 3,500 studying abroad

Education reform and the transition to the market economy since 1991, particularly the opening of private schools, have begun to change the previous pattern of education and its institutions. A decline in the birth rate of the population (q.v.) has also begun to reduce the number of school-age children attending school, down to 424,800 in 1993-1994. For further details about higher (tertiary) education, *see* Universities.

EG. River in Mongolia. The Eg (Egiyn *gol*), 475 km, entirely within Mongolia, is the only outlet of Lake Hövsgöl (q.v.). Leaving the lake at Hatgal, it flows east and enters the river Selenge (q.v.) in northern Bulgan Province (q.v.). The Eg has been considered suitable for construction of a hydroelectric power station.

ELBEGDORJ, RENCHINOGIYN (1888-1938). A Barguzin Buryat, Elbegdorj first worked in a newspaper office in Troitskosavsk but traveled in Mongolia in the autonomous period. In 1919 he returned to attend the Buryat Great Hural in Deed-Üüd, then moved to Irkutsk in 1920. Elbegdorj was appointed an interpreter with the MPRP delegation of Danzan and Chagdarjav (qq.v), which went to Moscow and met Russian Communist leader Nikolay Bukharin in November 1920. He attended the first Congress of the Mongolian People's Party (q.v.) as representative of the Comintern (q.v.) and was elected to the Central Committee in 1923. According to one source (where he is called Rinchino), from 1922-1925 he was chairman of the Mongolian Military-War Council, although prior to this he had been appointed to a post in the Buryat government. At the third MPP Congress Elbegdorj is said to have spoken out on behalf of the "oppressed" Mongols of Inner Mongolia (q.v.). Subsequently he was considered to be a proponent of Pan-Mongolism (the idea of uniting all Mongols in one state). Such ideas were condemned at the fourth Congress (1925) as "bourgeois-nationalist" and contrary to communist policy, and Elbegdorj's membership of the MPRP Central Committee (qq.v.) was not renewed. In 1928 he was exiled to Moscow, where he worked at the Association for National and Colonial Studies and later met Badrah and Shijee (qq.v.). One of the victims of the Mongolian purges of the 1930s and 1940s (q.v.), Elbegdorj was sentenced to death by the Military Collegium of the USSR Supreme Court in Moscow on July 2, 1938, according to details released by the Russian government in 1993. The date of his execution was not recorded.

ELBEGDORJ, TSAHIAGIYN (1963-   ). Mongolian politician, leader of the Mongolian Democratic Association (q.v.). Born in Zereg district of Hovd Province (q.v.), Elbegdorj graduated in 1988 from the journalism faculty of L'vov Higher Military Political School (Ukraine). He had worked in 1981-1982 as a machinist in the engineering repair works of Erdenet mining and enriching combine and served in the army as a private soldier from 1982-1983. He became a correspondent of the Defense Ministry newspaper *Ulaan Od* (Red Star) in 1988. At the birth of Mongolian democracy in 1990, he was elected a member of the Presidium of the General Coordinating Council of the Mongolian Democratic Movement (Association) and editor in chief of the MDM paper *Ardchilal* (Democracy), then MDA general coordinator in 1991. In the general elections the same year, he was elected a deputy of the People's Great Hural (q.v.) and a member of the State Little Hural (q.v.), and he served on the SLH social policy standing committee from 1990-1992. Elbegdorj was elected a member of the Mongolian Great Hural (q.v.) as a pro-Mongolian Democratic Party (q.v.) independent for a four-year term on June 28, 1992, in constituency 17 (Hövsgöl) and was a member of the two MGH standing committees: foreign policy and security, and legal affairs. In June 1994, however, Elbegdorj resigned his seat in the Mongolian Great Hural following recriminations over his participation in an opposition hunger strike against government control of the media and dictatorship of Hural business, and in connection with claims that he had betrayed state secrets.

ELDEV-OCHIR, BAT-OCHIRYN (1905-1937). Mongolian party leader from 1928-1937. Born in Zasagt-Han Province (q.v.), Eldev-Ochir was from 1922-1925 the secretary of the local cell of the Mongolian Revolutionary Youth League (q.v.). He studied at the Party School of the Mongolian People's Revolutionary Party (q.v.) and in the USSR at the Communist University of the Toilers of the East from 1925-1928. He was elected member of the Presidium and concurrently secretary of the MPRP Central Committee (qq.v.) from December 1928 to March 1930, and reelected to the Presidium in March 1930, 1932-1934, and in October 1937. He was appointed head of the Internal Security Directorate from 1930-1932, then reelected secretary of the Central Committee in June 1932. He died of illness in 1937, according to a recent account, although previously he was thought to have been a victim of Choybalsan's (q.v.) purges.

ELECTRICITY. Power generation in Mongolia is based on large coal-fired stations forming a central high-voltage grid, with individual small diesel generators supplying outlying towns and settlements. One of the country's first large power stations was built in Ulan Bator (q.v.) in the 1930s to supply the industrial combine. A narrow-gauge railway was laid in Ulan Bator from the coal-mines at Nalayh (q.v.) in 1938. During the industrialization of Mongolia in the 1960s-1980s three large new power stations were built with Soviet aid in Ulan Bator. The No. 4 power station, which burns lignite, doubled the country's generating capacity. Much of the coal for Ulan Bator's power stations now comes by rail from the mines at Baganuur (q.v.), where construction of a new large coal-fired power station has been planned (six 130 MW sets). The total installed capacity of coal-fired power stations is 935.6 MW. Annual electricity generation fell over the period from 1990-1993 from 2,814.2 to 2,313.7 million kWh.

Some electricity is imported from Russia, with which the central grid is linked via Sühbaatar (q.v.) and Gusinoorzersk in the Buryat Republic (q.v.). The grid links Ulan Bator with Darhan and its own coalmine at Sharyn Gol (qq.v.), as well as other towns and settlements of northern Mongolia, and has two main spurs: south to the Hentiy Province fluorite mines and Saynshand in Dornogov' Province (qq.v.); and west to Erdenet copper mining town in Bulgan Province (qq.v.), with a further link to a small Chinese-built hydroelectric station at Harhorin. Mongolia is also planning to build a second hydroelectric station, on the river Eg (q.v.). In 1991-1992 electricity generation was frequently interrupted by breakdowns caused by the lack of spare parts and the chronic shortage of diesel and petrol, which disrupted mine and railway transport and closed the local diesel generating stations. Herdsmen who had bought small wind generators for domestic use fared better than those who had invested larger sums in more powerful portable petrol generators.

ENEBISH, LHAMSÜRENGIYN (1947-   ). Deputy prime minister since 1992. Born on June 1, 1947, in Bulgan Province (q.v.), Enebish graduated in 1970 from the Mongolian State University with a degree in building engineering (water supply). He first worked in the administrative department of Ulan Bator City Executive Administration (qq.v.) from 1970-1985; he was appointed deputy chairman of the Executive Administration in 1985 and served as chairman (Mayor) from September 1990-1992. He was elected a deputy of the People's Great Hural (q.v.) in July 1990 and a member of the MPRP Central Committee (qq.v.) in April 1990, reelected in 1991 and 1992. He was also made chairman of the Mongolian-Chinese Friendship Society in 1990. Enebish was elected a member of the Mongolian Great Hural (q.v.) for the MPRP for a four-year term on June 28, 1992, in constituency 25 (Ulan Bator). He is a member of the MGH standing committee for foreign policy and security. He was appointed deputy prime minister and minister of administration on October 20, 1992, and elected a member of the Party Leadership Council of the MPRP Little Hural (qq.v.) the same month. The Ministry of Administration was abolished, however, after the adoption of the Law on the Government in

May 1993. Enebish was appointed chairman of the State Commission for the Introduction of the Mongolian Script for Official Business in November 1992.

ENHBAYAR, NAMBARYN (1958-   ). Minister of culture since 1992. Born on September 15, 1958, in Ulan Bator (q.v.), Enhbayar graduated in 1980 from the Gor'kiy Higher School of Literature in Moscow. He first worked as a literary translator and editor in the translation bureau of the Committee of the Mongolian Writers' Union from 1980-1983; he was appointed head of the MWU's foreign relations department in 1983 and vice president of the Mongolian Translators' Association in 1990. He took up his first government post as chief deputy chairman of the Culture and Art Development Committee from November 1990-August 1992. Enhbayar was elected a member of the Mongolian Great Hural (q.v.) for the MPRP (q.v.) for a four-year term on June 28, 1992, in constituency 23 (Ulan Bator). He is a member of two MGH standing committees: foreign policy and security, and education, science, and culture. He was appointed minister of culture on August 5, 1992, by the first session of the Mongolian Great Hural. Enhbayar was appointed a deputy chairman of the State Commission for the Introduction of the Mongolian Script for Official Business in November 1992.

ENHMANDAH, BALDANGIYN (1955-   ). Mongolian politician. Enhmandah graduated from the Mongolian State University in 1973, Leningrad State University in 1978, and the Academy of Social Sciences (of the CPSU) in Moscow in 1991 with a higher degree in philosophy. After working as a lecturer in the Mongolian State University from 1978-1983, he held the posts of Second and First Secretary of Ulan Bator City Committee of the Mongolian Revolutionary Youth League (q.v.) from 1983-1988. In 1991 he was appointed head of the vocational education auditing service at the Ministry of Education (since 1992, the Ministry of Science and Education). In November 1993 he was elected a member of the MPRP's Party Leadership Council (qq.v.) and to the post of secretary of the MPRP.

ENHNASAN, JAMSRANGIYN 1954-   ). Deputy procurator general since 1993. Born in Ulan Bator (q.v.), Enhnasan graduated from Irkutsk (q.v.) State University in 1979 with a degree in law. He began work in the Construction Troops' Procurator's office in 1979, served in the office of the Military Procurator General from 1980-1983, then worked as the military procurator of Erdenet garrison from 1983-1986. On his return to Ulan Bator he was appointed deputy military procurator general and concurrently construction troops' procurator from 1986-1988, concurrently director of the General Auditing Department, then first deputy military procurator general from 1988-1991. After serving as an adviser to the legal affairs standing committee of the Mongolian Great Hural (q.v.) from 1991-1992, in October 1992 Enhnasan was appointed deputy head of the legal research and information department of the MGH Secretariat. Following the reorganization of the legal system in keeping with the provisions of the new fourth Constitution (q.v.), he was appointed to the new post of deputy procurator general in July 1993.

ENHSAYHAN, MENDSAYHANY (1955-   ). Mongolian politician. Born in Ulan Bator (q.v.), Enhsayhan graduated in 1978 with an economics degree from Kiev State University (Ukraine) and also obtained a higher degree in economics in the USSR in 1987. He first worked from 1978 as an economist, research worker, and deputy head of a directorate at the Ministry of Foreign Trade (Ministry of Foreign Economic Relations and Supply); he was next appointed director of the Market Research Institute of the once more renamed Ministry of Trade and Cooperation. In 1990 he was elected a deputy of the People's Great Hural (q.v.), a member of the State Little Hural (q.v.), and chairman of the SLH economic standing committee. Enhsayhan was elected a member of the Mongolian Great Hural (q.v.) for the Mongolian Democratic Party (q.v.) for a four-year term on June 28, 1992, in constituency 26 (Ulan Bator). He is a member of two MGH standing committees: environmental protection, and budget and finance. He became the chairman of the MDP in April 1992, and a member of the General Council of the Mongolian National Democratic Party (q.v.) on its formation in October 1992. He remained director of the Political Academy of the Mongolian Democratic Association (q.v.). Following President Ochirbat's (q.v.) victory in the 1993 presidential elections, Enhsayhan replaced Tümen (q.v.) in July as head of the Presidential Secretariat and resigned his seat in the MGH.

ERDENE ZUU. Mongolia's oldest Buddhist monastery, founded by Avtay Khan in 1586, built near the ruins of the Mongol capital Karakorum in the Orhon (qq.v.) valley. One of the few monasteries to survive the destruction of religious establishments in the 1930s, Erdene Zuu was closed for many years but reopened as a religious museum in the 1960s. In 1992 a group of lamas (*see* Lamaism) returned to Erdene Zuu to rebuild the religious community there. The nearest town is called Harhorin.

ERDENEBATHAAN (BATUKHANOV, NIKITA FEDOROVICH). Buryat intellectual, given the name Erdene (''precious'') because of his learning. He arrived in Niyslel Hüree (q.v.) in 1914 to work as a teacher, but was appointed secretary of the provisional revolutionary government in March 1921. As interpreter and adviser to the delegation led by Soliyn Danzan and Sühbaatar (qq.v.), he visited Moscow in November 1921 for the signing of the Mongolian-Soviet treaty of friendship. In 1924 Erdenebathaan was elected to membership of the Little Hural (q.v.) and given an appointment in the new Ministry of Education. In 1925 he arranged for groups of Mongolian children to go to Germany and France for several years to study. He became minister of education in 1926 and visited his pupils abroad, organizing the publication of Mongolian maps and an atlas and the manufacture of a Mongol typewriter while in Germany. He was relieved of his duties in 1929 and accused of Right Opportunism (q.v.). In 1930 he was sent to Leningrad, where he taught Mongolian at the Institute of Oriental Languages. Erdenebathaan was arrested by the NKVD in 1937 and sent to a prison camp at Ukhta (Komi Republic).

ERDENEBILEG, TÖMÖR-OCHIRYN (1967-). Mongolian politician. Erdenebileg finished Darhan (q.v.) 10-year school in 1983 and graduated from the Chinese studies department of the Mongolian State University in 1989. Subsequently he worked in the Institute of Philosophy and Sociology of the Academy of Sciences (q.v.), the government's Center for State Policy and Social Affairs Studies, and the foreign trade policy department of the Ministry of Trade and Industry. He joined the Mongolian National Democratic Party in 1992 (q.v.). In the 1992 elections to the Mongolian Great Hural (q.v.), he took fourth place in the three-seat constituency No. 19 (Darhan). Following the resignation from the MGH of Natsagiyn Jantsannorov (q.v.) in October 1993, Erdenebileg's membership of the MGH was approved. He is the youngest member.

ERDENET. Name given to the Mongolian-Soviet joint stock company set up in November 1973 to develop the copper and molybdenum mine at Erdenetiyn Ovoo and build and run the concentrating combine, the core plant in the construction of the new town of Erdenet (q.v.). At first the director general was a Soviet citizen and his first deputy Mongolian, but since the company became a *kontsern* (concern) in 1992, the director general has been a Mongolian, Shagdaryn Otgonbileg. Copper ore mined and concentrated at Erdenet is shared between Mongolia and Russia. Mongolia's share is sent by rail to Dzhezkazgan or Balkhash in Kazakhstan for smelting, while the Russian share is smelted in the Urals. The work force of 7,200 includes 800 "foreign experts" (Russian engineers and technicians). Income from the mining operation accounts for about half of Mongolia's foreign exchange revenue. The concern's auxiliary activities include the cement and lime works at Hötöl, Zelter coal mine, and Erdenet building company. It has opened offices in Moscow, Peking, Berlin, London, St. Petersburg, Yekaterinburg, and Almaty to gain access to the metals markets. Annual production capacity is planned to reach 27 million tons of ore and 120,000 tons of copper.

ERDENET. Center of Orhon Province (q.v.). Founded in 1976, Erdenet was a "town under national jurisdiction" comprising four wards (*horoo*), Bayan-Öndör, Hyalganat, Jargalant, and Nayramdal. In May 1994, these were redesignated to form the new Orhon Province, and Hyalganat was transferred to Hangal *sum* of the surrounding Bulgan Province. The town is linked to the Trans-Mongolian Railway by a branch line from Salhit in Selenge Province (q.v.). The town was built to serve the copper and molybdenum mine of Erdenetiyn Ovoo, and has grown to include factories producing foodstuffs and carpets, as well as sawmills at Hyalganat. Livestock numbers reached 92,100 head (1992) and arable land 4,200 hectares (1989). The population was 50,005 (1991).

ERDENIYN OCHIR. Order of merit instituted by the government of Autonomous Mongolia (q.v.) in 1913. It continued to be awarded by the revolutionary government until new medals were introduced in 1924.

EREENTSAV. Mongolia's lowest district center. Ereentsav in Dornod Province (q.v.), situated at an altitude of 600 m above sea level, is the lowest district center in Mongolia.

EXECUTIVE ADMINISTRATION. This local government administrative body was until 1992 part of the system of Hurals of People's Deputies (q.v.).

- F -

FELT. A material made by pressing and rolling wool, used for carpets and articles of clothing and for covering the Mongolian round tent (*ger*, q.v., or yurt). The *ger* wall felt is called *tuurga*, from which is derived the Mongol expression *esgiy tuurgatan*, "people of the felt walls," embracing the Mongols, Kazakh (qq.v.), Kirghiz, and other nations who traditionally live in *ger*. Mongolian felts are of varied density and number of layers and sometimes of different colors on the obverse and reverse. Felt carpets are embroidered with camelhair thread in vivid traditional patterns and may be decorated with appliqué.

Originally produced by domestic methods, felt is now mostly manufactured. Output in the early 1990s averaged about 500,000 m and
some 400,000 pairs of felt boots a year.

FIVE-YEAR PLANS. Not counting the first failed attempt for 1931-
1935, the Mongolian People's Revolutionary Party (q.v.) and Mongolian government launched eight five-year plans over the period
from 1948-1990, plus one three-year plan to correct their alignment
with the five-yearly congresses of the MPRP and the Soviet five-year
plans—First: 1948-1952; Second: 1953-1957; Three-Year Plan:
1958-1960; Third: 1961-1965; Fourth 1966-1970; Fifth: 1971-1975;
Sixth: 1976-1980; Seventh: 1981-1985; and Eighth: 1986-1990. The
collapse of the MPRP's role as the ruling party in 1990 and the beginning of the transition to a market economy marked the abandonment of socialist planning methods.

FODDER. In Mongolia livestock (q.v.) has traditionally been maintained by natural grazing in all seasons and weathers, although hay
making has become an established practice. The growing of fodder
and silage crops increased in importance with the establishment near
large towns of mechanized dairy farms relying on supplies of concentrates. Production, storage, and distribution, as well as the creation
of emergency reserves, were associated with the general introduction
of industrialized farming methods, which became fashionable in the
1970s-1980s. However, the economic disruption of the transition to a
market economy has practically forced the abandonment of most large
mechanized dairy farms, which have not been able to procure and
transport fodder in the quantities required, nor sell their produce prof-
itably. The practice of fodder growing was not limited to state farms
(q.v.); the arable land farmed by cooperatives (q.v.) across the country was mostly used for fodder crops. With 117,800 hectares sown to
fodder and silage crops, national production reached 780,000 tons in
1990, but fell to 140,000 tons in 1992. Hay mowing also declined from
1990-1992, from 893,000 to 644,000 tons. The fall in production was
also due to the breaking up of large farms by privatization and to shortages of fuel for sowing, harvesting, and transport.

FOREIGN TRADE. The Mongolian government introduced a foreign
trade monopoly in the 1920s, driving Russian, other European, and
particularly Chinese merchants out of the country. Mongolia traded
only with the USSR until the establishment of diplomatic and trade relations with China after the Second World War. Mongolia's membership of Comecon (q.v.) provided wider opportunities for trade with
Eastern Europe, including the import of machinery and vehicles in ex-

change for raw materials, but some 85 percent of trade turnover remained with the Soviet Union. While opening up a little to the West in the 1980s, Mongolia was able to devote only 1 or 2 percent of its trade to the purchase of certain equipment, chemicals, and pharmaceuticals unavailable from its Comecon partners, as well as cigarettes and Scotch whiskey for the increasingly important tourist trade. The value of imports far exceeded that of exports, and the imbalance was funded from long-term loans from the USSR, estimated by Soviet sources to have reached some 10 billion rubles by 1990.

The introduction in 1991 of foreign trade settlements in hard currency reduced Mongolia's foreign trade capacity considerably, there being virtually no reserves, and the country's economy suffered particularly badly from the shortage of oil, all of which had been imported from the USSR. Total oil imports fell sharply from a peak of more than 800,000 tons in 1989, amounting to 570,000 tons in 1992 and 512,700 tons in 1993. Petrol imports fell from 321,800 tons tin 1990 to 178,600 tons in 1992 and 174,300 tons in 1993.

Total trade turnover in 1992 was worth US$767 million, 57 percent with Russia, 12 percent with China, and 9 percent with Japan, the main trading partners. Provisional figures for 1993 indicate a trade turnover of US$722 million, 48 percent with Russia, 24 percent with China, 7.5 percent with Kazakhstan, 4.9 percent with Japan, and 2.9 percent with the US. Exports worth US$360.9 million went mainly to Russia (37 percent), China (31 percent) and Kazakhstan (15 percent), while imports worth US$360.9 million were mostly from Russia (60 percent), China (17 percent), and the US (5 percent). Mongolia's chief exports to Russia were 184,000 tons of copper concentrate, 1,265 tons of molybdenum concentrate, 58,500 *tarvagan* (marmot) skins, and 394,630 meters of carpet.

Mongolia imports all kinds of manufactured goods from heavy machinery to aircraft and motorcycles, refrigerators, sewing machines, and paper, and some foodstuffs. Mongolian exports are mainly livestock (q.v.), raw materials, and mining (q.v.) industry products. There is also revenue from transit flights by foreign airlines (q.v.) and tourism (*see* Juulchin). In an effort to attract more foreign investors, Mongolia offered tax holidays and other incentives under the 1993 Law on Foreign Investment (*see* Appendix 5).

FOUR ASSOCIATIONS. Mongolian political movement. The Four Associations was the name given to the loose coalition formed by the Mongolian Democratic, New Progress (qq.v.), Youth and Students' Associations in 1993 under the leadership of Sangajavyn Bayartsogt. It later sought to broaden its base through contacts with other organizations like the Women's Movement for Social Development, the

Committee of Teachers' Representatives (formed for the teachers' strike in 1993), and the Mongolian Students' Trade Union.

FRUIT. Although the Mongols came to know many kinds of fruit during the expansion of the Mongol Empire, few are native to Mongolia, and for climatic reasons even the experimental planting of apple trees has not proved to be viable. Yet, this lack is partially offset by an abundance of wild berries of several kinds. The sea buckthorn (*chatsargana*) is grown commercially to make a sweet juice and a fruit wine. The Kazakhs (q.v.) of western Mongolia (Bayan-Ölgiy and Hovd Provinces, qq.v.) grow melons. Soft drinks like lemonade are made with imported extracts.

- G -

GACHUURT. District (*düüreg*) of Ulan Bator (q.v.). Established in 1992, this urban district of some 950 households consists of two wards (*horoo*) incorporating the Shar Hooloy, Töv (central), Bayandöhöm, Artsat, and Huanday areas of the former Gachuurt ward of Ulan Bator centered on a state farm situated some 15 km east of the capital.

GALINDIV, SOYRYN (1907-1941). Minister of health. One of the 32 victims of the Mongolian purges of the 1930s and 1940s (q.v.) sent to the USSR for trial and sentence, details of which were released by the Russian government in 1993. Sentenced to death by the Military Collegium of the USSR Supreme Court in Moscow in July 5, 1941, and executed on July 30.

GALSANPUNTSAG, DELEGIYN (1913-1941). Head of investigation department, Ministry of Internal Affairs. One of the 32 victims of the Mongolian purges of the 1930s and 1940s (q.v.) sent to the USSR for trial and sentence, details of which were released by the Russian government in 1993. Sentenced to death by the Military Collegium of the USSR Supreme Court in Moscow on July 5, 1941, and executed on July 27.

GAMIN. Mongol rendering of the Chinese *kuomin*, meaning the Kuomintang (Guomindang), National Party of the Republic of China founded by Sun Yat-sen, particularly with reference to the Chinese troops who entered Mongolia in 1919.

GANBAATAR, AR"YAAGIYN (1959-). Mongolian politician. Born in Ulan Bator (q.v.), Ganbaatar graduated from Lodz University in 1983 with a degree in mathematics. He began working as a teacher at Ulan

Bator No. 76 School from 1983-1984, then at the Mongolian State University from 1984-1990. He was chairman of the Executive Council of the Mongolian Social Democratic Movement (q.v.) from November 1990 until the movement merged with the Mongolian Social Democratic Party (q.v.) in September 1991; he was elected vice-chairman of the MSDP in 1992. Ganbaatar was made a member of the Mongolian Great Hural (q.v.) on the resignation of Mendsayhany Enhsayhan (q.v.) in July 1993. He had failed to be elected in the 1992 general elections in the multiseat Ulan Bator No 26 constituency, and indeed received fewer votes than the former chief deputy minister of law, Dulamym Sugar, but the latter did not want to take the vacant seat.

GANBAT, TSERENSODNOMYN (1957-   ). Mongolian politician. Ganbat trained as a translator and became a member of the MPRP Central Committee (qq.v.) in 1992 and secretary of the MPRP theoretical magazine *Bodrol, Byasalgal* (Interpretation and Contemplation). He was elected a member of the Mongolian Great Hural (q.v.) for the MPRP for a four-year term on June 28, 1992, in constituency 24 (Ulan Bator). He is a member of two MGH standing committees: education, science, and culture, and foreign policy and security.

GANBAYAR, NANZADYN (1953-   ). Procurator-general since 1993. Born in Ulan Bator (q.v.), Ganbayar graduated with a degree in law from Irkutsk (q.v.) State University in 1976. From 1976-1978 he worked as section and department head at the Supreme Court and was a member of the Supreme Court from 1978-1984. In 1984 he was appointed chairman and chief arbitrator of Ulan Bator City Court, but in 1987 he moved to the MPRP Central Committee (qq.v.), where he worked as an aide in the administrative organizations department. Elected a member of the State Little Hural (q.v.) from 1990-1992, he was made chairman of its Standing Committee on Legal Affairs and was actively involved in the drafting of new legislation. In September 1992, he was appointed chief deputy minister of culture, and remained in this post until his appointment to the post of Mongolian procurator-general in June 1993, when he suspended his MPRP membership.

GANBOLD, BAASANJAVYN (1955-   ). Mongolian politician. Ganbold trained as a journalist and became editor of the Mongolian People's Revolutionary Party (q.v.) fortnightly newspaper *Bodlyn Solbitsol* (Cross Opinions). He was elected a member of the Mongolian Great Hural (q.v.) for the MPRP for a four-year term on June 28, 1992, in constituency 26 (Ulan Bator). He is a member of three MGH standing committees: environmental protection; education, science, and culture; and health and social security.

GANBOLD, DAVAADORJIYN (1957-). Mongolian politician. Born in Ulan Bator (q.v.), Ganbold went to school in Moscow and graduated from the faculty of economics of Moscow State University in 1979. He lectured in political economy at the Mongolian State University from 1979-1984, then obtained the higher degree of Candidate of Economics from Moscow State University in 1987. From February 1988 to September 1990, he was a lecturer at the MPRP Central Committee's (qq.v.) Higher Party School. As chairman of the Mongolian National Progress Party (q.v.) from May 1990 to October 1992, he was one of the first advocates of a market economy in Mongolia. He was elected a deputy of the People's Great Hural (q.v.) in July 1990, but shortly afterward surrendered his seat when appointed chief deputy prime minister from 1990-1992; his responsibilities included the economy, planning, finance, trade and international cooperation, catering and supply, and local government, and he chaired the government commissions on privatization, foreign aid coordination, food distribution, and economic relations with Russia. Ganbold was elected a member of the Mongolian Great Hural (q.v.) for the MNPP for a four-year term on June 28, 1992, in constituency 18 (Hentiy). He is a member of two MGH standing committees: assemblies and administration, and economic policy. He was elected president of the Mongolian National Democratic Party (q.v.) on its formation in October 1992.

GANBOLD, GAANJUURYN (1956-). Mongolian politician. Ganbold trained as a lawyer, becoming deputy chairman of the Mongolian Lawyers' Association in 1992. He was made a member of the MPRP Central Committee (qq.v.) in 1990 and 1992, following a period as an official at Gachuurt state farm, near Ulan Bator (q.v.). He was elected a member of the Mongolian Great Hural (q.v.) for the MPRP for a four-year term on June 28, 1992, in constituency 23 (Ulan Bator). He is a member of two MGH standing committees: assemblies and administration, and legal affairs. In December 1993, he was elected chairman of the MGH Subcommittee on Human Rights, replacing Radnaasümbereliyn Gonchigdorj (Social Democrat).

GANBYAMBA, NAVAANSAMDANGIYN (1958-). Mongolian politician. Ganbyamba studied history. He was made a secretary of Hentiy MPRP (qq.v.) Committee, then a deputy of the People's Great Hural (q.v.) from 1990-1992 and a member of the State Little Hural (q.v.) from January-July 1992, as well as a member of the MPRP Central Committee (q.v.) in 1992. He was elected a member of the Mongolian Great Hural (q.v.) for the MPRP for a four-year term on June 28, 1992, in constituency 18 (Hentiy). He is a member of two MGH standing committees: education, science, and culture, and foreign policy and security.

GANDAN MONASTERY. Gandantegchinlen (Tushitamahayanavipa) monastery in Ulan Bator (q.v.), built in 1834-1838, is named after Dga'-ldan, the Tibetan monastery of Tsongkhapa, founder of the reformed Gelugpa (Yellow Hat) sect. It has been the center of Mongolian Lamaism (q.v.) since 1944, when it was reopened after five years' closure. Gandan is still the country's biggest active monastery and religious training center with 130 lamas.

GANDI, TÖGSJARGALYN (1960-). Mongolian politician. Gandi became a journalist and later head of a department of the newspaper *Ardyn Erh* (q.v.). She was elected a pro-MPRP (q.v.) independent member of the Mongolian Great Hural (q.v.) for a four-year term on June 28, 1992, in constituency 25 (Ulan Bator). She is a member of two MGH standing committees: education, science, and culture, and foreign policy and security.

GAN-ÖLZIY, CHIMEDTSERENGIYN. Mongolian politician. Gan-Ölziy has the higher degree of candidate of philosophy and was a political worker at the MPRP Central Committee (qq.v.) until 1992. He was made a member of the Mongolian Great Hural (q.v.) for the MPRP in December 1992 on the resignation of Dashiyn Byambasüren (q.v.). In the general elections of June 28, 1992, Gan-Ölziy had won fourth place in the three-seat constituency 18 (Hentiy), after Byambasüren, Davaadorjiyn Ganbold, and Ganbyamba (qq.v.).

GAVAA, RASHMAAGIYN (1949-). Mongolian military commander. Born in Bayan-Dalay district of Ömögov' Province (q.v.), Gavaa attended the Military Communications Academy in Leningrad and the Academy of the Soviet Armed Forces General Staff and has a higher degree in technical sciences. After working as a section leader in the Mongolian Army Higher General School, he served as Commander of Army Communications, but returned to the renamed Combined Arms Higher School as commandant. In October 1990, Gavaa was appointed chief of the armed forces staff and chief deputy minister of defense. Following the government reorganization of August 1992, he resigned the latter post; he was reappointed chief of the armed forces staff once again in July 1993. In the same year he held talks on military cooperation with Col. Gen. Kolesnikov, the Russian armed forces chief of staff and first deputy minister of defense, and also visited US military installations in Hawaii. In February 1994 Gavaa was appointed a deputy minister of defense.

GAZARTARIALAN. Former province (*aymag*) in northern Mongolia. Founded in 1931, center Altanbulag (q.v.), this "land cultivation" ("agricultural") province was renamed Selenge Province (q.v.).

GENDEN, PELJIDIYN (1892-1937). Mongolian head of state from 1924-1927, prime minister from 1932-1936. Born in 1895 in present-day Taragt district of Övörhangay Province (q.v.), Genden joined the Mongolian Revolutionary Youth League (q.v.) in 1922 and the MPRP (q.v.) a year later, working as head of his local MRYL cell. He was chairman of the Presidium of the Little Hural (q.v.) and concurrently chairman of the Central Bureau of the Mongolian Trade Unions from November 29, 1924 to November 15, 1927; secretary of the MPRP Central Committee (q.v.) from December 11, 1928 to June 30, 1932; and prime minister from July 2, 1932 to March 22, 1936. He was elected to the Presidium of the MPRP Central Committee in September 1925, reelected in 1926-1934, and left in March 1936.

At his third and last meeting with Stalin (on December 30, 1935), Genden was accused of drunkenness and indifference to the threat of Japanese invasion. Genden was invited to stay at Foros on the Black Sea for a holiday—for a year. Genden was unhappy and wrote to Anandyn Amar (q.v.), his successor as prime minister, for help in getting back to Mongolia. Bat-Ochiryn Eldev-Ochir (q.v.), secretary of the MPRP Central Committee, was holidaying in nearby Yalta at the time, but took no action. On July 10, 1937, Genden was arrested in Sochi by a group of Mongolians on charges of counterrevolution and spying for the Japanese and told he would be flying to Mongolia. He was sentenced to death by the Military Collegium of the USSR Supreme Court in Moscow on November 26, 1937, however, and executed the same day. He was eventually buried at the Donskoy monastery in the south-western suburbs of Moscow. Genden was one of the 32 victims of the Mongolian purges of the 1930s and 1940s (q.v.) tried and sentenced in the USSR, details of whom were released by the Russian government in 1993. Genden was rehabilitated in 1962.

GENGHIS KHAN (1162-1227). Named after a defeated Tatar enemy by his father Yesügei, a minor chieftain, Temüchin adopted the title Genghis Kahn (Chinggis Han—and many other variants spellings via different languages, meaning "ruler of the oceans") in 1189, after he had unified the Mongol tribes. He was proclaimed Genghis Khan of All Mongols in 1206. The only substantial Mongol work about Genghis Khan and the early stages of the Mongol Empire is the partly legendary *Secret History of the Mongols* (called in Mongolian *Nuuts Tovchoo*), which survived only in a version transcribed into Chinese characters.

Genghis Khan was succeeded by his third son, Ögedei (1186-1241), as the second Great Khan of the Mongols in 1229; it was Ögedei Khan who built the walls of the Mongol capital Karakorum (q.v.). Genghis Khan's grandson Güyük (1207-1248), Ögedei's eldest son, was proclaimed the third Great Khan in 1246 at a ceremony witnessed by the Franciscan traveler John of Plano Carpini. After Güyük's death the succession passed to the line of Genghis Khan's youngest son, Tolui, Tolui's eldest son, Möngke (1209-1258), being proclaimed the fourth Great Khan in 1251. Möngke's brother Hülegü founded the dynasty of Ilkhans in Persia. Möngke was succeeded by another brother, Kublai (1215-1294), who was proclaimed Great Khan in 1260, in Kaiping. However, a fourth brother, Ariq-böke, was also proclaimed Great Khan, in Karakorum. Kublai defeated Ariq-böke in 1264, confirming his position as the fifth (and last) Great Khan and proclaiming himself the first Yuan Emperor.

Admired as the unifier of the Mongols and founder of the Mongol Empire, Genghis Khan has always had a special place in the hearts of all Mongols. He is the subject of a religious cult centered on Ejin Horo in Ih Ju League of Inner Mongolia (q.v.), where a mausoleum was built to house various supposed relics of Genghis Khan's times. It was damaged during the Second World War and in the "cultural revolution" but has been restored. In the twentieth century, the demands of communist ideology came into direct conflict with historical tradition. As the only ruling political party in Mongolia the MPRP (q.v.), guided by this ideology and spurred on by the Soviet Bolsheviks, in the name of "socialist democracy" and "internationalism" virtually destroyed what Manchu (q.v.) rule had left of the Mongols' native culture and spirit of independence. After the onslaught against Lamaism (q.v.) in the 1930s and the hardships of the Second World War, at a time of East-West confrontation when Stalinism was at its zenith, the party returned to matters of ideological reliability. In a resolution issued in 1949, the Politburo noted in the teaching of history and literature in schools a tendency "to deviate into bourgeois nationalist views." This was allegedly due to the lack of textbooks written from the Marxist-Leninist viewpoint, and confusion among intellectuals over the difference between national pride and "bourgeois nationalism"—boasting about the conquests of Genghis Khan and idealizing Mongol "feudalism" to the point of negating the achievements of the people's revolution in Mongolia, that is, the legitimacy of the party itself.

Changes following the death of Stalin and the Mongolian dictator Choybalsan (q.v.) gradually brought about some improvement in Mongolia's internal and international political situation, and in 1962 the MPRP Central Committee decided to celebrate the eight hundredth anniversary of Genghis Khan's birth. Daramyn Tömör-Ochir (q.v.), a member of the MPRP Politburo and Secretariat, was given the task of organizing the national celebrations, including the unveiling of a monument at Genghis Khan's supposed birthplace, Delüün Boldog in Hentiy Province (q.v.), with a speech by a leading historian for the occasion on May 31, and the publication of a set of Genghis Khan anniversary postage stamps. At about this time, however, Genghis Khan was attacked in the USSR as a "reactionary" whose Mongol-Tatar "yoke" of terror and extortion had laid waste to Russia. In a damage-limitation exercise the MPRP Politburo issued a new and negative evaluation of the founder of the Mongol state and deprived Tömör-Ochir of his party posts. He was said to have tried "to create an unhealthy mood in public opinion and to inflame nationalist passions," supported "nationalist tendencies directed at idealizing the role of Genghis Khan in Mongolian history," and organized "pompous celebration" of the anniversary.

The new official view of Genghis Khan was that in founding the Mongol state he had played a positive role in unifying the divided tribes. "But all his further activity was doubly reactionary and aimed at the seizure of foreign lands, the mass annihilation of the peoples of enslaved countries and the destruction of their material and cultural values." Thus to "deny or insufficiently emphasize the reactionary nature of Genghis Khan's activities is in essence to deviate from the party's position of principle and to encourage nationalism."

The three-volume official history of Mongolia published in 1969 dismissed the removal of Tömör-Ochir in a couple of lines, without even mentioning Genghis Khan. However, there are parallels to be found with the denunciation of the "personality cult" of Stalin in the USSR and the subsequent reevaluation of the role of Choybalsan in Mongolia. There was also the obvious political difficulty of how to handle the historical role of Yumjaagiyn Tsedenbal (q.v.) as well.

In December 1988, MPRP General Secretary Jambyn Batmönh (q.v.), responding to pressures from CPSU General Secretary Mikhail Gorbachev, called for greater openness (*glasnost'*) in Mongolia. For the first time since Tsedenbal was removed from power in 1984, he was blamed directly by name for the country's political and economic "stagnation." A resolution adopted by the MPRP Central Committee, after criticizing Tsedenbal's "willful and unprincipled" leadership, declared that having condemned national pride as "nationalism" for many years, the party was now reevaluating Genghis Khan and the Mongol Empire "so as to protect Mongolia's cultural heritage."

The MPRP resolution was soon overtaken by events—the birth of the democratic movement in Mongolia in 1989-1990 swept away the MPRP's self-proclaimed right to decide such matters. Ironically enough, one of the most popular songs of the movement was about

Genghis Khan, and lamented that for so long the "Blue Mongols" had not been allowed to "speak the name of their Lord."

GER. A Mongolian round felt-covered tent, or yurt (Russian: *yurta*), the family home of the nomadic herdsmen—and of townspeople lacking modern housing (q.v.). The *ger* has a wooden door about four feet high, but no windows. The walls are formed of five wooden lattice-work sections (*hana*, q.v.), measuring about five feet by five. The roof is supported on a cartwheel-shaped ring (*toono*, q.v.) mounted on two vertical posts, the wooden roof poles being mounted radially between the *toono* and the top of the latticework and tied in place. The frame-work is covered with large pieces of felt (q.v.) for warmth and canvas for protection against the elements, tied firmly with ropes around the circumference and across the top. The stove stands at the center, its chimney passing out through the *toono*, which is covered outside with a removable flap to let the air and light in. The stove burns the local fuel—coal, wood, *zag* (a desert shrub), or *argal* (q.v., dried dung). The large furniture (beds, storage chests, cupboards) is disposed along the interior walls, which may be decorated with a colorful material. The door and furniture are often brightly painted. The natural floor is cov-ered with felt or carpet, or a wooden floor is installed for longer-term occupation. A *ger* can be put up and taken down quickly and is easily transportable on camelback. In towns *gers* are usually pitched in indi-vidual small compounds protected by solid wooden fences to form parallel blocks separated by lanes. Town *gers* may have electricity and telephone connections, but lack water supplies or sewerage. Water is purchased from a communal supply point and household waste is buried in a communal dump. Each family has its own earth latrine.

GOATS. In Mongolia goats are raised for their hair and meat and are usu-ally herded together with sheep; the milk is made into curds and cheese. Goats are concentrated in the central and south-western provinces: Bayanhongor and Gov'-Altay (qq.v.) have the greatest numbers—712,915 and 633,169 (1993), respectively. There were altogether some 5.6 million goats in Mongolia at the end of 1992 and 6,107,041 in 1993. Selection and crossbreeding have developed domestic cashmere vari-eties like the Gurvan Sayhan, yielding 450 g of hair; the average for or-dinary breeds is 295 g (1990). The country produces some 1,300 tons of goat hair a year (1988-1990), though production of cashmere has de-clined from 300 tons in 1990 to 125 tons in 1992. Some 1.1-1.2 mil-lion goatskins are procured each year (1988-1990).

GOBI ALTAI MOUNTAINS. The Gov'-Altay range (*nuruu*) in Mon-golia. They are a continuation of the Mongol Altai Mountains (q.v.)

extending for some 700 km across southern Bayanhongor and Övörhangay provinces into Ömnögov' (South Gobi) Province (qq.v.). The
highest peak is Ih Bogd (q.v.).

GOBI ALTAI PROVINCE. *see* Gov'-Altay Province.

GOLD. In the nineteenth century mining (q.v.) operations were devel-
oped by foreign companies at many places in Mongolia, including
Altan-Uul in the south (Ömnögov'); Nühniy Nuruu, Alag Altay,
Sagsay Gol, Jargalant (Bayanhongor), Övör, Ar Har Chuluut, and
Ölziyt Gol in the west; Tsagaanchuluut in eastern Mongolia; and the
Yöröö, Haraa, and Hüyten river valleys as well as Zaamar (Töv), then
in the Ih Shav' (q.v.) territory. With the agreement of the Bogd
Gegeen (q.v.), the Russian-Mongolian gold mining company Mon-
golor began operations in 1901 at some 40 sites, including Sharyn Gol,
Terelj, Tolgoyt (Ih-Altat), and Yalbaga (Selenge Province, q.v.). Over
a period of 18 years, the company's 20,000 Russian and Chinese laborers produced 15.5 tons of gold.

Gold continues to be mined at or near many of these sites, although
during the communist period information about gold mining was a
state secret, and secrecy about gold, silver, and uranium in Mongolia
was reimposed by government decree in July 1991. The main operating mines are Tolgoyt, Ih Ajir, and Ih Olönt on the river Yöröö, and
Sharyn Gol (Selenge), Zaamar-Haylaast on the river Tuul (Töv), and
Muhar Ereg (Bayanhongor). Joint venture mining operations are situated at Boroo (Morrison Knudsen Corp.), Zaamar-Bumbat (Ataba-
yoka Co.), and Zaamar-Tuul (Mongolrostsvetmet Co., q.v., the former
Mongolsovtsvetmet) in Töv Province (q.v.). Development of gold
extraction is planned at Narantolgoy (Töv), Süjigtey and Tsagaanchuluut, as well as Salhit (Hentiy), Mogot and Bugant (Selenge), and
Dövönt (Bayanhonger). Mongolia's annual gold production amounted
to 722.5 kg in 1991, 775.5 kg in 1992, and 1,139.5 kg in 1993.

GOMBO, BYAMBADORJIYN (1953-). Mongolian politician.
Gombo trained as a teacher and became chairman of the district executive administration (q.v.) in Zag district, Bayanhongor Province
(q.v.). He was elected a member of the Mongolian Great Hural (q.v.)
for the MPRP (q.v.) for a four-year term on June 28, 1992, in constituency 3 (Bayanhongor). He is a member of two MGH standing
committees: assemblies and administration, and legal affairs.

GOMBOJAV, ERDENIYN (1950-). Minister of demography and labor since 1992. Born on July 14, 1950, in Tsetserleg district of Hövsgöl Province (q.v.), Gombojav graduated in economics from Warsaw

Higher School of Economics and Statistics in 1973 and from the Moscow Higher Party School in 1989. He was a specialist and department head at the State Committee for Labor and Social Security 1973-1987, then moved to the MPRP Central Committee (qq.v.), where he was an instructor in the socioeconomic department from 1989-1990. He worked as secretary of the Ulan Bator (q.v.) Association of Production Cooperatives from December 1990-August 1992. Gombojav, who is not a member of the Mongolian Great Hural (q.v.), was appointed minister of demography and labor on August 4, 1992, by the first session of the Mongolian Great Hural. In November 1993, Gombojav was elected to membership of the MPRP's Party Leadership Council (q.v.).

GOMBOJAV, JAMBYN (1941-   ). Mongolian politician. Gombojav graduated from Ulan Bator (q.v.) Higher School of Economics in 1964 and from the CPSU Central Committee's Higher Party School in 1974. He first worked as head of the statistics office and first deputy chairman of Dundgov' Executive Administration (qq.v.); later he became chairman of the Executive Administration of Dornogov', Süh-baatar, and then Töv Province (qq.v.), in August 1990 concurrently he was chairman of the Presidium of Töv Deputies' Hural. Gombojav was elected a deputy of the People's Great Hural (q.v.) from 1990-1992 and chairman (speaker) of the People's Great Hural from August 1990-November 1991; he was then appointed head of the government's local assemblies and administrations department (until July 1992). He was promoted from candidate to member of the MPRP Central Committee (qq.v.) in March 1990, and reelected to the Central Committee in 1991 and 1992. Gombojav was elected a member of the Mongolian Great Hural (q.v.) for the MPRP for a four-year term on June 28, 1992, in constituency 12 (Sühbaatar). He was then elected by the MGH to be its vice-chairman and also became deputy chairman of the Parliamentary Group.

GOMBOJAV, MÖNH-OCHIRYN (1906-1940). Son of a Halh (q.v.) prince, Mergen Gün, Gombojav studied at the Communist University of Toilers of the East in Leningrad from 1923. Besides Russian and French, he knew Chinese, Tibetan, and Manchu (q.v.). In 1926-1927 he visited Paris and Berlin and inspected the schools where groups of Mongol children were being educated. He worked at the Mongolian Institute of Scriptures and Manuscripts (the future Academy of Sciences, q.v.) under Jamsrano (q.v.) until 1931, when he was exiled to Ulan-Ude (q.v.). In 1934 he was sent to Leningrad, where he worked at the Institute of Oriental Studies with Jamsrano. He was arrested and sentenced by the Military Collegium of the USSR Supreme Court in

Moscow on February 19, 1940, to eight years' imprisonment, and died on August 17, 1940, in Sevvostlag (Soviet North-Eastern Labor Camps Directorate, Magadan/Kolyma). Gombojav was one of the 32 victims of the Mongolian purges of the 1930s and 1940s (q.v.) sent to the USSR for trial and sentence, details of whom were released by the Russian government in 1993.

GOMBOSÜREN, DALAY CHIN VAN. Member of the General Administration Office in Charge of Halh (q.v.) Affairs set up in November 1911 as a kind of provisional government of Mongolia as Manchu (q.v.) rule collapsed. He was appointed minister of the army in the first government of the Bogd Khan (q.v.).

GOMBOSÜREN, TSERENPILIYN (1943-   ). Minister of foreign relations since 1990. Born on January 5, 1943 in Hujirt district of Övörhangay Province (q.v.), Gombosüren graduated in 1966 from Moscow Higher School of Publishing and in 1976 from the CPSU Central Committee's Higher Party School; he also completed a course at the Diplomatic Academy of the USSR Ministry of Foreign Affairs. He first worked as an engineer and department head at the State Publishing House from 1967-1976, but then went to the Ministry of Foreign Affairs, where he became head of the First Department (USSR and Eastern Europe). From 1982-1984 he was deputy minister of foreign affairs for Asian affairs, and then appointed counselor at the Mongolian embassy in Moscow from 1984-1987. On return to Ulan Bator (q.v.), he was made deputy head of the foreign relations department of the MPRP Central Committee (qq.v.) from 1987-1988. He was appointed minister of foreign affairs from 1988-1990, then minister of foreign relations from November 1990-August 1992. He had been a candidate member of the MPRP Central Committee from 1986-1990, member of the MPRP Central Committee from March 1990-August 1991, and a member of the Politburo (Presidium) and secretary of the MPRP Central Committee from March-December 1990. Gombosüren was elected a member of the Mongolian Great Hural (q.v.) for the MPRP for a four-year term on June 28, 1992, in constituency 25 (Ulan Bator), and was reappointed minister of foreign relations on August 4, 1992, by the first session of the Mongolian Great Hural. He is a member of three MGH standing committees: foreign policy and security, legal affairs, and economic policy.

GONCHIGDORJ, RADNAASÜMBERELIYN (1954-   ). Mongolian politician, MSDP leader. Born in Tariat district of Arhangay Province (q.v.), Gonchigdorj graduated from the Mongolian State University in 1975 and has a higher degree in physics and mathematics. He was a teacher at the MSU from 1975-1988, when he was appointed director of the Institute of Mathematics of the Mongolian Academy of Sciences (q.v.). At the birth of Mongolian democracy in 1990 he was elected chairman of the Executive Council of the Mongolian Social Democratic Movement (q.v.). The same year, he was elected a deputy of the People's Great Hural (q.v.) and a member of the State Little Hural (q.v.), then chairman of the State Little Hural and ex officio vice president of Mongolia (1990-1992). Over the same period he was also chairman of the Rehabilitation Commission, investigating the purges of the 1930s-1950s. Gonchigdorj was elected a member of the Mongolian Great Hural (q.v.) for the Mongolian Social Democratic Party (q.v.) for a four-year term on June 28, 1992, in constituency 1 (Arhangay). He is a member of three MGH standing committees: education, science, and culture; foreign policy and security; and internal affairs, and was also chairman of the Sub-Committee on Human Rights until December 1993. In March 1994 Gonchigdorj was elected Chairman of the MSDP, replacing Batbayar (q.v.).

GOVERNMENT (ZASGIYN GAZAR). Official name of the executive from March 24, 1925 to July 2, 1932, and since September 10, 1990. From March 13, 1921 to April 19, 1921, it was known as the People's Government Affairs Provisional Administrative Office; from April 19, 1921 to July 16, 1921, People's Provisional Government; from July 16, 1921 to March 24, 1925, People's Government; from July 2, 1932 to September 10, 1990, Council of Ministers.

GOVERNMENT 1990 (JANUARY-MARCH). On its resignation in March 1990 Dumaagiyn Sodnom's last unreformed Council of Ministers (CM) comprised the following members, most of whom had been in office since its formation in 1986:
Sodnom, Dumaagiyn, Chairman, Council of Ministers (q.v.)
Jasray, Puntsagiyn, First Deputy Chairman, CM (q.v.)
Byambasüren, Dashiyn, Deputy Chairman, CM (q.v.)
Gungaadorj, Sharavyn, Deputy Chairman, CM (q.v.)
Peljee, Myatavyn, Deputy Chairman, CM
Süren, Choynoryn, Deputy Chairman, CM

Ministers:
Baatar, Byambajavyn, Communications
Bathuyag, Sodovyn, Power and Mining Industries and Geology
Dagvadorj, Nyam-Osoryn, Light Industry
Davaasüren, Byambyn, Education
Demchigdorj, Tümengiyn, Communal Economy and Services
Gombosüren, Tserenpiliyn, Foreign Affairs (q.v.)

Gungaadorj, Sharavyn, Agriculture and Food Industry (q.v.)
Jambaldorj, Origiyn, Law and Arbitration
Jamsranjav, Agvaanjantsangiyn, Public Security
Mavlyet, Uthany, Environmental Protection
Molomjamts, Demchigjavyn, Finance
Molomjamts, Luvsangombyn, Defense
Ochirbat, Punsalmaagiyn, Foreign Economic Relations and Supply (q.v.)
Sharavsambuu, Badrahyn, Trade and Procurement (q.v.)
Sum"yaa, Budyn, Culture
Tserennadmid, Choyjiljavyn, Health

State Committee Chairmen:
Dash, Mönhdorjiyn, Science, Technology and Higher Education Committee
Jasray, Puntsagiyn, Planning and Economic Committee (q.v.)
Namjim, Tömöriyn, First Deputy (minister), Planning and Economic Committee
Nyamsambuu, Luvsanbaldangiyn, Construction Committee

GOVERNMENT 1990 (MARCH/APRIL-SEPTEMBER). Sharavyn Gungaadorj's interim Council of Ministers (CM) comprised the following members:
Gungaadorj, Sharavyn, Chairman, Council of Ministers (q.v.)
Byambasüren, Dashiyn, First Deputy Chairman, CM (q.v.)
Pürevdorj, Choyjilsürengiyn, Deputy Chairman, CM (from May) (q.v.)
Sharavsambuu, Badrahyn, Deputy Chairman, CM (q.v.)
Zardyhan, Kinayatyn, Deputy Chairman, CM (q.v.)

Ministers:
Baatar, Byambajavyn, Communications
Badamhand, Choyjamtsyn, Labor (August-September)
Baljinnyam, Begziyn, Culture
Bathuyag, Sodovyn, Heavy Industry
Bavuu, Nadmidiyn, Trade and Cooperation
Bazarhüü, Ayuurzanyn, Finance (q.v.)
Gombosüren, Tserenpiliyn, Foreign Affairs (q.v.)
Jambaldorj, Origiyn, Law and Arbitration
Mavlyet, Uthany, Environmental Protection
Molomjamts, Luvsangombyn, Defense
Nyamdavaa, Pagvajavyn, Health and Social Security (q.v.)
Nyamsambuu, Luvsanbaldangiyn, Construction
Radnaaragchaa, Danzangiyn, Agriculture, Light and Food Industries
Urtnasan, Norovyn, Education
Yondonsüren, Dogoyn, Roads and Transport

State Committee Chairmen:
Batsuur', Jam"yangiyn, Technical Progress and Standardization (q.v.)
Byambasüren, Dashiyn, Planning and Economic Committee (March) (q.v.)
Byambasüren, Dashiyn, Socio-Economic Development Committee (April-September)
Mönhjargal, Sambuugiyn, First Deputy Chairman (minister), Socio-Economic Development Committee

GOVERNMENT 1990-1992. The following members of Government were approved by the People's Great Hural (q.v.) in September-October 1990 (for details see the individual entries):
Byambasüren, Dashiyn, Prime Minister
Ganbold, Davaadorjiyn, Chief Deputy Prime Minister
Dorligjav, Dambiyn, Deputy Prime Minister
Pürevdorj, Choyjilsürengiyn, Deputy Prime Minister

Ministers:
Amarsanaa, Jügneegiyn, Law
Batsuur', Jam"yangiyn, National Development
Bayarbaatar, Sed-Ochiryn, Trade and Industry
Bazarhüü, Ayuurzanyn, Finance
Gombosüren, Tserenpiliyn, Foreign Relations (abroad, approved in November)
Jadambaa, Shagalyn, Defense
Jigjid, Byambyn, Power
Nyamdavaa, Pagvajavyn, Health
Radnaaragchaa, Danzangiyn, Agriculture
Tsolmon, Tserendashiyn, Labor
Urtnasan, Norovyn, Education

State Committee Chairman (minister):
Batjargal, Zambyn, Environmental Protection
Some previous ministries were downgraded to committee or directorate: Badar-Uugan, Badraagiyn, Chairman, Culture and Art Development Committee; Shavarjaa, Ragchaagiyn, Head, Construction and Urban Development Commission; Baatar, Byambajavyn, Head, Chief Directorate of Communications; Nyamdavaa, Galsandagvyn, Head, Chief Directorate of Transport.

GOVERNMENT 1992-1993. The following members of Government were approved by the Mongolian Great Hural (q.v.) in July—August 1992 (for details see individual entries):
Jasray, Puntsagiyn, Prime Minister

Pürevdorj, Choyjilsürengiyn, Deputy Prime Minister
Enebish, Lhamsürengiyn, Deputy Prime Minister (from October)

Ministers:
Batjargal, Zambyn, Environment
Damiran, Tserendashiyn, Construction and Town Planning
Davaasambuu, Dalrayn, Finance
Enebish, Lhamsürengiyn, Administration (from October 1992-May
    1993)
Enhbayar, Nambaryn, Culture
Gombojav, Erdeniyn, Demography and Labor
Gombosüren, Tserenpiliyn, Foreign Relations
Jadambaa, Shagalyn, Defense
Jigjid, Byambyn, Fuel and Power
Luvsanjav, Namsrayjavyn, Law
Nyamdavaa, Pagvajavyn, Health
Ölziyhutag, Nadmidiyn, Science and Education
Ööld, Tseveenjavyn, Food and Agriculture
Sandalhan, Razdakiyn, Roads, Transport and Communications
Tsogbaatar, Dorjiyn, Geology and Mineral Resources
Tsogt, Tsevegmidiyn, Trade and Industry
Ulaan, Chültemiyn, Chairman, National Development Board

GOVERNMENT 1993-1994. In accordance with Article 18 of the Law
on the Government adopted by the Mongolian Great Hural (q.v.) on
May 6, 1993, the Mongolian government comprised 15 ministries plus
five directorates belonging to the "basic structure." The article listed
all the ministries of the Government from 1992-1993 (q.v.) except the
Ministry of Administration.
    A reorganization of the Government in January 1994 amalgamated
the Ministry of Roads, Transport, and Communications with the Ministry of Construction and Town Planning to form a new Ministry of
Infrastructure Development (Minister, Razdakiyn Sandalhan); and the
Ministry of Fuel and Power with the Ministry of Geology and Mineral
Resources to form a new Ministry of Power, Geology, and Mining
(Minister, Byambyn Jigjid).
    The name of the Ministry of Law was to have been altered (from
Huul' züyn yaam to *Huul' tsaazyn yaam*), perhaps to emphasize law
enforcement. The police remained under the direct control of the Gov-
ernment (see below).
    The directorates of the "basic structure" were increased to six:
National Development Board (Chültemiyn Ulaan)
Central Directorate of Intelligence (Maj.-Gen. Dalhjavyn Sandag)
Chief Directorate of Police (Maj.-Gen. Baastyn Pürev)

Directorate of Radio and Television Affairs (Byambajavyn Övgönhüü)
Directorate of Statistics (Badamtsedengiyn Tsend-Ayuush)
Montsame News Agency (Chuluunbatyn Erdene)
   Four directorates were designated part of the "infrastructure":
Chief Directorate of Customs (Gonchigiyn Seseer)*
Chief Directorate of Taxation (Lhanaasürengiyn Pürevdorj)
Directorate of Border Troops (Maj.-Gen. Palamyn Sündev)
Directorate of Civil Defense (Maj.-Gen. Gombosürengiyn Damdin-
   süren)

*from July 1994 Badrahyn Sharavsambuu (q.v.)

GOVERNMENT, LOCAL. For local government structures before
1992, *see* Hural of People's Deputies; after 1992, *see* Hural of Citizen's Delegates.

GOV' (GOBI). The Mongolian word from which the name Gobi Desert
is derived. Gobi terrain extends to the lakes of north-western Mongolia and the Gobi Altai Mountains (q.v.), besides covering much of
southern Mongolia as well as central and western Inner Mongolia
(q.v.). The Gobi region embraces 40 percent of Mongolia's territory,
30 percent of its livestock (q.v.), and 11 percent of its population. The
Mongols distinguish as many as 30 different kinds of *gov'*, embracing
a wide range of desert-steppe and mostly gravelly semidesert with typ-
ical shrubs and plants like *zag* (Zaisan saxaul or Haloxylon) and *har-
gana* (Caragana). True sandy desert (*els*) and salt pans (*hujir*) account
for only a relatively small part of the country's territory. The Gobi region was a sea in the Paleozoic Age and lakeland in the Mesozoic, and
the habitat of many different kinds of Cretaceous dinosaurs (q.v.).

GOV'-ALTAY (GOBI ALTAI). Province (*aymag*) in south-western
Mongolia. Formed in 1931 as Altay Province (q.v.) and abolished in
1935, the province was reestablished as Gov'-Altay in 1940, named
after the Gobi Altai Mountains (q.v.) in the southern part of the province
and the Gobi [Gov', (q.v.)] region beyond them. The province borders
on China (Hami Prefecture of Xinjiang Uighur Autonomous Region
and Gansu Province). With a territory of 142,000 sq km and population
of 65,123 (1991), it has 17 rural districts (*sum*); until 1992 there was one
ward (*horoo*), Guulin; the provincial center is Altay (q.v.), the former
Yösönbulag. The designated occasional crossing points on the border
with China are Burgastay (for Daoyemao) and Naransevstey. There are
deposits of coal (Tsahiurt, Hüren Gol, and Maan't), lignite (Zeegt), and
asbestos (Tayshir and Tonhil). Livestock numbers reached 1,770,800
head (1992) and arable land 4,800 hectares (1989).

GOV'-ALTAY ECONOMIC COOPERATION ZONE. One of six economic cooperation zones into which Mongolia was divided on the basis of a government ordinance issued in November 1991 [the others being the Central, Bayan-Ölgiy, Övörhangay, Sühbaatar, and Ulan Bator economic cooperation zones, (q.v.)]. It consists of Gov'-Altay, Zavhan, Hövsgöl, and Bayanhongor Provinces (qq.v.). Each zone has a cooperation office headed by the secretary of the zonal cooperation council.

GOV'-SÜMBER. Province (*aymag*) in central Mongolia. Established in May 1994, the province consists of Bayantal, Shiveegov', and Sümber, three former *horoo* of Dornogov' Province redesignated as *sum* (qq.v.); the provincial center is Choyr (q.v.), a former "town under national jurisdiction."

GÖLGÖÖ, JANTSANGIYN (1950-   ). Mongolian foreign trade expert. Gölgöö was born into an Ööld (q.v.) family in Erdenebüren district of Hvod Province (q.v.). In the 1960s he is reputed to have coauthored a resolution, drafted in secret, that called for equal opportunities for ordinary young men and women in selection for higher education at home and abroad. Previously this had been reserved for the relatives of the country's top communist leaders. He graduated from the economics faculty of the Institute of Foreign Relations in Moscow in 1968. On return to Mongolia he worked in various departments of the State Committee for Foreign Economic Relations. He was awarded a higher degree for a feasibility study of the streamlining of Mongolia's foreign economic relations system. He was a deputy minister of foreign trade and from January 1988, following reorganization of the ministry, deputy minister of foreign economic relations and supply. He was appointed president of the Mongolian Chamber of Trade and Industry in 1989. In 1993, he was appointed trade representative at Mongolia's embassy in London.

GRAIN. In Mongolia grain growing is not a traditional occupation, but there is evidence that in several areas Mongolian laborers were engaged in grain production for local consumption during the Manchu (q.v.) period. Large-scale grain production is associated with the formation of state farms (q.v.) and particularly with the industrialization of Mongolian farming methods and Soviet-style "virgin lands" cultivation campaigns. The main grain-growing state farms are concentrated in the north-central and eastern provinces, where wheat predominates, although barley and oats are also grown in small quantities. The average yield of 10-15 quintals (metric hundredweight) per hectare is low, but the growing season is short (110 days) and the crop may be lodged by rainstorms or early snow. The soil is mostly thin and subject to wind erosion, and the land is cultivated in alternating strips of plough land and fallow with little use of fertilizer. The area of land sown to grain reached 654,100 hectares in 1990, producing a gross harvest of 718,300 tons. In 1992 the gross harvest declined to 493,900 tons, however; state procurements were insufficient to meet the needs of the milling industry and public demand, and grain (including rice) had to be imported. The gross cereal harvest in 1993 amounted to 454,000 tons.

GUNGAADORJ, SHARAVYN (1935-   ). Chairman of the Council of Ministers 1990. Born in Ihhet district of Dornogov' Province (q.v.), Gungaadorj graduated in 1959 from the Timiryazev Academy of Agriculture in Moscow. After working at the MPRP Central Committee (qq.v.) in 1967-1968, he had various appointments including deputy minister of agriculture, first deputy minister of state farms in 1980, first secretary of Selenge (q.v.) MPRP Committee in 1981, and minister of agriculture in 1986. Gungaadorj then served as deputy chairman of the Council of Ministers from October 1987 to March 1990 and concurrently minister of agriculture and food industry from December 1987. From October 1986, he also served concurrently as the chairman of the Central Council of the Union of Livestock Production Associations (*negdel*, q.v.). He was chairman of the Council of Ministers (head of government) from March 21, 1990 to September 10, 1990, in the interim administration between the collapse of the leadership of Jambyn Batmönh and Dumaagiyn Sodnom (qq.v.) and the first free general elections and formation of the government of Dashiyn Byambasüren (q.v.). He had been elected to the MPRP Central Committee in 1990 and was a deputy of the People's Great Hural from 1981-1990. Toward the end of 1990, he was chosen to be the first chairman of the Civil Council, a presidential advisory body. The Civil Council was abolished a year later, and Gungaadorj was appointed ambassador to North Korea at the beginning of 1992.

GUTAL. Mongolian leather boot with upturned toe, worn with the *deel* (q.v.) or by wrestlers. The boot is incised with traditional patterns and worn with a felt (q.v.) sock, whose protruding top is often embroidered.

GÜN (KUNG). A noble title of the third grade created by the Manchu (q.v.). There were two classes, *tüsheegün* and *gün*.

GÜNDENBAL, SODNOMTSERENGIYN (1950-   ). Mongolian politician. Gündenbal trained as an economist. He was chairman of the

Bulgan Provincial Executive Administration (qq.v.) from January 1991-July 1992, and elected to the MPRP Central Committee (qq.v.) in 1992. He was elected a member of the Mongolian Great Hural (q.v.) for the MPRP for a four-year term on June 28, 1992, in constituency 4 (Bulgan). He is a member of two MGH standing committees: budget and finance, and assemblies and administration.

GÜRRAGCHAA, JÜGDERDEMIDIYN (1947-   ). Mongolian cosmonaut. Born in Gurvanbulag district of Bulgan Province (q.v.) on December 5, 1947, Gürragchaa joined the Mongolian People's Army in 1966, after graduating from the local secondary school. In 1971 he was sent to the USSR for training as a helicopter radio-electronics mechanic. In 1973 he was accepted by the Zhukovskiy Air Force Academy in Moscow, and after graduating he worked as an equipment engineer in the MPR's air arm. Promoted to captain, in April 1978 he began three years' training at the Yury Gagarin Cosmonauts' Training Center in the USSR under the Intercosmos program. Captain Gürragchaa was launched into space with the Soviet cosmonaut Dzhanibekov aboard the spaceship *Soyuz-39* from Baykonur in Kazakhstan in March 1981; they spent seven days with two other Soviet cosmonauts, Kovalenok and Savinykh, in the Salyut-6 space station. The research program included Mongolian projects in the field of earth resources photography (Erdem), diffusion of lead and tin, and vanadium pentoxide crystal growing (Altay 1 and 2), spectrometry (Spektr-Mon, Solongo), and the tonic effects of vitamin extracts from sea buckthorn berries (Chatsargana). For his space flight, Gürragchaa was promoted to colonel and (with his earthbound stand-in, Ganzorig) received the titles of MPR Pilot-Cosmonaut and Hero of the MPR.

There being few openings for spacemen in Mongolia, Gürragchaa was appointed deputy head of the administrative organs department of the MPRP Central Committee (qq.v.) from June 1981-1983. In March 1983, he was elected chairman of the Central Council of the Society for the Promotion of State Defense, an official body for the promotion of paramilitary sports; he remained in this post until the society was disbanded in 1990, having been promoted to the rank of major general in March 1984. In December 1982, Gürragchaa was appointed deputy chairman (deputy speaker) of the People's Great Hural (q.v.), and he held this position until the formation of the new PGH in the autumn of 1990, following Mongolia's first democratic elections. He was made chairman of the Electoral Commission for organizing and supervising these elections. Gürragchaa was also elected a member of the MPRP Central Committee in 1981 and 1986 and a deputy of the People's Great Hural in 1981-1992. In December 1990, he was elected chairman of the Central Council of the Mongolian-Soviet Friendship

Society. Following the disintegration of the Soviet Union, the society was renamed the Federation of Societies for Friendship between Mongolia and the CIS Countries, and Gürragchaa was elected its leader in February 1992.

- H -

HADAG. A folded silk scarf, usually white or pale blue, presented as a sign of respect to a high-ranking visitor or religious leader, or as an offering in a Lamaist temple (Russian rendering: *khadak*).

HALH (KHALKHA). Mongol ethnic group, and the territory they inhabit. The Halh comprise the majority of the population of Mongolia, 78.8 percent (1,610,400), according to the 1989 census, and Halh Mongolian is the national literary language of Mongolia. Although Halh was first recorded as a toponym more than 2,000 years ago, it was only in the second half of the fourteenth century that the word was used for the people (Halh *tümen*, Halh *uls*) then forming the Halh nation. Later they became divided into North (*ar*) and South (*övör*) Halh, the former inhabiting Outer Mongolia (q.v.) and the latter Inner Mongolia (q.v.). The dialects are usually described as eastern, central, and western. They differ little phonetically or grammatically, but there are big lexical variations. Some ethnographers and linguists include the Hotgoyd, Darhad, and Dariganga (qq.v.), as well as the Sartuul, Arig, and Iljgen among the Halh.

HALH. River in Mongolia. The Halhyn *gol*, 233 km within Mongolia, rises in the Hinggan Mountains in China's Inner Mongolia (q.v.) and flows northwest, crossing into Dornod Province (q.v.) and forming the border between Mongolia and China for a short distance before entering Lake Buyr (q.v.).

HALHYN GOL, BATTLE OF. The battle fought between units of the Japanese Imperial Army and the combined forces of the Soviet Red Army and Mongolian People's Army in the area of the river Halh (q.v.) (Halhyn Gol, Khalkhin Gol), on the border between Mongolia's Dornod (Eastern) Province (q.v.) and the Japanese puppet state of Manchukuo (q.v.) in May–August 1939. The battle is also known as the Battle of Nomonhan, named after a local hill and border post. There had been clashes since December 1935, due to Japanese probing in the same general area, which stimulated the signing of the Soviet-Mongolian mutual assistance protocol in March 1936. The building of the broad-gauge railway from the Soviet border to Bayantümen (later Choybalsan) and of a narrow-gauge extension to

Tamsagbulag at this time were evidently connected with Soviet rein-forcement plans. Superior tactics by the Soviet commander, General (later Marshal) Georgiy Zhukov, ensured the eventual defeat of the Japa-nese forces. It is generally considered that the battle halted Jap-anese plans for the invasion of the USSR, with which Japan signed a neutrality pact in April 1941. Official histories of the communist pe-riod depict the battles as a great victory against "imperialism" by com-munist forces, but a more balanced account of events is needed to gain a true picture.

HAMBA LAMA. The abbot of Gandan monastery in Ulan Bator, the center of Lamaism (qq.v.) in Mongolia.

HAMJLAGA. A vassal (serf) or personal retainer of a *tayj* or the *zasag* of a *hoshuu*, giving with his family lifelong service under Manchu (qq.v.) law.

HAMNIGAN. Tungusic ethnic group. The Hamnigan, Evenki, related to the Manchu (q.v.), total around 300 families inhabiting Dadal and Binder districts of Hentiy Province (q.v.), Bayan-Uul, Tsagaan-Ovoo, Bayandün, and Dashbalbar districts of Dornod Province (q.v.), Möngönmor't district of Töv Province (q.v.), and Yöröö district of Se-lenge Province (q.v.). They have become Mongolized, and, except for a few old people, speak a form of Buryat (q.v.).

HANA. Meaning wall, the sections of wooden lattice forming the wall frame of a *ger* (q.v.), their number indicating the size of the *ger* and perhaps also the status of the owner. The standard-sized *ger* has five *hana*.

HANDDORJ, MIJIDDORJIYN (TSERENDORJIYN), HOSHOY CHIN VAN (1871-1915). Born in present-day Bulgan province (q.v.), Hand-dorj inherited the title of his grandfather Tserendorj, Governor of Tüsheet Han Province (q.v.), in 1892. He was the leader of the dele-gation sent by the Bogd Gegeen (q.v.) to St. Petersburg in July 1911, to try to obtain the support of Russia and West European countries for Mongolian independence. A member of the General Administration Office in Charge of Halh (q.v.) Affairs set up in November 1911 as a kind of provisional government of Mongolia as Manchu (q.v.) rule collapsed, he was appointed minister of foreign affairs in the first gov-ernment of the Bogd Khan (q.v.). He concluded the Mongolian-Russian treaty of 1912 and led a Mongolian delegation to Russia in 1913 to obtain aid. He was assassinated in February 1915. His suc-cessor as foreign minister was Tserendorj Gün (q.v.).

HANGAY. Mountains situated in central Mongolia, extending for some 500 km across eastern Zavhan, northern Bayanhongor, Arhangay, and Övörhangay provinces (qq.v.). The highest peak is Otgon Tenger (q.v.). Also, Hangay is the name for the mountain-steppe and forest-steppe pastureland, as typified by the Hangay Mountains region.

HAN-HENTIY-UUL. Former province (*aymag*) in eastern Mongolia. This large province, center Öndörhaan (q.v.), was founded in 1923 on the territory of the former Tsetsen-Han (q.v.) *aymag*. In the administrative reforms of 1931, the five large provinces were broken up into 12 (later 18) smaller ones. This province formed parts of the present-day Dornod, Hentiy, and Sühbaatar provinces (q.v.).

HAN-TAYSHIR-UUL. Former province (*aymag*) in western Mongolia. This large province, center Javhlant, later Uliastay (q.v.), was founded in 1923 on the territory of the former Zasagt-Han (q.v.) *aymag*. In the administrative reforms of 1931, the five large provinces were broken up into 12 (later 18) smaller ones. This province formed parts of the present-day Zavhan, Gov'-Altay, Hovd, and Hövsgöl provinces (q.v.).

HAN-UUL. District (*düüreg*) of Ulan Bator (q.v.). Established in 1992, this southern urban district of some 14,900 households (1992) is named after the Bogd Han Uul mountain overlooking Ulan Bator and consists of 12 wards (*horoo*), incorporating Yaarmag and Zaysan residential (*ger*) and No. 19 (apartment) areas (*horoolol*), Niseh (Buyant-Uhaa airport), the industrial combine, and other southern parts along the river Tuul (q.v.) of the former Ajilchin district (*rayon*) of the capital.

HAR. Lake in Mongolia. Har *nuur*, one of the country's six largest lakes, has a surface area of 575 sq km and is situated at a height of 1,132 m above sea level. This freshwater lake, fed by the river Chono Harayh from Lake Har-Us (q.v.) and having an outlet into the saline Lake Dörgön, forms part of the boundary between Hovd and Zavhan provinces (qq.v.).

HARACHIN. Mongol ethnic group. This group living near the border with China is related to the Harachin of Inner Mongolia (q.v.) and numbered some 400, according to the 1989 census. See also China: Mongol Ethnic Groups.

HAR-US. Lake in Mongolia. Har-Us *nuur*, one of the country's six largest lakes, has a surface area of 1,852 sq km. This freshwater lake, fed by the river Hovd and having an outlet into Lake Har (q.v.), is situated at a height of 1,157 m above sea level in the northern part of Hovd Province (q.v.). It has a circumference of 3,068 km and breadth of 25.8 km, but averages only 2.2 m deep. It freezes over in November to a thickness of 80-100 cm, but due to temperature variations, the ice cracks everywhere, producing the dark patterns across the surface that give the lake its name—"black water." Agbash and Tsagaan islands in the lake have become reserves for rare flora and fauna such as the lotus, muskrat, and white *hulan* (wild ass), but in recent years shallow areas of the lake have been drying up.

HEADS OF STATE. Mongolian presidents from 1924-1994. Since the death of the Bogd Khan Javzandamba Hutagt (qq.v.) in 1924, Mongolia has had 11 heads of state (chairmen of the Presidium of the State Little Hural from 1924-1951, chairmen of the Presidium of the MPR People's Great Hural from 1951-1990, president of Mongolia 1990-   ); for details see individual entries:
Genden, Peljidiyn—November 29, 1924 to November 15, 1927;
Damdinsüren, Jantsangiyn—November 16, 1927 to January 23, 1929;
Choybalsan, Horloogiyn—January 24, 1929 to April 27, 1930;
Laagan, Losolyn—April 27, 1930 to July 2, 1932;
Amar, Anandyn (Agdangiyn, Agdanbuugiyn)—July 2, 1932 to March 22, 1936;
Dogsom, Dansranbilegiyn—March 22, 1936 to July 9, 1939;
Bumtsend, Gonchigiyn—July 6, 1940 to September 23, 1953;
Sambuu, Jamsrangiyn—July 7, 1954 to May 21, 1972;
Tsedenbal, Yumjaagiyn—June 11, 1974 to August 23, 1984;
Batmönh, Jambyn—December 12, 1984 to March 21, 1990;
Ochirbat, Punsalmaagiyn—March 21, 1990 to date.

HENTEY. Mountains in Mongolia. These mountains are situated in northern Mongolia, extending for some 200 km across Töv and Hentiy provinces (qq.v.) toward the border with Russia. The highest peak is Asralt Hayrhan (q.v.).

HENTIY. Province (*aymag*) in north-eastern Mongolia. Formed in 1931 and named after the Hentey Mountains (q.v.), the province is situated on the border with Russia (Krasnyy Chikoy and Kyra districts of Chita Region). With a territory of 82,000 sq km and population of 74,227 (1991), it has 19 rural districts (*sum*); until 1992 there were four wards (*horoo*), Berh, Bürenhaan, Herlen, and Herlenbayan-Ulaan; the provincial center is Öndörhaan (q.v.). The minorities include the Buryad (q.v.). The designated permanent crossing point on the border with Russia is Heriyn Gol (for Gavan'), and seasonal crossing points are

Balj Gol (for Balzhikan), Hürhree Nuur (for Ust'-Bukukun), Agatsyn Gol (for Altan), and Hojgor Toyrom (for Tyrin). The fluorite mines at Hajuu-Ulaan (Bor-Öndör) are linked by a branch line to Ayrag (Dornogov' Province) on the Trans-Mongolian Railway. There are deposits of lignite (Chandgantal), fluorite (Berh, Batnorov, Bayan-Ovoo, and Galshar), tin (Modot), lead (Jargalthaan), and other nonferrous metals (Tsenhermandal). Livestock numbers reached 1,350,700 head (1992) and arable land 50,200 hectares (1989).

HEREM. Meaning wall, a massive wall of mud, stone, or brick, e.g., the Great Wall of China (*Tsagaan herem*—"white wall"), or by extension a fortification or fortress, e.g., the Moscow Kremlin—whose name is derived from this Mongol word. The ancient Mongol capital Karakorum (q.v.) was named after its "black wall."

HERLEN. River in Mongolia. The Herlen *gol* (Kerulen), one of the country's five longest rivers, 1,090 km within Mongolia, rises in the Hentey mountains (q.v.) in northern Mongolia and flows south, forming the boundary between Töv and Hentiy provinces (q.v.), and then east, passing through Öndörhaan and Choybalsan (qq.v.); it crosses the border between Dornod Province and China's Inner Mongolia (qq.v.) and enters Dalay *nuur* (Hulun Nur), a lake that is linked (except in years of severe drought) with the rivers Ergun (Argun') and Heilongjiang (Amur), the Sea of Okhotsk and Pacific Ocean. The basins of the Herlen, Tuul, and Onon (qq.v.), the "three rivers," are considered to embrace the original homeland of the Mongols.

HORIN. Derived from *horin*, or twenty, an administrative unit of 20 households used in the period from 1927-1932.

HOROO. An urban district of Ulan Bator (q.v.) until the formation of the *rayon* (q.v.) in 1965. Also, an urban-type settlement in the countryside administratively separate from the rural district (*sum*, q.v.) until the abolition of most *horoo* in May 1994. Since 1992, a ward, subdivision, of a borough or urban district (*düüreg*, q.v.) of Ulan Bator. Among other meanings, *horoo* can be a committee (e.g., the MPRP Central Committee, qq.v.) or a regiment.

HOROOLOL. A housing estate, or *mikrorayon* (q.v.), of blocks of apartment buildings, or a district of *ger* (q.v.) compounds arranged in rows.

HORSES. The Mongolian horse is small but sturdy and used for riding and as a draught animal; horsemeat is eaten by Kazakhs (q.v.) but not usually by Mongols. Fermented mare's milk, or koumiss (q.v.), is widely made and drunk in horse-breeding regions during the summer. Working horses are selected from the herd, captured with the help of a lasso pole (*uurga*, q.v.), saddled, and broken in. While resting they are tied to a tethering line near the *ger* (q.v.) or hobbled overnight; after being worked they are released to run with the herd again. Horses are concentrated in the central provinces: Töv and Övörhangay (qq.v.) have the greatest numbers—207,293 and 191,255 (1993). There were altogether some 2.2 million horses in Mongolia in 1992 and 2,190,325 in 1993. The country produces 115,000-130,000 horsehides a year (1988-1990), and horsehair is also exported.

The ancestral Mongolian wild horse (*tah'*), named *equus Przewalskii* after its discoverer, a Polish officer serving in the Russian Tsarist army who traveled widely in Inner Asia, is now believed to be extinct. There have been no sightings in its habitat—the Jungarian desert south of the Gobi-Altai mountains (q.v.)—for some 40 years. In an effort to reestablish the Przewalskii horse in Mongolia from hybrid stock preserved in the USA and Europe, several individuals were flown to Ulan Bator in 1993 and released into a nature reserve on Bogd Han Uul (q.v.) for acclimatization.

HORSHOOLOL. Former ward (*horoo*) of Ulan Bator (q.v.). "Cooperative" ward, one of the 10 wards abolished in 1965 on the formation of Ajilchin, Nayramdal, Oktyabr' and Sühbaatar (qq.v.) districts (*rayon*), each with smaller numbered *horoo*.

HORSHOOLOLIMPEKS. Foreign trade company set up by the former Ministry of Communal Economy and Services to export products of light industry cooperatives and recyclable waste. After the abolition of the ministry, it traded as Horshooimpeks, exporting products of the cooperatives and importing consumer goods.

HOSHUU. A "banner," territorial-administrative unit in prerevolutionary and early postrevolutionary Mongolia, equivalent of a district, subdivision of an *aymag* (q.v.). The *hoshuu* (Russian rendering: *khoshun*), then numbering 72, were abolished in February 1931, when the existing four *aymag* were abolished and new smaller *aymag* formed.

HOSHUUD (HOSHUTS). Mongol ethnic group. A West Mongol Oyrd (q.v.) (Oirat) group concentrated mostly in western districts of Zavhan Province, east of Lake Har (qq.v.).

HOT. The word *hot* (Russian rendering: *khoto*) usually means a town (or city), but can also be applied to a group of *ger* (q.v.) or even to a sheepfold. In 1993, a *hot* was defined administratively as a settlement of the urban type with a population of more than 15,000.

HOTGOYD (KHOTOGOITS). Mongol ethnic group. The Hotgoyd, a Halhized Oyrd (q.v.) (Oirat) group, are concentrated mostly in southern districts of Hövsgöl Province and north-eastern districts of Zavhan Province (qq.v.). There were some 400, according to the 1989 census.

HOTON. Turkic ethnic group. The Hoton accounted for 0.2 percent (6,100) of the population of Mongolia, according to the 1989 census. The Hoton are concentrated mostly in the central districts of Uvs Province (q.v.) and speak a northern dialect of Oyrd (q.v.) (Oirat).

HOUSING. According to statistics at the end of 1993, just under 58 percent of the population were living in 258,000 traditional felt tents, or *ger* (q.v.); 29.3 percent (600,800 people) were accommodated in state or cooperative housing, of which there was 3,662,900 square meters; and 13.3 percent (311,000 people) were living in private housing, totaling 1,461,000 square meters. Because of difficulties with the supply of metal structures, pipe, window glass, fittings, etc., since 1990 industrial construction of multistory housing blocks has virtually ceased.

HOVD. Center of Hovd Province (q.v.). Founded in 1685 by the Jungarian (q.v.) Khan Galsan Boshigt, previously known as Jargalant, and named after the river Hovd, Hovd was accorded town status in 1961. Its height above sea level is 1,406 m, the average January and July temperatures are −25.4 and 18.9 deg C, respectively, and the average annual precipitation is 119.0 mm. The distance from Ulan Bator (q.v.) is 1,175 km.The population is about 24,000. Local industries include vehicle repairs, wool washing, meat packing, and the production of animal protein and foodstuffs.

HOVD (KHOBDO). Province (*aymag*) in western Mongolia. Formed in 1931, and initially including parts of the present-day Bayan-Ölgiy Province (q.v.), the province extends from Lake Har Us (q.v.) to the border with China (Altai District of Ili Kazakh Autonomous Prefecture, Changji Hui Autonomous Prefecture, and Hami Prefecture, Xinjiang Uighur Autonomous Region). With a territory of 76,000 sq km and population of 80,777 (1991), it has 16 rural districts (*sum*); the provincial center, after which it is named, is Hovd. The local minorities include the Kazakh, Zahchin, Altai Urianhay, Torguud, Ööld, and Myangad (qq.v.). A poor road provides access to Xinjiang (Ürümqi) via Bulgan district (for Chingol). The designated occasional crossing points on the border with China are Baytag (for Uliastay) and Bulgan (for Takashikene). There are deposits of coal (Darvi and Jargalant Hayrhan), lignite (Höshööt), silver and zinc (Baytag Bogd Uul). Livestock numbers reached 1,688,600 head (1992) and arable land 9,400 hectares (1989).

HOVD. Border district (*hyazgaar*) in western Mongolia (1760-1911), formerly part of the Züüngar (Jungarian or Oyrd, qq.v) state, which embraced the territory of the present-day Hovd and Bayan-Ölgiy Provinces (qq.v.). It was included in the territory of Chandman'-Uul (q.v.) *aymag* in 1925.

HÖDÖÖ. The countryside, rural. In Russian books about Mongolia, it is often rendered as *khudon*.

HÖH NUUR. Lowest point of Mongolia. This saline lake in northeastern Dornod Province (q.v.), some 50 km south of the Chuluunhoroot (Solov'yevsk) crossing on the border with Russia's Chita Region, is 560 m above sea level.

HÖHHOT (HUHEHOT, GUISUI). Capital of the Inner Mongolia Autonomous Region (q.v.) in China, founded by Altan Khan of the Tümet in 1554. It was at Höhhot ("blue town") that Altan Khan in 1578 received the Tibetan leader Sonam Gyatso, whom he accorded the title Dalai Lama (*see* Lamaism). It is now an industrial city and its population is overwhelmingly Chinese.

HÖVSGÖL. Lake in Mongolia. Hövsgöl *nuur*, the country's second-largest lake with an area of 2,620 sq km is also the country's deepest, 238 m. This freshwater lake, fed by numerous small streams and having one outlet, the river Eg (q.v.), is situated at a height of 1,645 m above sea level in the northern part of Hövsgöl Province (q.v.), which is named after it. Small-scale shipping operations with a tug and two barges for the carriage of goods and fuel link the ports of Hatgal, on the southern shore, and Hanh, at the northern end, not far from the Russian border.

HÖVSGÖL. Province (*aymag*) in northern Mongolia. Formed in 1931 and named after Lake Hövsgöl (q.v.), the province is situated on the border with Russia (Kaa-Khem and Todzha districts of the Tuva Republic, (q.v.), and Oka and Tunka districts of the Buryat Republic, q.v.). With a territory of 101,000 sq km and population of 106,558 (1991), it has 22 rural districts (*sum*); until 1992 there was one ward (*horoo*), Hanh; the provincial center, now Mörön (q.v.), was initially

Hatgal. The local minorities include Tannu Urianhay (Tuvans), Darhad, and Hotgoyd (qq.v.). Hatgal port on the southern shore of Lake Hövsgöl has a cargo shipping link with Hanh (Turtu) on the northern shore; Hanh has a road link with Mondy (Buryat Republic), providing access to Irkutsk. The designated permanent crossing point on the border with Russia is Hanh (via Mungen-Daba for Mondy), and seasonal crossing points are Bayanzürh (for Tarisyn Rashaan), Turandavaa (for Turan), Högshin Üüriyn Gol (for Harbit), and Heegt (for Sanaga). There are deposits of coal (Egiyn Gol, Tünel, Höh Tolgoy, and Mogoyn Gol), lead (Chandman'-Öndör), iron (Bayan-Uul), and phosphorite (Urandösh). The wool-washing plant at Hatgal, Mongolia's oldest industrial enterprise, has been declared harmful to the environment and is due for closure. Livestock numbers reached 1,747,600 head (1992) and arable land 31,900 hectares (1989).

HÖVSGÖL. Border district (*hyazgaar*) in northern Mongolia. This district (1760-1911) incorporated the Darhad *Shav'* and Urianhay (qq.v.).

HUNTING. Traditionally pursued by all Mongols, in modern times hunting has largely been restricted to professional hunters employed by enterprises procuring furs. Some 800,000 to 1 million Mongolian steppe marmot (*tarvagan*) are shot or trapped each year, 8,000-17,000 squirrels, and around 4,000 wolves (1988-1989). Foreign hunters traveling with approved safari companies may be licensed to shoot single examples of the wild sheep (*argal'*, q.v.) and the snow leopard (*irves*), which is no longer protected.

HURAL. The word *hural* means a gathering, or assembly, hence a religious service, or even a small monastery. The related word *huraldaan*, meaning a meeting or session, is also found in its Central Asian Turkic form *kuriltai*. During the period of Mongolian autonomy, the Bogd Khan (q.v.) formed two chambers of officials, the Deed Hural (upper assembly) and Dood Hural (lower assembly), to advise him on policy as required. After the death of the Bogd Khan, Mongolia adopted a republican form of government and established a national assembly, the Great (Ih) Hural (q.v.). This selected a legislative or executive assembly called the Little (Baga) Hural (q.v.).

HURAL, CITIZENS' DELEGATES'. Local government assembly. Following the introduction of local government reforms earmarked in the 1992 Constitution (q.v.), local government assemblies were instituted in Ulan Bator (q.v.) and the provinces and at their district and lower levels. Reflecting the new balance of power at the center between parliament and president, the activities of Hurals of Citizens' Delegates are subject to approval by the local governor. (For details *see* Appendix 4, text of the 1992 Constitution.) Previously, under the 1960 Constitution, local government was effected through Hurals of People's Deputies (q.v.).

HURAL, GREAT, 1924-1992. The convocations of the national assembly, the MPR or National (*ulsyn*) Great Hural 1924-1960 and People's (*ardyn*) Great Hural 1960-1992, were numbered as follows:

MPR *(ulsyn)* Great Hural:
1st: November 8 to 28, 1924 (90 delegates nominated, 77 attended)
2nd: November 6 to 18, 1925 (94 delegates nominated, 88 attended)
3rd: November 1 to 13, 1926 (99 delegates nominated, 81 attended)
4th: November 1 to 16, 1927 (100 delegates nominated, 88 attended)
5th: December 14, 1928 to January 24, 1929 (102 nominated, 85 attended)
6th: opened April 7, 1930 (number of delegates not traced)
7th: December 20 to 27, 1934 (291 delegates attended)
8th: June 20 to July 6, 1940 (532 delegates)
9th: February 12 to 19, 1949 (515 delegates nominated, 498 attended)

Sessions renumbered after electoral reform (dates of first sessions):
1st: July 5 to 6, 1951 (295 deputies elected June 10)
2nd: July 5 to 6, 1954 (295 deputies elected June 13)
3rd: July 7 to 8, 1957 (233 deputies elected June 16)

People's *(ardyn)* Great Hural:
4th: July 5 to 6, 1960 (267 deputies elected June 19)
5th: July 1 to 2, 1963 (270 deputies elected June 9)
6th: July 1 to 2, 1966 (287 deputies elected June 26)
7th: July 4, 1969 (297 deputies elected June 22)
8th: July 2 to 3, 1973 (336 deputies elected June 24)
9th: June 27, 1977 (354 deputies elected June 19)
10th: June 29, 1981 (370 deputies elected June 21)
11th: July 1, 1986 (370 deputies elected June 22)
12th: September 30, 1990 (430 deputies elected July 22 and 29)

Although the assembly was called the Mongolian (National) Great Hural from 1924-1960, following the adoption of the name People's Great Hural (*Ardyn Ih Hural*) in 1960, most Mongolian and Russian sources called it the PGH, retrospectively. For assembly sessions from 1992 onward, *see* Great Hural 1990-1992, and Great Hural 1992.

HURAL, GREAT 1990-1992. The elections to the twelfth People's Great Hural were held in July 1990 under the terms of the April 1990 amendments to the (third) Constitution (q.v.) of 1960. In the 430 constituencies, a total of 2,364 candidates (MPRP 1,963, allies 49, opposition parties 352, and independents 49) stood in the first round on July 22: in 43 constituencies there was one candidate, in 115 constituencies two candidates and in 272 constituencies three or more. The two candidates who received the most votes in each constituency went forward to a runoff in the second round on July 29: in 213 constituencies both candidates were from the MPRP (q.v.), and in another 8 both were from opposition parties; in 60 constituencies MPRP candidates stood unopposed in the second round (of the 860 candidates who went into the second round, 628 represented the MPRP). In the final result the MPRP won 357 seats (84.6 percent) in the PGH with 61.7 percent of the total ballot, the pro-MPRP MRYL (q.v.) won 9 seats, the opposition parties 26 seats, and independents 39. Discrepancies in published results are due to the holding of new elections in 63 of the constituencies in August-September because of irregularities, lack of a majority, or the election of new deputies to replace those appointed to high office, including President Ochirbat (q.v.).

The twelfth People's Great Hural was to meet at least four times in its five-year lifetime. The duties of its 430 deputies included proclamation and amendment of the Constitution, election of the president, vice president and Little Hural (q.v.), and appointment of the prime minister and other officials. The first session took place in September 1990 when, following the election of its chairman, Jambyn Gombojav (q.v.), four vice-chairmen and five standing commissions, it set about the formation of the Little Hural. The last session of the twelfth People's Great Hural ended in January 1992 with the adoption of the fourth Constitution (q.v.).

HURAL, GREAT 1992- . The Mongolian (National) Great Hural (*Mongol Ulsyn Ih Hural*), the current national assembly, was elected in June 1992 for a four-year term. The Mongolian People's Revolutionary Party (MPRP) (q.v.) received 56.7 percent of the total ballot and other parties 40 percent. Of the 76 seats in 26 constituencies, 70 were won by the MPRP; one by an MPRP independent, Tögsjargalyn Gandi; one by the Mongolian Democratic Party (MDP) (q.v.), Mendsayhany Enhsayhan; one by a pro-MDP independent, Tsahiagiyn Elbegdorj; one by the Mongolian National Progress Party (MNPP) (q.v.), Davaadorjiyn Ganbold; one by the Mongolian Social Democratic Party (MSDP) (q.v.), Radnaasümbereliyn Gonchigdorj; and one by the United Party (UP), Sanjaasürengiyn Zorig. In October 1992, the MDP, MNPP, and UP formed the Mongolian National Democratic Party (q.v.). The first session of the Mongolian Great Hural opened on July 20, 1992, for the election of officers and formation of the government. Under the terms of the 1992 Constitution (q.v.), the MGH meets every half year for at least 75 days. For a list of members, *see* Appendix 1.

HURAL, LITTLE 1924-1950. First convened in 1924 and abolished under the electoral reforms of 1951, the National (State) Little Hural (*Ulsyn Baga Hural*) was elected by the Great Hural (q.v.). It formed a Presidium of five members (from 1927, three), of whom the chairman was in effect head of state, and selected the prime minister. Its sessions were held as follows:

1st: November 29, 1924 (elected by 1st Great Hural)
2nd: March 20 to 28, 1925
3rd: October 5 to 7, 1925
4th: November 19, 1925 (elected by 2nd Great Hural)
5th: May 3 to 4, 1926
6th: October 6 to 8, 1926
7th: November 13, 1926 (elected by 3rd Great Hural)
8th: June 1 to 10, 1927
9th: November 16, 1927 (elected by 4th Great Hural)
10th: February 21, 1928
11th: June 1 to 8, 1928
12th: January 24, 1929 (elected by 5th Great Hural)
13th: August 1929
14th: September 20 to 26, 1929
15th: April 27, 1930 (elected by 6th Great Hural)
16th: January 19 to 27, 1931
17th: (special) July 1 to 2, 1932
18th: March 20, 1934
19th: December 28, 1934 (elected by 7th Great Hural)
20th: March 22, 1936
21st: July 15 to 18, 1936
22nd: March 7 to 24, 1939
23rd: July 6, 1940 (elected by 8th Great Hural)
24th: February 11 to 14, 1941
25th: January 13 to 17, 1942
26th: March 6 to 9, 1943
27th: December 24 to 28, 1943
28th: February 1 to 6, 1945
29th: April 19 to 21, 1948
30th: February 1949 (elected by 9th Great Hural)
31st: November 19 to 21, 1949
32nd: February 4 to 6, 1950

HURAL, LITTLE 1990-92. In keeping with amendments to the 1960 (third) Constitution (q.v.) adopted in 1990, the People's Great Hural (q.v.) elected in 1990 selected a Little Hural of 50 members, of which three-quarters had to be PGH deputies to form a standing legislature. On the basis of proportional representation of the total ballot for parties participating in the elections, its 50 seats were apportioned as follows: Mongolian People's Revolutionary Party 31, Mongolian Democratic Party 13, and Mongolian National Progress and Social Democratic Parties (qq.v.) 3 each. The Little Hural met twice a year for sessions of at least 75 days. Its chairman, Radnaasümbereliyn Gonchigdorj (q.v.), was ex officio the vice president of Mongolia. There were also a vice-chairman, Kinayatyn Zardyhan (q.v.), and a secretary, Byaraagiyn Chimid (q.v.). The Little Hural functioned from its first session in September 1990 until its abolition in July 1992, following the adoption of the 1992 (fourth) Constitution (q.v.) and the holding of new elections for the single-chamber Mongolian Great Hural (q.v.). For a list of members of the Little Hural, *see* Appendix 2.

HURAL, LITTLE, MPRP. The MPRP Little Hural formed in October 1992 is the successor to the MPRP Central Committee (qq.v.). Previously the name Little Hural (q.v.) was that of the legislature selected by the Great Hural (q.v.). It was also used previously by the MPRP, however, when in 1930-1932 it held Little Hurals or assemblies of members.

HURAL, PEOPLE'S DEPUTIES'. Under the 1960 Constitution (q.v.) local government was organized through hurals (assemblies) of people's deputies, with "executive administrations" (q.v.), a presidium, and a chairman. The executive administration was responsible for the day-to-day running of the province, town, district, etc., and had departments dealing with local agriculture, industry, transport, army recruitment, police, and so on. The MPRP (q.v.) exercised its monopoly of power from the local MPRP committee through its members in the hurals. The 1992 Constitution (q.v.) brought about local government reforms, including the institution of Hurals of Citizens' Delegates (q.v.).

HURTS, CHOYNJINGIYN (1939-). Mongolian politician. Born in Sühbaatar Province (q.v.), Hurts trained as a geological engineer, graduating from Moscow Institute of Geology. He was dean of a faculty at the Polytechnical Institute, deputy minister of fuel, power, and geology in the 1970s, and minister of geology and mining industry from July 1976-July 1980. He was a deputy of the People's Great Hural (q.v.) from 1990-1992. He was also director of the Institute of Geology and Minerology. He was elected a member of the Mongolian Great Hural (q.v.) for the MPRP (q.v.) for a four-year term on June 28, 1992, in constituency 12 (Sühbaatar). He was the chairman of the MGH standing committee for environmental protection from June

1992 to October 1993, and is a member of the MGH standing committee for economic policy.

HURTS, DAMDINDORJIYN (1958-). President of the Chamber of Commerce and Industry since 1994. Born in Mörön, Hövsgöl Province (qq.v.), Hurts studied at Kiev State University from 1976-1982 and at the Indian Foreign Trade Institute from 1992-1993. He has a law degree. He was a legal consultant in the Tyehnikimport (q.v.) foreign trade company from 1983-1986, then worked at the Ministry of Foreign Trade. In 1988 he moved to the Chamber of Commerce and Industry, where he became secretary-general.

HUTAGT. A *hutagt*, or "blessed one" (sometimes rendered via Russian *khutukhtu*) was a highranking Mongolian incarnated "saint," or *huvilgaan* (q.v.), but especially the Javzandamba Hutagt (q.v.), also known as the Bogd Gegeen or Bogd Khan (qq.v.), who was outranked in the hierarchy of Lamaism (q.v.) only by the Dalai and Panchen Lamas. The discovery of incarnations of *hutagt* was banned "permanently" under the Law on the Separation of the Church and State adopted in December 1934.

HUVILGAAN. An incarnation or "living Buddha," often the head of a monastery or temple. The discovery of incarnations of *huvilgaan* and *hutagt* (q.v.) was banned "permanently" under the Law on the Separation of the Church and State adopted in December 1934.

HUV'SGALT MONGOL. The "Revolutionary Mongolia" (in Russian: *Revolyutsionnaya Mongoliya*) tank regiment presented to the Soviet Union by the Mongolian government during the Second World War. The money raised by a decision of the Little Hural (q.v.) in January 1942 paid for 53 tanks of the T-34 type, handed over at a ceremony in January 1943. The regiment was assigned to the 112th (later 44th) Brigade of the Soviet Army, which fought from Kursk to Kiev, the Carpathians, Poland, and Berlin.

HÜREE. Monastery or enclosure. Any monastery, but especially the seat of the Bogd Gegeen (q.v.), also known as Ih Hüree, "the great monastery," the religious capital of Outer Mongolia (q.v.). It was renamed Niyslel Hüree (capital monastery) in 1911, after the proclamation of independence and the establishment of the government of Autonomous Mongolia (q.v.) under the Bogd Khan (q.v.). On the proclamation of the Mongolian People's Republic in 1924, it was given the name Ulan Bator (qq.v.).

Züün (Eastern) Hüree was a district of Niyslel Hüree. A group of

Mongolian revolutionaries including Danzan, Dogsom, Jam"yan, and
Shühbaatar (qq.v.), formed in 1919, was named after it. They joined
forces with the Konsulyn Denj group in 1920 to form the Mongolian
People's Party (qq.v.).

HÜYTEN. Mongolia's highest mountain. This glaciated 4,374 m peak
of the Mongol Altai Mountains (q.v.) is situated in Bayan-Ölgiy
Province (q.v.), some 10 km south-east of Tavan Bogd (q.v.).

HYARGAS. Lake in Mongolia. Hyargas *nuur*, one of the country's six
largest lakes, has a surface area of 1,407 sq km. This saline lake, fed
by the freshwater Lake Ayrag and river Zavhan (q.v.) and having no
outlets, is situated at a height of 1,028 m above sea level in the southern part of Uvs Province (q.v.).

- I -

IDEVHTEN, DOLOONJINGIYN (1953-). Mongolian politician. Idevhten trained as a mechanical engineer. He was chairman of the Ömnögov' (q.v.) MPRP Committee from October 1990-1992. He became
a member of the MPRP Central Committee (qq.v.) in November 1990
and was reelected in 1991 and 1992. He was elected a member of the
Mongolian Great Hural (q.v.) for the MPRP for a four-year term on
June 28, 1992, in constituency 11 (Ömnögov'). He is a member of
two MGH standing committees: food and agriculture, and economic
policy.

IH BOGD. Mountain in Mongolia. This 3,957 m peak is the highest in
the Gobi Altai Mountains (q.v.) and is situated in southern Bayanhongor Province (q.v.), 135 km south of Bayanhongor town; it is
sometimes called Tergüün Bogd.

IH HÜREE *see* Hüree *and* Ulan Bator.

INDEPENDENCE PROCLAMATION. The Mongolian proclamation
of independence was issued on December 1, 1911, by the General Administration Office in Charge of Halh (q.v.) Affairs (set up in November as a kind of provisional government). Calling for peace and
harmony, and stating that Mongolia should not be ruled by Manchu-
Chinese officials, it said: "Because our Mongolia was originally an independent nation, we have now decided after consultation to establish
a new independent nation based on our old tradition, without the interference of others in our own rights." (For the text, *see* Onon and
Pritchatt, *Asia's First Modern Revolution*.)

INDUSTRY. Mongolia's main industries are mining (q.v.), generation of electricity (q.v.), production of building materials, the processing of livestock (q.v.) produce into semifinished goods, foodstuffs and consumer goods including soap and candles, and output of chinaware and glassware. The country had no industry to speak of before the building of the Ulan Bator (q.v.) "industrial combine" in the 1930s, and there was no large-scale industrial development until the building of Darhan in the 1960s and Erdenet (qq.v.) in the 1970s. This was accompanied by efforts to modernize provincial towns like Choybalsan and Sühbaatar (qq.v.). The shortage of investment has now cut building industry operations considerably. Traditionally an exporter of wool and hides, in recent years Mongolia has striven to increase production of finished goods for export, including clothing and blankets. Output of the main industrial products has declined sharply since 1990, however. Figures for 1990, 1992, and 1993 are as follows:

Building materials:
Breeze blocks: 40,200,000, 14,900,000, and 9,700,000
Bricks: 110,900,000, 39,100,000, and 23,700,000
Cement: 440,800, 132,500, and 82,300 tons
Chipboard: 5,520, 880, and 140 cubic meters
Lime: 102,900, 67,800, and 51,200 tons
Plywood: 3,422, 1,054, and 221 cubic meters

Materials of animal origin:
Cashmere: 307, 97.6, and 121.5 tons
Felt: 745,100, 494,800, and 241,400 meters
Kid leather: 418,400, 494,500, and 64,400 square meters
Lambskin: 1,510,500, 994,900, and 287,200 square meters
Raw hides: 727,600, 439,900 and 99,400 square meters
Washed wool: 9,733, 7,057, and 3,466 tons

Light industry products:
Camelhair blankets: 91,200, 90,600, and 48,700
Carpets: 1,971,200, 1,037,000 and 1,000,000 square meters
Felt boots: 588,500, 409,100 and 252,100 pairs
Knitwear: 4,284,600, 1,411,700 and 990,700 garments
Leather boots and shoes: 4,222,500, 2,244,700 and 1,030,800 pairs
Leather coats: 35,700, 40,100 and 9,400
Leather jackets: 264,500, 141,100 and 160,100
Matches: 25.8, 17.6 and 22.3 million boxes
Sheepskin coats: 138,100, 99,400 and 86,600
Woolen cloth: 1,111,500, 705,800 and 289,900 meters

Foodstuffs:
Beer: 6,254,200, 3,042,800 and 2,287,200 liters
Bread: 63,295, 60,860, and 46,007 tons

Confectionery: 19,432, 10,720, and 6,173 tons
Flour: 189,800, 181,900, and 138,800 tons
Pasta: 6,224, 3,304, and 1,540 tons
Soft drinks: 20,068,900, 9,666,100, and 6,697,100 liters
Vodka: 6,438,400, 6,686,600 and 5,250,800 liters

IRKUTSK. Russian town founded in 1661 on the river Angara, west of Lake Baikal, Mongolian name Erhüü. There are several historical links between Irkutsk and Mongolia. Choybalsan (q.v.) went to school there; there was an office of the Comintern (q.v.), and the MPP (q.v.) conspirators met in the town in 1920 and published their newspaper there. In the communist period of Mongolia's history, hundreds of young people were educated and trained there, including Tsedenbal (q.v.). Mongolia still maintains a consulate in Irkutsk.

- J -

JADAMBAA, JAM"YANGIYN (1947-). Mongolian politician. Jadambaa trained as a building engineer. He was appointed an organizer in the MPRP Central Committee (qq.v.) in 1990 and then chairman of Darhan (q.v.) MPRP Committee from November 1990-1992. He became a member of the MPRP Central Committee in 1990 and was reelected in 1991 and 1992. He was elected a member of the Mongolian Great Hural (q.v.) for the MPRP for a four-year term on June 28, 1992, in constituency 19 (Darhan). He is a member of three MGH standing committees: internal affairs, assemblies and administration, and food and agriculture. In 1993 he was appointed deputy leader of the MPRP group in the MGH.

JADAMBAA, SHAGALYN (1940-). Minister of defense since 1990. Born on April 4, 1940, in Haliun district of Gov'-Altay Province (q.v.), Jadambaa graduated from the USSR Combined Arms Academy in 1970 and the USSR Armed Forces General Staff Academy in 1976. He had served as a soldier in the Border Troops from 1960-1964 and an instructor at the Mongolian People's Army Combined Arms School from 1964-1970. He was an operations officer on the People's Army General Staff from 1970-1973; deputy head of the operations department from 1973-1976, then first deputy chief of staff from 1976-1981, deputy minister of defense from 1981-1986, and chief of staff, and concurrently first deputy minister of defense from 1986-1990. His promotions in the military hierarchy were reflected in the MPRP (q.v.) structure: candidate member of MPRP Central Committee from 1981-1986, member from 1986-1990; he was also a deputy of the People's Great Hural (q.v.) from 1986-1990. He was appointed minister of defense with the rank of lieutenant general in September 1990. His responsibilities included the drafting of national security policy, military cooperation with foreign countries, and military policy and organization in the era of democracy and openness. He was reappointed on August 4, 1992, by the first session of the Mongolian Great Hural (q.v.), of which he is not a member.

JALBAJAV, NANZADDORJIYN (1950-). Mongolian politician. Jalbajav became a military political instructor and later head of a department at the Military University. He was elected a member of the Mongolian Great Hural (q.v.) for the MPRP (q.v.) for a four-year term on June 28, 1992, in constituency 22 (Ulan Bator). He is a member of two MGH standing committees: education, science and culture, and foreign policy and security.

JALHANZ HUTAGT. Title of Damdinbazar (q.v.).

JAMSRAN, GENDENGIYN (1915-1941). Secretary of the Ministry of Internal Affairs. One of the 32 victims of the Mongolian purges of the 1930s and 1940s (q.v.) sent to the USSR for trial and sentence, details of which were released by the Russian government in 1993. Sentenced to death by the Military Collegium of the USSR Supreme Court in Moscow in July 5, 1941, and executed on July 27.

JAMSRANO, PEVEENIY (1880-1942). Founder of the Mongolian Academy of Sciences (q.v.). An Aga Khori Buryat (q.v.), Jamsrano (Tsyben Jamtsrano) was a scholar, collector of Mongol epics, songs, and stories, researcher into shamanism, and translator of European literature into Mongol. He worked at the University of St. Petersburg, and from 1907-1908 he taught Mongol there. After traveling in Inner Mongolia (q.v.) from 1909-1910, Jamsrano lived in Urga (q.v.) from 1912-1917, running a school and publishing a Mongol newspaper called *Shine Tol'* (New Mirror) with Russian sponsorship. A "democratic socialist" rather than a communist, Jamsrano attended the first MPP (q.v.) Congress in March 1921 and is said to have authored the party program, or Ten Aspirations (qq.v.). In November 1921, Jamsrano founded the *Sudar Bichgiyn Hüreelen,* that is, the Institute (or Committee) of Scriptures and Manuscripts, and as the permanent secretary under the directorship of Onguudyn Jam"yan (q.v.) became its "guiding spirit." In March 1932, Jamsrano was dismissed and ordered to Leningrad, where he worked at the Institute of Oriental Studies until his arrest. One of the victims of the Mongolian purges of the 1930s and 1940s (q.v.), Jamsrano was sentenced by the Military Collegium of the USSR Supreme

Court in Moscow on February 19, 1940, to five years' imprisonment, and he died in Sol'-Iletsk prison (Orenburg) on May 14, 1942. Details were released by the Russian government in 1993.

JAM"YAN, ONGUUDYN (JAM"YAN GÜN) (1864-1930). First director of the Academy of Sciences (q.v.), Jam"yan taught Sühbaatar (q.v.) Mongol and arithmetic in his "*ger* (q.v.) school" in Ih Hüree (q.v.) from 1907-1909. Later, Jam"yan worked in the Ministry of Finance of Autonomous Mongolia (q.v.) and was awarded the title of Zaysan. In 1919, he joined the Züün Hüree (q.v.) secret revolutionary group, which with the Konsulyn Denj (q.v.) group combined to form the Mongolian People's Party (q.v.). When the MPP revolutionaries drew up their appeal for Soviet aid in 1920, it was Jam"yan who obtained an audience with the Bogd Khan (q.v.) and persuaded him to affix his seal to it. According to some sources, Jam"yan was imprisoned by the Chinese and under torture may have betrayed some of his comrades. Released after the Chinese left Niyslel Hüree (q.v.), he became a member of the Mongolian Ministry set up by Baron von Ungern-Sternberg (q.v.). However, Jam"yan was appointed deputy minister of finance in the first people's government of 1921, then minister of education until 1926. He was the author of several primary school textbooks on the Mongol language (q.v.). From November 1921 to 1930, he was also director of the Institute of Scripture and Manuscripts, forerunner of the Academy of Sciences (q.v.), although some sources describe its permanent secretary, Jamsrano (q.v.), as the "guiding light."

JANTSANNOROV, NATSAGIYN (1946-). Mongolian politician and musician. He became a composer and later musical director of the State Folksong and Dance Ensemble. Jantsannorov was made secretary, then chairman of the Mongolian Union of Composers from November 1983-July 1990. He became a member of the MPRP Central Committee (qq.v.) in 1991 and was reelected in 1992. He was elected a member of the Mongolian Great Hural (q.v.) for the MPRP for a four-year term on June 28, 1992, in constituency 19 (Darhan). He was a member of two MGH standing committees: education, science, and culture, and budget and finance. In October 1993, he resigned from the MGH on the grounds of ill health. His seat in the MGH was taken by Tömör-Ochiryn Erdenebileg (q.v.).

JARGALANT. Former name for the town of Khobdo or Hovd (q.v.).

JARGALANT. District (*düüreg*) of Ulan Bator (q.v.). Established in 1992, this urban district of some 1,300 households (1992) consists of two wards *(horoo)* incorporating Arshaant, Emeelt, and other residential and commercial parts of the former Partizan ward of Ulan Bator centered on a state farm situated some 25 km north of the capital.

JAS. Monastery property. At the beginning of the 1930s, there were more than 7,700 *jas* as well as some 800 monasteries and 80,000 lamas. As the campaign to break the power of Lamaism (q.v.) got under way, by 1932 the number of lamas permanently resident in monasteries fell to 20,000 and the number of *jas* was reduced to 2,700. The government gave the livestock from the *jas* to the newly formed collective farms (*hamtral*) and to poor *ard* (q.v.), but it was widely treated as stolen property and neglected.

JASRAY, PUNTSAGIYN (1933-). Prime minister since 1992. Born on November 26, 1933, in Bugat district of Gov'-Altay Province (q.v.), Jasray graduated in 1961 from Moscow Higher School of Economics and Statistics with a degree in agricultural economics. He was appointed chairman of the State Prices Committee from 1970-1975 (chairman of the State Prices and Standards Committee from 1975-1976), then head of the planning and finance department of the MPRP Central Committee (q.v.) from 1976-1978. In 1978, he moved to the post of first deputy chairman of the State Planning Commission. On promotion to chairman of the Commission in 1984, he was appointed deputy chairman of the Council of Ministers (vice-premier) concurrently. Taking up the post of chairman of the new State Planning and Economic Committee in 1988, he was promoted to first deputy chairman of the Council of Ministers concurrently. He was elected a deputy of the People's Great Hural (q.v.) four times from 1973-1986 and awarded the Order of the Red Banner of Labor Merit (twice) and the Order of the Pole Star (q.v.). He had joined the MPRP in 1951 and was elected a member of the MPRP Central Committee by the 1976, 1981, and 1986 congresses; he became a candidate member of the Politburo in December 1989.

With the collapse of communist power in March 1990, he resigned his MPRP and government posts to become president of the Association of Mongolian Production and Services Cooperatives (March 1990-1992). He was not reelected to the MPRP Central Committee in 1991 and 1992. Jasray was elected a member of the Mongolian Great Hural (q.v.) for the MPRP for a four-year term on June 28, 1992, in constituency 26 (Ulan Bator). He was appointed prime minister on July 20, 1992, by the first session of the MGH.

JAVHLANT. Former name for the town of Uliastay (q.v.).

JAVHLANT-SHARGA. Former province (*aymag*) in eastern Mongolia. Founded in 1941 by the amalgamation of districts (*sum*) from Hentiy and Dornod provinces, this province was renamed Sühbaatar Province (qq.v.) in 1943, to mark the fiftieth anniversary of the birth of Damdiny Sühbaatar (q.v.).

JAVZANDAMBA HUTAGT. Title of the "living Buddhas of Urga," leaders of Lemaism (q.v.) in Mongolia, also known as the Bogd Gegeen or Bogd Khan (qq.v.). The title Javzandamba (from the Tibetan *Rje btsun dam pa*), was first awarded in 1650 to Zanabazar (q.v.), the first Bogd Gegeen, after religious study in Tibet.

JIGJID, BYAMBYN (1945-). Minister of Power, Geology, and Mining since 1994. Born on February 5, 1945, in Jargalant district of Arhangay Province (q.v.), Jigjid graduated in 1969 from the Urals Polytechnic in Sverdlovsk as a heating engineer. He first worked in the central power distribution system from 1969-1975, and became chief engineer, then manager of Ulan Bator (q.v.) City heating network from 1975-1984. After serving as deputy minister of communal economy and services until 1990, he was briefly chairman of the Society for the Promotion of Industry and Services, then minister of fuel and power from September 1990-August 1992. He was elected a member of the MPRP Central Committee (qq.v.) in 1992. Jigjid was reappointed minister of fuel and power on August 3, 1992, by the first session of the Mongolian Great Hural (q.v.), of which he is not a member. In a reshuffle in January 1994, Jigjid's ministry was amalgamated with the Ministry of Geology and Mineral Resources to form the Ministry of Power, Geology, and Mining, and he was appointed minister.

JIGJIDJAV, TSENGELTIYN (1894-1933). Mongolian prime minister from 1930-1932. Born in present-day Halzan district, Sühbaatar Province (q.v.), Jigjidjav graduated from the Finance Ministry's school of accountancy in 1924, during which time he attended the first Great Hural (q.v.). He joined the MPRP (q.v.) and was appointed the accountant of the Mongolian Central Cooperative (Montsenkoop, q.v.) in 1925 and elected chairman of the General Committee of the Mongolian Central Cooperative in 1928. He served as prime minister of Mongolia from April 27, 1930 to July 2, 1932; he was also a member of the Presidium of the MPRP Central Committee (q.v.) and a member of the Little Hural (q.v.). Later in 1932 he was appointed minister of trade, road transport, and communications development, a post that he held until his death on May 22, 1933; he was shot with a handgun in his *ger* in the Ulan Bator suburbs. After his death, he was accused of counterrevolutionary crimes, and his name was linked with the Lhümbe (q.v.) case.

JUNGARIA. Historical territory of the Oirat (Oyrd, q.v.) or Western Mongols, also known as Jungars or Jungarians (Dzungar, Züüngar), embracing western areas of modern Mongolia, the part of Xinjiang north of the Tian Shan Mountains, and adjacent areas of Kazakhstan and the Altay Republic (q.v.). The Jungarian Khanate was established in 1635 and expanded greatly after 1671 under Galdan Boshigt (Boshgot) Khan, whose army was destroyed by the Manchu (q.v.) in 1697.

JUULCHIN. The Mongolian state tourism corporation (sometimes spelled Zhuulchin) set up in 1954 and subordinated to the Ministry of Foreign Trade and its successors. Until the 1990s, it was the only organization handling foreign tourism in Mongolia. About 8,000 foreign tourists visited Mongolia in 1993. Currently, tourism and hunting bring Mongolia an annual revenue averaging US$3.5-4 million.

- K -

KALMYK (HAL'MG, HALIMAG). The Kalmyk are Oirat (Oyrd, q.v.) Mongols from Jungaria (q.v.), some 300,000 of whom settled in Russia in the seventeenth century (although 125,000 later returned to Jungaria). The name Kalmyk is derived from a Turkic word meaning "they stayed behind." Some 174,000 Kalmyk now live in the Kalmyk Republic (q.v.), but perhaps as a consequence of their exile in Soviet Central Asia, most no longer speak their own language. *See also* Russia: Mongol Ethnic Groups.

KALMYK REPUBLIC. Part of the Russian Federation situated on the northwestern side of the Caspian Sea, area 75,900 sq km. The capital is Elista. About 174,000 (half) of the population are Kalmyk (q.v.), who occupied the territory in the seventeenth century. The Kalmyk "Autonomous *Oblast'* " (AO) was founded in November 1920 (capital Astrakhan') and the status of "Autonomous Soviet Socialist Republic" (ASSR) awarded in October 1935. Under German occupation from December 1942 to January 1943, the ASSR was abolished and the population exiled mostly to Soviet Central Asia for alleged collaboration with the enemy. The AO was reestablished in January 1957 and ASSR status restored in July 1958. Like similar republics in the former RSFSR seeking to promote their sovereignty, it opted in the early 1990s to style itself the Kalmyk Republic, or Hal'mg Tangch

(Kalmyk Nation). Economic and cultural relations with Mongolia are now developing under a bilateral agreement signed in 1992.

KARAKORUM (QARAQORUM). The town, perhaps first built in 1220, that was made the Mongol capital in 1235 by Ögedei Khan. Situated in the Orhon (q.v.) valley, it is not to be confused with the Karakoram mountain range in Kashmir. The name Karakorum (Har Horum) is probably derived from the word *herem* (q.v.), that is, Harherem ("black wall"). The Mongol capital was destroyed in 1380 by Ming troops and was rediscovered in the nineteenth century. Bricks and tiles from the ruins of Karakorum were reused in the building nearby of Mongolia's first Lamaist monastery, Erdene Zuu (q.v.), founded in 1586. The site of Karakorum was excavated superficially by Mongolian and Soviet archaeologists in the 1940s, but detailed long-term excavations are now planned with the participation of Japanese archaeologists. The nearest modern settlement is Harhorin, a rural district center in northern Övörhangay (q.v.).

KAZAKH (HASAG). Turkic ethnic group. The Kazakh constitute the majority of the population (some 75 percent) of Bayan-Ölgiy Province (q.v.) and a large minority in neighboring Hovd Province (q.v.). They accounted for 120,500 (5.9 percent) of the population of Mongolia, according to the 1989 census, but large-scale emigration from Bayan-Ölgiy to Kazakhstan in 1991-1993 has reduced this figure by as much as 54,200. There have been several migrations. In the eighteenth century, Kirei and Naiman Kazakh left Kazakhstan, then under pressure from Russia, to settle in Xinjiang (Chinese Turkestan); in the 1860s some Kirei crossed the Mongol Altai Mountains (q.v.) and settled in the Hovd (q.v.) basin. In Mongolia, the Kazakh have mostly continued their traditional occupations of herding and hunting, while some have engaged in melon growing and others have taken up employment in the mining industry in other parts of the country. The Muslim among the Kazakh are Sunni, and in recent years small groups have been making the hajj. The mosques were destroyed in the 1930s, but some are being rebuilt. *See also* Mongolian Muslim Society.

KAZAKH NATIONAL UNITY MOVEMENT. Movement inaugurated in October 1990 in Bayan-Ölgiy (q.v.) Province to promote Kazakh (q.v.) autonomy in Mongolia, adoption of Kazakh as the local official language, and the appointment of a Kazakh to the post of vice president of Mongolia. The movement launched its own publication in Kazakh in April 1991.

KOMPLEKSIMPORT. Foreign trade company set up by the former State Committee for Foreign Economic Relations to import sets of industrial equipment and turnkey projects and arrange the technical training of Mongolians abroad.

KONSULYN DENJ. The "consul's terrace," an eastern district of the Mongol capital, Niyslel Hüree (q.v.), named after the river terrace on which the Russian Consul's residence was situated. Also the name used to describe a group of Mongolian revolutionaries including Bodoo, Chagdarjav, Choybalsan, and Losol (qq.v.) formed in 1919. They joined forces with the Züün Hüree (q.v.) group in 1920 to form the Mongolian People's Party (q.v.).

KOUMISS. Fermented mare's milk (*ayrag*). A slightly intoxicating drink made domestically in a cowhide bag in the herdsman's *ger* (q.v.). Koumiss (from the Tatar word *kumiz*), long the focus of traditions and ceremonies, was described by William of Rubruck, Marco Polo, and other medieval European visitors to the Mongol Empire. It contains 98 mg of vitamin C per liter and has certain medicinal properties, so that it is available at some Mongolian health resorts. A report on its properties was delivered to the Edinburgh Medical Society in 1788. In the summer months, when the Mongols mostly eat *tsagaan idee* (dairy produce) and little meat, koumiss is consumed in large quantities by the male population.

KYAKHTA (HIAGT). Town in the Buryat Republic (q.v.) of the Russian Federation, situated on the northern side of the border opposite the Mongolian town of Altanbulag (q.v.). Founded as Fort Troitsk (Mongol name, Deed Shivee), the original Russian settlement developed a "trading suburb" (*sloboda*) for merchants dealing with Manchu (q.v.) China called Kyakhta (Ar Hiagt), after the local river. The Manchu equivalent was Övör Hiagt. The Russian settlement was renamed Troitskosavsk in honor of Prince Savva Raguzinskiy, who signed the 1727 Russo-Manchurian Treaty of Kyakhta (*see* Chronology). It was accorded town status in 1851. The Russo-Sino-Mongolian Treaty was signed in Kyakhta in 1915. The town of Troitskosavsk-Kyakhta was renamed Kyakhta in 1934.

KYZYL. The capital of the People's Republic of (Tannu) Tuva from 1921-1944 and now of the Republic of Tuva (q.v.), previously called Belotsarsk and from 1918-1926 Khem-Beldir ("confluence"). The town of Kyzyl ("red") with a population of about 85,000 is situated at the confluence of the Kaa Khem (Greater Yenisey) and Biy Khem (Lesser Yenisey), which form the Ulug Khem ("big river") or Upper

Yenisey. (The name Yenisey itself means "big river" in the Evenki language.)

- L -

LAAGAN, LOSOLYN (1887-1940). Mongolian head of state from 1930-1932. Born in the present-day Buyant district of Hovd Province (q.v.), Laagan joined the Mongolian People's Revolutionary Party (q.v.) in 1923. He was appointed chairman of the Auditing Commission of the Hovd Provincial MPRP (q.v.) Committee in 1925, then chairman of the MPRP Central Auditing Commission in 1928. Laagan was elected to the Presidium of the MPRP Central Committee (q.v.) in March 1930 and was chairman of the Presidium of the Little Hural (q.v.) from April 27, 1930 to July 2, 1932. He was expelled from the MPRP Central Committee in June 1932 for Left Deviation (q.v.). Thereafter he held a minor post in Hovd Province from 1932-1934. In September 1937, he was arrested by the Ministry of Internal Affairs on charges of counterrevolution and was sentenced and executed on May 4, 1940. He was rehabilitated in 1962.

LAMAISM. The predominant religion of Mongolia, Tibetan Buddhism. Kublai Khan favored the Sakyapa ("red hat") sect, but it was the Mahayana "great vehicle" form of Buddhism of the Gelugpas ("yellow hats") that took hold in Mongolia. Altan Khan of the Tümd (Tumet Mongols of southern Mongolia) was converted in 1578 by the Tibetan leader Sonam Gyatso, whom he met in Höhhot (q.v.). Altan Khan awarded Sonam Gyatso the title "Dalai Lama," and Sonam Gyatso declared Altan Khan to be the "Brahma of the Gods." The incarnation of the Dalai Lama, Yonten Gyatso, was discovered in Mongolia, the great-grandson of Altan Khan. The Halh (q.v.) Khan Avtay founded Mongolia's first Buddhist monastery in 1586 at Erdene Zuu (q.v.).

In 1639 Zanabazar was proclaimed the first Bogd Gegeen (qq.v.) ("Holy Enlightened One") and leader of Mongolia's Buddhists. In 1650 he adopted the title Javzandamba Hutagt (q.v.). Lamaism displaced or absorbed shamanism in Mongolia and at the height of its powers controlled more than 700 monasteries and temples and tens of thousands of lamas and monastery serfs (*shav'*, q.v.). When Mongolia's independence was declared in 1911, the Bogd Gegeen was proclaimed Bogd Khan (q.v.), or head of state.

The 1926 Law Separating Church and State seemed to offer protection for Buddhism, but as amended in December 1934, it banned religious teaching in schools, prevented children from entering monasteries, and sought to end lamas' evasion of military service. Heavy taxes were imposed on the monasteries, and *artel'* (q.v.) established to employ poor lamas. Thereafter Mongolia's religious institutions were virtually all destroyed, their property (*jas,* q.v.) appropriated and the lamas either killed or secularized. In 1937, after a rebellion at Yögzör monastery, the government ordered that some 60 monasteries situated close to the Mongolian border should be moved over 100 km inland, allegedly for fear of invasion by the Japanese. To escape persecution, thousands of Mongols fled to Inner Mongolia (q.v.) and Xinjiang. In 1939 the Japanese sought the Dalai Lama's permission to seek the ninth incarnation of the Javzandamba Hutagt in Inner Mongolia.

The MPRP (q.v.) propagated atheism, but in the 1960s the communist government began low-level support for Lamaism, seeing it as a vehicle for propaganda in Asian Buddhist countries. The only active monastery, Gandan in Ulan Bator (qq.v.), was redecorated and a school for lamas was opened, but Mongolian Lamaists were not allowed to acknowledge the Dalai Lama as their spiritual leader until his first visit to Mongolia in 1979.

In the 1990s, with the birth of democracy and religious freedom in Mongolia, the rebuilding of the monasteries and training of young lamas began. Displays of popular enthusiasm for the Dalai Lama during his later visits to Mongolia, especially in 1991, greatly boosted the restoration of Lamaism. By mid-1993, some 140 monasteries and temples had been reactivated (many as *ger* temples, pending reconstruction) and 2,000 lamas had been trained; the lamas received cash subsistence from their monasteries, for the purchase of firewood and other necessities. Once Gandan was no longer the only active monastery, however, the Gandan abbot's role as "leader of Mongolian Lamaists" was challenged by the abbots of Amarbayasgalant and Dashchoylin monasteries. A dispute also arose over whether or not to recognize a supposed ninth Javzandamba Hutagt, said to be living in the Dalai Lama's community at Dharamsala. Meanwhile, the opening of a "red hat" monastery, Namdoldechin at Bayanhoshuu near Ulan Bator, was planned.

A political party for Buddhists was formed, the Mongolian Believers' Democratic Party (q.v.), although it did not do well in the elections. The 1993 Mongolian Law on State-Church Relations gives precedence to Lamaism, Islam, and shamanism before "non-native" religions like Christianity. Despite renewed interest in Buddhism — and a certain hostility toward Christian missionaries — for many Mongols it remains a matter of cultural heritage rather than religious faith.

LANGUAGE. Mongol is a member of the family of Altaic languages, which also includes the Turkic-Tatar and Manchu-Tungusic groups. Vowel harmony, agglutination, and absence of grammatical gender are common features. Mongol is spoken by some 6 million people in

Mongolia, Inner Mongolia (q.v.), and elsewhere in China, and in the Buryat and Kalmyk (qq.v.) Republics of Russia. Reflecting the history of the country, the language of the Halh (q.v.) Mongols has absorbed Chinese and Manchu (q.v.) terms from the Yuan and Qing periods, religious terminology from Sanskrit and Tibetan, and Russian words from the communist period. Lately, during the transition to a market economy, it has been increasingly influenced by English. Mongol has been written in a variety of scripts, although the classical script (q.v.) has survived from the times of Genghis Khan (q.v.) and was due to come back into official use in 1994. Several generations have learned to read and write in the modified Cyrillic script (q.v.), however, which is much closer to the modern spoken language.

LEFT DEVIATION. Name given in MPRP (q.v.) histories to the line of the MPRP leadership after the defeat of Right Opportunism (q.v.). In 1929-1932, the leadership pushed ahead with a premature transition from the "democratic" to the "socialist" stage of the Mongolian revolution in which private ownership was eliminated. Herdsmen were forced into communes and the monasteries were closed and their property (*jas,* q.v.) seized. These developments provoked "counterrevolutionary" uprisings in 1930 and 1932. In May 1932, the Comintern (q.v.) Executive Committee and CPSU Central Committee issued a joint resolution on the measures to be taken. They were accepted by the MPRP Central Committee (q.v.) at an extraordinary plenum in June, which expelled Badrah, Shijee, Laagan (qq.v.), and other leaders. The Left Deviation was followed by the New Turn (q.v.).

LHAGVAA, LHAGVASÜRENGIYN. Airline director. The son of Hero of Mongolia Lhagvasüren, onetime minister of defense, Lhagvaa was from 1979-1986 chairman of the Chief Directorate for Civil Air Transport under the Mongolian Council of Ministers, the body managing the Mongolian airline MIAT (q.v.). After the launching of privatization in 1990, he set up a private aviation company called Hangar'd (Garuda), of which he was appointed director general; MIAT also became a company. In June 1993, the management of MIAT was reorganized and placed under the control of a new Directorate of Civil Air Transport under the Ministry of Roads, Transport, and Communications. Lhagvaa was appointed head of this directorate. Since January 1994, the directorate has been subordinated to the Ministry of Infrastructure Development, which absorbed the former ministry.

LHAGVASÜREN, BAVUUGIYN (1944-). Mongolian politician. Lhagvasüren became a poet and was appointed chairman of the General Council of the Mongolian Writers' Union in January 1991. He was made a member of the MPRP Central Committee (qq.v.) in 1992. He was elected a member of the Mongolian Great Hural (q.v.) for the MPRP for a four-year term on June 28, 1992, in constituency 14 (Töv). He is a member of two MGH standing committees: education, science, and culture, and foreign policy and security.

LHAMSÜREN, BADAMYN. Mongolian politician. Lhamsüren first held high office as minister of foreign affairs from January 1950 to July 1953, concurrently serving as deputy chairman of the Council of Ministers from July 1951 to July 1954. He served again in the latter post over the period from July 1960 to April 1963, then was briefly chairman of the State Committee for Higher and Special Secondary Education (June-July 1963) before his election to the full-time post of chairman of the Presidium of the Mongol-Soviet Friendship Society, which he held from December 1963 to May 1972. He was made secretary of the MPRP Central Committee (qq.v.) (September 1962), then concurrently a candidate member of the Politburo (February 1963) until June 1976; he held these posts again briefly in 1981-1982. After working in Prague at the editorial offices of the journal *Problems of Peace and Socialism* from 1976-1981, he was appointed director of the MPRP Institute of Social Studies (May 1981-1984); thereafter he returned to Prague until 1986, when he was made an MPRP Central Committee aide. Lhamsüren is a member of the Academy of Sciences (q.v.) (department of social sciences) and was the editor in chief of *Information Mongolia,* published in 1990.

LHÜMBE, JAMBYN (1902-1934). Mongolian party leader from 1932-1933. Born in the present-day Hayrhan-Dulaan district of Övörhangay Province (q.v.), Lhümbe studied at the Party School in 1926-1927 and then was made the school's director in 1928. He was appointed to the Internal Security Directorate in 1929, but from 1929-1930 he studied in the USSR at the Communist University of Toilers of the East. On his return to Mongolia, he became chairman of the Central Council of Trade Unions from 1930-1932. He was elected a member of the Presidium of the MPRP Central Committee (qq.v.) in March 1930 and concurrently secretary of the MPRP Central Committee on June 30, 1932. In 1933, however, he was arrested by the Internal Security Directorate on charges of counterrevolution. He was sentenced to death by the Directorate's "Special Commission" on June 25, 1934, and executed on June 30. The Lhümbe "case" involved the arrest of a number of other innocent people. Lhümbe was rehabilitated in 1962.

LIVESTOCK. In terms of domesticated livestock, Mongolia is traditionally the "land of the five animals"—sheep, goats, cattle, horses, and camels (qq.v.). While cattle includes yaks (q.v.), the raising of pigs (q.v.) is a relatively new venture on a small scale. According to the year-end livestock census, the total number of the "five animals" reached a record 25,871,200 head in 1990, fell slightly to 24,475,200 in 1991, and rose again to 25,659,500 in 1992. These were rounded figures. The census results for the end of 1993, published at the beginning of February 1994, were more precise (total 25,174,688):

	1992	1993
Sheep	14,634,700	13,779,193
Goats	5,598,100	6,107,041
Cattle	2,814,000	2,730,456
Horses	2,197,800	2,190,325
Camels	414,900	367,673

In the spring of 1993 some 1,416,400 livestock died in severe weather in western Mongolia, and the number of surviving newborn stock as of October 1993 was only 7.6 million (87.5 percent of births, a much lower proportion than usual). Between 1992-1993, the number of families owning more than 1,000 head rose from seven to 48, and the largest private herd of 1,830 animals was owned by a herdsman from Bayanhongor Province (q.v.).

LOSOL, DAR'ZAVYN (1890-1940). Politician, victim of the purges. Born at Hujirt Tolgoy in Daychin Beys *hoshuu,* Setsen-Han Aymag (present-day Batnorov district of Hentiy Province, q.v.), into a herdsman's family on April 15, 1890, at the age of nine Losol became a novice at a local monastery and from twelve to eighteen received a Buddhist education at Gandan (q.v.). In 1908, Losol traveled at his own expense through Manchuria (q.v.) to Peking, and two years later visited St. Petersburg and Moscow; his journeys stimulated his interest in politics. Following Mongolia's declaration of independence in 1911, Losol joined the army of Autonomous Mongolia (q.v.) as a "soldier-lama," seeing action in 1913 with the troops of Manlaybaatar Damdinsüren (q.v.) against Chinese forces on the south-eastern border.

Losol became a member of the Konsulyn Denj (q.v.) secret revolutionary group of Dogsomyn Bodoo (q.v.) in 1918. The group combined with Sühbaatar's Züün Hüree group to form the Mongolian People's Party (MPP) (qq.v.) on June 25, 1920. Losol was a member of the MPP delegation, including Bodoo, Chagdarjav, Choybalsan, S. Danzan, Dogsom, and Sühbaatar (q.v.), which went to Soviet Russia in 1920 to contact the Bolsheviks. He was due to meet Soviet government leaders in Omsk, but fell ill and stayed in Irkutsk (q.v.). In November, Losol went to Troitskosavsk (Kyakhta, q.v.) for the first congress of the MPP, at which he was elected one of the three members of the Central Committee. In March 1921, Losol was appointed a member of the MPP Central Committee's Presidium and minister of finance. In January 1922, Losol, his wife, Davaajav, together with S. Danzan and Buyannemeh (qq.v.), were sent to the Moscow Conference of Eastern People's Revolutionary Organizations. In 1923, he was appointed director of the army hospital.

Losol was elected a deputy member of the Presidium of the MPRP Central Committee (qq.v.) from August 1924 to March 1925; from 1925-1939, he was chairman and then president of the Party Central Control Commission; and from 1925-1927, deputy chairman of the Presidium of the Little Hural (q.v.). In 1928-1937, he became a member of the Board of the State Bank and member of the control commission of the Cooperatives Association; and from 1936-1939, member of the Presidium and concurrently deputy chairman of the Presidium of the Little Hural. In 1928, Losol was the MPRP delegate at the fourth Congress of the Comintern (q.v.). His awards included the Orders of the Red Banner (civil), first class, and (military), second class, and the Order of the Pole Star (q.v.).

In July 1939, Marshal Horloogiyn Choybalsan (q.v.) arranged Losol's arrest on charges of counterrevolution. Together with MPRP Central Committee Secretary Dashiyn Damba and Minister of Trade and Industry Shagdarjav (qq.v.), Losol was tricked into boarding a Russian military aircraft ostensibly for a visit to Dornod (Eastern) Province (q.v.), but they were flown to Moscow and Losol was confined in Butyrki prison. In September 1939, Losol was deprived of his party membership, and he died on July 25, 1940, before his case went to trial. The USSR Procurator General ruled in 1956 that there had been no case to answer. The rehabilitation commission of the Presidium of the People's Great Hural (q.v.) restored his civil rights in 1962. The MPRP Central Committee's rehabilitation commission restored his party membership in 1989.

LUVSANDONOY, TSERENJAVYN (1903-1941). Deputy commander in chief of the Mongolian People's Revolutionary Army. One of the 32 victims of the Mongolian purges of the 1930s and 1940s (q.v.) sent to the USSR for trial, details of which were released by the Russian government in 1993. He died on July 18, 1941, in the Soviet Union before his case went to court.

LUVSANDORJ, HAS-OCHIRYN (1910-1937). Mongolian party leader from 1934-1936. Born in Tüsheet-Han Province (present-day Shaamar district of Selenge Province q.v.), Luvsandorj began work in 1926 as a scribe in the local seal office (administration) but in 1932 became chairman of the Provincial Committee of the Mongolian Revolutionary Youth League (MRYL) (q.v.). From 1933-1934 he was chairman of the Selenge MPRP Committee. He was then elected a member of the Presidium and secretary of the MPRP Central Committee (qq.v.) as well as editor of *Namyn Bayguulalt* (Party Organization) from October 5, 1934 to August 15, 1936. In the autumn of 1936, he was sent to the Soviet Institute of Oriental Studies, but while at home on holiday the following summer he was arrested by the Internal Security Directorate's "Special Commission" on charges of counterrevolution. He was sentenced and shot on November 16, 1937. He was rehabilitated in 1962.

LUVSANJAV, NAMSRAYJAVYN (1954-). Minister of law since 1992. Born on May 4, 1954, in Ulan Bator (q.v.), Luvsanjav graduated in 1977 from Irkutsk (q.v.) State University with a degree in law. After working in the State Procurator's Office from 1977-1980, he moved to the People's Control Committee where he became head of the legal department from 1980-1987 and secretary of the Committee from 1987-1990. Appointed deputy head of the legal department of the Presidium of the People's Great Hural (q.v.) in 1990, he became a senior aide in the Presidential Secretariat 1990 and the President's legal aide from December 1990-August 1992. He was elected a member of the MPRP Central Committee (qq.v.) in 1992. Luvsanjav, who is not a member of the Mongolian Great Hural (q.v.), was appointed minister of law on August 11, 1992, by the first session of the MGH.

LUVSANSHARAV, DORJJAVYN (DORGIJAVYN) (1900-1941). Mongolian politician. Born in Zasagt-Han Province (present-day Ih-Uul district of Hövsgöl Province, q.v.), Luvsansharav at the age of ten became a novice at Mörön (q.v.) monastery but in 1921 left to keep livestock. Having become an MPRP (q.v.) member in 1925, he was elected party cell secretary in Naran Jargalant Uul *hoshuu*, and in 1927 he was sent to the Central Party School. Here he opposed both the ideology of "Leftist" extremism in the party and the "Rightist" campaign in the student body, according to the MPRP (q.v.) history of the period. In 1928, Luvsansharav went to the USSR to attend the Communist University of the Toilers of the East. On his return, he worked as a specialist in Soviet affairs and Marxism-Leninism, from 1930 becoming head of a department at the MPRP Central Committee (q.v.) and then a member of the Presidium and deputy secretary of the MPRP Central Committee; he was elected a secretary of the MPRP Central Committee in June 1932 and was reelected to the Presidium in 1932-1937 and in July 1939. Luvsansharav's publications included a handbook on party cell organization and *The Lama Question*. In 1937 he went back to the USSR for a five-month practical training course in political and organizational work. On July 9, 1939, Luvsansharav was arrested by the Ministry of Internal Affairs on charges of counterrevolution. He was sentenced to death by the Military Collegium of the USSR Supreme Court in Moscow on July 5, 1941 and executed on July 30. Luvsansharav was one of the 32 victims of the Mongolian purges of the 1930s and 1940s (q.v.) sent to the USSR for trial and sentence, details of which were released by the Russian government in 1993. He was rehabilitated in 1962.

LÜN. District center in Töv Province (q.v.). It was the center of the former Bogd-Han-Uul Province (q.v.) from 1921-1931 and of Töv Province thereafter until the local administration was moved to Zuunmod (q.v.) in 1934.

LÜNDEEJANTSAN, DANZANGIYN (1957-). Mongolian politician. Born on November 25, 1957, in Ulan Bator (q.v.), Lündeejantsan graduated in 1980 from the Mongolian State University with a degree in law. He was awarded the higher degree of Candidate of Sciences for a study of legal provisions for environmental protection in 1987. From 1980 he was a teacher at the Mongolian State University, becoming secretary of the University MRYL (q.v.) Committee. In 1985, he was appointed a departmental procurator in the State Procurator's Office, then head of a department; later he became head of the sector for study of the socioeconomic legal mechanism at the Institute of State and Law of the Academy of Sciences (q.v.). From 1990-1992, he was a deputy of the People's Great Hural (q.v.) and member of the State Little Hural (q.v.) as well as a member of the SLH legal affairs standing committee; he was chairman of the SLH state organization standing committee from January-August 1992. He was elected a member of the MPRP Central Committee (qq.v.) in 1991 and 1992, and also a member of the MPRP Presidium from March 1991-1992. Lündeejantsan was elected a member of the Mongolian Great Hural (q.v.) for the MPRP for a four-year term on June 28, 1992, in constituency 10 (Övörhangay). He is chairman of the MGH standing committee for foreign policy and security (reelected October 1993) and a member of two MGH standing committees: environmental protection and legal affairs.

- M -

MAAN'T UUL. Westernmost point of Mongolia. This 3,244 m peak in the Mongol Altai Mountains (q.v.) is situated at the border between Bayan-Ölgiy Province (q.v.) and China's Xinjiang Uighur Autonomous Region at 48 deg 53 min North, 87 deg 44 min East, some 15 km south of Tavan Bogd (q.v.).

MAGSARJAV, SANDAGDORJIYN (HATANBAATAR) (1877-1927). Mongolian politician and military leader. Magsarjav was born in the present-day Hutag district of Bulgan province (q.v.). As minister of the western border, with Damdinsüren (q.v.), he liberated the town of Hovd (q.v.) in 1912. He commanded troops defending the southern border against Chinese incursions in 1915 and was awarded the Autonomous Mongolian government's "Shar Joloo" medal. In 1919, he was the first Mongolian military leader to establish contact with Soviet Russian units, the Red Partisans of A. D. Kravchenko and P. E. Shchetinkin. During the Chinese occupation in 1920, he was imprisoned on suspicion of having contact with Sühbaatar's (q.v.) revolutionaries. In 1921, he joined the Mongolian People's Party (q.v.) and was appointed deputy minister of war in the people's government. He commanded the unit that liberated Uliastay (q.v.) and much of northwestern Mongolia from the troops of Baron von Ungern-Sternberg (q.v.). He was appointed minister of war in 1922, candidate member of the MPRP Central Committee (qq.v.) from 1924-1925, and member from 1925. He was elected a member of the Presidium of the MPRP Central Committee from August 1924 to September 1925. He died on September 3, 1927, and is buried in a *ger*-shaped (q.v.) mausoleum in Bulgan (q.v.) town.

MANCHU (MANZHOU, MANJ). Tungusic nation whose leaders ruled China during the Qing (q.v.) dynasty, gaining control of the Eastern Mongols from 1624, Inner Mongolia (q.v.) from 1636, and Outer Mongolia (q.v.) from 1691. The Manchu imposed their own system of administration on the Mongols, and many Manchu terms entered Mongolian, including *amban* (governor), *mereen* (official of a *hoshuu*, q.v.), *zangi* (chief of a *sum* or *örtöö*, q.v.), and others listed elsewhere.

Over 4 million people claiming Manchu nationality live in the north-eastern provinces of China (the former Manchuria), but only a few living in a remote part of Heilongjiang still speak the Manchu language. The Manchu script is a rounded version of the classical Mongol script (q.v.), with diacritical marks.

MANCHUKUO (MANZHOUGUO). State on Mongolia's eastern border founded in 1932 as a Japanese protectorate in China's north-eastern provinces of Manchuria (Heilongjiang, Jilin, and Liaoning) and the northern part of present-day Inner Mongolia (q.v.). Russia had occupied Manchuria in 1900-1901 during the Boxer Rebellion, but after losing the war with Japan, had to cede the southern part to a Japanese protectorate. In September 1931, Japanese troops occupied the northern part. Hsingan Province in north-western Manchuria, with a predominantly Mongol population, was set up by the Japanese in 1932 (capital Wangyehhmiao). In 1934 the former Manchu (q.v.) emperor of China, Pu Yi, was enthroned as emperor of Manchukuo (Mongolian reign-title Enh Erdem). The capital was Changchun. The Russian-built Chinese Eastern Railway in Manchuria had become a Soviet-Chinese joint company in 1924, but the Soviet share was sold to Japan in 1935. In 1937, the Japanese advanced into Inner Mongolia and established another Mongol region, Mengchiang, centered on Kalgan. The armed clashes that took place from 1935 on the border between Manchukuo and Mongolia culminated in the Battle of Halhyn Gol (q.v.) in August 1939. The armistice of September 1939 was followed by a border agreement in 1940 and the Soviet-Japanese nonaggression pact of 1941. Soviet and Mongol troops invaded Manchukuo and Inner Mongolia in August 1945, and the Japanese-occupied territory was eventually returned to China.

MANDALGOV'. Center of Dundgov' Province (q.v.). Accorded town status in 1965. Its height above sea level is 1,393 m, the average January and July temperatures are −18.0 and 18.8 deg C, respectively, and the average annual precipitation is 163.8 mm. The distance from Ulan Bator is 240 km. The population is about 16,000. Local industry produces mainly foodstuffs.

MARDAY. Uranium-mining town in Dashbalbar district, Dornod Province (q.v.), built by Soviet construction workers. Marday is linked by a branch line to the railway between Choybalsan (q.v.) and the Russian border. Known as Erdes, the mining company was run as a secret Soviet concession from which Mongolians were excluded. At full capacity it was capable of producing 100,000 to 150,000 tons of uranium ore a year. It produced around 360,000 tons from 1988-1992, when the mines were closed and the entrances sealed with concrete. At the end of 1993, there were still some 2,000 Russian workers living there. After the establishment of a Mongolian company at Marday in 1993 the Mongolian population reached 320, but according to one report they were not allowed to buy food in the Russian shop.

MED'MOLIBDENSTROY. Russian name of the Soviet organization set up for the building of the copper and molybdenum combine at Erdenet (q.v.).

MEND, RENCHINGIYN (1901-1941). Minister of trade and industry. Born in the present-day Tayshir district of Gov'-Altay Province (q.v.),

Mend joined the MPRP (q.v.) in 1922 and was eventually appointed minister of trade, industry, transport, and communications. He was arrested during a visit to the USSR in August 1937 by the USSR People's Commissariat for Internal Affairs. He was sentenced to death by the Military Collegium of the USSR Supreme Court on July 5, 1941, and executed on July 30. He was one of the 32 victims of the Mongolian purges of the 1930s and 1940s (q.v.) sent to the USSR for trial and sentence, details of which were released by the Russian government in 1993.

MENDBILEG, MONDOONY (1949-). Mongolian politician. Mendbileg trained as a geophysicist, but was appointed vice-chairman of Töv Executive Administration (qq.v.) in 1992. He was elected a member of the Mongolian Great Hural (q.v.) for the MPRP (q.v.) for a four-year term on June 28, 1992 in constituency 14 (Töv). In October 1993, he was elected chairman of the MGH standing committee for environmental protection, of which he had been a member; he is also a member of the MGH standing committees for budget and finance, and food and agriculture.

MIAT. Mongolian national airline. Mongolian Civil Air Transport—*Mongol irgeniy agaaryn teever,* or MIAT—was for many years a military operation, and the history of its development is difficult to separate from that of the air arm of the People's Army, founded in 1925. Mongolia was given Junkers Ju-13 monoplanes by Soviet Russia in May 1925 to begin airmail, freight, and passenger services. Most air traffic was between Ulan Bator and Kyakhta and Ulan-Ude in the Buryat Republic, but routes from Ulan Bator to Hovd via Tsetserleg and Uliastay and to Bayantümen (Choybalsan) were opened in 1930 with Polikarpov R-1 (DH-9) aircraft, and to Zamyn-Üüd and the Altay (qq.v.) in 1933-1934. Civilianized R-5 (P-5) military biplanes were introduced in September 1934.

After the Second World War, the USSR gave Mongolia a US-built lend-lease C-47 Dakota, which was used to fly a Mongolian delegation to Chongqing in February 1946 for talks with Chiang Kai-shek and the Chinese government on mutual recognition. The main aircraft for airmail deliveries in the 1930s-1940s was the Polikarpov Po-2 biplane, with twice-weekly flights to Zavhan, Bayanhongor (q.v.), Hovd, etc. In 1956, Antonov An-2 biplanes were introduced for mail, freight, and passenger flights to Hovd, Hövsgöl (q.v.), Choybalsan, etc., as well as Ulan-Ude and became the mainstay of local air communications, medical and agricultural services for more than 30 years.

In 1957 the Air Communications Directorate was established under the Ministry of Military and Public Security Affairs to manage air transport operations. In the same year, the airports at Ulan Bator and

Saynshand (q.v.) were handed over to Mongolia by their Soviet operators and the USSR supplied five twin-engined Ilyushin Il-14 32-36-seat airliners. These aircraft were introduced on interprovincial flights, while the An-2 biplanes began to be used to link rural districts to their provincial centers. In 1964 twin-turboprop Antonov An-24 40-50-seat airliners entered service in Mongolia.

In January 1971, the Air Communications Directorate was renamed the Chief Directorate for Civil Air Transport (MIAT) and subordinated directly to the government. By 1975, MIAT was operating daily flights to Irkutsk, 17 provincial centers, and 170 herding cooperative and state farm (qq.v.) centers with a total route length of 35,500 km. In 1979, one An-30 was purchased from the USSR for aerial photography. In 1990, air freight traffic amounted to 8 million ton/kilometers and passenger traffic 571.4 million passenger/kilometers. MIAT's operations were severely affected in 1991-1992 by shortages of aviation fuel due to difficulties in foreign trade (q.v.).

As of 1994, MIAT had 12 Antonov An-24 twin-turboprop airliners, three An-26s, three Mil' Mi-8 heavy-lift helicopters, and 45 Antonov An-2 biplanes for local services, although fuel for the latter was in very short supply. One Tupolev Tu-154M was operating on the Ulan Bator-Moscow route, and a Boeing 727 presented by the South Korean government was being prepared for operational use. Facing the urgent need to modernize its fleet, MIAT purchased five Chinese-built Yu-12 airliners and put them into service on interprovincial routes. The Directorate for Civil Air Transport was placed under the control of the Ministry for Infrastructure Development in the reorganization of the government from 1993-1994 (q.v.).

The single runway at Ulan Bator (Buyant-Uhaa) is not wide, long, or strong enough for large modern US- or European-built jet aircraft, and heavy freight is brought in by Russian Antonov An-124. Because of its situation between Bogd Han Uul and the river Tuul (qq.v.) the airport cannot be improved much. Most provincial towns have only a dirt strip, although a 2,800 m runway was completed at Bayanhongor in 1993. The upgrading of ex-Soviet airfields at Nalayh and Choyr (qq.v.) has not proved viable.

MIKRORAYON. An urban housing estate, self-contained district of multistory apartment blocks with their own shops, services, cinema, etc., designed on the Soviet pattern and often mostly built by Soviet construction organizations. The word is Russian, meaning literally "micro-region," and derived from *rayon* (q.v.). The Mongolian equivalent is *horoolol*.

MINING. Mongolia has industrial reserves of coal, copper, fluorite and iron ore as well as numerous small deposits of gold (q.v.), silver, zinc, lead, tin, wolfram and other precious and rare metals whose mining is under state control. Current extraction (1993) includes hard coal and lignite, 5,608,500 metric tons; fluorite, 536,800 metric tons; copper concentrate 334,300 metric tons; molybdenum concentrate, 4,367 metric tons. Coal, especially lignite (Baganuur, Sharyn Gol, Nalayh, qq.v.), is burned in local and central power stations; in some years there is a surplus for export. Fluorite (Bor-Öndör, Hajuu-Ulaan) is exported to the Russian iron and steel industry. Both copper and molybdenum concentrates are produced at the joint Mongolian-Russian "combine" (mining and concentrating enterprise) at Erdenet (q.v.); the Russian share of the copper concentrate is smelted in the Urals, the Mongolian share in Kazakhstan (Balkhash, Dzhezkazgan). The Erdenet combine is Mongolia's biggest foreign-exchange earner. Local iron ore will be mined commercially as the small steel mill built by a Japanese firm in Darhan (q.v.) for scrap reduction goes on stream in 1993-1994. Current annual production of gold averages 1,100 kilograms and is expected to increase. Russia secretly developed two uranium mines in Mongolia, one at Choyr, Dornogov' Province, and the other at Marday, Dornod Province (qq.v.). For established mines *see* lists under each province.

MODTOY HAMAR. Easternmost point of Mongolia. A marker 1,290 m above sea level near Soyolz Uul (1,504 m) in the Hinggan Mountains is situated at the border between Dornod Province and China's Inner Mongolia (qq.v.) at 46 deg 43 min north, 119 deg 56 min east.

MONEL. Mongolian electronics corporation making components of computers and television sets.

MONGOL. A representative of the Mongol people; Mongolian, of or relating to the Mongols and Mongolia; the Mongol language (q.v.). The derivation of the word Mongol is disputed.

MONGOL ALTAI MOUNTAINS. The Mongol Altay range *(nuruu)* in Mongolia. They are a continuation of the Altai Mountains in Siberia and Kazakhstan extending for some 1,000 km along Mongolia's south-western border through Bayan-Ölgiy, Hovd, and Gov'-Altay provinces (qq.v.), then linking up with the Gobi Altai Mountains (q.v.). The highest peak is Hüyten (q.v.).

MONGOL AN. Foreign trade company exporting hunting products, importing hunting equipment and organizing hunting expeditions in Mongolia.

MONGOL ARD. The "Mongolian Arat" (Russian: *Mongol'skiy Arat*) fighter squadron presented to the Soviet Union by the Mongolian government during the Second World War. The money raised by a decision of the Little Hural (q.v.) in March 1943 paid for 12 Lavochkin La-5 aircraft, handed over at a ceremony in September 1943. The fighters, assigned to the 322nd Division at Smolensk, fought in Belorussia, Lithuania, East Prussia, and Poland, destroying 324 enemy aircraft in the air and on the ground.

MONGOL ETHNIC GROUPS. The eastern Mongols include the Barga and the Uzemchin (Ujumchin), who live in Dornod Province, and the Dariganga, in the southern part of Sühbaatar Province, along the border of Chinese Inner Mongolia (qq.v.). The northern Mongols are mainly the Buryad, inhabiting the northern areas of Hövsgöl, Selenge, Hentey, and Dornod provinces along the border with the Buryat Republic (qq.v.) and Chita region in Russia. The western Mongols are the peoples united under the name of Oirats or Oyrd who are concentrated in western regions of Mongolia, particularly Hovd Province (qq.v.). For details *see* individual entries, also China: Mongol Ethnic Groups, and Russia: Mongol Ethnic Groups.

MONGOL GAZRYN TOS. Mongolian *kontsern* in charge of petroleum exploration and development, established in 1991. Director General Doobatyn Sengee.

MONGOL SHARYN DAVAA. Northernmost point of Mongolia. There is a marker 2,200 m above sea level in a pass through the Greater Sayan range at the junction of the borders of Hövsgöl Province and Russia's Tuva and Buryat Republics (qq.v.) at 52 deg 9 min north, 98 deg 57 min east.

MONGOLBANK. The Mongolian national bank, formerly the State Bank of the MPR. The bank was founded in June 1924 as a Mongolian-Soviet joint stock company, the Mongolian Trade and Industry Bank. It issued the country's own currency, the tögrög (q.v.), in December 1925. The bank's capital rose from 500,000 tögrög in 1925 to 5.8 million in 1934. The bank was handed over to the Mongolian government in 1935, and renamed the State Bank from January 1, 1954. Mongolbank continues to issue bank notes and coins, decides credit policy, and regulates the operations of Mongolia's commercial banks (q.v.). The president of Mongolbank, Demchigjavyn Molomjamts, was previously minister of finance.

MONGOLIA. The homeland of the Mongol nation in various historical periods. In the Manchu period, Mongolia was divided into Inner and Outer Mongolia (qq.v.). Since the proclamation of the 1992 Constitution (q.v.), it is the official name of the independent state of Mongolia (Mongol Uls), previously (1924-1992) the Mongolian People's Republic (q.v.).

MONGOLIA, AUTONOMOUS. The name (Avtonomit Mongol Uls) given to Outer Mongolia (q.v.) in the period from the collapse of the Manchu Qing (qq.v.) dynasty, the Independence Proclamation, and the enthronement of the Bogd Khan (qq.v.) as head of state in 1911, to the return of Chinese troops to the capital Niyslel Hüree (q.v.). Hence sometimes also called Bogd Khan Mongolia (Bogd Haant Mongol). China and Russia rejected Mongolian independence in favor of autonomy within China. The government of Autonomous Mongolia was formed on December 16, 1911, and dissolved on February 19, 1920.

MONGOLIA, INNER. Historically, that part of Mongolian territory south of the Gobi (Gov', q.v.) that was closer to Peking and surrendered to Manchu (q.v.) control earlier (in 1636) than Outer Mongolia (q.v.), and was subsequently colonized, subjected to Chinese settlement, and thoroughly Sinicized. As an administrative unit Inner Mongolia (Dotood Mongol), also called Southern Mongolia (Övör Mongol), was abolished in 1913-1914 and its territory formed into Suiyuan, Jehol, and Chahar (Tsahar, q.v.) special regions. It was revived in 1947 as the Inner Mongolia Autonomous Region (q.v.).

MONGOLIA, INNER, AUTONOMOUS REGION. The establishment of the Inner Mongolia (q.v.) (Nei Mongol) Autonomous Region (IMAR) was proclaimed in May 1947 in Ulan Hot. Since then, the boundaries of the IMAR have been revised and the administrative divisions changed several times: after the founding of the People's Republic of China in October 1949, during the "cultural revolution," when the northern and western *aymag* were administered by neighboring provinces, and thereafter, when the IMAR's boundaries were restored. The IMAR has an area of 1,183,000 sq km. The capital is Höhhot (q.v.); Baotou (Bugat) is a large industrial town. According to the 1990 census, Mongols accounted for 3,379,738 of the IMAR's total population of 21,456,518, of whom 17,289,995 were Chinese (Han). The IMAR is divided into nine *aymag* (leagues), which are, from north to south-west: Hulun Buir (Hölönboyr), center Hailar; Hinggan, center Ulan Hot: Jirem (Shirem), center Tongliao; Ju Ud

(Zuu-Od), center Chifeng; Xilin Gol (Shiliyn Gol), center Xilin Hot; Ulanqab (Ulaan Tsav), center Jining; Ih Ju (Ih Zuu), center Dongsheng; Bayannur (Bayan Nuur), center Bayan Gol, Dengkou; and Alxa, center Bayan Hot. Hinggan *aymag,* named after the Great Khingan (Ih Hyangan) mountains, was formerly part of Hulun Buir. Alxa (Alashan) *aymag* was part of Bayannur. The former Qahar (Chahar, Tsahar) *aymag* was incorporated mostly in the southern part of Xilin Gol (one county to Ulanqab). *See also* China: Mongol Ethnic Groups.

MONGOLIA, OUTER. Historically, that part of Mongolian territory (Halh, Khalkha, q.v.) north of the Gobi (Gov', q.v.) that was farther away from Peking and surrendered to Manchu (q.v.) control later (1691) than Inner Mongolia (q.v.), was subsequently colonized but subjected less to Chinese settlement and Sinicization. Outer Mongolia (Gadaad Mongol), sometimes called Northern Mongolia (Ar Mongol), included Urianhay (q.v.), also known as Tannu-Tuva or Tuva (q.v.) (Tyva). After 1911, Outer Mongolia was renamed Autonomous or Bogd Khan Mongolia (qq.v.). The term should not be applied to the Mongolian People's Republic (q.v.) from 1924-1992, or the independent state of Mongolia (q.v.) since 1992.

MONGOLIA, PEOPLE'S REPUBLIC OF. Mongolian People's Republic or People's Republic of Mongolia (Bügd Nayramdah Mongol Ard Uls), official name of the independent Mongolian state from 1924-1992, previously known as Autonomous or Bogd Khan Mongolia and subsequently simply as Mongolia (qq.v.).

MONGOLIAN BELIEVERS' DEMOCRATIC PARTY (MBDP). Mongolian political party. The Believers' (Buddhist) Democratic Party was established in June 1990 under the leadership of Ts. Bayarsüren and developed from the Mongolian Believers' Union (q.v.) with the legalization of political parties. It was registered on February 14, 1991. For the June 1992 general elections, it formed an alliance with the Mongolian People's Party (q.v.) to field eight candidates (MBDP 5, MPP 3) and one independent, but they won no seats.

MONGOLIAN BELIEVERS' UNION. Mongolian social organization. The Union (Association) of Mongolian (Buddhist) Believers was established in 1990 under the leadership of Sandagiyn Bayantsagaan, who was elected President of the Executive Council from 1991-1992. It was the parent body of the Mongolian Believers' Democratic Party (q.v.). Its aims include the promotion of Buddhism in Mongolia, the restoration of monasteries destroyed in the 1930s, and the reestablishment of religious schools. The union's newspaper is *Arga Bilig* (Yin and Yang).

MONGOLIAN BOURGEOIS PARTY. Mongolian political party. An alternative name for the Mongolian Capitalists' Party (q.v.).

MONGOLIAN CAPITALISTS' PARTY. Mongolian political party. The Capitalists' (or Bourgeois, *höröngötön*) Party was established in March 1992 under the leadership of B. Jargalsayhan, president of the Buyan Company, with the aim of protecting the interests of small businesses, then being set up for the first time under the privatization laws. The party was registered on April 7, 1992. For the June 1992 general elections, the party fielded 13 candidates and five independents but won no seats. Following the elections, the Mongolian Capitalists' Party joined the Mongolian Independence, United Herdsmen's and Farmers', and United Private Owners' Parties (qq.v.) to form a loose coalition or political "Third Force" to counterpose the MPRP and Mongolian National Democratic Party (qq.v.). In late 1993, the four coalition parties formed a new party, the Mongolian United Heritage Party (q.v.).

MONGOLIAN DEMOCRATIC ASSOCIATION (MDA). Mongolian political movement. The first non-communist political organization in Mongolia, the Mongolian Democratic Association (Union) was the parent body of the Mongolian Democratic Party (MDP) (q.v.). The MDA was formed on December 10, 1989, by Sanjaasürengiyn Zorig (q.v.), a postgraduate student at the Mongolian State University who became general coordinator; Batboldyn Enhtüvshin, a lecturer who became deputy coordinator, also president of the Executive Committee of the Union of Teachers; and Gongorjavyn Boshigt, graduate of a Hungarian medical institute. The members of the Coordinating Council included Tsahiagiyn Elbegdorj and Erdeniyn Bat-Üül (qq.v.). As part of the coalition of Mongolian Democratic Forces (q.v.) in the July 1990 elections to the People's Great Hural (q.v.), nine of the MDA's candidates survived into the second round on the MDP ticket, and the MDA won two seats. In June 1991, Zorig was elected president of the MDA. In September 1991, Zorig resigned to found the Mongolian Republican Party (q.v.) and Elbegdorj became general coordinator. In the 1992 general elections, Elbegdorj won a seat in the Great Hural as a pro-MDP independent. In 1993, the MDA joined the coalition of Four Associations (q.v.). In a reshuffle of the leadership in November 1993, the MDA elected Elbegdorj to the post of chairman while also electing a president and vice president (D. Battulga and B. Battüvshin). The MDA's newspaper is *Ardchilal* (Democracy), previously *Shine Tol'* (New Mirror).

MONGOLIAN DEMOCRATIC FORCES. Mongolian political movement. The Democratic Forces was the name given to the loose coalition formed by the Mongolian Democratic, Social Democratic, and National Progress Parties and the Mongolian Democratic, Social Democratic, and New Progress Associations (qq.v.) to fight the MPRP (q.v.) in the 1990 general elections.

MONGOLIAN DEMOCRATIC PARTY (MDP). Mongolian political party. The Mongolian Democratic Party developed from the Mongolian Democratic Association (MDA) (q.v.) with the legalization of political parties. The founding congress of the MDP was held on February 18, 1990. Erdeniyn Bat-Üül (q.v.) was elected general coordinator and chairman of the Political Consultative Council. The party was registered on May 24, 1990. Part of the coalition of Mongolian Democratic Forces (q.v.) in the July 1990 general elections, the MDP put forward 191 candidates (including MDA members) for the first round, of which 57 survived into the second round. With 24.3 percent of the ballot, the party won 16 seats (3.8 percent) in the 430-seat People's Great Hural (q.v.); under proportional representation the MDP was given 13 seats in the 50-seat Little Hural (q.v.). The party campaigned for the revival of national consciousness and opposition to state monopoly. After policy disputes, Gongorjavyn Boshigt (*see* MDA) and his supporters were expelled from the MDP in April 1990, but allowed to rejoin some months later. In February 1992, the Civil Democracy wing of the MDP led by Boshigt merged with the Mongolian Free Labor Party (q.v.) and Sanjaasürengiyn Zorig's Mongolian Republican Party (q.v.) to form the United Party (q.v.). In May 1992, Dambiyn Dorligjav (q.v.) was elected deputy chairman and Dogsomyn Ganbold was elected secretary-general. For the June 1992 elections to the Great Hural (q.v.), the MDP formed an alliance with the Mongolian National Progress Party (MNPP) and the United Party (UP) to field 46 candidates (MDP 21, MNPP 13, UP 12) and five independents. Tsahiagiyn Elbegdorj (MDA, pro-MDP independent) and Mendsayhany Enhsayhan (qq.v.) won the MDP's two seats. In October 1992, the MDP merged with the MNPP, UP, and Mongolian Renewal Party (q.v.) to form the Mongolian National Democratic Party (qq.v.). The MDP's newspaper was *Shine Uye* (New Times).

MONGOLIAN DEMOCRATIC RENEWAL PARTY. Mongolian political party founded by Dashiyn Byambasüren (q.v.). At its first congress, held in Ulan Bator in June 1994, Byambasüren was elected leader of the party. Maj-Gen. (reserve) L. Pürevdorj, a commentator for the Montsame newspaper *Il Tovchoo,* was elected secretary-general.

MONGOLIAN DEVELOPMENT SOCIETY. Mongolian social movement. The Mongolian Development Society (Foundation) was formed in January 1993 by Dashiyn Byambasüren (q.v.), prime minister of Mongolia from 1990-1992. Byambasüren had resigned his seat in the Great Hural (q.v.) and his membership of the MPRP (q.v.) in December 1992, after expressing strong dissatisfaction with the policies of the MPRP government of Puntsagiyn Jasray (q.v.). Five members of the Great Hural, two former government members, and several other officials joined the society, as well as well-known sportsmen, and so on. Although the society was not ostensibly a political organization, some members with links to the MPRP subsequently lost their government-controlled jobs.

MONGOLIAN FREE LABOR MOVEMENT. Mongolian political movement. The Free Labor Movement founded in 1990 under the leadership of General Coordinator Nemehiyn Pürevdorj was the parent body of the Mongolian Free Labor Party (q.v.).

MONGOLIAN FREE LABOR PARTY (MFLP). Mongolian political party. The Free Labor Party, founded in May 1990 under the chairmanship of Hoorzayn Maam, developed from the Mongolian Free Labor Movement (q.v.) with the legalization of political parties. In the July 1990 People's Great Hural (q.v.) elections, the MFLP's two candidates in the first round with only 1.2 percent of the ballot failed to go forward to the second round and won no seats. In October 1990, Choydogiyn Döl was elected chairman, and Maam became vice-chairman; Döl had left the MPRP (q.v.) in 1989 after working abroad for the State Committee for Foreign Economic Relations and became a private businessman. In February 1992, the MFLP merged with the Civil Democracy wing of the Mongolian Democratic Party and the Mongolian Republican Party of Sanjaasürengiyn Zorig to form the United Party (qq.v.). The MFLP's newspaper was *Chölööt Hödölmör* (Free Labor).

MONGOLIAN GREEN ALLIANCE. Mongolian ecological movement. The Green Alliance (Movement) was set up in August 1990 under the leadership of General Coordinator G. Otgonbayar to provide a nongovernmental platform for people interested in environmental protection. It was the parent body of the Mongolian Green Party (q.v.). In November 1991, B. Jiyaandorj became president of the Mongolian Green Alliance.

MONGOLIAN GREEN PARTY (MGP). Mongolian political party. The Green Party, founded in March 1990 and registered on May 26,

1990, developed from the Mongolian Green Alliance (q.v.) with the legalization of political parties. In May 1990, Davaagiyn Basandorj was elected chairman. For the July 1990 elections to the People's Great Hural (q.v.), the MGP fielded two candidates for the first round and one survived into the second; the party received 1.2 percent of the ballot but opted not to take the single seat due to it. For the June 1992 general elections, the MGP fielded six candidates but won no seats. The party campaigned for environmental protection and the traditional use of natural resources. From 1991-1993, there were several changes in the leadership, the presidency passing from Ts. Mönhjargal to Mönhtüvshingiyn Ganbat and then L. Nyam. In August 1993, the MGP claimed a membership of 3,000. The MGP's newspaper is *Yörtönts* (The World).

MONGOLIAN HERDSMEN'S AND FARMERS' ASSOCIATION. Mongolian political movement. The Association of Herdsmen and Farmers (or Livestock-breeders and Crop-growers) was founded in March 1990 to protect the interests of agricultural workers, including those leaving state farms (q.v.) and livestock production cooperatives (*negdel,* q.v.) to live independently. It was the parent body of the Mongolian United Herdsmen's and Farmers' Party (q.v.). The association's first president, G. Batmönh, was the chairman of a *negdel* in Töv Province (q.v.). A statement issued by the association in December 1990 accused the MPRP (q.v.) of restoring communist dictatorship rather than establishing democracy. In May 1991, Tsedensonomyn Sühbaatar was elected president of the Executive Council, and D. Hürelbaatar became general coordinator. The association's newspaper is *Mongolyn Hödöö* (Mongolian Countryside).

MONGOLIAN INDEPENDENCE PARTY (MIP). Mongolian political party. The Independence Party was founded by an MPRP (q.v.) splinter group calling itself the "People's Union of 281 for the Protection of Mongolia's Independence" and held its first congress in March 1992. It was registered on April 1, 1992. For the June 1992 general elections, the MIP fielded 19 candidates and 8 pro-MIP independents but won no seats. It campaigned for cooperation with the MPRP, Russia, and China. Following the elections, the MIP joined the Mongolian Capitalists', United Herdsmen's and Farmers', and United Private Owners' Parties (qq.v.) to form a loose coalition or political "Third Force" to counterpose the MPRP and Mongolian National Democratic Party (q.v.). The chairman of the Political Executive Council, elected in June 1993, was Dashjaagiyn Zorigt. In August 1993, the MIP claimed a membership of 3,800. In late 1993, the four coalition parties formed a new party, the Mongolian United Heritage Party (q.v.).

MONGOLIAN MUSLIM SOCIETY. The Muslim Society was established in 1990 in the upsurge of freedom of religion accompanying the democratic movement, which brought about the collapse of the communist government. The society caters particularly to Mongolia's Sunni Kazakh, who mainly inhabit Bayan-Ölgiy Province (qq.v.) in western Mongolia but live in small communities elsewhere, including Ulan Bator as well as Nalayh (qq.v.) and other mining towns. The three or four mosques in Mongolia, one in Ulan Bator, were destroyed during the persecution of religion in the 1930s. Many Kazakh of the present generation are not religious, but public worship has recommenced, at least one new mosque is under construction in Ölgiy (q.v.), and Kazakh Muslim have begun performing the hajj. The chairman of the Muslim Society is a Kazakh, Hajji Hadiryn Sayraan.

MONGOLIAN NATIONAL DEMOCRATIC PARTY (MNDP). Mongolian political party. The Mongolian National Democratic Party was formed in October 1992 by the amalgamation of the Mongolian Democratic Party (MDP), Mongolian National Progress Party (MNPP), Mongolian Renewal Party (MRP) and United Party (UP) (qq.v.). Davaadorjiyn Ganbold (q.v.) of the MNPP was elected president and Tsedengombyn Baasanjav of the MRP, secretary-general. The party is managed by a 19-member General Council to which Erdeniyn Bat-Üül (MDP), Dashpuntsagiyn Ganbold (MNPP), Tserendashiyn Tsolmon (MRP), and Sanjaasürengiyn Zorig (UP) were among those elected (qq.v.). The post of secretary-general, which fell vacant in August 1993 when Baasanjav was appointed head of the correspondence department of the Presidential Secretariat, was filled in November 1993 by Erdeniyn Bat-Üül. The MNDP claimed a membership of 40,000 in August 1993. The party's newspaper is *Erh Chölöö* (Freedom).

MONGOLIAN NATIONAL PROGRESS PARTY (MNPP). Mongolian political party. The National Progress Party, formed in March 1990 under the chairmanship of Davaadorjiyn Ganbold (q.v.), developed from the Mongolian New Progress Association (q.v.) with the legalization of political parties. The party was registered on May 22, 1990. Dügersürengiyn Süh-Erdene was elected deputy chairman but replaced in 1991 by Dashpuntsagiyn Ganbold. The party is managed by an 11-member Presidium. As part of the coalition of Democratic Forces (q.v.) in the July 1990 general elections, the MNPP fielded 57 candidates for the first round, of whom 12 survived into the second, with 5.9 percent of the ballot winning 6 seats (1.4 percent) in the 430-seat People's Great Hural (q.v.). Under proportional representation, the MNPP was given 3 seats in the 50-seat Little Hural (q.v.). For the 1992 elections to the Great Hural (q.v.), the MNPP formed an alliance with the Mongolian Democratic (MDP) and United Parties (UP) to field 46 candidates (MNPP 13, MDP 21, UP 12) and five independents. Davaadorjiyn Ganbold won the MNPP's single seat. The party campaigned for pluralism, privatization, and a free market economy. In October 1992, the MNPP merged with the MDP, UP, and Mongolian Renewal Party to form the Mongolian National Democratic Party (qq.v.). The MNPP's newspaper was *Ündesniy Devshil* (National Progress).

MONGOLIAN NEW CONSTITUTION PARTY. Proposed Mongolian political party. Following the overwhelming victory of the MPRP (q.v.) in the 1992 general elections the opposition parties sought to strengthen their alliance. In July 1992, a meeting of opposition party leaders was held to discuss plans for a proposed New Constitution Party, i.e., a party that in opposing the MPRP would strongly support the 1992 Constitution (q.v.). The Mongolian Democratic, Social Democratic, National Progress, and Renewal parties and the United Party (qq.v.) were represented. These plans were not proceeded with, however. The opposition parties eventually formed new alliances, including the Mongolian National Democratic Party and the Third Force (qq.v.).

MONGOLIAN NEW PROGRESS ASSOCIATION (MNPA). Mongolian political movement. The New Progress Association (Movement, Union) was formed at the end of 1989 on amalgamation of the Union of Accord and New Progress Movement and was the parent body of the Mongolian National Progress Party (q.v.). Its leader until his death in 1994 was Damdinsürengiyn Batsüh, elected chairman in 1991 and 1993. The MNPA was part of the coalition of Mongolian Democratic Forces (q.v.) in fighting the July 1990 general elections. A faction called Mongolian Tradition was formed by PGH deputy Luvsandambyn Dashnyam. In 1991, Ts. Baatartogtoh was elected deputy chairman. In 1993, the MNPA joined the coalition of Four Associations (q.v.).

MONGOLIAN PEOPLE'S PARTY (MPP) (1920-1924). The party was founded on June 25, 1920, following the amalgamation of the Konsulyn Denj and Züün Hüree (qq.v.) groups of revolutionaries, in particular Bodoo, Chagdarjav, Choybalsan, Soliyn Danzan, Dogsom, Losol, and Sühbaatar (qq.v.). The MPP's 1st congress, held in Troitskosavsk (Kyakhta, q.v.) in 1921, laid down the course for the Mongolian revolution, in which victory was won in July 1921. For details, *see* Damdiny Sühbaatar. At the party's third congress in 1924, it was renamed the Mongolian People's Revolutionary Party (q.v.).

MONGOLIAN PEOPLE'S PARTY (MPP). Mongolian political party. The Mongolian People's Party was founded in November 1991 by a member of the Mongolian Democratic Association (q.v.), Lama D. Baasan, who was elected chairman of the Central Committee. The party, registered on April 3, 1992, was evidently established with a view to preventing the Mongolian People's Revolutionary Party (q.v.) from reverting to its former name from 1920-1924, the Mongolian People's Party (q.v.). The party also planned publication of the newspaper *Mongolyn Ünen* (Mongolian Truth), a former MPP/MPRP title. For the June 1992 general elections, the new MPP formed an alliance with the Mongolian Believers' Democratic Party (MBDP) (q.v.) to field eight candidates (MPP 3, MBDP 5) and one independent, but they won no seats.

MONGOLIAN PEOPLE'S REVOLUTIONARY PARTY (MPRP). The party was founded as the Mongolian People's Party (q.v.) in April 1920 and renamed at the party's third congress in 1924. During the period from 1924-1990, when it enjoyed a monopoly of power as the only constitutional political party and "leading force" in society, the party pursued Soviet-style policies variously described as "bypassing capitalism" and "building socialism" in the MPRP Programs (q.v.). See also separate entries for Damdiny Sühbaatar, as well as MPRP Congresses, Leaders, Presidium, Politburo, and Party Leadership Council.

After the collapse of the party leadership in March 1990, the MPRP split into factions; some members left the party to join or form new parties, while others attempted to reform the party's rules and program. Some of the reformers called for a return to the values of the MPP, but reversion to the old party's name was preempted by the registration of a new party called the Mongolian People's Party (q.v.). Although MPRP candidates won an overwhelming victory in the 1992 elections to the Mongolian Great Hural (q.v.), the number of seats they gained does not reflect the proportion of the vote for them countrywide. The MPRP claimed a membership in 1993 of some 80,000, only a few thousand fewer than in 1986, when the party was at the height of its powers. For many years the party's monthly ideological journal was called *Namyn Am'dral* (Party Life). The party's newspaper is *Ünen* (Truth) (q.v.).

In March 1994, MPRP Secretary-General Dash-Yondon (q.v.) declared: "The MPRP has given up its communist line and, in accordance with the resolutions of its congress, renewed and liberalized itself and adopted national democratic ideas. If our party is described in foreign countries as a communist party, this is only because of incorrect or distorted information. There is no communist party in power in Mongolia today."

MPRP CENTRAL COMMITTEE. The Central Committee *(töv horoo)* elected at the congresses of the Mongolian People's Revolutionary Party (q.v.) was the body responsible between congresses for the supervision of party affairs and the election of the party leaders—the members of the Politburo (Presidium) and Secretariat. Quite often it was plenary meetings of the Central Committee (CC), which tended to be held twice a year, rather than the less frequent MPRP congresses (q.v.) that made important policy decisions including the appointment and removal of party and government leaders. In recent decades the CC membership increased gradually, from 74 in 1966 and 83 in 1971 to 91 in 1976 and 1981, falling to 85 in 1986. The corresponding numbers of candidate (alternate, nonvoting) members from 1971-1986 were 55, 61, 71, and 65. In 1990 and 1991 there were 91 and 99 CC members, respectively. The twenty-first MPRP Congress (February 1992) elected 147 CC members. Candidate membership was abolished.

In October 1992 the MPRP Central Committee decided in the future to call the Central Committee the MPRP Little Hural *(baga hural);* the name Little Hural (q.v.) had been used from 1990 for the standing legislature elected by the Great Hural (national assembly), but this Little Hural was abolished following the adoption of the 1992 Constitution (q.v.). The MPRP Presidium was also renamed the Party Leadership Council (q.v.). The membership of the MPRP Little Hural was initially set at 169, including the 147 CC members elected by the congress in February. As amended in October 1992, the MPRP Rules said (Article 10) that all members of the Great Hural elected in June 1992 (q.v.) and all members of the government named in August 1992 (q.v.) who were members of the MPRP would be members of the MPRP Little Hural.

MPRP CONGRESSES. The congresses of the Mongolian People's (Revolutionary) Party were held as follows (the MPP was renamed MPRP at the third congress):
1st: March 1 to 3, 1921 (in Kyakhta, q.v.): 26 people present
2nd: July 18 to August 10, 1923: 93 delegates, 63 party groups
3rd: August 4 to September 1, 1924: 108 delegates, 4,000 members
4th: September 23 to October 2, 1925: 189 delegates, 7,600 members
5th: September 26 to October 4, 1926: 181 delegates, 11,600 members
6th: September 22 to October 4, 1927: 190 delegates, 12,000 members
7th: October 23 to December 10, 1928: 192 delegates, 15,269 members
8th: February 21 to April 3, 1930: 201 delegates, 12,012 members
9th: September 28 to October 5, 1934: 242 delegates, 7,976 members
10th: March 20 to April 5, 1940: 646 delegates, 13,385 members
11th: December 2 to 23, 1947: 475 delegates, 28,000 members
12th: November 19 to 24, 1954: 633 delegates, 31,714 members

13th: March 17 to 22, 1958: 617 delegates, 42,896 members
14th: July 3 to 7, 1961: 693 delegates, 43,800 members
15th: June 7 to 11, 1966: 747 delegates, 48,570 members
16th: June 7 to 12, 1971: 784 delegates, 58,000 members
17th: June 14 to 18, 1976: 813 delegates, 66,933 members
18th: May 26 to 30, 1981: 831 delegates, 76,240 members
19th: May 28 to 31, 1986: 841 delegates, 88,150 members
Extraordinary congress: April 10 to 13, 1990: 94,750 members
20th: February 25 to 27, 1991: 98,800 members
21st: February 27 to March 2, 1992: 80,000 members (January)

MPRP LEADERS. Chairmen and secretaries from 1921-1993. The individual leaders of the Mongolian People's Revolutionary Party (q.v.) since it was founded in March 1921 as the Mongolian People's Party have had titles varying from chairman to first secretary and general-secretary. From December 11, 1928 to April 8, 1940 (the seventh to tenth congresses), the collective leadership of the MPRP comprised three secretaries of the Central Committee (for details see individual entries):

Chairmen of the Central Committee:
Danzan, Soliyn, March 3, 1921 to September 1921
Bodoo, Dogsomyn, September 1921 to January 7, 1922
Dambadorj, Tseren-Ochiryn, March 15, 1922 to January 2, 1923
Danzan, Ajvaagiyn (Yapon), January 2, 1923 to August 31, 1924
Dambadorj, Tseren-Ochiryn, August 31, 1924 to October 1928

Secretaries of the Central Committee:
Badrah, Ölziytiyn, December 11, 1928 to June 30, 1932
Eldev-Ochir, Bat-Ochiryn, December 11, 1928 to March 13, 1930
Genden, Peljidiyn, December 11, 1928 to June 30, 1932
Shijee, Zolbingiyn, March 13, 1930 to June 30, 1932
Eldev-Ochir, Bat-Ochiryn, June 30, 1932 to 1937
Lhümbe, Jambyn, June 30, 1932 to 1933
Luvsansharav, Dorgijavyn, June 30, 1932 to 1937
Luvsandorj, Has-Ochiryn, October 5, 1934 to August 15, 1936
Baasanjav, Banzarjavyn, October 7, 1936 to February 22, 1940
Damba, Dashiyn, July 4, 1939 to April 8, 1940

General Secretary of the Central Committee:
Tsedenbal, Yumjaagiyn, General-Secretary, April 8, 1940 to April 4, 1954

First Secretaries of the Central Committee:
Damba, Dashiyn, April 4, 1954 to November 22, 1958
Tsedenbal, Yumjaagiyn, November 22, 1958 to May 30, 1981.

General Secretaries of the Central Committee:
Tsedenbal, Yumjaagiyn, May 30, 1981 to August 24, 1984
Batmönh, Jambyn, August 24, 1984 to March 14, 1990
Ochirbat, Gombojavyn, March 14, 1990 to April 13, 1990

Chairmen of the Central Committee:
Ochirbat, Gombojavyn, April 13, 1990 to February 28, 1991
Dash-Yondon, Büdragchaagiyn, February 28, 1991 to October 5, 1992

Secretary-General of the Party Leadership Council:
Dash-Yondon, Büdragchaagiyn, October 5, 1992 to date.

MPRP PARTY LEADERSHIP COUNCIL 1992-1993. The long series
of changes in the composition and designation of the members of the
Presidium of the Mongolian People's Revolutionary Party (MPRP)
Central Committee (qq.v.) which began with the collapse of the old or-
der in March 1990 culminated in October 1992 in the adoption of the
name Party Leadership Council *(namyn udirdah zövlöl)* in place of Pre-
sidium, paralleling a decision to rename the MPRP Central Committee
the Little Hural (q.v.). The composition of the PLC was as follows:
Dash-Yondon, Büdragchaagiyn (q.v.), Secretary-General
Yadamsüren, Jigjidsürengiyn (q.v.), Secretary
Bilegt, Tüdeviyn, PLC member
Boldbaatar, Jigjidiyn, PLC member
Byambajav, Janlavyn (q.v.), PLC member
Chuluunbaatar, G., PLC member
Dashdavaa, Sanduyjavyn, PLC member
Enebish, Lhamsürengiyn (q.v.), PLC member
Ölziy, Günteviyn, PLC member
Tüdev, Lodongiyn (q.v.), PLC member
Tümen, Büdsürengiyn (q.v.), PLC member
Ölziy was concurrently chairman of the Ulan Bator (q.v.) MPRP
    Committee

MPRP PARTY LEADERSHIP COUNCIL 1993- . The PLC was re-
shuffled at a meeting of the MPRP Little Hural held in November
1993. Of the members comprising the PLC in October 1992 (q.v.),
Yadamsüren, Bilegt, Chuluunbaatar, and Tümen were removed. Baldangiyn Enhmandah (q.v.) was elected to membership of the PLC and
subsequently to the post of secretary as well; the other new members
of the PLC were Nadmidiyn Bayartsayhan, Tserenhüügiyn Sharavdorj, and Erdeniyn Gombojav (qq.v.). Subsequently Damdingiyn
Demberel, leader of the MPRP party group in the Mongolian Great
Hural (qq.v.), was appointed a secretary of the PLC.

MPRP POLITBURO 1990 JANUARY-MARCH. In March 1990, when the communist leadership of Mongolia resigned in the face of the broad movement for democracy, the Political Bureau and Secretariat of the Mongolian People's Revolutionary Party Central Committee (CC) (q.v.) comprised the following members:
Batmönh, Jambyn (q.v.), General Secretary
Damdin, Paavangiyn, Politburo member, CC Secretary
Dejid, Bugyn, Politburo member, CC Secretary
Namsray, Tserendashiyn, Politburo member, CC Secretary
Sodnom, Dumaagiyn (q.v.), Politburo member
Jasray, Puntsagiyn (q.v.), Politburo candidate member
Lantuu, Lhamsürengiyn, Politburo candidate member
Balhaajav, Tserenpiliyn, CC Secretary
   Six of the eight—Batmönh, Damdin, Dejid, Namsray, Sodnom, and Balhaajav—were survivors of the party leadership elected by the MPRP Central Committee in 1986. Damdin became the director of Bambar Consultants; Dejid retired; Namsray, editor-in-chief of MPRP journals, died in November 1990; Lantuu, concurrently first secretary of the Ulan Bator (q.v.) MPRP Committee until March 1990, was appointed chairman of the Gov'-Altay Province Executive Administration (qq.v.); Balhaajav held the post of first deputy chairman of the Mongolian-Soviet Friendship Society until it was reorganized after the disintegration of the USSR.
   This Politburo's successor was the short-lived MPRP Politburo 1990 March-April (q.v.) headed by Gombojavyn Ochirbat (q.v.).

MPRP POLITBURO 1990 MARCH-APRIL. The Political Bureau and Secretariat of the Mongolian People's Revolutionary Party Central Committee (CC) (q.v.) installed in March 1990 after the resignation of Jambyn Batmönh (q.v.) and the MPRP Politburo 1990 January-March (q.v.) comprised the following five members:
Ochirbat, Gombojavyn (q.v.), General Secretary
Gombosüren, Tserenpiliyn (q.v.), Politburo member, CC Secretary
Mishigdorj, Nyamyn, Politburo member, CC Secretary
Ööld, Tseveenjavym (q.v.), Politburo member
Tüdev, Lodongiyn (q.v.), Politburo member
   Mishigdorj was appointed ambassador to Moscow in September 1990. This Politburo's successor was the MPRP Presidium 1990 April-November (q.v.).

MPRP PRESIDIUM 1990 APRIL-NOVEMBER. The MPRP leadership elected by the Mongolian People's Revolutionary Party Central Committee (CC) (q.v.) at the April 1990 Extraordinary Congress, which

changed the name of the Politburo to Presidium, comprised the following five members:
Ochirbat, Gombojavyn (q.v.), Chairman
Ööld, Tseveenjavyn (q.v.), Presidium member, CC Secretary
Sum"yaa, Budyn, Presidium member, CC Secretary
Gombosüren, Tserenpiliyn (q.v.), Presidium member
Tüdev, Lodongiyn (q.v.), Presidium member
    Sum"yaa was minister of culture until March 1990. This Presidium's successor was the MPRP Presidium from 1990-1991 (q.v.).

MPRP PRESIDIUM 1990-1991. In November 1990 the leadership of the Mongolian People's Revolutionary Party Central Committee (CC) (q.v.) underwent further changes, including the election of five new Presidium members (*see* MPRP Presidium 1990 April-November) to raise the total to nine:
Ochirbat, Gombojavyn (q.v.), Chairman
Bagabandi, Natsagiyn (q.v.), Presidium member, CC Secretary
Bathishig, Badamdorjiyn, Presidium member, CC Secretary
Dashdavaa, Sanduyjavyn, Presidium member, CC Secretary
Hongor, Oydovyn, Presidium member, CC Secretary
Dash-Yondon, Büdragchaagiyn (q.v.), Presidium member
Ööld, Tseveenjavyn (q.v.), Presidium member
Sum"yaa, Budyn, Presidium member
Tüdev, Lodongiyn (q.v.), Presidium member
    This Presidium's successor was the MPRP Presidium from 1991-1992 (q.v.).

MPRP PRESIDIUM 1991-1992. The MPRP's twentieth Congress at the end of February 1991 dismissed Gombojavyn Ochirbat (q.v.) from the post of chairman and made changes to the Presidium and Secretariat of the Central Committee (CC) (q.v.), raising the number of members to ten, with a further addition in July:
Dash-Yondon, Büdragchaagiyn (q.v.), Chairman
Bagabandi, Natsagiyn (q.v.), Presidium member, CC Secretary
Bathishig, Badamdorjiyn, Presidium member, CC Secretary
Dashdavaa, Sanduyjavyn, Presidium member
Lündeejantsan, Danzangiyn (q.v.), Presidium member
Pürevdorj, Choyjilsürengiyn (q.v.), Presidium member
Tüdev, Lodongiyn (q.v.), Presidium member
Tümen, Büdsürengiyn (q.v.), Presidium member
Yadamsüren, Jigjidsürengiyn (q.v.), Presidium member (from July)
Boldbaatar, Jigjidiyn, CC Secretary
    This Presidium's successor was the MPRP Presidium 1992 February-October (q.v.).

MPRP PRESIDIUM 1992 FEBRUARY-OCTOBER. The MPRP's twenty-first Congress in February-March 1992 retained the same ten leaders as the year before but changed some of their titles as follows:
Dash-Yondon, Büdragchaagiyn (q.v.), Chairman
Bagabandi, Natsagiyn (q.v.), Vice-Chairman
Bathishig, Badamdorjiyn,Vice-Chairman
Boldbaatar, Jigjidiyn, Vice-Chairman
Dashdavaa, Sanduyjavyn, Presidium member
Lündeejantsan, Danzangiyn (q.v.), Presidium member
Pürevdorj, Choyjilsürengiyn (q.v.), Presidium member
Tüdev, Lodongiyn (q.v.), Presidium member
Tümen, Büdsürengiyn (q.v.), Presidium member
Yadamsüren, Jigjidsürengiyn (q.v.), Presidium member
This Presidium's successor was the MPRP Party Leadership Council (q.v.).

MPRP PROGRAMS. Between 1921 and 1960 the Mongolian People's Party (later Mongolian People's Revolutionary Party) (qq.v.) adopted four programs of action for the party, which also served as outlines for reform of the state Constitution (q.v.). Their main provisions included the following:

First Program (adopted by the first MPP Congress in March 1921), also called the "Ten Aspirations" (q.v.) or "The Platform": 1) establishment of the rights and power of the people; 2) unity of the Mongolian tribes in one nation; 3) national self-government, possibly as an autonomous Mongolia in federal union with parts of China, Tibet, and Manchuria; 4) restoration of the Mongolian state; 5) cooperation with like-minded parties; 6) preservation of policies, religion, and customs in the people's interests, or their elimination if backward or harmful; 7) friendship with the revolutionary parties in China and Russia; 8) solidarity with other small oppressed nations; 9) the people's "right of freedom," and publication of the party's plans to resolve the problems of government, law, economy, health, etc.; 10) party membership only for those who honestly accept and support the party's policies.

Revised First Program (adopted by the second MPP Congress in July 1923): The First Program was revised to emphasize the country's noncapitalist development and to purge the party of "oppressor class elements" who had managed to join it.

Second Program (adopted by the fourth MPRP Congress in September 1925): goals for "bringing the Democratic Revolution to its conclusion and implementing the party's general line of developing the country along the noncapitalist path"; eradication of the remnants of the "secular and ecclesiastical reactionaries," "oppressive" foreign traders and moneylenders; creation of a new economy to strengthen national independence.

Third Program (adopted by the tenth MPRP Congress in March-April 1940): goals for uprooting the remnants of feudalism and "development along the noncapitalist path in order to prepare for entering socialism"; emphasis on development of livestock (q.v.) raising to make Mongolia an "agricultural-industrial" nation of "herdsmen, workers and intelligentsia"; praise to the Mongolian revolution and Soviet aid for protecting the Mongolian people against "aggressive predators" at home and abroad.

Fourth Program (adopted by the fifteenth MPRP Congress in June 1966): goals for the "completion of the building of socialism and preparations for advancing to communism," including the finishing of the "material-technical base of socialism," making Mongolia an "industrial-agricultural" nation; the strengthening of the alliance of "workers, collectivized herdsmen and working intelligentsia"; resolute struggle against survivals of the past alien to socialism; love and devotion to the homeland and the Soviet Union.

MONGOLIAN RENAISSANCE PARTY *see* Mongolian Renewal Party.

MONGOLIAN RENEWAL PARTY (MRP). Mongolian political party. The Renewal (Revival or Renaissance) Party was formed in December 1991 by dissident MPRP (q.v.) radicals, incuding Kinayatyn Zardyhan (q.v.), previously leader of the MPRP faction "For Restoration and Renewal of the Mongolian People's Party," and Logiyn Tsog, chairman of the Little Hural's Standing Committee on Legal Affairs from 1990-1991. Tserendashiyn Tsolmon (q.v.), minister of labor from 1990-1992, was elected chairman of the Executive Committee. The party was registered on January 18, 1992, but in October 1992 the MRP merged with the Mongolian Democratic and National Progress Parties and the United Party (qq.v.) to form the Mongolian National Democratic Party (q.v.).

MONGOLIAN REPUBLICAN PARTY. Mongolian political party. The Mongolian Republican Party was set up as a "middle-class party" in October 1991 by Sanjaasürengiyn Zorig (q.v.), who had left the Mongolian Democratic Association (q.v.). In November 1991 he appealed to the members of the People's Great Hural (q.v.), who were about to debate the new Constitution, to focus on the defense of human rights. In February 1992 the Mongolian Republican Party merged with the Mongolian Free Labor Party (q.v.) and the Civil Democracy wing of the Mongolian Democratic Party (q.v.) to form the United Party (q.v.).

MONGOLIAN REVIVAL PARTY *see* Mongolian Renewal Party.

MONGOLIAN REVOLUTIONARY YOUTH LEAGUE (MRYL). Founded in August 1921, the MRYL became the training ground for keen young members of the MPRP (q.v.) run on similar lines to the Soviet Komsomol. For a while, the MRYL tended to pursue its own political line, but in the 1930s the regular MRYL congresses (q.v.) were obliged to pursue policies and elect the MRYL's leaders according to the requirements of the MPRP. Over the communist period (1924-1992), the MRYL became institutionalized as the MPRP's youth propaganda arm, its newspaper being called *Zaluuchuudyn Ünen* (Youth Truth). The MRYL leaders often held high office in the MPRP and/or government concurrently. Although MRYL members were elected to the People's Great Hural (q.v.) in 1990, the MRYL was disbanded for a while and then reappeared as a new "reformed" youth organization. It has evidently lost its sense of direction, however.

MRYL CONGRESSES 1922-1988. The Mongolian Revolutionary Youth League (MRYL) (q.v.) held the following congresses following its founding on August 8, 1921:
1st: July 17-22, 1922: 600 members
2nd: July 18 to August 11, 1923: 2,000 members
3rd: September 15-30, 1924: 93 delegates, 3,000 members
4th: October 17-22, 1925: 128 delegates, 4,000 members
5th: October 11-16, 1926: 159 delegates, 5,010 members
6th: October 6-13, 1927: 114 delegates, 6,507 members
7th: December 14, 1928 to January 5, 1929: 150 delegates, 7,864 members
8th: August 1930: 19,525 members
9th: January 1935: 135 delegates, 6,100 members
10th: March 28-31, 1941: 299 delegates, 17,930 members
11th: April 27-30, 1948: 398 delegates, 25,332 members
12th: June 10-15, 1955: 543 delegates, 45,000 members
13th: December 26-31, 1958: 442 delegates, 61,485 members
14th: March 13-16, 1962: 467 delegates, 70,571 members
15th: November 22-26, 1966: 585 delegates, 80,000 members
16th: June 7-10, 1972: 662 delegates, 106,039 members
17th: May 24-27, 1978: 673 delegates, 170,000 members
18th: May 26-28, 1983: 700 delegates, 230,000 members
19th: June 1, 1988: 750 delegates, 269,000 members

MONGOLIAN SOCIAL DEMOCRATIC MOVEMENT (MSDM). Mongolian political movement. Formed in January 1990, the Mongolian Social Democratic Movement was the parent body of the

Mongolian Social Democratic Party (MSDP) (q.v.). The MSDM campaigned in the 1990 general elections as part of the coalition of Mongolian Democratic Forces (q.v.). The movement's first chairman, R. Hatanbaatar, a lecturer at the Mongolian State University, was replaced in August 1990 by Radnaasümbereliyn Gonchigdorj (q.v.), but in September 1990 Gonchigdorj was elected chairman of the Little Hural (q.v.) and vice president of Mongolia. Ar"yaagiyn Ganbaatar (q.v.) was chairman of the MSDM from November 1990-1991. In September 1991, the MSDM merged with the MSDP. The MSDM's journal was *Sotsial Demokrat.*

MONGOLIAN SOCIAL DEMOCRATIC PARTY (MSDP). Mongolian political party. The Mongolian Social Democratic Party developed from the Mongolian Social Democratic Movement (MSDM) (q.v.) with legalization of political parties. Bat-Erdeniyn Batbayar (q.v., also called Baabar) was elected chairman of the MSDP in March 1990. The MSDP was registered on May 25, 1990, and is a consultative member of the Socialist International. As part of the coalition of Democratic Forces (q.v.) in the July 1990 general elections the MSDP fielded 98 candidates in the first round, of whom 15 survived into the second (plus one MSDM member), with 5.5 percent of the ballot winning four seats (1 percent) in the 430-seat People's Great Hural (q.v.). Under proportional representation, the MSDP was given three seats in the 50-seat Little Hural (q.v.). The MSDM merged with the MSDP in September 1991. For the June 1992 elections, the MSDP fielded 27 candidates and three pro-MSDP independents; Radnaasümbereliyn Gonchigdorj (q.v.) won the MSDP's single seat. The party campaigned for a West European-style social democracy and for neutrality. The MSDM's first chairman, R. Hatanbaatar, and L. Byambajargal were elected deputy chairmen of the MSDP in July 1992, and Ar"yaagiyn Ganbaatar (q.v.), MSDM chairman from November 1990-1991, became a member of the MSDP's Political Council in September 1992. P. Ulaanhüü was elected deputy chairman in July 1993. In a reshuffle of the leadership in March 1994, Gonchigdorj replaced Batbayar as chairman of the MSDP and N. Altanhuyag and L. Byambajargal were elected vice-chairmen. In August 1993, the MSDP claimed a membership of 20,000. The MSDP's newspaper is *Ug* (The Word).

MONGOLIAN STUDENTS' UNION. The Union of Students was for many years a tool of the Mongolian Revolutionary Youth League (q.v.), but in March 1990, amid the development of the democracy movement, the union declared itself to be an independent public organization and demanded a multiparty political system and democratic elections, a free market, and safeguards for human rights in Mongolia. Under its general-secretary, Luvsanvandangiyn Bold, the union was extremely active in promoting these aims in coordination with the Mongolian Democratic and New Progress Associations and the Social Democratic Movement (qq.v.), forerunners of the country's first non-communist political parties. Many of the 10,000 or so Mongolian students studying in Eastern Germany, Czechoslovakia, Hungary, Poland, and so on, in the late 1980s were aware of the pressures for change in Eastern Europe and in touch with local student movements.

MONGOLIAN TRADE UNIONS (MTU). The first Mongolian trade unions were formed unofficially at Niyslel Hüree and the Mongolor gold mines at Yöröö (qq.v.) in 1917. The Union of Trade and Industry Workers was formally established in 1925. It had a membership of 3,312 workers from 45 factories and mines. The formation of the MTU was announced in April 1926, but the first MTU congress (q.v.) was not held until the following year. The MTU's governing body, the Central Council, published a newspaper called *Hödölmör* (Labor). Following the birth of democracy in 1990, the MTU were reorganized as the MTU Association (President, Gorchinsürengiyn Ad"yaa). Meanwhile, two more new trade union bodies were formed: the United Association of Mongolian Free Trade Unions, and the "Höh Mongol" (Blue Mongol) Free Trade Unions.

MONGOLIAN TRADE UNIONS CONGRESSES. The congresses of the MTU (q.v.) were held as follows (opening dates):
1st: August 15, 1927: 115 delegates, 4,396 members
2nd: September 25, 1929: 92 delegates, 5,685 members
3rd: October 1, 1935: 161 delegates, 7,900 members
4th: March 4, 1941: 192 delegates, 14,268 members
5th: February 24, 1948: 333 delegates, 27,000 members
6th: April 26, 1955: 501 delegates, 54,450 members
7th: April 26, 1959: 501 delegates, 84,000 members
8th: April 26, 1962: 633 delegates, 128,360 members
9th: October 18, 1966: 750 delegates, 171,300 members
10th: November 10, 1971: 802 delegates, 226,211 members
11th: May 12, 1977: 759 delegates, 318,000 members
12th: May 20, 1982: 763 delegates, 360,000 members
13th: May 13, 1987: 537,000 members

MONGOLIAN UNITED HERDSMEN'S AND FARMERS' PARTY (MUHFP). Mongolian political party. The Mongolian United Herdsmen's and Farmers' Party, formed at the end of 1990, developed from the Mongolian Herdsmen's and Farmers' Association (q.v.) with the legalization of political parties. The party's president, B. Gansüh, was elected in 1991 and reelected in 1992-1993. The party was registered on February 12, 1992. For the June 1992 general elections the MUHFP fielded ten candidates and ten pro-MUHFP independents, but won no seats. Following the elections, the MUHFP joined the Mongolian Capitalists', Independence and United Private Owners' Parties (qq.v.) to form a loose coalition or political "Third Force" to counterpose the MPRP and Mongolian National Democratic Party (qq.v.). In August 1993 the MUHFP claimed a membership of 6,600. In late 1993 the four coalition parties formed a new party, the Mongolian United Heritage Party (q.v.).

MONGOLIAN UNITED HERITAGE PARTY. Political party formed toward the end of 1993 on the amalgamation of the members of the Third Force (q.v.): the Mongolian Capitalists', Independence, United Herdsmen's and Farmers' and United Private Owners' Parties (qq.v.). It has also been referred to as the Conservative Party and Party of Tradition. Ochirbatyn Zayaa (q.v.), chairman of the former MUPOP, was elected leader of the new party, and Ch. Gombosüren its secretary-general.

MONGOLIAN UNITED PRIVATE OWNERS' PARTY (MUPOP). Mongolian political party. The Mongolian United Private Owners' Party was formed under the chairmanship of Mrs. Ochirbatyn Zayaa, director general of the Altan Shagay Co., in March 1992 and was registered on March 30, 1992. Its main aim is to unite private businessmen against state monopoly. In the 1992 general elections the MUPOP fielded 19 candidates and 1 independent but won no seats. Following the elections, the MUPOP joined the Mongolian Capitalists', Independence and United Herdsmen's and Farmers' Parties (qq.v.) to form a loose coalition or political "Third Force" to counterpose the MPRP and Mongolian National Democratic Party (qq.v.). In June 1993, P. Ayuurzana was elected chairman of the Executive Committee. The party's newspaper is called *Ömchlöh Erh* (Right of Ownership). In late 1993 the four coalition parties formed a new party, the Mongolian United Heritage Party (q.v.).

MONGOLIST. Mongolian: *mongolch erdemten,* Russian: *mongoloved.* Someone who makes an academic study of the Mongols (q.v.), their language, history, or culture, or carries out research into the politics, economics, international relations, or social development of Mongolia (q.v.), a "Mongolia-watcher." Mongolian studies have a long history in Russia and Western Europe, and are taught at various universities in the United Kingdom (SOAS, London, and Leeds and Cambridge universities), Germany (Bonn), France (Paris), and the USA (Indiana).

The first International Congress of Mongolists, held by the Mongolian Academy of Sciences (q.v.) in September 1959 in Ulan Bator (q.v.), brought together Mongolists from the West and from the Soviet world, including Mongolia itself, which had long been separated physically and ideologically by Stalinism. A few foreign Mongolists were invited to participate in the organization of similar congresses, and the next three (second to fourth congresses, 1970, 1976, and 1982) made progress in the dissemination of new research and discoveries. The congresses were financed by the MPR government, but despite the strong political pressures acting against academic freedom in Mongolia at the time, a beginning was made to exchanges of information and the publication of congress proceedings.

The fifth congress in 1987 established the International Association for Mongol Studies (IAMS). This is headed by a large executive committee that represents Mongolists from many countries but has no clearly defined role, and is managed by a small Secretariat based in Ulan Bator. By the time the sixth International Congress of Mongolists was held in 1992, the country's financial situation had become very difficult. As the transition to a market economy began, the severe shortages of foreign exchange, paper, and so on, affected academic publishing in particular, although the birth of democracy and multiparty politics in Mongolia had made little impact on the organization of the IAMS. An international conference of Mongolists was held by the IAMS and J. Nehru University in New Delhi in February 1995. The IAMS publishes a Bulletin *(Medeelel)* and an annual collection of papers *(Mongolica)*.

Both the Mongolia Society in the USA and the Anglo-Mongolian Society have regular publications of interest to specialists and the general public.

MONGOLNEFT'. Mongolian-Soviet joint stock company set up in 1949 to develop extraction and refining of oil (q.v.) at Züünbayan (q.v.). It was handed over to the Mongolian government in 1957.

MONGOLRADIO. The radio broadcasting division of the government's Radio and Television Affairs Directorate. Radio broadcasts for the home audience in Mongolian began in February 1933. The main service is broadcast across the country from a long-wave transmitter, although FM stations have been set up in Ulan Bator (q.v.) and some other towns. A service in Kazakh (q.v.) is originated in Ölgiy (q.v.). Relays of Moscow home service (Mayak Radio) are broadcast for the Russian-speaking community; during the communist period, Radio Moscow's daily three hours of Mongolian broadcasts were also relayed. The external services of Mongolradio (Ulan Bator Radio) broadcast a few half-hour programs a week in English (for Europe, Australasia, and the Indian subcontinent), French (Europe and Africa), Russian, Chinese, and Japanese on shortwaves.

MONGOLROSTSVETMET. Joint stock company set up as Mongol-sovtsvetmet by Mongolia and the USSR in February 1973 for the extraction of nonferrous metals and minerals—fluorite at Bor-Öndör and Züün Tsagaandel and gold (q.v.) at Tolgoyt, as well as copper and molybdenum at Erdenet (q.v.). Mongolia later established similar joint stock mining companies with Bulgaria (Mongolbolgar-metall) and Czechoslovakia (Mongolchekhoslovakmetall). The Mongolsovtsvetmet company was renamed Mongolrostsvetmet in 1993.

MONGOLS, WORLD ASSOCIATION OF. International organization with headquarters in Ulan Bator (q.v.) set up by the World Assembly of Mongols, held in Mongolia in September 1993. The president of the Mongolian Development Society, Dashiyn Byambasüren (qq.v.), was elected the association's first president. The Mongols of Mongolia, Inner Mongolia, and the Buryat and Kalmyk (qq.v.) republics of Russia, as well as Mongol communities in the USA, Taiwan, and elsewhere were represented. The aims of the association are essentially cultural, but with a strong interest in environmental protection in Mongol-inhabited territories.

MONGOLTELEVIZ. The television broadcasting division of the government's Radio and Television Affairs Directorate. Television broadcasts started in September 1967 in the Ulan Bator (q.v.) area and were later extended to main provincial towns by microwave links. In 1970 satellite relays of Soviet Television and Intervideniye broadcasts to Mongolia began via an Orbita ground station in Ulan Bator, and then in the 1980s via small Ekran receivers set up all over the country. Since 1992 the transmissions of Mongolteleviz (logo TVM) have been relayed by Asiasat, providing nationwide coverage, although people living in remote areas without electricity cannot receive them.

MONGOLTRANS. Mongolian-Soviet joint stock company founded in December 1929. The Soviet side provided 50 vehicles and a repair shop. The company serviced both road and river transport, built and repaired bridges and roads, and opened a bus service in Ulan Bator (q.v.) in 1930. In 1936, when 60 percent of the staff were Mongols, the company's 320 vehicles carried out 10.7 million ton/kilometers of goods transport. Mongoltrans was handed over to the Mongolian government in 1936 and became the State Motor Transport Organization.

MONGSOVBUNER. Mongolian-Soviet joint stock company founded in 1932 to develop wholesale (Mongolian: *bönöör*) trade. It took over the wholesale business of Montsenkoop (q.v.) and by January 1934 had 900 employees. However, it was handed over to the Mongolian government and became part of the State Trade Directorate in September 1934.

MONROSNEFT'. Mongolian-Russian joint enterprise set up in 1994 for the prospecting, production, and refining of oil (q.v.) and gas in Mongolia.

MONTSAME. The Mongolian news agency. Founded in 1916 as MONTA (Mongolian Telegraph Agency), the agency was renamed Montsame in 1921. Montsame is derived from the contraction of its Mongolian name, *Mongol tsahilgaan medeeniy agentlag*. As the only official source for party and government information, Montsame dominated the media in the post-revolutionary period and published its own Mongolian-language newspapers (in the classical script). In 1942 it launched *Novosti Mongolii* (News from Mongolia) in Russian. Montsame was reorganized along modern lines in October 1957 to send official information abroad by wire services and to some extent collect foreign news, although it relied heavily on the Soviet agency Tass. Montsame also published a monthly magazine in English, *Mongolia,* and a weekly newspaper in Chinese, *Menggu Xiaozibao,* but they and *Novosti Mongolii* ceased publication in 1990. Since then, still under government control, Montsame has continued to combine newsgathering and publishing activities, producing the thrice-monthly newsprint magazine *Il Tovchoo* (Openness) and the weekly English newspaper *The Mongol Messenger.*

MONTSENKOOP. Mongolian Central Cooperative. The Russian name for the Mongolian Mutual Aid Cooperative, founded in December 1921. The statutes of Montsenkoop were adopted at the organization's first congress in April 1922. It was reorganized in 1932 as the Union of Consumer Cooperatives, in Russian *Monkoopsoyuz.*

MORIN HUUR. Traditional Mongolian musical instrument. The *morin huur,* or "horse-head fiddle," has two strings and is played with a bow in the manner of a cello or viola, but being smaller and shorter, the rectangular body rests in the player's lap. The neck is surmounted by a scroll carved in the shape of a horse's head, which gives it its name. In skilled hands the instrument is versatile and may be used to perform both Mongolian folk tunes and European classical music. There is also a double-bass-sized version.

MÖNH HAYRHAN. Mongolia's second-highest mountain. This glaciated 4,204 m peak of the Mongol Altai Mountains (q.v.) is situated
on the boundary between Bayan-Ölgiy and Hovd provinces some 120
km south of Hovd (qq.v.) town; it is sometimes called Sühbaatar Peak.

MÖNH SAR'DAG. Mountain in Mongolia. This 3,491 m peak is the
highest in the Mongolian part of the Sayan range and is situated due
north of Lake Hövsgöl on the border between Hövsgöl Province and
Russia's Buryat Republic (qq.v.).

MÖNHÖÖ, Dorjiyn (1943-   ). Mongolian politician. Mönhöö was a pe-
diatrician in Selenge Province (q.v.) and later became president of the
Mongolian Red Cross Society. In 1985 she was appointed deputy minister of health, then president of the Central Council of the Mongolian
Women's Association from 1990-1992. She was a member of the
MPRP Central Committee (qq.v.) from 1990-1992 and a deputy of the
People's Great Hural (q.v.) from 1990-1992. She was elected a member
of the Mongolian Great Hural (q.v.) for the MPRP for a four-year term
on June 28, 1992, in constituency 13 (Selenge). In October 1993, she
was elected chairman of the MGH standing committee on population,
health, labor, and social security, of which she had been a member; she
is also a member of the budget and finance standing committee.

MÖRÖN. Center of Hövsgöl Province (q.v.). Accorded town status in
1961, Mörön is on the river Delgermörön. Its height above sea level
is 1,283 m, the average January and July temperatures are −23.8 and
16.9 deg C, respectively, and the average annual precipitation is 234.5
mm. The distance from Ulan Bator (q.v.) is 525 km. The population
is about 21,500. Local industries include flour milling and foodstuffs
production.

MYANGAD (MINGAT). Mongol ethnic group. The Myangad, a West
Mongol Oyrd (q.v.) (Oirat) group, accounted for 0.2 percent (4,800)
of the population of Mongolia, according to the 1989 census. The
Myangad are concentrated mostly in Myangad district of Hovd
Province, north of Lake Har-Us (qq.v.).

- N -

NAADAM (NADOM). Mongolian sports festival. The *eriyn gurvan
naadam,* or "three manly sports," of wrestling, archery, and horserac-
ing featured in particular at the National Day celebrations on July 11
in Ulan Bator (q.v.). Mongolian wrestlers wear a traditional garment
called *zodog* (jacket) and *shuudag* (briefs) as well as *gutal* (q.v.)

(boots). The archers shoot their arrows at traditional targets of stacked leather cups called *sur*. The wrestling and archery competitions are held at the city stadium. The mass horseraces are held over a 30 km cross-country course with child riders aged five to thirteen.

NALAYH. District *(düüreg)* of Ulan Bator (q.v.). A coal-mining center situated south-east of the capital, to which it was linked by a 43 km narrow-gauge railway line in July 1938; there is now a branch line to the Trans-Mongolian Railway. Nalayh was accorded town status in 1962, then established as an urban district of Ulan Bator in 1992 with some 5,850 households (1992) and five wards *(horoo)* incorporating Terelj, Shohoy, Arjanchivlan, and other residential areas and the military cantonment of Nalayh town. Its population is about 20,000.

NAMHAYNYAMBUU, TSERENDASHIYN (1947-   ). Mongolian politician. Namhaynyambuu did not complete his secondary education but became a herdsman in Songino district, Zavhan Province (q.v.). He was elected to membership of the MPRP Central Committee (qq.v.) in 1986 and 1990. He was elected a member of the Mongolian Great Hural (q.v.) for the MPRP for a four-year term on June 28, 1992, in constituency 9 (Zavhan). He is a member of two MGH standing committees: health and social security, and food and agriculture.

NAMJIL, BADRAHYN (1902-1941). Head of general department, Political Directorate, Mongolian People's Revolutionary Army. One of the 32 victims of the Mongolian purges of the 1930s and 1940s (q.v.) sent to the USSR for trial and sentence, details of which were released by the Russian government in1993. Sentenced to death by the Military Collegium of the USSR Supreme Court in Moscow on July 5, 1941 and executed on July 27.

NAMJIM, TÖMÖRIYN. Mongolian economist. Director of the Institute for the Development and Location of Productive Forces until 1982, Namjim was appointed deputy chairman of the State Planning Commission from July 1982-1985, then first deputy chairman (with the rank of minister) from 1985-1988. When the commission was renamed in January 1988, he was reappointed first deputy chairman of the State Planning-Economic Committee, a post he held until April 1990. Namjim worked in the department of social sciences (economics) of the Mongolian Academy of Sciences (q.v.), of which he was elected a corresponding member, then member and member of its Presidium.

NAMNANSÜREN, TÖGS-OCHIRYN, SAYN NOYON HAN (1878-1919). Mongolian prime minister from 1912-1915. Namnansüren was a member of the delegation sent by the Bogd Gegeen (q.v.) to St. Petersburg in July 1911 to seek the support of Russia and West European countries for Mongolian independence. He was appointed prime minister in the government of the Bogd Khan (q.v.) in1912; previously the functions of prime minister had been carried out by the minister of internal affairs, Tserenchimed (q.v.). Namnansüren led a delegation to St. Petersburg from November 1913 to January 1914 in an unsuccessful attempt to obtain Russian support for the union of Outer and Inner Mongolia (qq.v.). In 1915 the post of prime minister was abolished, and he was appointed minister of the army.

NAMSRAY, ERDENE VAN. Minister of justice in the first government of the Bogd Khan (q.v.). His successor (until 1920) was Setsen Han Navaanneren. Namsray was imprisoned by the Chinese in 1920.

NARANGEREL, SODOVSÜRENGIYN (1953-). Mongolian politician. Narangerel trained as a lawyer. He was elected a member of the Mongolian Great Hural (q.v.) for the MPRP (q.v.) for a four-year term on June 28, 1992, in constituency 25 (Ulan Bator). He has been vice rector of the Academy of State and Social Studies (q.v.) under the Secretariat of the MGH. He is a member of two MGH standing committees: internal affairs and legal affairs, and was chairman of the Sub-Committee for Struggle against Bribetaking and Abuse of Office until December 1993.

NASANTOGTOH, NERENMÖRIYN (1904-1941). Deputy minister of internal affairs. One of the 32 victims of the Mongolian purges of the 1930s and 1940s (q.v.) sent to the USSR for trial and sentence, details of which were released by the Russian government in 1993. Sentenced to death by the Military Collegium of the USSR Supreme Court in Moscow on July 5, 1941, and executed on July 30.

NATSAGDORJ, DASHDORJIYN (1906-1937). Mongolian journalist and writer. Born in present-day Bayandelger district of Töv Province (q.v.), Natsagdorj was employed as a scribe in the Ministry of War and became secretary to the commander in chief from 1921-1922. Working in the MPRP Central Committee (qq.v.) from 1922-1925, he was employed successively as an aide and secretary to the Secretariat of the Central Committee and to the government, editor of *Ardyn Tsereg* (People's Army), deputy chairman of the Mongolian Revolutionary Youth League (q.v.) Central Committee, and chairman of the Central Bureau of the Pioneers (youth organization). He was elected a member of the Presidium of the MPRP Central Committee in August 1923, then became a deputy member from August 1924 to March 1925. After studying in Germany and the USSR from 1925-1929, he was engaged as an interpreter at the iron works in 1929, then appointed literary editor of the MRYL's *Zaluuchuudyn Ünen* (Youth Truth) in 1930. From 1931-1937, he worked at the Committee of Sciences (the future Academy of Sciences, q.v.) as a translator and head of the history section. Sometimes described as the "first classic of the socialist period," Natsagdorj was the author of an opera about the 1921 revolution called *Uchirtay Gurvan Tolgoy* (known via its Russian translation as *Three Sad Hills*), which is still performed today. He also wrote a famous poem, *Miniy Nutag* (My Homeland), describing the beauty of Mongolia's mountains and rivers. The cause of his death in 1937 is still unclear.

NAYRAMDAL. Former district *(rayon)* of Ulan Bator (q.v.). "Friendship" *rayon,* named in honor of friendship with the Soviet Union, was formed in 1965 and abolished in 1992. It consisted of Nos. 19-22 wards *(horoo)* and embraced the eastern residential areas of the capital now incorporated in Bayanzürh-Uul (q.v.) urban district *(düüreg).*

NAYRAMDAL. Former ward *(horoo)* of Ulan Bator (q.v.). "Friendship" ward, one of the ten wards abolished in 1965 on the formation of Ajilchin, Nayramdal, Oktyabr', and Sühbaatar (qq.v.) districts *(rayon),* each with smaller numbered *horoo.*

NEGDEL. Production association. A *negdel* is a livestock-raising collective run as a cooperative farm (q.v.).

NEW TIMES. Mongolian political movement. The name New Times was given to one of the first "informal" political groups, founded in 1988 by Erdeniyn Bat-Üül (q.v.), later leader of the Mongolian Democratic Party (q.v.). By means of posters and leaflets, the group criticized the policies of the running MPRP (q.v.), especially the ineffectual measures outlined by the MPRP Central Committee (q.v.) plenum of December 1989.

NEW TURN. Name given in MPRP histories to the policy pursued by the MPRP after the June 1932 extraordinary plenum of the MPRP Central Committee (qq.v.) at which the "errors" of the Left Deviation (q.v.) were "corrected." Leftist policies had led to uprisings in the countryside and the intervention of the Comintern (q.v.).

NIYSLEL HÜREE *see* Hüree *and* Ulan Bator.

NOMENKLATUR. From the Russian *nomenklatura* (name list), the system having been developed by Stalin after he was put in charge of "cadre" policy in 1922: secret lists of communist officials and the posts held by them from rural district level upward to the highest echelons. Maintained by the leadership of the ruling party at various levels, it ensured full control over personnel appointments and the placement of party officials in top government, trade union, and other jobs.

NOOSIMPEKS. Foreign trade company exporting wool, yarn, carpets, blankets, etc., and importing machinery and chemicals for the wool industry.

NOROVSAMBUU, JAMBALYN (1942-   ). Mongolian politician. Born in Darvi district of Hovd Province (q.v.), Norovsambuu trained as a veterinary surgeon at the Institute of Agriculture, Ulan Bator (q.v.). He first worked in Dornod Province (q.v.) and was made chief vet of the province in 1970. He was appointed director of Bayan Uul state farm in 1974. In 1978, he went to study at the CPSU Central Committee's Academy of Social Sciences, Moscow, and on graduation was appointed deputy minister of state farms. When this ministry was disbanded, he returned to the countryside, and was appointed director of Tsagaantolgoy state farm in Selenge Province (q.v.). Two years later he became chairman of Hovd Province Executive Administration (qq.v.); then he was appointed chairman of Selenge MPRP Committee from November 1986-1992. He was elected a member of the MPRP Central Auditing Commission from 1986-1990 and a member of the MPRP Central Committee (qq.v.) in 1991 and 1992. He had joined the MPRP in 1963. He was a deputy of the People's Great Hural (q.v.) from 1990-1992 and a member of the State Little Hural (q.v.) from January-July 1992. He was elected a member of the Mongolian Great Hural (q.v.) for the MPRP for a four-year term on June 28, 1992, in constituency 16 (Hovd). He was the chairman of the MGH standing committee for food and agriculture from June 1992 to October 1993 and is a member of the MGH standing committee for foreign policy and security.

NORTHERN TERRITORIAL-PRODUCTION COMPLEX. An industrial and agricultural development region established in the 1980s in northern Mongolia and modeled on the numerous TPCs set up in the USSR. It embraced Hövsgöl, Bulgan, and Selenge provinces and the towns of Erdenet and Darhan (qq.v.), responsible for 30 percent of the country's industrial production. An alternative approach in planning to the Economic Regions (q.v.) but equally unsuccessful, it was eventually abandoned and superseded by the system of Economic Cooperation Zones (q.v.) introduced in 1991.

NOYON. Although sometimes translated via Russian *knyaz'* as "prince," a member of the Mongol nobility rather than a royal household. In modern times used as the equivalent of "mister."

NYAMDAVAA, PAGVAJAVYN (1947-). Minister of health since 1992. Born on January 11, 1947, in Baruunbüren district of Selenge Province (q.v.), Nyamdavaa graduated in 1971 from the Mongolian Higher School of Medicine; he obtained his degree of Doctor of Medicine in 1989. Specializing in bacteriology, he lectured at the Higher School of Medicine from 1971-1974. He then moved to the State Institute of Hygiene, Infections, and Bacteriology, where he was head of a laboratory, research worker, learned secretary, and then deputy director from 1978-1987. He was appointed deputy minister of health from 1987-1990 and minister of health and social security from April-September 1990. As minister of health in the government of Dashiyn Byambasüren (q.v.) from September 1990-August 1992 his responsibilities included the drafting of policies on demography and genetics, cooperation with the World Health Organization, and the development of oriental medicine. He was a member of the MPRP Central Committee (qq.v.) from 1990-1992. Nyamdavaa was reappointed minister of health on August 4, 1992, by the first session of the Mongolian Great Hural (q.v.), of which he is not a member. He is a member of the Academy of Sciences (q.v.).

NYAMDORJ, TSENDIYN (1956-). Mongolian politician. Nyamdorj trained as a lawyer. He was chief deputy minister of law from 1990-1992. He was elected a member of the Mongolian Great Hural (q.v.) for the MPRP (q.v.) for a four-year term on June 28, 1992, in constituency 21 (Ulan Bator). In October 1993 he was elected chairman of the MGH standing committee on legal affairs, of which he had been a member; he is also a member of the standing committee on foreign policy and security.

NYAMZAGD, SÜHRAGCHAAGIYN (1951-). Mongolian politician. Nyamzagd trained as an economist. Director of the State Policy and Social Studies Research Center, he was elected to the MPRP Central Committee (qq.v.) in 1992. He was elected a member of the Mongolian Great Hural (q.v.) for the MPRP for a four-year term on June 28, 1992, in constituency 9 (Zavhan). He is a member of two MGH standing committees: budget and finance, and economic policy.

- O -

OCHIRBAT, GOMBOJAVYN (1929-   ). Mongolian politician. Born in Nömrög district of Zavhan Province (q.v.), Ochirbat first worked as a secondary school teacher in Nömrög and in neighboring Gov'-Altay Province (q.v.). A graduate of the Mongolian State University, he also studied at Moscow State University from 1952-1958. On return to Mongolia, he became a lecturer at the Mongolian State University, then editor in chief of the State Committee on the Press from 1958-1962. After serving as deputy editor in chief of *Ünen* (Truth) (q.v.) from 1962-1964, he was appointed head of the MPRP's (q.v.) ideological department from 1962-1969. From 1969-1972 Ochirbat studied at the Institute of Social Sciences of the MPRP Central Committee (q.v.), graduating with a higher degree in philosophy. In 1972, he was elected chairman of the Central Council of the Mongolian Trade Unions (MTU) (q.v.). He was sacked from this job in 1982, under the influence of Yumjaagiyn Tsedenbal (q.v.), and for the next three years he worked in the Ministry of Education and the Institute of Social Sciences. Following Tsedenbal's own removal from office, from 1985-1988 Ochirbat was acting deputy head of the cadres department of the MPRP Central Committee, following which he was appointed the Mongolian representative on the editorial board of the international communist journal *Problems of Peace and Socialism* in Prague. Ochirbat had joined the MPRP in 1949 and was elected to full membership of the Central Committee from 1966-1990. Following the resignation of the Politburo of Jambyn Batmönh (q.v.) in March 1990, he was elected general secretary of the MPRP and chairman in April 1990, but was not reelected in February 1991. He was also a deputy of the People's Great Hural (q.v.) for many years and a member of its Presidium from 1977-1982.

OCHIRBAT, PUNSALMAAGIYN (1942-   ). Head of state since 1990. Ochirbat was born on January 23, 1942, in Tüdevtey district, Zavhan Province (q.v.), the son of Gonsyn Gendenjav and Tsogtyn Punsalmaa; his father died when he was five, and in 1951 he adopted his mother's name. Ochirbat completed nine years' schooling in Ulan Bator (q.v.) in 1960 and then studied at Leningrad Higher School of Mining, graduating with a degree in mining engineering in 1965. He was awarded a higher degree (Candidate of Technical Sciences) for a study of the Erdenet (q.v.) copper and molybdenum mine in 1975.

   He first worked as an adviser at the Ministry of Industry in 1966, and was appointed chief engineer of Sharyn Gol coal mine in January 1967. In April 1972 he was appointed deputy minister and in April 1976 minister of fuel and power industry and geology. In January

1985 he was transferred to the post of chairman of the State Committee for Foreign Economic Relations, and following a ministerial reorganization was made Minister of Foreign Economic Relations and Supply in December 1987; he was concurrently chairman of the Mongolian side of the Mongolian-Yugoslav intergovernmental cooperation committee.

Ochirbat had been a deputy of the People's Great Hural (q.v.) since 1976. Following the resignation of the old MPRP (q.v.) leadership under Jambyn Batmönh (q.v.) in March 1990 and the subsequent resignation of state and government leaders, he was made chairman of the Presidium of the People's Great Hural (q.v.), that is, head of state, on March 21, 1990. He was reelected to the PGH in the July 1990 general parliamentary elections. On September 3, 1990, the PGH elected him to the newly created post of president of the Mongolian People's Republic for a five-year term in accordance with the amended 1960 Constitution (q.v.), which required the president to resign his seat in the PGH.

Ochirbat joined the MPRP in 1965 and was elected to the MPRP Central Committee (q.v.) in 1976, 1981, 1986, April 1990, and February 1991; he suspended his MPRP membership and was withdrawn from the Central Committee in September 1991 in accordance with the law banning people in high office from membership in political parties, adopted following the attempted anti-Gorbachev coup in the Soviet Union.

The 1992 Constitution (q.v.), which came into force in February, set the term of the presidency at four years and changed the country's name from the MPR to Mongolia, and Ochirbat became president of Mongolia and commander in chief. The Constitution Implementation Law of 1992 called the first general presidential elections in June 1993.

Ochirbat was nominated for the 1993 presidential elections, after deselection by the MPRP, by a coalition of the Mongolian National Democratic Party and Mongolian Social Democratic Party (qq.v.). Of the 50 delegates present at the nomination meeting (25 from the MNDP and 25 from the MSDP), 30 voted for Ochirbat. The MNDP had been formed in October 1992 on the amalgamation of the Mongolian Democratic Party, National Progress Party and Renewal Party and the United Party (qq.v.). In the elections on June 6, winning 57.8 percent of the vote, Ochirbat defeated the MPRP candidate, Lodongiyn Tüdev (q.v.), who gained 38.7 percent.

Ochirbat has been awarded the Mongolian Order of the Pole Star (q.v.), the Hungarian Order of Labor Merit, the Republic of Korea's Order of Moogunghwa, and an honorary doctorate from the ROK Dan Kook University.

OCHIRHÜÜ, TÜVDENGIYN (1948-   ). Mongolian policitian. Born in Sharga district, Gov'-Altay Province (q.v.), Ochirhüü graduated in cybernetics from Leningrad State University in 1972 and from the CPSU Central Committee's Academy of Social Sciences in 1980. From 1972 he worked as a specialist and section chief in the State Prices Committee, later State Committee of Prices and Standards of the State Planning Commission. After working as an instructor in the cadres and economics departments of the MPRP Central Committee (q.q.v.) from 1980-1990, he was appointed head of a directorate at the State Committee for Socio-Economic Development (March-September 1990). He was a deputy of the People's Great Hural (q.v.) and member of the State Little Hural (q.v.) as well as chairman of the SLH social policy standing committee from 1990-1992. He became a member of the MPRP Central Committee in 1992. Ochirhüü was elected a member of the Mongolian Great Hural (q.v.) for the MPRP for a four-year term on June 28, 1992 in constituency 22 (Ulan Bator). He is a member of three MGH standing committees: foreign policy and security, health and social security, and economic policy.

ODONBAATAR, RENCHINSAMBUUGIYN (1961-   ). Mongolian politician. Educated in Hövsgöl Province (q.v.), Odonbaatar graduated from the Mongolian State University in 1983 with a degree in trade economics. After working for two years as an accountant in Hövsgöl provincial trade department, he did his military service from 1984-1986 and was then employed in the Trade Procurement Directorate in Ulan Bator. Odonbaatar attended trade management courses in Novosibirsk from 1987-1988. On return to Mongolia he was appointed head of the trade and procurement offices in Erdenebulgan district from 1988-1990 and in the town of Mörön (qq.v.) from 1990-1991. In 1991 he was appointed the director of the provincial brokers' office. Odonbaatar joined the Mongolian Democratic Party in 1992, becoming a member of the Mongolian National Democratic Party (qq.v.) on their amalgamation and being elected chairman of the MNDP Committee in Hövsgöl Province. Odonbaatar was made a member of the Mongolian Great Hural in June 1994 on the resignation of Tsahiagiyn Elbegdorj (qq.v.). In the 1992 general elections, Odonbaatar had taken fourth place in the three-seat Hövsgöl constituency.

OIL. Mongolia's oil deposits are in the south-east, at Züünbayan (q.v.) and Tsagaan Els, near Saynshand (Dornogov' Province, q.v.), and at Tamsagbulag (Dornod Province, q.v.). Mongolneft' (q.v.) began extraction in 1956 and production amounted to 22,600 tons in 1957 and 35,400 in1958. Petrol and diesel were refined at Züünbayan refinery. Output soon declined, however, to 28,600 tons in 1961, 18,000 in

1964, and 15,900 in 1965. Thereafter production levels were not revealed, and after 1967 oil extraction was no longer even mentioned. Meanwhile, imports of Soviet oil rose from 63,700 to 160,000 tons a year from 1958-1964. By the end of the 1980s Soviet oil imports exceeded 800,000 tons a year. Since the beginning of the transition to a market economy, Mongol Gazryn Tos (q.v.) has invited foreign oil companies to participate in further prospecting and development of Mongolia's oil fields, in the belief that considerable reserves may have remained untouched.

OIROTS. Name sometimes given to the Turkicized Mongol Altaytsy, the native people of the Altay Republic (q.v.) in the Russian Federation who are related to the Oirats (Oyrd, q.v.). *See also* Russia: Mongol Ethnic Groups.

OKTYABR'. Former district *(rayon)* of Ulan Bator (q.v.). "October" *rayon,* named in honor of the Soviet 1917 revolution, was formed in 1965 and abolished in 1992. It consisted of Nos. 23-30 wards *(horoo)* and embraced the western residential areas of the capital now incorporated in Bayangol and Songino-Hayrhan (qq.v.) urban districts *(düüreg).*

OKTYABR'. Former ward *(horoo)* of Ulan Bator (q.v.). "October" ward, one of the ten wards abolished in 1965 on the formation of Ajilchin, Nayramdal, Oktyabr', and Sühbaatar (qq.v.) districts *(rayon),* each with smaller numbered *horoo.*

OLNOO ÖRGÖGDSÖN. "Elevated by many," the reign title of the Bogd Khan of Autonomous Mongolia (qq.v.), from whose accession the years were numbered until his death in 1924. (Subsequently "years of the Mongolian state" until the European calendar came into use.)

ONON. River in Mongolia. The Onon *gol,* 296 km within Mongolia, rises in the Hentey Mountains in north-western Hentiy Province (q.v.) and flows north-east, crossing the boundary of Hentiy Province into Dornod Province (q.v.) and thence into Russia's Chita Region near Mangut; it joins the river Ingoda to form the Shilka, and the Shilka joins the Argun' (Ergun) to form the Amur (Heilongjiang). The basins of the Onon, Herlen, and Tuul (qq.v.), the "three rivers," are considered to embrace the original homeland of the Mongols.

ORHON. Province *(aymag)* in north-central Mongolia. Established in May 1994, the province consists of three former *horoo* reorganized into *sum* (qq.v.): Bayan-Öndör and Nayramdal *horoo* combined as Bayan-

Öndör *sum;* and Jargalant *horoo* redesignated as a *sum;* the provincial center is Erdenet (q.v.), a former "town under national jurisdiction."

ORHON. River in Mongolia. The Orhon, the country's longest river, 1,124 km, entirely within Mongolia, rises in the Hangay Mountains in central Mongolia and flows north, passing the ruins of Karakorum, the Mongol imperial capital, and the monastery of Erdene Zuu, turning east in the area of Bulgan town and entering the river Selenge near Sühbaatar in Selenge Province, not far from the border with Russia's Buryat Republic (qq.v.). The Orhon valley has many ancient monuments, including Bronze Age burials, Turkic stelae inscribed in runic script, and the remains of Uighur towns.

ORVOG GASHUUNY BOR TOLGOY. Southernmost point of Mongolia. There is a marker 802 m above sea level in the Gobi (Gov') at the border between Ömnögov' Province and China's Inner Mongolia (qq.v.) at 41 deg 35 min north, 105 deg 0 min east.

OSMAN (OSPAN), ISLAM. Kazakh (q.v.) warlord from Altai district, Xinjiang. Osman had taken refuge from Chinese KMT forces on Mongolian territory, and in August 1943 the Mongolian leaders Choybalsan and Tsedenbal (qq.v.) and Minister of Internal Affairs B. Shagdarjav decided to establish contact with him. Deputy Minister of Internal Affairs Colonel D. Düynherjav (later minister with the rank of major general) went to Hovd (q.v.), and messengers were sent to Osman's camp. Subsequently, Choybalsan drove to Bulgan district of Hovd Province in February 1944 and had a meeting with Osman at Alag Tolgoy. However, nothing came of these contacts. In 1947-1948 cross-border incursions became more frequent, and in June 1948 Osman's forces were defeated in a pitched battle in the Baytag Bogd (Peitashan) Mountains on Hovd Province's southern border. After unsuccessful attempts to negotiate with the Soviet and East Turkestan authorities, Osman fled to Qinghai in the hope of reaching India, but was caught and executed in Ürümqi in 1951.

OTGON TENGER. Mountain in Mongolia. This 4,021 m peak is the highest in the Hangay Mountains and is situated in Zavhan Province, 60 km south-east of Uliastay (qq.v.); it is sometimes called Enhtayvan (peace) peak.

OTOG. The equivalent in the Ih Shav' (q.v.) of *hoshuu* (q.v.).

OTOR. Practice whereby *negdel* (q.v.) herdsmen drove the herds to better pasture over great distances for lengthy periods while their families were accommodated in small permanent settlements with a school, shop, clinic, library, *ulaan bulan* (q.v.), etc. The Mongolian equivalent of the Russian *otgonnoye zhivotnovodstvo*.

OYRD (OYRAD, OIRAT). Mongol ethnic group. The Oirats or Western Mongols account for some 9.5 percent of the population of Mongolia. They comprise the Dörvöd (Derbet) west of Lake Uvs and Torguud (Torgut) on the western border between Hovd (Khobdo) Province and China; the Zahchin (Dzakhchin), part of the Torguud, living in southern Hovd Province; the Ööld (Eleuth) dwelling mostly in northern Hovd Province but in small groups also in Bayan-Ölgiy Province; the Myangad (Mingat) from north of Lake Har-Us; and the Bayad (Bait), to the east of Lake Uvs (qq.v.). The language of the Oirats is closer to Middle Mongolian and the classical written language than Halh, from which there are considerable phonetic, grammatical, and lexical differences. In the seventeenth century the Oirats of Jungaria (q.v.) adopted the "clear script" *(tod bichig)* alphabet of Zayapandita (q.v.). The Altay people or Oirot (q.v.) are Turkicized Oyrd. *See also* China: Mongol Ethnic Groups; Russia: Mongol Ethnic Groups.

- Ö -

ÖLGIY. Center of Bayan-Ölgiy Province (q.v.). Accorded town status in 1961. Ölgiy's height above sea level is 1,710 m, the average January and July temperatures are − 17.8 and 14.5 deg C, respectively, and the average annual precipitation is 107.1 mm. The distance from Ulan Bator (q.v.) is 1,380 km. The population is about 26,500. Local industries include wool scouring and the production of bricks, ferroconcrete, and foodstuffs.

ÖLZIYHUTAG, NADMIDIYN (1938-   ). Minister of Science and Education since 1992. Born on August 15, 1938 in Erdenedalay district, Dundgov' Province (q.v.), Ölziyhutag graduated in 1962 from the Mongolian State University and was later awarded a doctorate in biology. He started work as a lecturer, then was head of a department at the Mongolian State University from 1962-1974. Moving to the Institute of Botany of the Mongolian Academy of Sciences (q.v.) in 1974, he was appointed learned secretary, then deputy director and later director from 1978-1985. After a three-year secondment as a senior research worker at the Institute of Botany of the USSR Academy of Sciences from 1985-1988, he was reappointed director of the Mongolian Institute of Botany from 1988-1992. Ölziyhutag, who is not a member of the Mongolian Great Hural (q.v.), was appointed Minister of Science and Education on August 10, 1992, by the first session of the MGH. In November 1992 he was appointed a deputy chairman of the State Commission for the Introduction of the Mongolian Script for Official Business.

ÖMNÖGOV' (SOUTH GOBI). Province *(aymag)* in southern Mongolia. Formed in 1931, and initially including parts of the present-day Dundgov' Province (q.v.), the province is situated on the border with China (Bayannur and Alxa Leagues of Inner Mongolia Autonomous Region; during the Chinese "cultural revolution," Ömnögov' bordered on Gansu Province and Ningxia Hui Autonomous Region). With a territory of 165,000 sq km and population of 43,562 (1991), it has 14 rural districts *(sum);* the provincial center is Dalanzadgad (q.v.), the "camel (q.v.) capital" of Mongolia. The designated occasional crossing point on the border with China is Gashuun Suhayt (for Gants Mod). There are deposits of coking coal (Tavan Tolgoyt in Tsogttsetsiy *sum*), coal (Mandal-Ovoo), gold (Altan uul), tin (Nomgon), lead (Borzongiyn Gov'), and salt (Gurvantes). Livestock numbers reached 900,000 head (1992) and arable land 300 hectares (1989).

ÖNDÖRHAAN. Center of Hentiy Province (q.v.). Previously known as Tsetsen-Hany Hüree, the center of the former Tsetsen-Han Province until 1921, and the center of the former Han-Hentiy-Uul (qq.v.) Province until 1931, Öndörhaan was accorded town status in 1961. Its height above sea level is 1,027 m, the average January and July temperatures are −23.2 and 18.8 deg C, respectively, and the average annual precipitation is 254.2 mm. The distance from Ulan Bator (q.v.) is 315 km. The population is about 15,000. Local industries include flour milling and foodstuffs production.

ÖÖLD (ELEUTH). Mongol ethnic group. The Ööld, a West Mongol Oyrd (q.v.) (Oirat) group speaking the northern dialect, accounted for 0.4 percent (9,100) of the population of Mongolia, according to the 1989 census. The Ööld are concentrated mostly in northern Hovd Province and western Bayan-Ölgiy Province (qq.v.)

ÖÖLD, TSEVEENJAVYN (1942-   ). Minister of Food and Agriculture since 1992. Born on February 4, 1942 in Bayan-Öndör district, Övörhangay Province (q.v.), Ööld graduated in 1966 from the Timiryazev Academy of Agriculture in Moscow with a degree in agronomy. Having worked as a section head, department head, and chief agronomist at the Ministry of Agriculture from 1966-1979, he became an instructor and deputy head of the agricultural department of the MPRP Central Committee (qq.v.) from 1979-1983. After serving as chairman of the Töv (q.v.) MPRP Committee from 1983-1989, he was appointed deputy chairman in 1989 and chairman from 1989-1990 of the MPRP Party Control Committee. Elected a member of the MPRP Central Committee in 1990 (and reelected in 1991 and 1992), he became a member of the Presidium of the MPRP Central Committee from March 1990-1991 and secretary of the Central Committee from April-November 1990. He was also a deputy of the People's Great Hural (q.v.) from 1984-1992 and a member of the State Little Hural (q.v.) from 1990-1992. Ööld, who is not a member of the Mongolian Great Hural (q.v.), was appointed Minister of Food and Agriculture on August 3, 1992 by the first session of the MGH.

ÖRTÖÖ. A stage, a distance of 30-40 kilometers, and by extension the system of horse-relay postal stations. Horse-relay duty *(morin örtööniy alba)* or the provision of horses for riders on official business was a form of corvée, or *alba* (q.v.), which continued until 1949. The Russian form *urton* may also be found.

ÖVÖRHANGAY. Province *(aymag)* in central Mongolia. Formed in 1931, the province's name means the front or southern slopes of the Hangay Mountains, on which it is situated. With a territory of 63,000 sq km and population of 100,341 (1991), it has 18 rural districts *(sum)*; until 1992 there were two wards *(horoo)*, Bayanteeg and Dölgöön; the provincial center is Arvayheer (q.v.). Local historical monuments include the imperial capital Karakorum and Erdene Zuu (qq.v.) monastery. There are deposits of lignite (Bayanteeg and Övdög Hudag), a brick works (Övdög Hudag) and flour mill (Harhorin). Livestock numbers reached 2,045,400 head (1992) and arable land 29,600 hectares (1989).

ÖVÖRHANGAY ECONOMIC COOPERATION ZONE. One of six economic cooperation zones into which Mongolia was divided on the basis of a government ordinance issued in November 1991 (the others being the Central, Bayan-Ölgiy, Gov'-Altay, Sühbaatar, and Ulan Bator economic cooperation zones, q.q.v.). It consists of Erdenet town and Övörhangay, Arhangay, Bulgan, and Ömnögov' provinces (qq.v.). Each zone has a cooperation office headed by the secretary of the zonal cooperation council.

- P -

PARTIZAN. Former ward *(horoo)* of Ulan Bator (q.v.). In 1992 this ward was renamed Janchivlin (q.v.) and designated a district *(düüreg)* of the capital.

PIGS. In Mongolia pig farming is not a traditional occupation but was developed when the general introduction of industrialized farming methods became fashionable in the 1970s-1980s. The pigs are mostly left to forage in the open steppe rather than kept in enclosures. The country had 134,700 pigs in 1990, when pig meat production was 5,000 tons; roughly one-third of the pigs were owned by *negdel* (q.v.), one-third were privately owned, and the remainder were kept by state farms (q.v.) and other state organizations. By 1993 the figure had fallen to 28,600, 86.7 percent privately owned.

POLE STAR, ORDER OF THE. This government decoration (Mongolian name *Altan Gadas*) instituted in 1936 is awarded to soldiers and civilians for outstanding services to the development of the country's defense, economy, culture, or health services. The badge of the order was redesigned in 1940 and 1970 to take account of changes in the state coat of arms.

POPULATION. Mongolia's population as of January 1, 1995, was estimated at 2,288,000. At the last two censuses (January 5, 1979 and 1989) the population was recorded as 1,594,800 and 2,043,400, respectively. In 1991, in the course of registration for the receipt of privatization vouchers, issued to all Mongolians, the population was recorded as 2,103,297.

The country, having a total area of 1,566,500 square kilometers, the average density of the population in 1993 was 1.4 persons per square kilometer. This figure is rather misleading, however, since nearly three-quarters of a million people live in the three main towns, Ulan Bator, Darhan, and Erdenet (qq.v.).

In 1993, 43.4 percent of the population were aged 0-16 years; 13.4 percent were pensioners; and 5.8 percent students of working age.

In 1992, there were 95,805 pregnancies, 63,384 births (66.2 percent), 28,103 abortions (29.3 percent), and 4,318 miscarriages (4.5 percent). The birthrate has fallen, from 41.2 births per 1,000 of the population in 1970-1974 to 28.9 per 1,000 in 1992. The rate of population growth has also fallen, from 2.9 percent in 1970-1974 to 2.1 percent in 1992, and the trend is expected to continue, to 1.9 percent in 1994-1999.

POULTRY. In Mongolia poultry farming is not a traditional occupation but was developed when the general introduction of industrialized farming methods became fashionable in the 1970s-1980s. Hens are mostly kept in batteries in industrial premises, but "free-range" ducks and geese were kept by some state farms (q.v.) in the northern river valleys. The country had 326,200 poultry in 1990, mostly on state farms in Töv and Selenge provinces (qq.v.), and only 12,700 were privately owned. Egg production fell from 34.8 million in 1990 to 16.8 million in 1992. By 1993 the number of poultry had fallen to 131,500, 14.3 percent privately owned.

PRESIDENCY. The Mongolian presidency was instituted in September 1990 on the election by the new Mongolian Great Hural of Punsalmaagiyn Ochirbat (q.v.), former chairman of the Presidium of the People's Great Hural (q.v.). His election was in accordance with amendments to the 1960 Constitution (q.v.) adopted in May 1990. Direct presidential elections were held for the first time in June 1993, following the adoption in January 1992 of the new fourth Constitution (q.v.). Ochirbat was reelected, for a four-year term. Presidential candidates are nominated by the political parties having seats in the MGH. The powers and duties of the president are defined in articles 30-37 of the 1992 Constitution (*see* Appendix 4). *See also* Heads of State.

PRIME MINISTERS. Mongolian prime ministers 1921- . Mongolia has had 15 prime ministers (1921-1932, 1990-1993) and premiers (chairmen of the Council of Ministers 1932-1990) since the formation of the provisional revolutionary government in March 1921 (for details see individual entries):
Shagdarjav (Chagdarjav), Dambyn, March 13 to April 16, 1921
Bodoo, Dosomyn, April 16, 1921 to January 7, 1922
Damdinbazar, Sodnomyn (Jalhanz Hutagt), March 3, 1922 to June 23, 1923
Tserendorj, Balingiyn, September 28, 1923 to February 13, 1928
Amar, Anandyn (Agdangiyn), February 21, 1928 to April 27, 1930
Jigjidjav, Tsengeltiyn, April 27, 1930 to July 2, 1932
Genden, Peljidiyn, July 2, 1932 to March 22, 1936
Amar, Anandyn (Agdangiyn), March 22, 1936 to March 7, 1939
Choybalsan, Horloogiyn, March 24, 1939 to January 26, 1952
Tsedenbal, Yumjaagiyn, May 27, 1952 to June 11, 1974
Batmönh, Jambyn, June 11, 1974 to December 12, 1984
Sodnom, Dumaagiyn, December 12, 1984 to March 21, 1990
Gungaadorj, Sharavyn, March 21 to September 10, 1990
Byambasüren, Dashiyn, September 10, 1990 to July 20, 1992
Jasray, Puntsagiyn, July 20, 1992 to date

PRIVATE FARMING. Generally small-scale livestock-raising and occasionally arable-farming by private individuals or families living in the countryside. In Mongolia's transition to a market economy the property of cooperative *(negdel)* and state farms (qq.v.) is being privatized. While communal livestock (q.v.) has been shared out among the former members of the *negdel* and individual herdsmen may now own over a thousand head, the distribution of immovable property and machinery has proved to be a difficult problem.

The number of families engaged in private livestock-raising rose from 74,700 in 1990 to 153,600 in 1993. The number of herdsmen increased from 147,500 to 347,900, and on average there are 72 head of livestock per herdsman. Some 16.5 percent of these families have electric light and 10.6 percent have a television set, while 51.6 percent have a radio receiver.

The growth of subsistence farming, the country's economic dislocation and shortage of consumer goods have been discouraging farmers from selling their produce and livestock for slaughter, and basic commodities like flour, meat, and milk have been in short supply in the towns. Lacking insurance cover, some herdsmen in western Mongolia lost all their animals in the severe blizzards and frosts of the winter/spring of 1993 and were faced with ruin. Townspeople may also own livestock or vegetable plots where suitable land is available.

PROMMONGOLSTROY. Mongolian-Soviet joint stock company for industrial construction established in 1936 to build Hatgal wool-washing factory and the industrial "combine" and No. 1 heat and power station in Ulan Bator (q.v.). The company was handed over to the Mongolian government in 1937, becoming the State Building Trust.

PROVINCES. The territory of Mongolia is currently divided into 21 provinces *(aymag)* and the capital, which, according to the 1992 Constitution (q.v.), are "self-governing territorial administrative socio-economic complexes." In English alphabetical order the provinces are (alternative forms in brackets, followed by provincial center):

Arhangay	Tsetserleg
Bayanhongor	Bayanhongor
Bayan-Ölgiy	Ölgiy
Bulgan	Bulgan
Darhan-Uul	Darhan
Dornod (Eastern)	Choybalsan
Dornogov' (East Gobi)	Saynshand
Dundgov' (Central Gobi)	Mandalgov'
Gov'-Altay (Gobi Altai)	Altay
Gov'-Sümber	Choyr
Hentiy	Öndörhaan
Hovd (Khobdo)	Hovd
Hövsgöl (Khubsugul)	Mörön
Orhon	Erdenet
Ömnögov' (South Gobi)	Dalanzadgad
Övörhangay	Arvayheer
Selenge	Sühbaatar
Sühbaatar	Baruun-Urt
Töv (Central)	Zuunmod
Uvs (Ubs Nur)	Ulaangom
Zavhan	Uliastay

For details about the provinces and provincial centers *see* individual entries. The provinces are divided into rural districts, or *sum* (q.v.); for a full list of rural districts, *see* Administrative Gazetteer, Appendix 6.

During the Manchu (q.v.) period the territory of Outer Mongolia (q.v.) consisted in the main of four *aymag* named after their ruling princes: Sayn-Noyon-Han, Setsen-Han (Tsetsen-Han), Tüsheet-Han, and Zasagt-Han (qq.v.). In the postrevolutionary period some boundaries were changed and new names adopted: Bogd-Han-Uul, Chandman'-Uul, Han-Hentey-Uul, Han-Tayshir-Uul, and Tsetserleg-Mandal (qq.v.) *aymag*.

PURGES OF THE 1930S AND 1940S. In this period, at least 35,000 Mongols fell victim to the plots, conspiracies, and false charges contrived by Horloogiyn Choybalsan (q.v.), the Mongolian Ministry of the Interior, and the "Special Commission" to fight espionage and counterrevolution. The "Special Commission" alone dealt with 25,824 cases between September 1937 and April 1939, sentencing 20,474 of the accused to be shot, 5,103 to ten years' imprisonment, 240 to periods of up to ten years, and declaring seven innocent. Between 1939 and 1990, 4,000 cases were reviewed and the victims exonerated. In 1990-1993, the new atmosphere of democracy and justice greatly accelerated rehabilitations and 22,867 more people were rehabilitated: 16,961 lamas, 27 government officials, 417 army officers and men, and 5,241 herdsmen and workers.

It was estimated that from 1934-1939, altogether 155 Mongols were arrested for counterrevolutionary activities in Mongolia but tried and sentenced in Russia. Of the 155, it is known that 30 were shot, 108 received long terms of imprisonment, 13 were released, and 4 died "under investigation." Of the 108 who were imprisoned, 30 died in Komi, Perm', and other parts of the Gulag archipelago, 4 returned to Mongolia in 1955, 29 were released on the completion of their sentences, and 2 died in the USSR in 1980; there is no information about the remaining 43. Between 1956-1963, 41 of the 155 were rehabilitated in Mongolia. In September 1993 the Russian authorites released to Mongolia the names of 32 Mongols tried and sentenced in the USSR and the official total then rose from 155 to 194, although the discrepancy has not been explained. It has emerged that the total includes Buryats like Elbegdorj and Jamsrano (qq.v.), who were arrested in the USSR several years after working in Mongolia. Other victims of the purges who died in Russia, including Prime Ministers Amar and Genden (qq.v.), whose names and details were passed to Mongolia by the Russian authorities in 1993, are also listed in individual entries.

PÜREV, BAASTYN (1942-). Mongolian police chief since 1990. Born in Tonhil district of Gov'-Altay Province (q.v.), Pürev attended the Trade Vocational School in Ulan Bator (q.v.) and first worked as an accountant in the State Department Store. After graduating from the institute of the Soviet Ministry of Internal Affairs, he worked for two years in the Mongolian Ministry of Public Security at the Chief Directorate of the Militia (Police) in Ulan Bator. He then moved for a further two years to the MPRP Central Committee (qq.v.) as an instructor and organizer. He was awarded a higher degree of Candidate of Sciences after studying at the CPSU Central Committee's Academy of Social Sciences. In January 1981 he was appointed head of the organization department of the Council of Ministers. He was elected chairman of Gov'-Altay Executive Administration (qq.v.) in July 1989. Following the disbanding of the Ministry of Public Security in April 1990, Pürev was appointed head (with the rank of major general) of the Chief Directorate of Police, placed directly under government control, and his appointment confirmed by the new government in October 1990.

PÜREVDORJ, CHOYJILSÜRENGIYN (1948-). Deputy prime minister since 1992. Born on July 20, 1948 in Mörön district, Arhangay Province (q.v.), Pürevdorj graduated in 1970 from the Urals Higher Polytechnic, Sverdlovsk, with a degree in electrical engineering. He first worked as an engineer and deputy director of Ulan Bator (q.v.) No. 3 heat and power station from 1970-1980, then as chief engineer of the central power distribution system from1980-1983. He was appointed deputy minister of fuel and power from 1983-1987 and deputy minister of power, mining and geology from 1987-1990. Following the collapse of communist power he was deputy minister of heavy industry (for the last two weeks of April) before being appointed deputy chairman of the Council of Ministers from May-September 1990. In the first freely elected government, he was deputy prime minister for industry from October 1990-August 1992; his responsibilities included the development of heavy and light industry, construction, transport and communications, science, nuclear power, the environment, and prisons. He was elected a member of the MPRP Central Committee (q.q.v.) and member of the MPRP Presidium in 1991 and 1992. Pürevdorj was elected a member of the Mongolian Great Hural (q.v.) for the MPRP for a four-year term on June 28, 1992 in constituency 1 (Arhangay). He was reappointed deputy prime minister on August 3, 1992 by the first session of the Mongolian Great Hural. He is a member of three MGH standing committees: envir-onmental protection, economic policy, and education, science, and culture.

PÜREVDORJ, ZUNDUYN (1900-1941). Minister of livestock and cultivation. One of the 32 victims of the Mongolian purges of the 1930s and 1940s (q.v.) sent to the USSR for trial and sentence, details of which were released by the Russian government in 1993. Sentenced to death by the Military Collegium of the USSR Supreme Court in Moscow on July 5, 1941 and executed on July 27.

- Q -

QING (CH'ING). The dynastic title ("pure") adopted by the Manchu (q.v.) emperors of China. The Qing dynasty is usually dated from the death of the Ming emperor in 1644, although the dynasty's foundation was proclaimed by Abakhay Khan in 1636, and his successor came to the Manchu throne in 1643. The last Qing emperor, Pu Yi, abdicated on February 12, 1912 (not counting a 12-day restoration), although the Republic of China was proclaimed by Sun Yat-sen on January 1, 1912. For the Qing emperors and their reign titles, *see* the Chronology.

- R -

RADNAARAGCHAA, DANZANGIYN (1940-). Mongolian politician. Born in Ih-Uul district of Zavhan Province (q.v.), Radnaaragchaa was educated at Ulan Bator (q.v.) Finance and Economics School and the Higher School of Economics. After working for the Mongolian Revolutionary Youth League (q.v.) he became deputy chairman of the State Committee for Information, Radio and Television from 1978-1983. He was next appointed chairman of the Zavhan Province Executive Administration (q.v.) but in 1987 moved to the Ministry of Agriculture. He was one of two first deputy ministers of agriculture and food industry in April 1990 when the minister, Sharavyn Gungaadorj (q.v.), was appointed chairman of the Council of Ministers and the ministry was recognized; Radnaaragchaa was then appointed minister of agriculture and light and food industries. He is a member of the MPRP (q.v.). In September 1990 he was reappointed with the title of minister of agriculture, serving in the government of Dashiyn Byambasüren (q.v.) until the elections of 1992. He was not reappointed again, and when Puntsagiyn Jasray (q.v.) became prime minister, Radnaaragchaa replaced him in the post of president of the Supreme Council of the Association of Production and Services Cooperatives.

RAILWAYS. Mongolia's railways, which are of the Russian broad (1,520 mm) gauge, are run by the Ulan Bator Railway Co. and have a total route length (1993) of 1,807 km. The main trans-Mongolian line

(1,110 km) runs from Sühbaatar (q.v.) (Naushki) on the Russian border (link with the Trans-Siberian and the sea ports of the Russian Far East) through Ulan Bator to Zamyn-Üüd (q.v.) (Ehrlien, Ereen) on the Chinese border (transit route to Peking and the sea port of Tianjin). There are branches to Sharyn Gol (63 km), Erdenet (164 km), Baganuur (qq.v.) (85 km), Bor-Öndör (60 km), and Züünbayan (63 km). At Ereen (Erenhot) station in Inner Mongolia (q.v.), the interface between the broad gauge and China's standard (1,435 mm) gauge, there are transshipping facilities and rolling stock lifting equipment for changing the bogies. The eastern railway in Dornod Province runs from Chuluunhoroot/Ereentsav (Borzya) on the Russian border to Choybalsan (238 km), with a branch line to Marday (qq.v.) (110 km). A narrow-gauge line built during the Second World War from Choybalsan to Tamsagbulag is no longer in use.

In 1990 rail freight traffic amounted to 5,088 million ton/kilometers (of which 1,086 million was transit freight) and passenger traffic to 524.1 million passenger/kilometers, carrying 14.5 million tons of freight and 2.6 million passengers. In 1991-1992 rail freight transport fell to 10.3 and 8.6 million metric tons because of shortages of diesel due to difficulties in foreign trade (q.v.). In 1993 rail freight traffic amounted to 2,531 million ton/kilometers and passenger traffic to 582.5 million passenger/kilometers. The Directorate of Railways was placed under the control of the Ministry of Infrastructure Development in the reorganization of the government from 1993-1994 (q.v.).

RAYON. Former name for the urban districts of Ulan Bator (q.v.). The word is derived from the Russian *rayon,* meaning also a rural district, the subdivision of an *oblast'*.

RIGHT OPPORTUNISM. Name given in MPRP (q.v.) histories to the line of the MPRP leadership during the period from 1924-1928. The source of Right Opportunism was said to be petit bourgeois nationalism, including attempts to equate communist and religious doctrine. The Rightists advanced the policy of "Get rich!" and encouraged capitalism, and allegedly sought to undermine relations with the USSR, weaken the anti-feudalist struggle, and oppose the Comintern (q.v.). Right Opportunism was attacked by Badrah (q.v.) at the seventh MPRP Congress (October-December 1928), and Dambadorj (q.v.) and other leaders were expelled. Soon after, at the fifth Great Hural (December 1928-January 1929), Choybalsan was elected chairman of the Little Hural (qq.v.). Right Opportunism was followed by Left Deviation (q.v.).

RINCHINDORJ, NAMSRAYN (1948-   ). Mongolian politician. Born in Aldarhaan district of Zavhan Province (q.v.), Rinchindorj graduated from Irkutsk (q.v.) State University in 1973 with a degree in law. On his return to Mongolia he began work at the Institute for the Study of Crime under the State Procurator's Office. In 1976 he was engaged as an expert at the Council of Ministers. From 1990 he was employed as a government desk officer. In August 1992 he was appointed secretary-general of the Mongolian Great Hural (q.v.).

ROADS. Mongolia is estimated to have over 49,000 km of "roads," but only 1,300 km of this total are properly surfaced with concrete or asphalt. Hardtop roads run from Ulan Bator north to the Russian border, west to Erdenet (qq.v.), and to a few other nearby locations, but they are otherwise confined to the central areas of large towns. On main interprovincial roads, the rivers have been bridged and the surface has been graded and rolled, but elsewhere lorries, buses, and cars follow severely rutted cross-country routes to local destinations. The main border-crossing points by road are at Kyakhta/Altanbulag (qq.v.) and Mangut/Onon (Ölziy) for Russia and Zamyn-Üüd/Ehrlien (Ereen) for China. The roads into Mongolia from the Altay Republic (Kosh-Agach to Tashanta and Tsagaannuur), from the Tuva Republic (Kyzyl to Khandagayty and Ulaangom), and from Irkutsk and the Buryat Republic (qq.v.) (Mondy to Hanh on Lake Hövsgöl) follow traditional routes and are important lines of supply of petrol and other imports to remoter parts of the country. In 1990 road freight traffic amounted to 1,772 million ton/kilometers and passenger traffic to 915 million passenger/kilometers. Road transport in 1991-1992 was sharply reduced by shortages of petrol due to difficulties in foreign trade (q.v.). In 1993 road freight traffic amounted to 268.4 million ton/kilometers and passenger traffic to 700.5 million passenger/kilometers.

RUSSIA. Mongolian border with Russia. The border with Russia extends for 3,485 km from Height 4104.0 north of the Tavan Bogd in the west to Height 646.7 at Tarvagan Dah (qq.v.) in the east, as does the southern border with China (q.v.). Some 677 km of the border is water, 41 rivers flowing into Mongolia and 15 flowing out. The border with Russia is divided for administrative purposes on the Mongolian side into the Uvs section from the Tavan Bogd to Asgatyn Davaa (junction of Zavhan and Hövsgöl Provinces with the Tuva Republic qq.v.), the Selenge section from Asgatyn Davaa to Minj (marker 988 at the junction of Selenge and Hentiy Provinces with the Buryat Republic, qq.v.), and the Eastern section from Minj to Tarvagan Dah. On the Russian side it is divided into the Kyzyl (q.v.) section from the Tavan Bogd to the Ih Sayaany Nuruu or Sayan Mountains (marker 332 at the junction of the Tuva and Buryat Republics with Hövsgöl Province at Mongol Sharyn Davaa (qq.v.), the Kyakhta (q.v.) section from the Ih Sayaany Nuruu to Yolt (marker 1019 on Chita Region's border with Hentiy Province), and the Mangut section from Yolt to Tarvagan Dah. Joint demarcation of the sector from Asgatyn Davaa to marker 332 was completed in 1959-1960, and of the remainder in 1977-1979. For crossing points, *see* the Mongolian provinces Bayan-Ölgiy, Uvs, Zavhan, Hövsgöl, Bulgan, Selenge, Hentiy, and Dornod.

RUSSIA: MONGOL ETHNIC GROUPS. The Buryats (Buriad, q.v.) were conquered by Jochi, Genghis Khan's (q.v.) son, in 1207 and colonized by the Russians from the seventeenth century. The Buryats in the USSR now number around 453,000. They live mostly in the Buryat Republic and the districts centered on Aginskoye and Ust'-Ordynskiy in Irkutsk (qq.v.) and Chita Regions. The main groups are the Bulagat, Ekhirit, and Khoriburyat or Khorintsy. The Bulagat settled on the river Lena and its tributaries; their name, perhaps meaning "sable hunters," is a variant of Buryat. The Ekhirit settled on the river Barguzin and tributaries; their name may mean "squirrel hunters." The Khorintsy (their Russian name) were mostly from the east bank of Lake Baikal and nomadized into Mongolia proper in the middle of the seventeenth century, returning to the Nerchinsk area some 25 years later, and finally settled in the Aginskiye steppes in the eighteenth century. Some Buryats are Buryatized Tungus or Tuvan (q.v.) people. The Buryats were basically shamanist rather than Buddhist, but were later brought by Russian influence to Orthodox Christianity, especially those dwelling west of Lake Baikal.

Some Jungar (Züüngar) or Oirat (Oyrd, q.v.) Mongols settled in Buryat territory in the fifteenth century. More settled in Nizhneudinsk and Zungarbukhotskiy districts in the seventeenth to eighteenth centuries, after the collapse of the Jungarian state.

The Kalmyks are Jungarian (Oyrd, q.v.) Mongols originally from western Mongolia, some 300,000 of whom settled in Russia in the seventeenth century, although 125,000 of them returned to Jungaria in 1771. They now live mostly in the Hal'mg Tangch or Kalmyk Republic (q.v.), the former "Autonomous Soviet Socialist Republic," southwest of the Volga in the Caspian steppes, and number about 200,000. After Stalin's abolition of the Kalmyk ASSR in December 1943 for alleged wartime collaboration with the Germans, they were settled in Rostov, Astrakhan', and Volgograd regions and parts of Siberia and Central Asia. Their republic was restored in 1957, but as a result of the scattering of the population, only about 10 percent still speak their mother tongue.

There are about 3,000 Halh (q.v.) (Khalkha) Mongols in Russia.

The so-called Oirot people of the Altay Republic (qq.v.) are Turkicized Mongol Oyrd. Their language is now Turkic, but the vocabulary of livestock herding, for example, and the life-style of the herdsmen are basically Mongol. Their territory was called the Autonomous Oirat *Oblast'* from 1922, and renamed the Gornyy Altay (part of the Altayskiy Kray) in 1948. The Soviet name of the people, Altaytsy, is derived from this.

The Tuvans (Urianhay) of the Republic of Tuva (qq.v.) (Tyva, former Tuvan ASSR) are Mongolized Turks numbering some 207,000. The total number of Mongols in the USSR in 1989 was 805,000.

RUSSIA. Residents in Mongolia. There were around 2,000 ethnic Russian citizens of Mongolia at the end of 1992. Most had lived in Mongolia for several generations and were engaged in farming or other skilled trades. Russians began settling in Mongolia in the second half of the nineteenth century, and there was an influx of traders during the period of autonomy. In Urga (q.v.) they organized local government and services for themselves. The number of Russians in Mongolia rose from 1,772 in 1926 to 2,969 in 1927. According to census figures, Russians comprised 1.6 percent of the population (13,400) in 1956, 0.9 percent (8,900) in 1963, and 1.8 percent (22,100) in 1969, but their citizenship was unclear. The number of Russian citizens of Mongolia does not include the 100,000 or so men of the Soviet Army stationed in Mongolia in the 1970s-1980s, or the 50,000 or so economic and technical experts sent to work in Mongolia by the Soviet Union. By the end of 1992 all the Soviet Army units had been withdrawn and most of the civilian experts had left because of Mongolia's inability to pay them. The remainder are employed in Ulan Bator, Darhan, Erdenet, and Marday (qq.v.). At the beginning of August 1993, altogether 4,561 Russian citizens were working in Mongolia, mainly in trading firms.

- S -

SAMBUU, JAMSRANGIYN (1895-1972). Politician and statesman. Born into a herdsman's family in Delgerhangay-Uul Hoshuu of Bogd-Han-Uul Aymag, the present-day Büren district of Töv Province (q.v.), on June 27, 1895, Sambuu learned to read and write and was employed in the *hoshuu* (q.v.) secretariat. In the period from 1922-1937, Sambuu joined the MPRP (q.v.), worked in the Ministry of Finance where he was aide to the minister, became chairman of the administration of Bogd-Han-Uul and later Omnögov' provinces (qq.v.), and then head of a department in the Ministry of Livestock and Cultivation from 1936-1938. In 1938, he was appointed ambassador (minister plenipotentiary) to the Soviet Union. Returning to Mongolia in 1946, he headed a department in the Ministry of Foreign Affairs from

1946-1949 and was appointed deputy foreign minister from 1949-1951. From 1951-1953 he served in Pyongyang as ambassador and from 1953-1954 he was deputy chairman of the Society for Cultural Relations with the USSR (Mongolian-Soviet Friendship Society). He was first elected a deputy of the People's Great Hural (q.v.) in 1951 and appointed chairman of its Presidium (head of state) on July 7, 1954. Later the same year, he was elected to the MPRP Central Committee (qq.v.) and Politburo, remaining a member until his death. He was the author of several books including *Advice to Herdsmen on Livestock Care* and *On the Question of Religion and Lamas*. His awards included the Order of Sühbaatar (q.v.) (four times), the Order of the Red Banner of Labor (twice), and the Order of the Pole Star (q.v.), as well as the Soviet Orders of Lenin, the October Revolution, the Red Star, and the Red Banner of Labor. He also won a Lenin Peace Price in 1966. He died in office of cancer on May 21, 1972, and was given a state funeral on May 24.

SANDALHAN, RAZDAKIYN (1943-   ). Minister of infrastructure development since 1994. Born on November 19, 1943 in Tsengel district of Bayan-Ölgiy Province (q.v.), Sandalhan, a Kazakh (q.v.), graduated in 1967 from Irkutsk (q.v.) Polytechnic with a degree in motor vehicle engineering. He first worked as a foreman and engineer at Ulan Bator City No. 5 transport depot, and chief engineer at Nalayh (q.v.) No. 14 transport depot from 1967-1972, then director of Nalayh No. 14 depot from 1972-1979. He returned to Ulan Bator (q.v.) in 1979 to be director of the capital's motor vehicle repair and technical servicing station until 1982, on appointment as director of the motor transport combine. He was also director of the interurban motor transport directorate from 1987-1989, and a specialist and department head at the Ministry of Roads and Transport from 1989-1990. After briefly serving once again as motor transport combine director in 1990, he was appointed deputy director then chief deputy director of the Roads and Transport Directorate from October 1990-August 1992. Sandalhan, who is not a member of the Mongolian Great Hural (q.v.), was appointed minister of roads, transport, and communications on August 4, 1992, by the first session of the MGH. In a reshuffle in January 1994, Sandalhan's ministry was amalgamated with the Ministry of Construction and Town Planning to form the Ministry of Infrastructure Development, and Sandalhan was appointed minister.

SAYN-NOYON-HAN. Former province (*aymag*) in central-western Mongolia. One of four large provinces (named after their Mongol princes) during the period of Qing (Manchu) (qq.v.) rule, center Sayn Noyony Hüree (later Arvayheer, q.v.). The province was abolished in 1923, when the territory was renamed Tsetserleg-Mandal (q.v.) Province.

SAYNSHAND. Center of Dornogov' Province (q.v.). Previously known as Dalaysaynshand, it was accorded town status in 1961. Its height above sea level is 938 m, the average January and July temperatures are − 18.4 and 23.2 deg C, respectively, and the average annual precipitation is 116.1 mm. The population is about 15,000. There is a station on the Trans-Mongolian Railway and a branch line to Züün-Bayan, site of an oil field and refinery in the 1950s. The local industries include railway rolling stock repairs and foodstuffs production.

SCRIPT, CLASSICAL. According to tradition, the vertical Mongolian alphabetical script was derived from the Uighur script and introduced among the Mongols in the time of Genghis Khan (q.v.) by the captive Uighur scribe Tatatunga. The 24 letters of the classical alphabet, which begins with the vowels, have initial, medial, and final forms. This script, reflecting the grammar and pronunciation of the medieval period, continued in official use in Mongolia until the introduction of the Latin and then Cyrillic scripts (qq.v.). For the following 50 years or so, the use of classical Mongolian was neglected and almost all publications were in the Cyrillic alphabet, although study of the classical language was allowed once again in universities in the 1980s. In the nationalist fervor of the democratic revolution of 1990 and immediate post-communist period, it was decided that classical Mongolian would be reintroduced nationwide, and its teaching began in schools. Preparations were made to publish government business in classical Mongolian from 1994, and a government commission was set up for this purpose. The transition is being promoted by the Mongolian Script Society. Classical Mongolian in the vertical script has remained in general use among the Mongols of China (*see* China: Mongol Ethnic Groups).

SCRIPT, CLEAR. The modified Mongolian classical script (q.v.) called *tod bichig* devised in 1648 by the Zayapandita (Zaya Bandid) Luvsanperenlei of the Oirat (Oyrd, q.v.) and that became widespread among the western Mongols. It was used by the Kalmyks (q.v.) of Russia until 1927, when a Cyrillic script (q.v.) was introduced.

SCRIPT, CYRILLIC. The Russian Cyrillic alphabet (with two extra letters to represent the sounds ö and ü) whose adoption in the MPR was decreed in March 1941 but that came into general use only after the Second World War. It displaced a modified Latin script (q.v.) popularized in Mongolia in the 1930s. Introduction of the Cyrillic alphabet in Mongolia was evidently justified on political grounds, following its general application to minority languages in the USSR. Initially, long vowels were represented by a single barred letter (e.g., ō), later they came to be doubled (oo). Despite its complicated orthographic rules, the Cyrillic script proved to be a better medium for modern spoken Mongolian or Halh (q.v.) (Khalkha) than the classical Mongolian script (q.v.) it displaced. Since the birth of democracy in Mongolia in the 1990s allowed freedom of expression of nationalist feeling, there has been a strong movement for a return to official use of classical Mongolian. Despite its link with the imposition of Soviet Russian policies in Mongolia, however, the Cyrillic alphabet is still widely used and supported.

The Cyrillic scripts used officially for Buryat and Kalmyk (qq.v.) in the Russian Federation since the abandonment of the Latin alphabet in 1938 differ from one another and from the Mongolian version (as does the Cyrillic transcription used by Poppe in his Mongolian grammar in Russian). Kalmyk also used a slightly different Cyrillic alphabet from 1927-1930. The Cyrillic script was also introduced briefly in Inner Mongolia (q.v.) in the 1950s.

SCRIPT, LATIN. Use of the Latin alphabet (with six extra letters—č, ĕ, î, and š, plus specially designed letters for ö and ü) was decreed in July 1940. This followed several years of experimental use in Mongolia in accordance with a resolution of the sixth Great Hural (April 1930) and the decision on script reform of the First Cultural Conference of Mongol Peoples, held in Moscow in January 1931 and attended by Halh Mongol, Buryat, and Kalmyk (qq.v.) representatives. The decree was rescinded almost immediately in favor of a modified Cyrillic script (q.v.). In the post-communist period in Mongolia, supporters of this modified Latin alphabet have been encouraging its adoption once again, citing the worldwide use of English, especially as the language of computers. Meanwhile, computer applications have generated a number of new but unofficial schemes for the compatible transliteration of both classical Mongolian and the Cyrillic script into the Latin alphabet. In Russia, Buryat was written in a modified Latin alphabet from 1929-1938 and Kalmyk from 1930-1938.

SCRIPT, RUNIC. The Old Turkic alphabet of several sixth- to eighth-century inscriptions found in Mongolia, similar in appearance but unrelated to Scandinavian runes. The Turkish state occupied much of the territory of present-day Mongolia and was succeeded by Uighur and Kighiz states before the coming of the Mongols. The runes were discovered at Höshöö Tsaydam in the valley of the river Orhon (q.v.) on a Turkic stele, which also had an inscription in Chinese. It said that it had been set up in honor of the Turkish Khan Bilge-Mogilyan (684-734) and general Kul-Tegin (685-731). Another Turkic stele honoring the chief Tonyukuk was found at Nalayh, south-east of Ulan Bator (qq.v.). The deciphering of the script was completed in 1895 by the Danish scientist V.L.P. Thomsen and V. V. Radlov (W. Radloff) of the Russian Academy, and it became known as the Orhon runic script. A similar stele from Tariat marks in verse the coronation of Khan Toryan and the building of his palace on the river Tes.

SELENGE. Province (*aymag*) in northern Mongolia. Formed in 1931 as Gazartarialan ("agricultural") Province, the province was abolished in 1956 and its territory shared between Bulgan and Töv provinces (qq.v.), then reinstated in 1959. Named after the river Selenge (q.v.), it is situated on the border with Russia (Dzhida and Kyakhta districts of the Buryat Republic, q.v., and Krasnyy Chikoy district of Chita region). With a territory of 42,800 sq km and population of 91,189 (1991), it has 16 rural districts (*sum*); until 1992 there were three wards (*horoo*), Dulaanhaan, Tünhel, and Yöröö; the provincial center is Sühbatar (q.v.). The local minorities include the Buryad (q.v.). The border with Russia is crossed by the Trans-Mongolian Railway at Sühbaatar (Naushki) for Ulan-Ude and the Trans-Siberian Railway, and by a motor road at nearby Altanbulag (Kyakhta) (qq.v.); branch lines link the Trans-Mongolian Railway with Sharyn Gol lignite mine and Erdenet copper mine (Bulgan Province) (qq.v.). The designated permanent crossing points on the border with Russia are Zelter (for Zheltura), Hongor Ovoo (for Botsiy), Sühbaatar (for Naushki), Altanbulag (for Kyakhta), Hutag-Öndör (for Kiran), and Hüder (for Tsagaanchuluutay), and seasonal crossing points Tsagaan Aral (for Naushki), Uyalga Gol (for Altay), and Urjin (for Zhindo). There are deposits of gold (q.v.) (Bugant, Tolgoyt, Yöröö Gol, Sharyn Gol, and Boroo), iron ore (Bayan Gol, Hüder Gol, Yöröö, and Örmögtey), coal (Bayangol, Hangay, and Ulaan-Ovoo) and wolfram (Salaa). The largest towns are Darhan (q.v.), Hötöl (cement), and Züünharaa (timber). Local industry includes a building combine (Dulaanhaan), woodworking (Yöröö and Tünhel), leather goods (Altanbulag), foodstuffs (Altanbulag), and animal feed (Shaamar and Salhit). Livestock numbers reached 459,300 head (1992) and arable land 195,900 hectares (1989).

SELENGE. River in Mongolia. The Selenge *mörön*, one of the country's five longest rivers, 593 km within Mongolia, is navigable as far upstream as Selenge river port in Bulgan Province (q.v.). Fed by the river systems of the Ider, rising in the Hangay Mountains (q.v.), the Delgermörön, rising west of Lake Hövsgöl (q.v.), and the lake's only outlet, the Eg (q.v.), the Selenge flows northeast through southern Hövsgöl and northern Bulgan provinces; it crosses the border between Selenge Province and Russia's Buryat Republic near the town of Sühbaatar (qq.v.) and enters Lake Baikal, which is linked via the rivers Angara and Yenisey with the Arctic Ocean.

SETSEN-HAN. Mongolian prince, and former province named after him. A variant spelling from transcription of the old Mongolian script form of the name Tsetsen-Han (q.v.).

SHAALUU, OONOYGIYN (1950-   ). Mongolian politician. Shaaluu trained as a radio engineer. He was chairman of Uvs (q.v.) MPRP Committee from October 1991-July 1992 and became a member of the MPRP Central Committee (qq.v.) in 1992. He was elected a member of the Mongolian Great Hural (q.v.) for the MPRP for a four-year term on June 28, 1992, in constituency 15 (Uvs). He is a member of two MGH standing committees: assemblies and administration, and economic policy.

SHAGDARJAV, DAMDINSURENGIYN (1902-1941). Minister of trade. Born in 1902 in the present-day Choybalsan district of Dornod Province (q.v.), Shagdarjav joined the MPRP in 1925 and eventually became a member of the Presidium of the MPRP Central Committee (qq.v.) and Minister of Trade and Transport. He was arrested in July 1939 together with Losol (q.v.) by the Ministry of Internal Affairs, sentenced to death in Moscow by the Military Collegium of the USSR Supreme Court on July 5, 1941, and executed on July 27. He was one of the 32 victims of the Mongolian purges of the 1930s and 1940s (q.v.) sent to the USSR for trial and sentence, details of which were released by the Russian government in 1993.

SHARAVDORJ, TSERENHÜÜGIYN (1954-   ). Mongolian politician. Sharavdorj trained as a lawyer at Irkutsk (q.v.) State University. After working as deputy chairman of Selenge Provincial Court and chairman of Dornod Provincial Court, he became a member and then deputy chairman of the Supreme Court. He was elected a member of the Mongolian Great Hural (q.v.) for the MPRP (q.v.) for a four-year term on June 28, 1992, in constituency 6 (Dornogov'). He is a member of two MGH standing committees: foreign policy and security, and legal affairs. In November 1993, Sharavdorj was elected a member of the MPRP's Party Leadership Council (q.v.).

SHARAVSAMBUU, BADRAHYN (1947-   ). Deputy chairman of the Council of Ministers 1990. Born in Ider district of Zavhan Province (q.v.), Sharavsambuu trained as a trade accountant at Ulan Bator Trade Technical School in the 1960s and graduated from Irkutsk State Higher School of the National Economy with a degree in economics in 1975. After graduation, he worked at the Ministry of Trade and Procurement as a senior expert and head of the internal trade directorate, and subsequently was promoted to the rank of deputy minister in 1979 and minister in 1984. In 1990 he served as deputy chairman of the Council of Ministers in the short-lived government of Sharavyn Gungaadorj (q.v.). He took up the post of first secretary (economics) in the Mongolian embassy in Moscow from 1991-1994. Sharavsambuu, who received a doctorate in market consumer studies in 1992, was appointed head of the Chief Directorate of Customs, replacing Gonchigiyn Seseer, in July 1994.

SHARYN GOL. Town in Selenge Province (q.v.). Founded in the 1960s, this town serving the Sharyn Gol opencast lignite mines was initially subordinated administratively to Darhan (q.v.). The town is the terminus of a branch line of the Trans-Mongolian Railway.

SHAV'. A vassal (literally, a novice or disciple) of a monastery estate. They were free of corvée (*alba,* q.v.) and liability to do military service but were taxed by the Lamaist Church. There were perhaps 89,000 of them in 1921. The Ih (Great) Shav', also called Bogdyn Shav', were the estates ruled by the Bogd Gegeen (q.v.), especially those in the area of Lake Hövsgöl (q.v.).

SHEEP. In Mongolia sheep are raised for their wool and meat and mutton is the staple food, while the milk is made into curds and cheese. Sheep, mainly of the Mongolian fat-tail variety, are concentrated in the central and western provinces: Zavhan and Övörhangay (qq.v.) have the greatest numbers—1,257,031 and 1,170,800, respectively (1993). There were altogether some 14.6 million sheep in Mongolia at the end of 1992 and 13,779,193 in 1993. Selection and crossbreeding have developed domestic semifine-fleece varieties like the Orhon; astrakhan (karakul) lambs are raised in the Gobi (Gov', q.v.) regions. The country produces some 19,000-20,000 tons of sheep's wool a year (1988-1990) with an average shear of 1.5 kg per head (1990); live weight on procurement is 39 kg (1990). Some 4 million sheepskins are procured each year (1988-1990), production of sheepskin coats averaging 100,000 a year (1990-1992). The Mongolian wild sheep (*argal'*, q.v.) is hunted in the Gobi-Altai Mountains (q.v.).

SHIJEE, ZOLBINGIYN (1901-1941). Mongolian party leader from 1930-1932. Born in the present-day Tsagaannuur district of Selenge

Province (q.v.), Shijee was a partisan in the 1921 revolution. After the revolution he became a prison director, joined the Mongolian People's Party (q.v.) in 1923, then worked for the MPRP Central Committee (qq.v.) before studying at the Communist University of Toilers of the East in the USSR. In 1928 he was elected secretary of the Central Council of the Mongolian Trade Unions, but in 1928-1929 he was appointed head of the Internal Security Directorate, then chairman of the Board of the State Bank from 1929-1930. He was elected member of the Presidium and secretary of the MPRP Central Committee from March 13, 1930 to June 30, 1932, when he was expelled for Left Deviation (q.v.) and apparently exiled in Moscow. In 1937 he was arrested on charges of counterrevolution. He was sentenced to death by the Military Collegium of the USSR Supreme Court in Moscow on July 9, 1941 and was executed on July 27. He was rehabilitated in 1963.

SHIRENDEV, BAZARYN (1912-   ). Mongolian historian and politician. Born on May 14, 1912 in Shine-Ider district, Hövsgöl Province (q.v.), Shirendev was sent to Nüht monastery school but ran away several times and eventually was given a place in the first secular school in the province. He continued his studies for two years at Tsetserleg agricultural school. Shirendev began his working life as manager of Chuluut district commune in 1930-1931, but in 1932 he was sent to the Mongolian Workers' Faculty in Ulan-Ude (Buryat Republic) (qq.v.). He then studied at the Lunacharskiy Institute in Moscow and the history faculty of the Teacher Training Institute in Irkutsk (q.v.). On return to Mongolia at the beginning of the Second World War, Shirendev was appointed an assistant to Marshal Horloogiyn Choybalsan (q.v.) and given tasks in the Gobi (Gov', q.v.) areas, but in 1943 he was sent to Moscow to study the CPSU's wartime work.

Shirendev was appointed rector of the Mongolian State University from 1944-1951, minister of education from 1951 to 1953, then first deputy chairman of the Council of Ministers from 1954-1957. He was also chairman of the Mongolian Peace Committee from 1950-1957. Shirendev was a deputy of the People's Great Hural (q.v.) and was elected deputy chairman (speaker) in 1966 and from 1981-1986 and later; he was elected a member of the MPRP Central Committee (qq.v.) at several congresses, and member of the Politburo and secretary of the Central Committee from 1954-1958.

Shirendev obtained the degree of Doctor of History at the Institute of Oriental Studies in Moscow. He was elected a member of the Academy of Sciences (q.v.) in 1961, then president of the Academy from 1961-1982, also chairman of the Permanent Committee of the International Congress of Mongolists from 1970-1982. He wrote several works expressing the official view of Mongolian history, including *Mongolia on the Boundary of the 19th and 20th Centuries, History of the Mongolian People's Revolution,* and *Bypassing Capitalism.* Shirendev received the degree of Dr. Litt. *honoris causa* from the University of Leeds, England, in May 1970 and the Mongolian Order of Sühbaatar (q.v.) on his sixtieth birthday in 1972.

Although he had been described officially as a "renowned scientist and brilliant and talented organizer and administrator," in January 1982 he was ousted from the presidency of the Academy on the instructions of Yumjaagiyn Tsedenbal (q.v.) for his alleged "lack of principle and party spirit." After Tsedenbal's fall from power in 1984, Shirendev resumed his literary activity and was able to return to work in the Academy of Sciences, not as president but as a counselor at the Institute of Oriental Studies.

SHIRNENDAMDIN BEISE (DA LAM). Deputy minister of justice who replaced Da Lam Dashjav (q.v.) as leader of the Mongolian delegation at the Mongolian-Russian-Chinese treaty conference in Kyakhta (q.v.) in 1915; he signed the treaty with Tüsheet Van Chagdarjav (q.v.). He accompanied the Jalhanz Hutagt Damdinbazar (q.v.) to the January 1921 meeting with Baron von Ungern-Sternberg (q.v.) to discuss the formation of a new government. In November 1921 Shirnendamdin was a member of Danzan's (q.v.) delegation, which met Lenin and signed the Mongolian-Soviet treaty of friendship.

SODNOM, DUMAAGIYN (1933-   ). Chairman of the Council of Ministers from 1984-1990. Born in Örgön district of Dornogov' Province (q.v.) on July 14, 1933, Sodnom attended school in Bayanmönh district, then went to the Finance and Economic Technical College in Ulan Bator (q.v.) from 1946-1950. After working as an accountant at the Ministry of Finance from 1950-1954, he studied at Irkutsk (q.v.) Higher School of Finance and Economics, graduating in economics. On his return to Mongolia he worked as an economist at the Ministry of Finance from 1958-1959, head of a department from 1959-1963 and minister of finance from 1963-1969. He then served as first deputy chairman of the State Planning Commission with the rank of minister from 1969-1972. Having been appointed chairman of the State Planning Commission in 1972, he was appointed concurrently deputy chairman of the Council of Ministers in 1974. When Jambyn Batmönh (q.v.) was elected chairman of the Presidium of the People's Great Hural (q.v.), following the ousting of Yumjaagiyn Tsedenbal (q.v.), Sodnom was appointed chairman of the Council of Ministers on December 12, 1984 and elected a member of the MPRP (q.v.) Politburo. He retained these posts until the resignation of the Politburo and government on March 21, 1990. Sodnom had joined the MPRP in 1954 and had been elected a member of the MPRP Central Committee (q.v.) and a deputy of the PGH from 1966-1990. In the post-socialist period, Sodnom was director of the Mongolian Gazryn Tos (q.v.) petroleum company from 1990-1991, then appointed aide to Prime Minister Puntsagiyn Jasray (q.v.) in 1992.

SODNOM, GOMBYN (1903-1932). Politician and minister. Born in the present-day Darhan district of Hentiy Province (q.v.), Sodnom joined the revolutionary partisans in 1921 and after the victory of the revolution was sent to Moscow to study at the Communist University of the Toilers of the East. After his return he was made secretary of the Mongolian Revolutionary Youth League (q.v.) and elected to the Presidium of the MPRP Central Committee (qq.v.). On the formation of the ministry in 1930 he was appointed minister of trade and industry and was instrumental in the establishment of Ulan Bator (q.v.) industrial combine and Hatgal wool-washing mill and the organization of radio broadcasting in Mongolia. After dealing successfully with an outbreak of "counterrevolution" in Ömnögov' Province in the early spring of 1932, in May Sodnom was sent by the government to Arhangay Province (qq.v.), where he was seized by another group of "counterrevolutionaries" and killed.

SONGINO-HAYRHAN. District (*düüreg*) of Ulan Bator (q.v.). Established in 1992, this western and north-western urban district of some 28,600 households (1992) is named after a local range of hills and consists of 20 wards (*horoo*) incorporating Tolgoy, Orbit (satellite receiving station), Bayanhoshuu, the meat-packing plant, brickworks, and other western parts of the former Oktyabr' district (q.v.) (*rayon*) of the capital.

SOSORJAV, TSENDIYN (1911-1941). Aide to the head of the investigation department, Ministry of Internal Affairs. One of the 32 victims of the Mongolian purges of the 1930s and 1940s (q.v.) sent to the USSR for trial and sentence, details of which were released by the Russian government in 1993. Sentenced to death by the Military Collegium of the USSR Supreme Court in Moscow on July 5, 1941, and executed on July 28.

SOUTH GOBI PROVINCE *see* Ömnögov' Province.

SOVD, GALDANGIYN (1930-   ). Chairman of the Constitutional Court since 1992. Sovd was born in Zavhan district of Uvs Province (q.v.). After completing his three years of military service, he worked in the provincial procurator's office and then went to law school. He was sent to study at Sverdlovsk Institute of Law and on graduation worked at the Mongolian State Procurator's Office. He also served as first deputy chairman of the Supreme Court. In 1964 he became a lecturer at the Mongolian State University. He was awarded the higher degree of Candidate of Sciences and in 1989 was appointed director of the Institute of State and Law of the Academy of Sciences (q.v.). In July 1992 he was nominated by President Punsalmaagiyn Ochirbat (q.v.) in accordance with the new Constitution (q.v.) to be a member of the Constitutional Court, which elected him its chairman.

SOVMONGOLMETALL. Mongolian-Soviet joint stock company founded in 1949 for the prospecting and extraction of nonferrous and rare metals. Its capital of 23 million tögrög was shared by the Mongolian Ministry of Industry and the Soviet Ministry of Ferrous Metallurgy. The company mined fluorite (for the Soviet steel industry) at Bürentsogt and Tümentsogt in Sühbaatar Province (q.v.) and tin at Chuluunhoroot and Modot in Dornod Province (q.v.). Its buildings and equipment were handed over to the Mongolian government in 1957.

SOYOMBO. Symbol of Mongolian independence (sometimes spelled *soyonbo*). The *soyombo* has been used as the Mongolian emblem on the state seal, national flag, identity cards, passports, and other official documents since 1911. The *soyombo* is a mystic device centered on a yin and yang symbol, with vertical bars left and right, horizontal bars and "arrow heads" above and below, the whole surmounted by the sun, moon, and flames. Initially it stood on a wreath of lotus; from 1945-1992 it was surmounted by a communist five-pointed star. It may be much older, but the *soyombo* is usually attributed to Zanabazar, the first Bogd Gegeen (qq.v.), who developed on its basis a script for the Mongol language (q.v.) similar to the Devanagari script of Sanskrit. In the communist period the origins of the *soyombo* were "socialized," the yin and yang being described as "two vigilant fish." According to one theory, the various parts of the *soyombo* represent, besides the sun and moon, the five elements (wood, fire, earth, iron, and water). *See also* Animal Cycle.

STATE FARMS. Mainly arable farms run by the state on an industrial basis (*sangiyn aj ahuy*). There were 53 of these, plus 20 fodder farms (*tejeeliyn aj ahuy*), with a total of 35,200 workers (1990) concentrated in the central and northern provinces of Mongolia where natural conditions suit large-scale production of grain and vegetables (q.v.); some were engaged in raising poultry (q.v.). On average a state farm had 15,400 hectares of arable land, 92 tractors, and 36 grain harvesters, as well as 26,200 head of livestock and 500 workers (1985). In 1990 the state farms owned 5.1 percent of the country's livestock, that is 1.32 million head. The first state farms were established in 1922-1923 and numbered ten in 1940. Their numbers increased rapidly with the introduction of industrial farming methods and the development of large-scale grain farming, rising to 25 by 1960 and doubling to 52 by 1985. The transition to a free-market economy, which began in 1990, has encouraged the dissolution of the state farms, and some state farm workers have gone in for private farming (q.v.). However, the government is concerned with preserving large-scale grain farming in the interests of efficiency.

STORMONG. Mongolian-Soviet joint stock company (name derived from the Russian *torgovlya,* trade) founded in 1927 for trade and economic cooperation, selling Soviet goods in Mongolia and procuring raw materials for Soviet industry through the Mongolian cooperatives. Stormong was the successor of the Russian wool trading company Sherst', but in turn was closed down in 1933 on the establishment of Mongolsovbuner.

SULTAN, TAUKEYN (1944-   ). Mongolian politician. Born in Tsengel district of Bayan-Ölgiy Province (q.v.), Sultan who is a Kazakh (q.v.) graduated from Ölgiy (q.v.) secondary school in 1962 and trained as an economist at Ulan Bator (q.v.) Higher School of Economics. He began his working life at Arhangay Province (q.v.) trade and procurement office, then moved to the Ministry of Trade and Procurement and later became Ulan Bator's director of trade and public catering. Moving to work as head of a department in the Ulan Bator MPRP Committee, he was next appointed first secretary of Ulan Bator's Sühbaatar District (q.v.) MPRP Committee 1986. In 1988 he became second secretary, then first secretary (chairman) of the Bayan-Ölgiy MPRP Committee June 1990-1992. Previously a candidate member from 1986-1990, he was made a member of the MPRP Central Committee (qq.v.) in 1990, 1991, and 1992. He was elected a member of the Mongolian Great Hural (q.v.) for the MPRP for a four-year term on June 28, 1992 in constituency 2 (Bayan-Ölgiy). He is a member of two MGH standing committees: foreign policy and security, and economic policy.

SUM. Derived from *sum,* meaning an arrow, a rural district. In Manchu (q.v.) times the four *aymag* (q.v.) were divided into *hoshuu* (q.v.), and the *hoshuu* into *sum* (Russian rendering: *somon*). In the postrevolutionary period the *sum* was divided into *bag* (q.v.) and subdivided into *arvan* (q.v.). From 1931 onward, as divisions of the new *aymag,* the *sum* became the basic rural district. However, on the formation of the *negdel* (q.v.), the basic administrative unit in rural areas became the *sum-negdel* (q.v.). The role of the *sum* was restored on the dissolution of the *negdel* and confirmed in the 1992 Constitution (q.v.).

SUM-NEGDEL. Rural administrative unit. In the course of the consolidation of the agricultural production associations, or *negdel* (q.v.), in the 1950s the territories of the *sum* (q.v.) and *negdel* were combined and their boundaries made coterminous. The posts of head of the *sum* administration and chairman of the *negdel* council were combined. Initially there were 263 *sum-negdel*. They were abolished with the dissolution of the *negdel* and the reorganization of local government in accordance with the 1992 Constitution (q.v.).

SUUR'. Derived from *suur'*, meaning base, a subdivision of a *brigad* (q.v.). A small group of rural households working together as a labor unit of a *negdel* (q.v.).

SÜHBAATAR. District (*düüreg*) of Ulan Bator (q.v.). Established in 1992, this central urban district of some 20,600 households (1992) is named after the hero of the 1921 revolution and consists of 15 wards (*horoo*) incorporating Doloon Buudal residential (*ger*) area and Nos. 5 and 11 (apartment) areas (*horoolol*), Dambadarjaa, Züün Hüree, the government offices on Sühbaatar Square, and areas to the south of it of the former Sühbaatar district (q.v.) (*rayon*) of the capital.

SÜHBAATAR. Former district (*rayon*) of Ulan Bator (q.v.). This *rayon*, named in honor of the Mongolian revolutionary leader, was formed in 1965 and abolished in 1992. It consisted of Nos. 31-44 wards (*horoo*) and embraced the northern administrative and residential areas of the capital now incorporated in Sühbaatar and Chingeltey-Uul (qq.v.) urban districts (*düüreg*).

SÜHBAATAR. Former ward (*horoo*) of Ulan Bator (q.v.). One of the ten wards abolished in 1965 on the formation of Ajilchin, Nayramdal, Oktyabr', and Sühbaatar (q.v.) districts (*rayon*), each with smaller numbered *horoo*.

SÜHBAATAR. Province (*aymag*) in south-eastern Mongolia. Formed in 1942 as Javhlant-Sharga *aymag* from parts of Hentiy and Dornod provinces (q.v.), the province was renamed in 1943 on the fiftieth anniversary of Damdiny Sühbaatar's (q.v.) birth. It is situated on the border with China (Xilin Gol League of Inner Mongolia Autonomous Region). With a territory of 82,000 sq km and population of 53,496

(1991), it has 12 rural districts (*sum*); the provincial center is Baruun-Urt (q.v.). The local minorities include the Dariganga and Uzemchin (qq.v.). The designated occasional crossing point on the border with China is Bichigt (for Züün Hatavch). There are deposits of coal (Ölziyt and Yögzör), lignite (Talbulag and Tüvshinshiree), fluorite (Bürentsogt), iron ore (Bürentsogt and Sühbaatar), zinc (Tömörtiyn Ovoo), wolfram (Bürentsogt and Tümentsogt), and other nonferrous metals (Yögzör and Erdenetsagaan). Livestock numbers reached 1,098,700 head (1992) and arable land 15,800 hectares (1989).

SÜHBAATAR. Center of Selenge Province (q.v.). Accorded town status in 1959, it is the lowest town in Mongolia at 626 m above sea level. The average January and July temperatures are −23.3 and 19.1 deg C, respectively, and the average annual precipitation is 304.7 mm. The population is about 20,000. The town is situated on the Trans-Mongolian Railway and is the customs and immigration control point for traffic to and from Russia (Naushki station in the Buryat Republic, q.v.). Local industries include production of building materials and matches, distilling, railway rolling stock repairs, woodworking, and flour milling.

SÜHBAATAR, DAMDINY (DAMDINGIYN). Mongolian revolutionary leader. Sühbaatar was born on February 2, 1893 (according to some other sources on February 17, 1894) into the family of a serf from Yost Beysiyn *hoshuu* (q.v.) in Setsen Han Province (present-day Sühbaatar Province q.v.). His father, Damdin, had managed to find manual work at his province's office in Ih Hüree (q.v.). From 1890-1896, the family lived in the district now called Amgalanbaatar, and thereafter in various other suburbs including Konsulyn Denj (q.v.). There is some confusion over whether his name was originally Sühbaatar ("axe hero") or just Süh ("axe"). It was chosen after his father Damdin lost his axe in the river Uliastay, a tributary of the Tuul (q.v.), which flows through the eastern suburbs of Ih Hüree. His mother Handjav died when he was eight years old. His elder brother Dendev became a lama.

In 1907 Sühbaatar began to take lessons in Mongolian and arithmetic from Onguudyn Jam"yan (q.v.), but two years later he was sent out to work, first at *örtöö* (q.v.) stations, then gathering firewood and cutting hay. At the beginning of 1912, Sühbaatar was drafted into the army of Setsen Han Province and attended the Military Training School at Hujirbulan, not far from Niyslel Hüree (q.v.), where Russian instructors taught the Mongol soldiers how to use Russian-made firearms. He won the reputation of a skilled rider and marksman, and on graduation he was appointed platoon commander of a machine-gun company. He and his wife Yanjmaa (q.v.) had a son, Galsan, born in 1913. Sühbaatar was placed under the command of Magsarjav (q.v.) in 1917 and saw action on the eastern border in the area of Tamsagbulag and Halhyn Gol (q.v.). In 1918 he was transferred by the Ministry of the Army to a typesetting job in Niyslel Hüree, printing laws and religious texts for the government of the Bogd Khan (q.v.).

In October 1919 Chinese General Hsü Shu-cheng entered Niyslel Hüree and demanded the resignation of the Mongolian government. A dispute broke out between the members of the Bogd Khan's upper and lower advisory assemblies, the Deed and Dood Hurals (q.v.), over whether or not to agree to this. Sühbaatar and Dogsom (q.v.) are said to have opposed this Chinese demand in the Dood Hural, but were overruled. The government of Autonomous Mongolia (q.v.) formally resigned on February 19, 1920, and the army was disbanded, leaving Sühbaatar without work.

In late 1919 Sühbaatar had helped form a secret nationalist group called the Züün Hüree (q.v.) group, and in 1920 this group and another, called the Konsulyn Denj (q.v.) group, joined forces and made contact with Russian revolutionaries, including a Comintern (q.v.) agent, Sorokovikov. He advised them to send a delegation to the Comintern office in Irkutsk (q.v.). On June 25, 1920, the amalgamated group formed itself into the Mongolian People's Party (q.v.), and an oath of secrecy and unity was sworn. The MPP drew up an appeal for Soviet assistance and with Jam"yan's help it was presented to the Bogd Khan, who affixed his seal.

Sühbaatar left Hüree with the appeal in July for Troitskosavsk (Deed Shivee, near Russian Kyakhta). He arrived in mid-August and met up with six MPP comrades, who had traveled separately. They set out by boat for Deed Ud (now Ulan-Ude), where they consulted the local Comintern representative Shumyatskiy. They then went on to Irkutsk, where the Mongols' needs were discussed with a representative of the Soviet People's Commissariat for Foreign Affairs. At this point the MPP delegation decided to split up: while Sühbaatar and Choybalsan (q.v.) stayed in Irkutsk to study Red Army tactics, Bodoo (q.v.) and Dogsom would go back to Niyslel Hüree, and Soliyn Danzan, Losol and Chagdarjav (qq.v.) would go to Omsk. However, Losol fell ill and stayed in Irkutsk, too. Chagdarjav and Danzan went to Omsk, then on to Moscow, where they were received by Vladimir Lenin, returning to Irkutsk in November. (History books from the communist period avoid going into detail about this meeting, because neither Sühbaatar nor Choybalsan took part, and Chagdarjav and Danzan were later purged.) While in Irkutsk, Sühbaatar, Choybalsan, and Losol prepared for the founding congress of the MPP and started publishing *Mongolyn Ünen* (q.v.).

On February 9, 1921, Sühbaatar was made commander in chief of the Mongol Ardyn Juramt Tsereg, as the Mongolian People's Army (q.v.) was first called, and set out to recruit soldiers, crossing the border into Mongolia and fighting occasional battles against Chinese troops. His command was confirmed by the first congress of the MPP, held on March 1, 1921, in Deed Shivee (Troitskosavsk), and on March 13 he was made a member of the provisional people's government. On March 18 Sühbaatar's revolutionary volunteer force drove the Chinese troops garrison out of Kyakhta (q.v.), allowing the MPP and provisional government to base themselves on Mongolian soil close to the border. Much of the rest of the country was still under the control of Baron Roman von Ungern-Sternberg (q.v.). In coordination with the Soviet Red Army, Sühbaatar's volunteer force beat off repeated attacks in the Kyakhta area until a lull in the fighting toward the end of June enabled them to advance on Niyslel Hüree, which they captured on July 6. Sühbaatar was appointed minister of the army in the revolutionary government formed on July 9.

In October 1921, Sühbaatar as army minister went to Moscow as a member of another Mongolian delegation, headed by the MPP leader and Minister of Finance Soliyn Danzan. (History books from the communist period ignored Danzan and claimed that Sühbaatar was the delegation leader.) The delegation members included Deputy Foreign Minister Tserendorj (q.v.), Da Lam Shirnendamdin (q.v.), and adviser and interpreter Erdenebathaan (q.v.). The delegation was received by Vladimir Lenin, who told them about the national liberation struggle, advised them on their party's main tasks, and told them not to rename it the Mongolian communist party until Mongolia had developed a proletariat (the details were not released until the ninth MPRP Congress in 1934). A treaty of friendship between Mongolia and Soviet Russia was signed on November 5, 1921.

Sühbaatar returned to his task of building a regular army in Mongolia. In September 1922 the government awarded him the title of Zorigt Baatar, "Resolute Hero." Sühbaatar died on February 20, 1923, of illness (although a 1943 biography claimed he had been poisoned) and was buried at Altan-Ölgiy cemetery near Ulan Bator (q.v.). The monument to him in Ulan Bator's Sühbaatar Square was unveiled in 1946, and the Sühbatar-Choybalsan Mausoleum in the 1950s. The role of Sühbaatar and Choybalsan as Mongolia's revolutionary leaders was greatly exaggerated in communist history books, while the part played by Bodoo, Danzan, and other revolutionaries was for many years belittled, distorted, or ignored.

SÜHBAATAR ECONOMIC COOPERATION ZONE. One of six economic cooperation zones into which Mongolia was divided on the basis of a government ordinance issued in November 1991 (the others being the Central, Bayan-Ölgiy, Gov'-Altay, Övörhangay, and Ulan Bator economic cooperation zones, qq.v.). It consists of Sühbaatar, Hentiy, and Dornod provinces (qq.v.). Each zone has a cooperation office headed by the secretary of the zonal cooperation council.

SÜHBAATAR, ORDER OF. The highest government decoration in the MPR, this order named after Damdiny Sühbaatar (q.v.) was instituted in May 1941 and is awarded to military and labor heroes (*baatar*, q.v.). According to some sources the first recipients, in September 1945, were Choybalsan, Bumtsend, Yanjmaa, and Tsedenbal (qq.v.); during his political career Tsedenbal was awarded a total of six. The recipients of the order and their children were entitled to free education in all Mongolian institutes and were given priority in selection for education abroad.

- T -

TAMGA. Traditional seals. The use of stone or metal seals by Mongol rulers dates back to the times of the Mongol Empire—a letter sent by Güyük Khan to the Pope in 1246 bears the stamp of a seal in the Mongol script, declaring that all should fear the decree of the Mongol Khan who rules by the mandate of Eternal Heaven (Mönh Tenger). After the disintegration of the empire, the use of personal seals continued among the khans of Halh (q.v.) and the Oirats (Oyrd, q.v.). The seal of the Bogd Khan (q.v.) was inscribed in the 'Phags-pa, *soyombo*, and Mongolian classical scripts (q.v.). After the 1921 revolution, the "people's government" designed its own seals on the basis of the *soyombo* (q.v.).

The word *tamga* is also used for livestock brands to identify ownership. This traditional practice was banned for much of the communist period but reintroduced by the *negdel* (q.v.) in the 1980s to try to ensure proper care of collectively owned animals. Branding has become widespread since the dissolution of the *negdel* and many different brands are used, ranging from modern letters and numbers to ancient geometric designs.

TAMGYN GAZAR. Meaning seal office, the secretariat, or administrative center of a town, province, or rural district, where the local administrator's seal (*tamga*, q.v.) was kept. This prerevolutionary term has been reintroduced since the local government reforms brought about by the 1922 Constitution (q.v.). The presidency and some ministries and government departments also have "seal offices."

TARVAGAN DAH. This elevation 646.7 m above sea level at the junction of the borders of Mongolia (Dornod Province, q.v.), Russia (Chita

Region), and China (Inner Mongolia Autonomous Region) marks the eastern terminus of Mongolia's borders with Russia and China (qq.v.) at 49 deg 52 min north and 116 deg 45 min east.

TAVAN BOGD. Mountains in Mongolia. This range of the Mongol Altai Mountains (q.v.) is situated in the area of the junction of the borders of Mongolia (Bayan-Ölgiy Province, q.v.), Russia (Altay Republic, q.v.), and China (Xinjiang Uighur Autonomous Region). The highest peak, sometimes called Nayramdal (friendship) peak, 4,374 m, is crossed by the Mongolian-Chinese border. This peak is a short distance south-east of an unnamed 4,104 m peak, which marks the junction of Mongolia's borders with Russia and China (qq.v.) and their western starting point at 49 deg 8 min north and 87 deg 45 min east.

TAYJ (TAIJI, T'AI-TZU). "Heir apparent," one of the hereditary aristocracy claiming descent from Genghis Khan (q.v.) or one of his brothers, owning *hamjlaga* (q.v.) but not necessarily estates as well.

TEN ASPIRATIONS. Name sometimes given to the first MPRP Program (qq.v.), drafted in March 1921, before the revolution had been fought and won. "After we have established the rights and power of the people of Mongolia's many *aymag* (q.v.) and have eradicated the masses' bitter sufferings," Point One declared, "we will strive to develop our strength so that we can live peacefully as other peoples do, increase our wisdom, become more developed and create happiness equally for all." Point Two went on to say that the Mongolian people were "striving to establish a nation of one house ruled by the Mongolian people themselves. In no circumstances should Mongolia be enslaved and oppressed by imperialists of other nations. Therefore our People's Party will strive in the future to join all Mongolian tribes into one nation." For extracts from the Ten Aspirations *see* Brown and Onon, *History of the Mongolian People's Republic*.

TES. River in Mongolia. The Tes *gol,* 430 km within Mongolia, rises in the Bulnayn Nuruu, a northern formation of the Hangay Mountains in southern Hövsgöl Province, and flows west, crossing into the Tuva Republic (as the Tes-Khem) and out again into Uvs Province, then running parallel with the border before entering Lake Uvs (qq.v.).

THIRD FORCE. Mongolian political movement. After the 1992 elections, in which they failed to win any seats, the Mongolian Capitalists', Independence, United Herdsmen's and Farmers', and United Private Owners' Parties formed a loose coalition or "political Third Force" to counterpose the MPRP and Mongolian National Democratic Party (qq.v.). In 1993 the four parties of the Third Force amalgamated in the Mongolian United Heritage Party (q.v.).

TIME ZONES. Based on the meridian of Hürel-Togoo observatory on Bogd Haan Uul Mountain (q.v.), longitude 107 degrees and three minutes east, Ulan Bator (q.v.) time is seven hours (eight minutes and 12 seconds) ahead of Greenwich mean time. However, following the former Soviet practice of one hour's permanent summer time, Ulan Bator time is maintained at eight hours ahead of Greenwich time. For six months a year Mongolia also adopts one hour's local summer time.

The territory of Mongolia is divided into three time zones, which were established by government decision in October 1961. Zone One keeps Hovd time, an hour behind Ulan Bator time, in western Mongolia: Bayan-Ölgiy, Uvs, Hovd, Gov'-Altay, and Zavhan provinces (qq.v.). Zone Two keeps Ulan Bator time in central Mongolia: Hövsgöl, Bulgan, Selenge, Arhangay, Hentiy, Töv, Bayanhongor, Övörhangay, Dundgov', Ömnögov', and Dornogov' provinces (qq.v.). Zone Three keeps Choybalsan time, an hour ahead of Ulan Bator time, in eastern Mongolia: Dornod and Sühbaatar provinces (qq.v.).

TOGTOH, NORJMOOGIYN (1946-). Mongolian politician. Togtoh trained as a building engineer and became director of the Institute of Construction. He was elected a member of the Mongolian Great Hural for the MPRP (qq.v.) for a four-year term on June 28, 1992 in constituency 8 (Dundgov'). He is a member of three MGH standing committees: environmental protection, education, science, and culture, and economic policy.

TOLBO. Lake in the Mongol Altai Mountains of Bayan-Ölgiy Province (qq.v.), site of a famous battle in 1921. Having suffered defeat at the hands of the revolutionary army and its Soviet Russian allies, the forces of Baron von Ungern-Sternberg (q.v.) and White Guard (Tsarist) Generals Bakich, Kaygorodov, and Kazantsev, numbering some 3,000 men, had fled to western Mongolia. A mixed Mongol and Soviet Red Army unit of 300 men under Hasbaatar and Baykalov made contact with the Whites at the beginning of September 1921 near Saruul Güngiyn Hüree (monastery) on the shores of Lake Tolbo and took shelter inside the monastery's mud brick walls. Rejecting surrender terms and beating off repeated attacks, the besieged defenders held out for 44 days until relieved by the Red Army's 185th Cavalry Regiment. Hasbaatar was killed during the action.

TOLGOYT. Former ward (*horoo*) of Ulan Bator (q.v.). One of the ten wards abolished in 1965 on the formation of Ajilchin, Nayramdal,

Oktyabr', and Sühbaatar (q.v.) districts (*rayon*), each with smaller numbered *horoo*.

TOONO. The cartwheel-shaped wooden top of a *ger* (q.v.) frame, mounted on two posts, which supports the radial roof poles and thereby the felt (q.v.) covering. It lets daylight into the *ger* and the chimney of the stove passes through it. It may be covered with an exterior canvas flap.

TORGUUD (TORGUT). Mongol ethnic group. The Torguud, a West Mongol or Oirat (Oyrd, q.v.) group speaking the southern dialect, accounted for 0.5 percent (10,200) of the population of Mongolia, according to the 1989 census. The Torguud are concentrated mostly in Bulgan district, south-western Hovd Province (q.v.), close to the border with China. *See also* China: Mongol Ethnic Groups *and* Russia: Mongol Ethnic Groups.

TOSONTSENGEL. Town in Mongolia. Accorded town status in 1965, Tosontsengel is situated in north-eastern Zavhan Province (q.v.) on the river Ider. It is an important timber-producing center with a population of about 10,000. The distance from Ulan Bator (q.v.) is 695 km.

TOVUUSÜREN, TSEDEVIYN (1947-   ). Mongolian politician. Born in Bayandelger district, Sühbaatar Province (q.v.), Tovuusüren graduated in 1975 from Moscow Higher School of Food Industry Technology with a degree in engineering. In 1975 he started work as a foreman, technologist, then confectionery production chief of Darhan town food combine. Later he was an engineer and head of a department at the Ministry of Light and Food Industry, then head of directorate and chief engineer of the renamed Ministry of Agriculture and Food Industry. He became a member of the MPRP Central Committee (qq.v.) in 1992. He was a member of the State Little Hural (q.v.) and a member of the SLH social policy committee from 1990-1992. Tovuusüren was elected a member of the Mongolian Great Hural (q.v.) for the MPRP for a four-year term on June 28, 1992 in constituency 24 (Ulan Bator). He is a member of two MGH standing committees: health and social security, and food and agriculture.

TÖGRÖG. Mongolian national currency. The Mongolian tögrög or tughrik (one tögrög equals 100 möngö) was put into circulation in 1925 following the establishment of the Mongolian State Bank (Mongolbank, q.v.), and from 1928 it was the only legal tender. Previously various foreign currencies including Maria Theresa dollars and gold rubles had been in circulation, although still older forms of exchange like tea bricks and silver ingots still existed. Circulation of the tögrög was strictly controlled by the Mongolian government with Soviet backing throughout the communist period, and its foreign exchange rate was fixed artificially. In the 1960s, for example, it was valued by the State Bank at an official rate of US$1 = four tögrög. In the post-communist transition to a market economy since 1990 under the guidance of the International Monetary Fund the value of the tögrög has been reduced step by step to a more realistic exchange rate. Recent devaluations included US$1 = 40 tögrög (June 1991), US$1 = 150 tögrög (January 1993), and US$1 = 390 tögrög on true flotation in May 1993, since when it has been stable in a situation of relatively low inflation. The devaluation of the tögrög has also had the effect of bringing Mongolia's true per capita GNP ($100) down to the bottom of the world list.

TÖMÖR, SOROGJOOGIYN (1953-). Mongolian politician. Born in Tes district of Uvs Province (q.v.), Tömör entered the Mongolian State University in 1971 to study law but graduated from the Azerbaijan State University in Baku. He returned to the MSU and was awarded the higher degree of Candidate of Law in 1979. He was an advisor to the Secretariat of the State Little Hural (q.v.) from 1990-1992 and became a member of the MPRP Central Committee (qq.v.) in 1992. He was elected a member of the Mongolian Great Hural (q.v.) for the MPRP for a four-year term on June 28, 1992 in constituency 15 (Uvs). He was the chairman of the MGH standing committee for legal affairs from June 1992 to October 1993, and is a member of the MGH standing committee for assemblies and administration.

TÖMÖR-OCHIR, DARAMYN. Mongolian politician. Tömör-Ochir was the member of the MPRP (q.v.) Politburo and Secretariat charged in February 1962 with the task of organizing the national celebrations of the 800th anniversary of Genghis Khan's (q.v.) birth on May 31 of that year. Unfortunately for him, when the preparations were already in full swing (and a set of Genghis Khan anniversary postage stamps had already been printed), the Soviet Communist Party newspaper *Pravda* published a fierce attack on Genghis Khan and the "Mongol-Tatar" empire, which had placed Russia under its "yoke" for several centuries. The MPRP cancelled the celebrations and issued a new and negative evaluation of the founder of the Mongol state. In September 1962, Tömör-Ochir was deprived of his membership in the Politburo and Secretariat for allegedly intriguing against other party leaders, being a careerist, and trying "to create an unhealthy mood in public opinion and to inflame nationalist passions." More particularly, he was also denounced for supporting "nationalist tendencies directed at idealizing the role of Genghis Khan in Mongolian history" and organizing "pompous celebration" of the anniversary; and for pursuing an "anti-Marxist nationalist line in the guise of struggle against the Choybalsan (q.v.) personality cult." This was despite the fact that the Politburo resolution of February 14, 1962, on organizing the anniversary celebrations had been signed by Tsedenbal and Sambuu (qq.v.), as well as Tömör-Ochir and six other Politburo members and candidate members. Tömör-Ochir retired into obscurity, and eventually was murdered with an axe under mysterious circumstances. Some nationalists who believe in a conspiracy would like his murder reinvestigated. He was rehabilitated by the March 1990 meeting of the MPRP Central Committee (q.v.).

TÖMÖR ZAM. Former ward (*horoo*) of Ulan Bator (q.v.). "Railway" ward, one of the ten wards abolished in 1965 on the formation of Ajilchin, Nayramdal, Oktyabr', and Sühbaatar (qq.v.) districts (*rayon*), each with smaller numbered *horoo*.

TÖRMANDAH, TSOGBADRAHYN (1951-   ). Mongolian politician. Törmandah became a political journalist and later worked for Mongolian Free Television Channel of Information and Exchange. He was elected a member of the Mongolian Great Hural (q.v.) for the MPRP (q.v.) for a four-year term on June 28, 1992 in constituency 7 (Dornod). He is a member of three MGH standing committees: education, science, and culture, foreign policy and security, and economic policy.

TÖRTOGTOH, GENDENGIYN (1948-   ). Mongolian politician. Törtogtoh became a historian. He was appointed editor in chief of MPRP Central Committee (qq.v.) periodicals and first deputy editor of the MPRP newspaper *Ünen* (Truth) (q.v.) in 1991 and a member of the MPRP Central Committee in 1991 and 1992. He was elected a member of the Mongolian Great Hural (q.v.) for the MPRP for a four-year term on June 28, 1992 in constituency 17 (Hövsgöl). He is a member of three MGH standing committees: education, science, and culture, foreign policy and security, and economic policy.

TÖV (CENTRAL). Province (*aymag*) in central Mongolia. Formed in 1931, the province surrounds the capital, Ulan Bator (q.v.). From 1956-1960, it included parts of the present-day Selenge Province (q.v.). With a territory of 81,000 sq km and population of 105,789 (1991), it has 25 rural districts (*sum*); until 1992 there was one ward (*horoo*), Arhust; the provincial center is Zuunmod (q.v.). The province also administers the former Soviet Army No. 7 cantonment of

215 buildings—the second largest in the country—in Sergelen district, south-east of Ulan Bator, handed over to the Mongolian authorities. The Trans-Mongolian Railway runs through the province, giving access to the coal mines at Nalayh, but not to Zuunmod; another branch line runs to the lignite mine at Baganuur (q.v.), Bayandelger district. There are deposits of gold (Janchivlin, Sergelen, Möngönmor't, Zaamar, and Zuunmod), wolfram (Ih Hayrhan), tin (Janchivlin), other nonferrous metals (Arhust), fluorite (Tsagaandel, Bayantsagaan district), bitumen (Bayan Erht, Bayanjargalan district), and lime (Tsagaan Bulag, Maan't), as well as a glass works (Nalayh), woodworking (Möngönmor't), and production of foodstuffs (Nalayh) and animal feed (Bayantsogt and Erdenesant). Livestock numbers reached 1,687,900 head (1992) and arable land 200,300 hectares (1989).

TRANSPORT. For information about transport to and in Mongolia, *see* Airlines, MIAT, Railways, *and* Roads.

TSAATAN (TSAATANGUUD, REINDEER PEOPLE). This very small group (80 or so families) of Turkic Urianhay or Tuvans live with their reindeer in the taiga of north-western Hövsgöl Province (qq.v.).

TSAGAANHÜÜ, RAVDANGIYN (1933-). Mongolian politician. Born in Hanbogd district of Ömnögov' Province (q.v.), Tsagaanhüü trained as an economist and has a doctorate in economics. He was deputy, then first deputy minister of agriculture for some 14 years before being appointed head of the MPRP Central Committee's (qq.v.) agricultural (agricultural policy) department from 1986-1990; he was elected a member of the MPRP Central Committee in March 1990. He served as chief deputy minister of National Development from 1990-1992. He was elected a member of the Mongolian Great Hural (q.v.) for the MPRP for a four-year term on June 28, 1992 in constituency 11 (Ömnögov'). He is a member of two MGH standing committees: food and agriculture, and economic policy.

TSAHAR (CHAHAR, QAHAR). Mongol ethnic group. This group living near the border with China is related to the Chahar of Inner Mongolia (q.v.) and numbered some 400, according to the 1989 census. *See also* China: Mongol Ethnic Groups.

TSEDENBAL, YUMJAAGIYN (1916-1991). Mongolian premier from 1952-1974 and president from 1974-1984. Born in Davst district of Uvs Province (q.v.) on September 17, 1916, Tsedenbal was educated at the Institute of Finance and Economics in Irkutsk (q.v.). He began his working career as a teacher at Ulan Bator (q.v.) Financial College, but was appointed deputy minister, then minister of finance, and concurrently chairman of the Board of the Bank of Trade and Industry from 1939-1940. He joined the Mongolian Revolutionary Youth League in 1931 and the MPRP (qq.v.) in 1939, and was elected a member of the MPRP Central Committee (q.v.), member of the Presidium, and general secretary of the MPRP on April 8, 1940. He was responsible for the introduction of the Cyrillic script for writing modern Mongolian and the displacement of the classical Mongolian script (qq.v.). During the war years from 1941-1945, he served as head of the Political Directorate and deputy commander in chief of the Mongolian People's Army with the rank of lieutenant general and was awarded the Soviet Order of Lenin. He was appointed chairman of the State Planning Commission in 1945, and deputy chairman of the Council of Ministers in 1948. Following the death of Horloogiyn Choybalsan (q.v.) he became chairman of the Council of Ministers (premier) from May 27, 1952 to June 11, 1974. Meanwhile, in 1954 the post of MPRP first secretary passed to Dashiyn Damba (q.v.), and only after Damba's removal was Tsedenbal elected first secretary of the MPRP Central Committee from October 1958-1981 (general secretary from 1981-1984).

"Unshakably loyal to Marxism-Leninism and socialist internationalism," Tsedenbal was always very close to the Soviet leadership and a strong proponent of Soviet political and economic policies, describing the USSR as Mongolia's "elder brother." After the death of Jamsrangiyn Sambuu (q.v.), and apparently following the example of Soviet leader Leonid Brezhnev, whom he admired, Tsedenbal was elected chairman of the Presidium of the People's Great Hural (head of state) in 1974 and resigned the premiership in favor of Jambyn Batmönh (q.v.). Despite his protestations to the contrary, Tsedenbal built his own "personality cult." He was awarded the title of Hero of the Mongolian People's Republic and presented with the Order of Sühbaatar (q.v.) on his fiftieth birthday (1966) for his "special services to the party, state, and Mongolian people" and made an honorary member of the Academy of Sciences (q.v.). Ten years later, he received another Order of Sühbaatar at a "grand ceremony" marking his sixtieth birthday, an exhibition about him was opened in Ulan Bator, and a bronze bust was unveiled in Ulaangom (qq.v.); Brezhnev gave him another Order of Lenin. Tsedenbal promoted himself Army general and then created for himself the title of marshal of the MPR in 1979. On his sixty-fifth birthday (1981), Marshal Tsedenbal was given yet another Order of Sühbaatar (he was awarded six altogether).

In August 1984, while he was on holiday in Moscow, Tsedenbal's removal from the MPRP Central Committee and PGH Presidium was engineered by Batmönh, "on account of the state of his health and with his agreement." However, it was Tsedenbal's political health that was suffering more. He had never been able to divorce himself from his past association with the "cult of personality" and methods of the dictator Horloogiyn Choybalsan. During his own long political career, Tsedenbal also ruthlessly purged prominent politicians and academics, generally exiling them rather than executing them but ruining many lives nonetheless. His autocratic style of leadership was increasingly out of place in the international arena that Mongolia had finally entered. Moreover, his Russian wife, Anastasya Tsedenbal-Filatova, was widely considered to have been allowed too much power in a political system from which the wives of the leaders were usually excluded. However, four years passed after his ouster before Batmönh and Mongolia's official media began to blame him by name for the political and economic "stagnation" from which the country was suffering.

The Tsedenbals stayed on in their flat in Moscow, where their son Slava was working at the headquarters of Comecon (q.v.), while Yumjaagiyn Tsedenbal's health continued to decline. A film made by a Mongolian Television team at their Moscow flat showed him as doddery and forgetful and his wife as bossy and protective. Mongolia's new democratic government planned to try him and other members of the Politburo on various charges connected with the communist regime's activities, but by February 1991 he was considered too ill to face trial and he died on April 21, 1991. His body was returned to Mongolia and he was buried in Ulan Bator. Since his death, his other son, Zorig, also resident in Moscow, has been trying to rally support for a new and more positive evaluation of Tsedenbal's achievements.

TSEDENDAGVA, GÜRJAVYN (1946-   ). Mongolian politician. Born in Bayanovoo district, Bayanhongor Province (q.v.), Tsedendagva graduated from Ulan Bator (q.v.) Finance and Economics School in 1965 as an agricultural accountant and worked as an accountant in the Bayanhongor (q.v.) network of inter-*negdel* (q.v.) enterprises and in the clothing factory of the Ministry of Defense. He studied at the Mongolian State University from 1968-1973, obtaining a degree in industrial engineering, and was a student of the CPSU Central Committee's Academy of Social Sciences in Moscow from 1979-1982, gaining a higher degree in economics. Over the period from 1973-1990 he was a teacher, later Learned Secretary, at the MPRP Central Committee's (q.v.) Higher Party School (renamed the Great Hural's Higher Political School). He also took short courses on market relations in South Korea and the USA. He was chairman of Bayanhongor Province Executive Administration from 1990-1992 and a member of the MPRP Central Committee in 1991 and 1992. Tsedendagva was elected a member of the Mongolian Great Hural (q.v.) for the MPRP for a four-year term on June 28, 1992 in constituency 3 (Bayanhongor). He is the chairman of the MGH standing committee for economic policy (development and infrastructure) (reelected in October 1993) and a member of the MGH standing committee for budget and finance. In October 1993 he led the Mongolian team to the fourth Anglo-Mongolian Round Table Conference on economic and cultural cooperation, held in London.

TSENDSÜREN, GÜRJAVYN (1903-1941). Head of first department, Ministry of Internal Affairs. One of the 32 victims of the Mongolian purges of the 1930s and 1940s (q.v.) sent to the USSR for trial and sentence, details of which were released by the Russian government in 1993. Sentenced to death by the Military Collegium of the USSR Supreme Court in Moscow on July 5, 1941, he was executed on July 29.

TSERENCHIMED, DA LAM (1869-1914). Born in present-day Hövs-göl Province (q.v.), Tserenchimed became a lama and trained as a clerk, working in the office of the Shanzav (administrator) of the Ih Shav' (q.v.). Tserenchimed was a member of the delegation sent by the Bogd Gegeen (q.v.) to St. Petersburg in July 1911 to try to obtain the support of Russia and West European countries for Mongolian independence. Tserenchimed became a member of the General Administration Office in Charge of Halh (q.v.) Affairs set up in November 1911 as a kind of provisional government of Mongolia as Manchu (q.v.) rule collapsed and was appointed minister of internal affairs in the first government of the Bogd Khan (q.v.). His ministry gradually developed into a "prime ministry" until the formal appointment of a prime minister, Tögs-Ochiryn Namnansüren (q.v.), in 1912. Tserenchimed then reverted to his role of minister of internal affairs. He tried to visit Tokyo, to gain Japanese recognition of Mongolia's independence, but because of Russian objections he was turned back in Harbin. After his death his successor in the post was Beligt Gün Da Lam Dashjav (q.v.).

TSERENDORJ, BALINGIYN (1868-1928). Mongolian prime minister from 1923-1928. Born in the Ih Shav' (the Bogd Gegeen's territory), Tserendorj worked from 1885-1911 as a scribe and translator in the Manchu (q.v.) litigation office. In 1911, he entered the Foreign Ministry of Autonomous Mongolia (q.v.), being appointed deputy minister in 1913 and minister of foreign affairs from 1913-1915, after the death of Handdorj (q.v.). He participated in the Mongolian-Russian-Chinese treaty conference in Kyakhta (q.v.) in 1915 and was a member of the Mongolian ministry set up in 1921 by Baron von Ungern-

Sternberg (q.v.) in his short-lived "provisional government of Mongolian army administration." Under the revolutionary government in 1921 he became deputy minister of foreign affairs, then from August 1921 to January 1922 he held a senior position in the Foreign Ministry (Prime Minister Bodoo, q.v., was concurrently foreign minister). As a member of the Mongolian delegation to Soviet Russia in the autumn of 1921 he participated in intergovernmental talks and met Lenin. He served from 1922-1923 as minister of foreign affairs. Following the death of Damdinbazar (q.v.), Tserendorj was appointed prime minister on September 18, 1923, and remained in this post until he died on February 13, 1928. He was elected to the Presidium of the MPRP Central Committee (qq.v.) in February 1923 and reelected from 1923-1926 and in October 1927.

TSETSEN-HAN. Former province (*aymag*) in eastern Mongolia. One of four large provinces (named after their Mongol princes) during the period of Qing (Manchu) (qq.v.) rule, center Tsetsen Hany Hüree (later Öndörhaan, q.v.). The province was abolished in 1923, when the territory was named Han-Hentiy-Uul (q.v.) *aymag*.

TSETSERLEG. Center of Arhangay Province (q.v.). Previously known as Zayayn Hüree and the center of the former Sayn-Noyon-Han Province (q.v.) until 1923, then the center of the former Tsetserleg-Mandal Province (q.v.) until 1931, Tsetserleg was accorded town status in 1961. Its height above sea level is 1,691 m, the average January and July temperatures are − 15.6 and 14.7 deg C, respectively, and the average annual precipitation is 344.0 mm. The distance from Ulan Bator (q.v.) is 400 km. The population is about 21,500. Local industries include animal protein and foodstuffs production.

TSETSERLEG-MANDAL. Former province (*aymag*) in central-western Mongolia. This large province, center Zayayn Hüree, later Tsetserleg (q.v.), was founded in 1923 on the territory of the former Sayn-Noyon-Han (q.v.) *aymag*. In the administrative reforms of 1931, the five large provinces were broken up into 12 (later 18) smaller ones. This province formed parts of the present-day Bayanhongor, Gov'-Altay, Zavhan, Arhangay, and Övörhangay Provinces, and (1924-1929) part of Hövsgöl Province (qq.v.).

TSOGBAATAR, DORJIYN (1954-). Minister of geology and mineral resources from 1992-1994. Born on January 5, 1954, in Ulan Bator (q.v.), Tsogbaatar graduated in 1977 from the Mongolian State University with a degree in mining engineering. He first worked as an engineer and deputy department head from 1977-1980, then chief

engineer from 1980-1986 at the Mongolian-Soviet copper and molybdenum mining and concentrating combine at Erdenet (q.v.). In 1986
he became a specialist at the Ministry of Geology and Mining Industry, and in 1989 chief mining specialist of the Mongolchekhoslovakmetall (Mongol-Czechoslovak metal-mining) company. From October 1990-August 1992 he was deputy director of the State Control
Directorate. Tsogbaatar, who is not a member of the Mongolian Great
Hural (q.v.), was appointed minister of geology and mineral resources
on August 20, 1992, by the first session of the Mongolian Great Hural.
In a reshuffle in January 1994, Tsogbaatar's ministry was amalgamated with the Ministry of Fuel and Power to form the Ministry of
Power, Geology, and Mining, and Tsogbaatar was dismissed.

TSOGT, TSEVEGMIDIYN (1958-   ). Minister of trade and industry
since 1992. Born on February 28, 1958, in Ulan Bator (q.v.), Tsogt
graduated in 1979 from Moscow Higher School of the National Economy and in 1990 from the USSR Foreign Trade Academy. After
working at the Mongolian Chamber of Commerce from 1979-1981,
he became a specialist at the Ministry of Foreign Trade from 1981-
1985. He then served for three years in the Mongolian commercial
representation in the USSR from 1985-1989 and was appointed
deputy head of a directorate in the reorganized Ministry of Foreign
Economic Relations and Supply from 1989-1990. In early 1990 he
was briefly an aide to the minister of trade and cooperation, and then
in October 1990 appointed head of the foreign trade policy directorate
in the new Ministry of Trade and Industry. Tsogt, who is not a member of the Mongolian Great Hural (q.v.), was appointed minister of
trade and industry on August 5, 1992 by the first session of the MGT.

TSOLMON, TSERENDASHIYN (1953-   ). Mongolian politician. Born
in Arhangay Province, Tsolmon obtained a basic degree in electrical
engineering in Irkutsk (qq.v.). On return to Mongolia, he worked at
Ulan Bator (q.v.) meat-packing combine. He then entered the MPRP
Central Committee's (qq.v.) Higher Party School, graduating in 1982,
and for two years was head of a department of the Mongolian Revolutionary Youth League (q.v.) Central Committee. In 1984 he was sent
to the Soviet Diplomatic Academy where he obtained a higher degree
in economics in 1987. He served as minister of labor from September
1990-1992, introducing new legislation on pensions and labor and setting up a new bureau to handle the employment of Mongolians abroad.
A member of the MPRP, Tsolmon joined other radicals in the party in
December 1991 to found the breakaway Mongolian Renewal Party
(q.v.), of which he was elected chairman of the Executive Committee.
When the MRP amalgamated with other parties in October 1992 to

form the Mongolian National Democratic Party (q.v.), Tsolmon became a member of the MNDP General Council.

TUUL. District (*düüreg*) of Ulan Bator (q.v.). Established in 1992, this urban district of some 850 households in the capital's outer southwestern suburbs is named after the river Tuul (q.v.) and consists of two wards (*horoo*) incorporating the central and surrounding areas. Previously Tuul was itself a ward (*horoo*) of the capital.

TUUL. River in Mongolia. The Tuul *gol,* one of the country's five longest rivers, 819 km, entirely within Mongolia, rises in the Hentey Mountains in Töv Province and flows first south and then west, passing through Ulan Bator (qq.v.); thence it flows north, passing Lün and forming the boundary between Töv and Bulgan Provinces, before entering the Orhon in Orhontuul district of south-western Selenge Province (qq.v.). The basins of the Tuul, Onon, and Herlen (qq.v.), the "three rivers," are considered to embrace the original homeland of the Mongols.

TUVA REPUBLIC. Part of the Russian Federation situated on Mongolia's northern border, area 170,000 sq km. The capital is Kyzyl (q.v.). Some 207,000 (two-thirds) of the population are Tuvans (q.v.). Tuva (Tannu-Tuva) was originally part of Outer Mongolia (q.v.) and known as Urianhay (q.v.). Under Russian protectorate from 1914, then Soviet control in August 1921, it became the People's Republic of Tannu-Tuva, then in 1926 the Republic of Tuva. Diplomatic relations were established and a friendship treaty concluded with the Mongolian People's Republic in 1926. In October 1944 Tuva was incorporated as an "Autonomous *Oblast' "* into the Soviet Russian republic (RSFSR), allegedly at the request of its inhabitants, although the request was evidently contrived by Stalin. In October 1961 Tuva became an "Autonomous Soviet Socialist Republic," but like similar republics in the RSFSR seeking to promote their sovereignty, it opted in the early 1990s to style itself the Republic of Tuva (Tyva). The Soviet administrative districts (*rayon*) were replaced by the former Mongolian-style *hoshuu* and *sum* (qq.v.). Economic and cultural relations with Mongolia are now developing under a bilateral agreement signed in 1992.

TUVANS. Turkic ethnic group. The Tuvans, Soyot, or Tannu Urianhay (q.v.) inhabit the northern borders of Mongolia's Hövsgöl Province and the Republic of Tuva (qq.v.). The Tuvans in the Republic of Tuva number about 207,000. Their life-style is similar to that of Mongols — mostly they are Lamaist, live in felt tents (*ger*), and raise livestock (qq.v.). The Tuvans used classical Mongolian with its vertical script until their language was reduced to a modified Latin script in 1930 and then a modified Cyrillic script (qq.v.), decreed in 1941.

TÜDEV, LODONGIYN (1935-). Mongolian politician and writer. Born in March 1935 in Naran-Öndör district, Gov'-Altay Province (q.v.), Tüdev went to school in Yösönbulag (now Altay, q.v., center of Gov'-Altay Province), then attended Ulan Bator (q.v.) teacher training school from 1950-1953 and the Higher Teachers' School from 1953-1956. He first worked as a teacher in Altay secondary school from 1956-1959, then as a specialist at the Teacher Retraining Institute, Ulan Bator from 1959-1960. He was appointed literary secretary of the MPRP newspaper *Ünen* (Truth) (q.v.) from 1960-1963, then editor of the literary paper *Soyol Utga Zohiol* (Culture and Literature) from 1963-1964. He studied at the CPSU Central Committee's Academy of Social Sciences in Moscow from 1964-1967 and was awarded the degree of candidate of philology; he obtained his doctorate in 1984. On return from Moscow he became an instructor at the MPRP Central Committee (qq.v.) from 1967-1968, then deputy chairman from 1968-1974, and chairman from 1974-1975 of the Committee of the Mongolian Writers' Union. He had been a member of the Buro of the Mongolian Revolutionary Youth Union from 1972-1975 and was elected first secretary from 1975-1984. He was also chairman of the Mongolian Afro-Asian Solidarity Committee from 1971-1973 and chairman of the Mongolian Peace Committee from 1973-1976. He was appointed editor in chief of *Ünen* in 1984 and served as chairman of the Mongolian Journalists' Union from November 1984-April 1990.

Since the 1950s, he has published many stories, books, and novels on conventional communist themes, and he was the author of the MPRP official guidelines for Mongolian writers, including *MPRP Policy in the Field of Literature* (1970) and *National and International Aspects of Mongolian Literature* (1975). He was awarded the title of Merited Cultural Worker (1989), and Order of Sühbaatar (q.v.) (1981), and Order of the Red Banner of Labor Merit, as well as the Soviet Order of People's Friendship (1979).

A member of the MPRP since 1958, he was elected a candidate member of the MPRP Central Committee from 1972-1976 and a member of the MPRP Central Committee from 1976-1992, and is a member of the MPRP Little Hural (q.v.). Following the resignation of the MPRP leadership under Jambyn Batmönh (q.v.), he became a member of the MPRP Politburo in March 1990, member of the MPRP Presidium (the renamed Politburo), and editor in chief of MPRP publications in April 1990, and has been a member of the MPRP Leadership Council (the renamed Presidium) since October 1992. Tüdev was elected a deputy of the People's Great Hural (q.v.) from 1963-1969 and 1973-1992, and a member of the Presidium of the PGH from 1977-1986; he was chairman of the Executive Committee of the Parliamentary Group of the PGH from 1986-1990. He has also been involved in the work of various international communist front organizations, as a member of the Executive Committee of the Afro-Asian Writers' Organization from 1972-1974; member of the Presidium of the World Peace Council from 1974-1976; and vice president of the International Journalists' Organization from 1986-1990.

Tüdev was nominated for the 1993 presidential elections by a meeting of the MPRP Little Hural (q.v.) at which 117 votes were cast for him and 56 for Punsalmaagiyn Ochirbat (q.v.), who subsequently was nominated by the opposition parties. In the elections of June 6, Tüdev with 38.7 percent of the vote was defeated by President Ochirbat, who won 57.8 percent.

TÜMEN, BÜDSÜRENGIYN (1957-   ). Mongolian presidential aide from 1992-1993. Born in Nalayh district of Ulan Bator (qq.v.), Tümen, after completing his schooling in Ulan Bator, studied for a degree in economics at Moscow Higher School of the National Economy from 1973-1978. He has also been awarded the higher degree of Candidate of Economics. He did research work at the Institute of Economics of the Mongolian Academy of Sciences (q.v.) from 1978-1985, then became sector chief and learned secretary of the renamed Institute of Economics of the State Planning and Economic Committee and the Academy of Sciences from 1985-1990. In April 1990 he was appointed a government aide, and from September 1990 senior aide to the president and chairman of the Presidential Learned Council (disbanded August 1992). He was elected a member of the Presidium of the MPRP Central Committee (qq.v.) in 1991 and of the MPRP's Party Leadership Council in October 1992. In July 1992 he was appointed head of the Presidential Seal Office (Secretariat) or President Punsalmaagiyn Ochirbat's (q.v.) "chief of staff," but was replaced in 1993 by Mendsayhany Enhsayhan (q.v.). In November 1993, he was removed from membership of the MPRP's Party Leadership Council (q.v.). His appointment to the post of ambassador to Poland was announced in February 1994.

TÜSHEET-HAN. Former province (*aymag*) in central Mongolia. One of four large provinces (named after their Mongol princes) during the period of Qing (Manchu) (qq.v.) rule, center Örgöö (Urga, q.v.). The province was abolished in 1923, when the territory was renamed Bogd-Han-Uul *aymag* (q.v.).

- U -

ULAAN, CHÜLTEMIYN (1954-   ). Chairman of the National Development Board since 1992. Born on April 22, 1954 in Baruun-Urt town, Sühbaatar Province (qq.v.), Ulaan graduated in 1972 from Irkutsk (q.v.) Higher School of the National Economy. Trained as an industrial engineer and economist, he first worked as a specialist and head of a department of the State Planning Commission from 1977-1985. He then moved to the MPRP Central Committee (qq.v.), where he was an instructor, head of a section, deputy head of a department, and finally economic affairs aide to Jambyn Batmönh (q.v.), chairman of the MPRP Central Committee, until Batmönh resigned in March 1990. He then went to Moscow and obtained a higher degree in market economics at the Russian Management Academy from 1990-1992. Ulaan, who is not a member of the Mongolian Great Hural (q.v.), was appointed chairman of the National Development Board on August 5, 1992 by the first session of the MGH.

ULAAN BULAN. Meaning red corner, a room of "culture and enlightenment" set up at factories, farms, schools, hostels, etc., on the model of the Soviet *krasnyy ugolok* to promote propaganda of the ruling MPRP's (q.v.) political and economic policies. Their number grew from 334 in 1950 to 1,262 in 1985.

ULAANGOM. Center of the Uvs Province (q.v.). Previously known as Ulaangomyn Hüree and the center of the former Chandman'-Uul Province (q.v.) from 1921-1931, Ulaangom was accorded town status in 1961. Its height above sea level is 939 m, the average January and July temperatures are −33.0 and 19.2 deg C, respectively, and the average annual precipitation is 135.3 mm. The distance from Ulan Bator (q.v.) is 1,140 km. Its population is about 23,000. Local industries include production of bricks and foodstuffs.

ULAN BATOR (ULAANBAATAR). Capital of Mongolia. Ulan Bator is Mongolia's biggest town, occupying an area of 2,058.4 sq km. The population is around 619,000 (1993), of which 56.7 percent (65,500 families in 1992) are housed in modern buildings, the remainder in *ger* (q.v.) compounds. The Mongolian Great Hural and Government (qq.v.) are located in the State Palace, which stands on the north side of Sühbaatar Square at the town center. The country's universities and Academy of Sciences (qq.v.), as well as ministries, main hospitals, hotels, libraries, museums, theaters, and other major institutions are also located near the center. The Gandan monastery and winter palace of the Bogd Khan (qq.v.) are in the suburbs. Ulan Bator is a major hub of transport and communications with railway links to the north and south and main motor vehicle routes to the east and west, as well as the country's only large operational civil aviation airport at Buyant-Uhaa, a few kilometers to the south-west.

The origins of Ulan Bator date back to the *örgöö* or temple *ger* of the Tüsheet Han Gombodorj's five-year-old son Zanabazar (q.v.), who was enthroned in 1639 as the first Bogd Gegeen (q.v.) or Buddhist leader of the Halh (q.v.) Mongols. It was originally situated at Shireet Tsagaan Nuur in the present-day Lün district of Arhangay Province (qq.v.). The Bogd Gegeen's temple *ger* and residence, called the Shar Bösiyn Ord, or "yellow cotton palace," were nomadic for 139 years, moving at least 40 times: in 1719-1720 they were situated at Daagandel and Usan Seert (Selenge Province), for example, in 1722 at Hoyt Tamir (Arhangay) and in 1729 at Hujirbulan, near present-day Ulan Bator. In 1706 the Ribogejigandanshadublin monastery was created within the Bogd Gegeen's religious community, which changed its name from Örgöö to Ih Hüree (great monastery). In 1778 it settled at its present site in the valley of the Selbe (a tributary of the Tuul, q.v.) and was renamed Ih Hüree Hot (the great monastery town), although it was not until 1837 that the first stone and brick temple buildings were constructed. The first two-story European-style house was built at Konsulyn Denj (q.v.) in 1863-1865, and the Russian Orthodox Holy Trinity Church was completed there shortly after. As the country's administrative center during and after the period of Autonomous Mongolia from 1911-1924 the town was called Niyslel Hüree (capital monastery).

At various times the Mongolian capital has also been known by other names: in Mongol Bogdyn Hüree, Da Hüree (from 1818) and Hutagtyn Hüree, in Chinese Kunlun (from Hüree), in Tibetan Ribogejigandanshadublin (the name of the founding monastery) or Chonmo, and in Russian and other European languages Urga (from Örgöö) or Kuren (from Hüree). In 1924 the new republican regime renamed it Ulaanbaatar Hot, meaning "Red Hero Town," perhaps in honor of the revolutionary leader Damdiny Sühbaatar (q.v), or possibly "Red Heroes Town." Although the widespread English spelling Ulan Bator seems directly related to the Russian form Ulan-Bator, it was approved by the Mongolian Post Office before the introduction of the Cyrillic script (q.v) for Mongolian.

In 1925, when the population was 61,000, Ulan Bator's districts, aside from Amgalanbaatar, were named after the town's big monasteries: Gandan Züün Hüree, and Dambadarjaalin, and Dashchoynhorlin, and Shadavlin *Hiyd*. Until 1965 it was divided into ten urban districts. From 1965-1992 it comprised four large *rayons,* Ajilchin, Nayramdal, Oktyabr', and Sühbaatar (qq.v.). Since the adoption of the 1992

Constitution (q.v.) and local government reforms, the capital has been composed of 12 urban districts (*düüreg*): Bagahangay, Baganuur, Bayangol, Bayanzürh-Uul, Chingeltey-Uul, Gachuurt, Han-Uul, Jargalant, Nalayh, Songino-Hayrhan, Sühbaatar, and Tuul (qq.v.).

The industrial combine, which began production in 1934, makes shoes and other leather goods, clothing, carpets, felt, woollen yarn and textiles, soap, etc. Newer industries include building materials, iron castings, vehicle repairs, distilling, woodworking, furniture making, brewing, meat packing, and the production of chinaware, glassware, matches, paper, confectionery, dairy produce, animal protein, and pharmaceuticals. In recent years cashmere garments and camel wool blankets have been produced for export. Livestock numbers reached 275,100 head (1992) and arable land 4,100 hectares (1989).

Ulan Bator's height above sea level is 1,351 m, the average January and July temperatures are −26.1 and 17.0 deg C, resepectively, and the average annual precipitation is 233 mm.

ULAN BATOR ECONOMIC COOPERATION ZONE. One of six economic cooperation zones into which Mongolia was divided on the basis of a government ordinance issued in November 1991 (the others being the Central, Bayan-Ölgiy, Gov'-Altay, Övörhangay, and Sühbaatar economic cooperation zones, qq.v). It consists of the Mongolian capital and its surrounding districts. Each zone has a cooperation office headed by the secretary of the zonal cooperation council.

ULAN BATOR RAILWAY. Mongolian-Soviet joint stock company set up in June 1949 with a half share each in the capital of 800 million tögrög for the construction of the Naushki-Ulan Bator (q.v.) railway line, which was opened in November 1949. The company's capital was increased to 1.4 billion tögrög in April 1953 for the construction of the Ulan Bator-Zamyn Uüd (q.v.) line, completed in December 1955. *See also* Railways.

ULAN-UDE. Capital of the Buryat Republic (q.v.). Founded in 1666 as the Udinskoye Cossack winter quarters, this settlement became known as Fort Verkhneudinskaya in 1689. It was made a provincial town in 1775, a district town of Irkutsk (q.v.) Province in 1783, and Verkhneudinsk (Mongolian name Deed Üüd) the capital of the Buryat "Autonomous Soviet Socialist Republic" in 1923. In 1934 it was renamed Ulan-Ude.

ULIASTAY. Center of Zavhan Province (q.v.). Uliastay was the center of Qing administration in Outer Mongolia, and a Manchu (qq.v.) governor was installed there in 1733. Later known as Javhlant and the center of former Zasagt-Han Province (q.v.) until 1921, then the center of the former Han Tayshir-Uul Province (q.v.) until 1931, Uliastay was accorded town status in 1961. Its height above sea level is 1,760 m, the average January and July temperatures are −23.1 and 15.4 deg C, respectively, and the average annual precipitation is 217.0 mm. The distance from Ulan Bator (q.v.) is 910 km. The population is about 20,500. Local industries include vehicle repairs and animal protein and foodstuffs production.

UNGERN-STERNBERG, BARON ROMAN VON (1885-1921). Born in Graz on December 19, 1885, into a noble Baltic German family from Pürkel in Livonia (present-day southern Estonia), the Baron became an officer in the Russian Tsarist army. Serving in Siberia during the Bolshevik revolution of 1917 and ensuing Russian Civil War, the Baron took his division of Cossack cavalry up to the river Onon (q.v.) into Mongolia in October 1920. In February 1921 he captured the Mongolian capital Niyslel Hüree and took the Bogd Khan (qq.v.) hostage. A cruel megalomaniac by all accounts, he recruited Mongolians into his forces with promises of loot and the restoration of Mongolia to the greatness of the Genghis Khan (q.v.) era, and slaughtered those who demurred. The "mad Baron" adopted Mongolian dress, but continued to wear his Russian badges of rank and decorations. In May 1921, as the Mongolian revolutionary army and supporting Soviet Red Army units at Altanbulag (q.v.) prepared for their assault on the capital, the Baron headed north from Niyslel Hüree with his forces to meet them. Beaten back, he turned west and in July 1921 lost another battle at Duh Nars, on the river Selenge (q.v.). In August he engaged Bolshevik forces near Lake Gusinoye (present-day Buryat Republic, q.v.) but retreated back into Mongolia and was captured at Tarialan on August 22. According to Mongol sources he was taken by the Bolsheviks to Novonikolayevsk (now Novosibirsk), tried and executed on September 15, 1921, although a German source says he was shot on September 17 in Irkutsk (q.v.).

UNITED PARTY (UP). Mongolian political party. The United Party was formed under the leadership of Sanjaasürengiyn Zorig (q.v.) in February 1992 on the amalgamation of the Republican and Free Labor Parties and the Civil Democracy wing of the Mongolian Democratic Party (q.v.). The party was registered on April 2, 1992. For the June 1992 elections to the Great Hural (q.v.), the UP formed an alliance with the MDP and Mongolian National Progress Party (q.v.) to field 46 candidates (UP 12, MDP 21, MNPP 13) and five independents. Zorig won the UP's single seat. In October 1992 the UP merged with the Mongolian Democratic, National Progress and Renewal Parties to form the Mongolian National Democratic Party (q.v.).

UNITED PATRIOTIC FRONT. Mongolian political movement. The United Patriotic Front (Patriotic Front, National Unity Front) was set up in February 1990 under the leadership of Luvsandambyn Huushaan (Coordinator 1990-1993) to promote a pro-MPRP (q.v.) line of "restructuring" and the dismantling of "administrative-command socialism" in cooperation with other "social forces." The leadership of the Front was reorganized in April 1993 and Academician Osoryn Shagdarsüren was elected president. The UPF's newspaper is *Erdeniyn Erih* (Precious Beads).

UNIVERSITIES. The Mongolian State University was founded in 1942 and named after Choybalsan (q.v.). During its early development the medical and veterinary faculties became independent "higher schools," and in 1982 the Russian language school and polytechnic were similarly reorganized. The university was renamed the Mongolian National University in 1991. It has five faculties—mathematics, natural sciences, physics, social sciences, and law.

The National Agricultural University, previously the Higher School of Agriculture, was set up on the basis of the State University's former veterinary faculty. It has five faculties—agronomy, economics, engineering, veterinary medicine, and zootechnics.

The National Medical University, previously the Higher Medical School, was set up on the basis of the State University's former medical faculty. It has five schools—medicine, traditional medicine, public health, dentistry, and pharmacy.

The Mongolian Technical University, previously the Higher Polytechnic Institute, was set up on the basis of the State University's former faculty of technology. It has four schools—electrical, mechanical, civil, and mining engineering.

The Army University, the former Higher Combined Arms School, has departments of artillery, communications, armored vehicles, air defense, and military engineering.

Several other "higher schools" are still functioning, including the Higher Schools of Foreign Languages (former Higher Russian Language School), Business Studies, and Theology (the latter at the monastery of Gandan, q.v.).

The number of university students in Mongolia rose from 5,900 at five higher education institutions in 1970 to 12,700 at nine institutions in 1990 (respectively, 1,500 and 3,500 studying at universities abroad). In the peak year of 1985, 15,000 students studied at eight institutions, and another 6,100 were studying abroad. There were 13,700 students attending full-time courses of higher education in 1993-1994, and 3,828 abroad, of whom 2,988 were studying in Russia.

Educational reform and the transition to the market economy since 1991 have brought about some changes to the previous pattern of education and its institutions, including the emergence of private schools, universities, and "colleges." The Economic College is the former Vocational School of Finance and Economics, and the College of Business and Commerce is the former Vocational School of Trade. *See also* Education.

URGA (ÖRGÖÖ). Former name of Ulan Bator (q.v.). Originally it meant the temple *ger* of the Bogd Gegeen (qq.v.), and thus was used as the name of the country's religious capital from 1639-1706; Urga is its Russian form. Until 1921, Urga (Niyslel Hüree) was also the center of the Tüsheet-Han Province (q.v.).

URIANHAY. Territory on Mongolia's Russian border inhabited by Tannu Urianhay or Tuvan people (qq.v.), which was part of Outer Mongolia under Manchu (qq.v.) rule from 1760 to 1911 and in the period of Mongolian autonomy thereafter. Despite Mongolia's wish after the 1921 revolution to preserve its territorial integrity, Russian settlement and political influence after 1914, followed by the victory of the Bolshevik revolution in Siberia, led to the establishment in 1921 of the People's Republic of Tannu-Tuva, later renamed the (People's) Republic of Tuva (q.v.).

URIANHAY, ALTAI. Mongol ethnic group. The Altai Urianhay accounted for 1.0 percent (21,300) of the population of Mongolia, according to the 1989 census. They are concentrated mainly in the northern districts of Bayan-Ölgiy Province and the central districts of Hovd Province and speak a southern dialect of Oyrd (qq.v.).

URIANHAY BÜGD. "All the Urianhay," a former district of northern Mongolia. In the seventeenth and eighteenth centuries the territory of "all the Urianhay" lay to the east of Lake Hövsgöl in the present-day Hövsgöl Province (q.v.).

URIANHAY, TANNU. Turkic ethnic group. The Tannu (Tagna) Urianhay or Tuvans are concentrated mostly in the northern districts of Hövsgöl Province (qq.v.) and numbered some 2,200, according to the 1989 census. Turkic speaking, they are related to the Tuvans of the Republic of Tuva (q.v.) in Russia. The Urianhay (Tuvan) reindeer breeders of Hövsgöl's Tsagaannuur district are called Tsaatan (q.v.) by the Mongols.

URTNASAN, JAMBALDORJIYN (1942-   ). Mongolian politician. Born in Buyant district, Hovd Province (q.v.), Urtnasan graduated in 1955 from the Higher Agricultural School and has a higher degree in veterinary science. In 1965 he became a research worker, later learned secretary of the Institute of Biology of the Academy of Sciences (q.v.) until 1986. After a spell at the Institute of Veterinary Research he became a deputy minister of agriculture for five years, then worked at the Council of Ministers. He was a deputy of the People's Great Hural (q.v.) from 1990-1992 as well as a member of the State Little Hural (q.v.) and a member of the SLH economics standing committee from 1990-1991. He was then elected chairman of the National Association of Agricultural Cooperative Members, only to become chairman of the PGH from November 1991-August 1992. He was made a member of the MPRP Central Committee (qq.v.) in 1992. Urtnasan was elected a member of the Mongolian Great Hural (q.v.) for the MPRP for a four-year term on June 28, 1992, in constituency 24 (Ulan Bator). He is a member of two MGH standing committees: environmental protection and food and agriculture.

URTNASAN, NOROVYN (1951-   ). Mongolian politician. Born in Sant district of Övörhangay Province (q.v.), Urtnasan trained as a teacher of Russian language and literature at the Lenin Higher Teacher-Training School in Moscow, graduating in 1977. He then worked as head of a department of the Mongolian Revolutionary Youth League (q.v.) Central Committee. He received a higher degree in philosophy (education studies) from the CPSU Central Committee's Academy of Social Sciences and on his return to Mongolia worked in the ideology department of the MPRP Central Committee (qq.v.). He is a member of the MPRP. He served as minister of education from September 1990-1992.

UST'-ORDYNSKIY. Center of the Ust'-Ordynskiy Buryat Autonomous District (*okrug*), part of Russia's Irkutsk Region, area 22,400 sq km, situated 69 km from Irkutsk (q.v.) town. Formed in September 1937 as the Ust'-Ordynskiy Buryat-Mongol National District, the district has a population of some 150,000, of whom 50,000 are Buryats, or Buriad (q.v.), called Irkutsk Buryats in Mongolia. They are from the Alar, Bokhan, Ekhirit, Bulagat, and Ol'khon *aymag* of the Buryat (Buryat-Mongol) Republic (q.v.), whose borders had been redrawn. The total Buryat population of Irkutsk Region is about 80,000.

UURGA. A lasso pole. A long pole with a loop of rope at the end used by riders to catch horses and other animals on the open range. The *uurgyn ulaa* was the use by officials on official business of horses and riders commandeered from households and settlements where there was no *örtöö* (q.v.).

UVS. Lake in Mongolia. Uvs *nuur*, the country's largest lake, has a surface area of 3,350 sq km. This saline lake, fed by the river Tes (q.v.) but having no outlet, is situated at a height of 759 m above sea level in the northern part of Uvs Province (q.v.), which is named after it.

UVS. Province (*aymag*) in north-western Mongolia. Formed in 1931, the province is situated on the border with Russia (Mongun-Tayga, Ovyur, Tes-Khem, and Erzin districts of the Tuva Republic, q.v.). With a territory of 69,000 sq km and population of 91,532 (1991), it has 19 rural districts (*sum*); the provincial center is Ulaangom (q.v.). The local minorities inlude the Hoton, Dörvöd, and Bayad (qq.v.). A difficult road into Tuva provides access via Handgayt (Khandagayty) to Kyzyl (q.v.) and Abakan (via the Us *trakt*). The designated permanent crossing points on the border with Russia are Böhmörön (for Kyzyl Hal), Harigiyn gol (for Mugur-Aksy), Borshoo (Borshoogiyn Gol) and Teel (for Handgayt), Teel (for Torgolyg), and Tes (for Shar suur'), and seasonal crossing points Davst and Tes (for Saryg-Hool'). There are deposits of coal (Harhiraa, Har Tarvagatay, Ömnögov', and Türgen) and lignite (Böhmörön and Nüürsthotgor) as well as woodworking industry (Tsagaanhayrhan). Livestock numbers reached 1,596,500 head (1992) and arable land 37,400 hectares (1989).

- Ü -

ÜNEN (TRUTH). Mongolian party newspaper. From its foundation in 1920, initially with the title *Mongolyn Ünen* (Mongolian Truth), this newspaper has been the organ of the Mongolian People's (Revolutionary) Party (qq.v.). The paper was renamed *Uria* (Call) from 1921-1922, then *Niysleliyn Shine Sonin* (Capital's New Newspaper), and *Ardyn Erh* (People's Power) from 1923-1925, finally settling on *Ünen* in 1925. In its heyday the daily *Ünen* was the mouthpiece of both the MPRP Central Committee (qq.v.) and the MPR Council of Ministers, the MPRP being until 1990 the only constitutional party and the "guiding force" in Mongolian society. It was required reading for all who wanted or needed to know the "party line" or read the official statements by the party and government leaders. Once the MPRP had lost its monopoly of political power, and following the rebirth of *Ardyn Erh* (q.v.) as the government newspaper, the circulation of *Ünen* fell from a peak of some 67,500 to around 9,000 copies, and the paper began to appear only once or twice a week.

ÜZEMCHIN (UJUMCHIN). Mongol ethnic group. The Üzemchin, an East Mongol group, are concentrated mostly in northern Dornod Province (q.v.). There were some 2,100 according to the 1989 census. *See also* China: Mongol Ethnic Groups.

- V -

VAN (WANG). A noble title of the first grade created by the Manchu (q.v.). There were two classes, *ch'inwang* and *chünwang*.

VANCHINHÜÜ, BANDIYN (1913-1941). Head of a department of the Special Branch. One of the 32 victims of the Mongolian purges of the 1930s and 1940s (q.v.) sent to the USSR for trial and sentence, details of which were released by the Russian government in 1993. Sentenced to death by the Military Collegium of the USSR Supreme Court in Moscow on July 5, 1941 and executed on July 30.

VEGETABLES. In Mongolia, vegetable growing is not a traditional occupation, but there is evidence that in several areas Mongolian laborers were growing vegetables for local consumption during the Manchu (q.v.) period. Although the herdsmen do not grow vegetables, they gather wild onions, garlic, mushrooms, etc. Large-scale vegetable production is associated with the formation of state farms (q.v.) and particularly with industrialization of Mongolian farming methods in the 1970s-1980s. Production is concentrated in the north-central Töv and Selenge provinces (qq.v.), to supply the shops and markets in the country's main towns. The area sown to potatoes, 11,300 hectares, yields over 100 quintals (metric hundredweight) per hectare (1990), but production of potatoes fell from 131,000 tons (1990) to 78,500 (1992) and 55,000 tons (1993). The area sown to green vegetables (mostly cabbage) in these provinces was 3,100 hectares (1990); production has also fallen, from 41,700 to 16,400 tons (1990-1992). The fall in state potato and vegetable production was due to the breaking up of large farms by privatization and to shortages of fuel for sowing, harvesting, and transport. On the other hand, production by private farmers is increasing, although output levels are not recorded at the moment. Cucumbers and tomatoes are also grown commercially under glass in the Ulan Bator (q.v.) area.

VOLODYA, HAMBARYN (1956-   ). Mongolian politician. Volodya trained as a lawyer and served as deputy chairman of Bayan-Ölgiy (q.v.) Court. He was elected a member of the Mongolian Great Hural (q.v.) for the MPRP (q.v.) for a four-year term on June 28, 1992 in constituency 2 (Bayan-Ölgiy). He is a member of three MGH stand-

ing committees: environmental protection, assemblies and administration, and legal affairs.

- W -

WESTERN ECONOMIC REGION. One of three economic regions into
which Mongolia was divided in the 1980s [the others being the
Central and Eastern Economic Regions, (qq.v.)]. It consisted of the
Hovd-Uvs (provincial) subregion, comprising Hovd, Uvs, and Bayan-
Ölgiy provinces; and the Zavhan-Biger (river-lake) subregion, comprising Zavhan and Gov'-Altay provinces (qq.v.). The region had 21
percent of the country's population and 32 percent of its livestock,
producing about 30 percent of the country's wool and meat. While
economic regionalization defined the geographical conditions of industrial and agricultural production, it did little to promote regional
development. The economic regions were eventually abandoned and
superseded by the system of Economic Cooperation Zones (q.v.) introduced in 1991.

- Y -

YADAMSÜREN, JIGJIDSÜRENGIYN (1950-   ). Mongolian politician. Born in Tariat district of Arhangay Province (q.v.), Yadamsüren
graduated from the Mongolian State University and the CPSU Central
Committee's Academy of Social Sciences in Moscow. He trained as
a teacher of finance and economics and political economy and has the
higher degree of Candidate of Economics. He was a lecturer, then
learned secretary of the MPRP Higher Party School from 1974-1990,
and deputy head, then head of the party organization department of the
MPRP Central Committee (qq.v.) from March 1990-1991. He served
as chairman of Ulan Bator (q.v.) MPRP Committee from April 1991
to October 1992. He was elected member of the MPRP Central Committee in 1990, 1991, and 1992, member of the MPRP Presidium in
July 1991, and secretary of the MPRP Central Committee in October
1992. He was a deputy of the People's Great Hural (q.v.) from 1990-
1992. In October 1992 he was elected chairman of the Presidium of
Ulan Bator Citizens' Delegates' Hural (q.v.). In November 1993 he
resigned from the posts of secretary and member of the MPRP's Party
Leadership Council (q.v.).

YAKS (SARLAG). Mongolia had some 500,000 yaks (Tibetan oxen),
accounting for about one-fifth of the country's cattle (q.v.) at the end
of the 1980s. The average full-grown yak weighs 276 kg and has long
hair reaching almost to the ground, but it is agile and well suited to life

in mountain pastures. The offspring of interbreeding with Mongolian cows are called *haynag*.

YANJMAA, NEMENDEYN (SÜHBAATARYN) (1893-1962). Wife of Damdiny Sühbaatar (q.v.). Born on February 15, 1893 in Ih Hüree (q.v.) into the family of a poor herdsman, Yanjmaa became a messenger for Sühbaatar's revolutionary group in 1919. When Sühbaatar secretly went to Russia in 1920, Yanjmaa and their son Galsan remained behind; forced to hide from Chinese troops hunting revolutionaries, she fell ill and only in 1921 was able with the help of Choybalsan (q.v.) and other revolutionaries to make her way to Kyakhta (Altanbulag) (qq.v.) to be reunited with Sühbaatar. She remained in Altanbulag until after the victory of the revolution, when she took up political work in the Mongolian Revolutionary Youth League (q.v.). In 1924 she joined the MPRP and was sent to Moscow by the MPRP Central Committee (qq.v.) to represent the party at the International Congress of Women, where she met Klara Zetkin and Nadezhda Krupskaya, and to participate in the fifth Congress of the Comintern (q.v.). Later she ran the women's section of the MPRP Central Committee, concentrating on the education of women. In 1925 she was involved in the formation of Mongolia's first trade union. From 1927-1930 she studied at the Communist University of the Toilers of the East in Moscow. She was elected to the MPRP Central Committee in 1925 and to its Presidium from August 1924 to September 1925, later to the Politburo from April 8, 1940-1954, and was a secretary of the Central Committee from 1941-1947. Yanjmaa was also elected a member of the Presidium of the Little Hural in 1940, a member of the People's Great Hural 1951-1962 and also of its Presidium, as well as president of the Mongolian Women's Committee. She was awarded the Order of Sühbaatar (q.v.) (twice), the Order of the Red Banner of Labor Merit (twice), and the Order of the Pole Star (q.v.), as well as the Soviet Order of the Red Banner and the WCP Jolio-Curie Medal.

YÖSONBULAG. Mongolian town. The former name of Altay (q.v.), center of Gov'-Altay Province (q.v.).

- Z -

ZAHCHIN (DZAKHCHIN). Mongol ethnic group. The Zahchin, a West Mongol Oyrd (q.v.) (Oirat) group related to the Torguud (q.v.) speaking a southern dialect, accounted for 1.1 percent (22,500) of the population of Mongolia, according to the 1989 census. They are concentrated mainly in the southern districts of Hovd Province (q.v.).

ZAMYN-ÜÜD. Town in Mongolia. Situated close to the Mongolian-Chinese border between Dornogov' Province and Inner Mongolia (qq.v.), the town is the customs and immigration control point for traffic on the Trans-Mongolian Railway to and from Ereen (Erenhot) station in Inner Mongolia.

ZANABAZAR (1635-1723). The first Bogd Gegeen (q.v.), Zanabazar was proclaimed the spiritual leader of Mongolian Lamaism (qq.v.) in 1639. Also named Luvsandambiyjaltsan, he was the son of the Mongol Tüsheet Khan Gombodorj (1594-1655), who claimed descent from Genghis Khan (q.v.). Zanabazar was awarded the title Javzandamba Hutagt (q.v.) in 1650. He devised the script based on the *soyombo* (q.v.) and was a talented sculptor of religious figures. Some fine examples of his bronze-casting skill are to be found in Mongolia's temples and museums. The modern Ulan Bator (q.v.) developed around his temple and palace.

ZARDYHAN, KINAYATYN (KINAYAT-ULY) (1940-   ). Mongolian politician. Born in Hovd district of Hovd Province (q.v.), Zardyhan, a Kazakh (q.v.), graduated from the Mongolian State University in 1965 and from the CPSU Central Committee's Academy of Social Sciences in 1975; he has a higher degree in philosophy and is a doctor of history. From 1965-1968 he was a lecturer for the Hovd Provincial MPRP (q.v.) Committee; from 1968-1975 he worked in the ideological department of the MPRP Central Committee (qq.v.); from 1975-1987 he was secretary of the Mongolian Central Trade Union Council (q.v.); and from 1987-1990 he was head of a department of the MPRP Central Committee's Institute of Social Sciences. He was one of the authors of a series of articles published in the MPRP monthly journal *Namyn Am'dral* (Party Life) in 1989 calling for an end to dogmatic interpretations of Marxism-Leninism and to the MPRP's political monopoly. In 1990-1991 he was leader of the MPRP faction "For the Continuation of Traditions and Renewal of the Mongolian People's Party," which broke away to form the Mongolian Renewal Party (q.v.) in December 1991. Appointed deputy chairman of the Council of Ministers from March-September 1990, he was elected a deputy of the People's Great Hural (q.v.), a member of the State Little Hural (q.v.), and vice chairman of the SLH from 1990-1992. In October 1992 he was appointed Mongolia's consul general in Tashkent, Uzbekistan.

ZASAG DARGA. Originally meaning the ruler of a *hoshuu* (q.v.), this title is now used for appointed governors of Ulan Bator (q.v.) and the 18 provinces as well as lower-level administrators since the local government reforms brought about by the 1922 Constitution (q.v.). The word *zasag* means power, authority, or even government—in full, *zasgyn gazar,* meaning the central government (q.v.).

ZASAGT-HAN. Former province (*aymag*) in western Mongolia. One of four large provinces (named after their Mongol princes) during the period of Qing (Manchu) (qq.v.) rule, center Zasagt Hany Hüree (later Yösönbulag, Altay q.v.). In the seventeenth and eighteenth centuries, the province included some territory of the present-day Hami Prefecture (Xinjiang Uighur Autonomous Region, China). The province was abolished in 1923, when the territory was renamed Han-Tayshir-Uul (q.v.) *aymag.*

ZAVHAN. Province (*aymag*) in north-western Mongolia. Formed in 1931, and initially including parts of the present-day Bayanhongor Province, the province, named after the river Zavhan, is situated between the Hangay Mountains (qq.v.) and the border with Russia (Erzin and Kaa-Khem districts of the Tuva Republic, q.v.). With a territory of 82,000 sq km and population of 93,541 (1991), it has 23 rural districts (*sum*); the provincial center, now Uliastay (q.v.), was initially Bayanzürh. The local minorities inlcude the Hotgoyd and Hoshuud (qq.v.). The designated permanent crossing point on the border with Russia is Artssuur' (for Tsagaantolgoy). There are lumber mills (Tosontsengel, q.v) and brickworks (Yaruu). Livestock numbers reached 2,085,000 head (1992) and arable land 45,200 hectares (1989).

ZAVHAN. River in Mongolia. The Zavhan *gol,* one of the country's five longest rivers, 808 km, entirely within Mongolia, is fed by the Buyant and Shar Us river systems rising in the Hangay Mountains in Zavhan Province (qq.v.). It flows north-west, forming the boundary between Zavhan and Gov'-Altay Provinces, before entering Lake Ayrag and Lake Hyargas in southern Uvs Province (qq.v.).

ZAYAA, OCHIRBATYN. Mongolian politician. Zayaa was elected leader of the newly formed Mongolian United Heritage Party (q.v.) toward the end of 1993. Previously she had been the leader of the Mongolian United Private Owners' Party (q.v.).

ZAYAPANDITA. The Zayapandita (Zaya Bandid) Luvsanperenlei, an Oirat (Oyrad, q.v.) prince also known as Ogtorguyn (Heavenly) Dalay, who devised the clear script (q.v.), or *tod bichig,* a modification of the classical Mongolian script (q.v.) for use by the western Mongols (Jungars, Oirats, and Kalmyks). Some 2,000 manuscript and xylographs in "clear script" are held by the State Public Library and the Institute of Language and Literature of the Mongolian Academy of Sciences in Ulan Bator (qq.v.). Most of the xylographs date from the time of the Jungarian Khan Galdantseren in the 1740s and are translations of Buddhist works such as the *Jadambaa* and *Altangerel*. However, there are 47 by Zayapandita himself, of the 177 he completed between 1652 and 1662, and biographic and colophon poetry by him.

ZEEREN. A kind of antelope, sometimes called the black-tailed antelope or dzheiran, inhabiting the steppe and semi-steppe regions of Mongolia, especially Gov'-Altay, Dundgov', Ömnögov', and Dornogov' provinces (qq.v.). A full-grown male reaches a height of 75 cm and a weight of 25-30 kg and can develop a speed of 60-70 kph for a distance of 10-15 km. They tend to congregate in herds of several hundred head in autumn. Their overall numbers have fallen considerably due to overhunting.

ZENEE, MENDIYN (1947-   ). Mongolian politician. Zenee trained as a teacher and became a research worker at the Northeast Asia Studies Center of the Academy of Sciences (q.v.). He became a member of the MPRP Central Committee (qq.v.) in November 1990-1992. He was elected a member of the Mongolian Great Hural (q.v.) for the MPRP for a four-year term on June 28, 1992, in constituency 14 (Töv). He is a member of three MGH standing committees: education, science, and culture; foreign policy and security; and internal affairs. He was elected chairman of the MGH Sub-Committee for Struggle against Bribetaking and Abuse of Office in December 1993.

ZOLJARGAL, NAYDANSÜRENGIYN (1964-   ). Director general of the Stock Exchange since 1991. Born in Ulan Bator (q.v.), Zoljargal attended a Russian school in Ulan Bator and entered the international economy faculty of Budapest Economic College, graduating in 1988. On his return to Mongolia he first worked as an accountant at the Mongolian State Bank (Mongolbank, q.v.). He was appointed director of the Mongolian Trade and Development Bank in 1990. He became director general of the Mongolian Stock Exchange on its foundation in January 1991.

ZORIG, SANJAASÜRENGIYN (1962-   ). Mongolian politician. Zorig graduated from the philosophy faculty of Moscow State University in 1985. He worked for a year as an instructor at the Ulan Bator MRYL Committee, and then in 1986 took up lecturing and postgraduate research in scientific communism at the Mongolian State University. The birth of democracy in Mongolia is particularly linked with Zorig, who abandoned Marxism-Leninism to found and lead the Mongolian Democratic Association (q.v.) in December 1989. In September 1991, however, he left the MDA to found the Mongolian Republican Party (q.v.), which he wanted to be a party with middle-class values focusing on human rights. In February 1992 the Republican Party merged with the Free Labor Party and the Civil Democracy wing of the MDA to form the United Party (q.v.), of which Zorig became the leader. Zorig was a deputy of the People's Great Hural (q.v.) and chairman of the Executive Committee of the Parliamentary Group from 1990-1992. He was elected a member of the Mongolian Great Hural (q.v.) for the UP for a four-year term on June 28, 1992, in constituency 23 (Ulan Bator). He is a member of three MGH standing committees: education, science, and culture; foreign policy and security; and internal affairs. During the summer of 1992, Zorig and other opposition party leaders negotiated over the formation of a new combined opposition party tentatively called the Mongolian New Constitution Party (q.v.), but this was not proceeded with. In October 1992, the Mongolian United, National Progress, Renewal, and Democratic Parties merged to form the Mongolian National Democratic Party (q.v.), and Zorig became a member of the MNDP General Council.

ZORIGTBAATAR, CHULUUNY (1958-   ). Mongolian politician. Zorigtbaatar trained as a lawyer and became head of the administrative department of the Selenge Executive Administration (qq.v.). He was elected a member of the Mongolian Great Hural for the MPRP (qq.v.) for a four-year term on June 28, 1992, in constituency 13 (Selenge). He is a member of two MGH standing committees: assemblies and administration, and legal affairs.

ZUD. Word usually translated as "starvation" or "fodder shortage," denoting weather or other conditions preventing livestock (q.v.) from grazing, in particular *gan zud,* when the ground is covered with a layer of ice after a warm spell in cold weather; *har zud*—"black zud," when there is a lack of snow in a waterless region; *tuurayn zud*—"hoof zud," when the pasture is trampled down as a result of overcrowding; and *tsagaan zud*—"white zud," when heavy snowfall prevents livestock from grazing.

ZUUNAY, GENDENSAMBUUGIYN (1944-1994). Mongolian politician. Born in Delger district of Gov'-Altay Province (q.v.), Zuunay graduated in 1970 from Ulan Bator (q.v.) Higher Medical School and has a higher degree in medicine from Moscow Medical Institute. He studied French at the Sorbonne and Russian and English at the Zhukov Academy, Moscow. In 1970 he became a physician at the State

Pathology Bureau, then a research worker at the Institute of Medicine, and in 1982 he was appointed head of medical services of the Mongolian Railway (q.v.). He became head of a department and then of a directorate at the Ministry of Health (Ministry of Health and Social Security) from 1987-1990. He was elected a deputy of the People's Great Hural, a member of the State Little Hural (qq.v.), and member of the SLH social policy committee from 1990-1992. He became a member of the MPRP Central Committee in 1992, then of the MPRP Little Hural (qq.v.). Zuunay was elected a member of the Mongolian Great Hural (q.v.) for the MPRP for a four-year term on June 28, 1992 in constituency 5 (Gov'-Altay). He served as chairman of the MGH standing committee for health and social security until October 1993 and as a member of the standing committees for environmental protection and for education, science, and culture. He died of illness on July 27, 1994.

ZUUNMOD. Center of Töv Province (q.v.). Accorded town status in 1965, Zuunmod is situated south of Bogd Han Mountain, which separates it from Ulan Bator (qq.v.). Its height above sea level is 1,529 m, the average January and July temperatures are −20.5 and 15.4 deg C, respectively, and the average annual precipitation is 270.8 mm. The population is about 15,500. Local industry produces mainly foodstuffs.

ZÜÜN HUREE *see* Hüree.

ZÜÜNHARAA. Town in Mongolia. Accorded town status in 1961, Züünharaa is situated in the southern part of Selenge Province (q.v.) and has a station on the Trans-Mongolian Railway. Its population is about 14,000. The main industries are timber processing, railway rolling stock repairs, and a distillery.

ZÜÜNSELBE. Former ward (*horoo*) of Ulan Bator (q.v.). One of the ten wards abolished in 1965 on the formation of Ajilchin, Nayramdal, Oktyabr', and Sühbaatar (qq.v.) districts (*rayon*), each with smaller numbered *horoo*.

Bibliography

The Mongol Empire was the biggest land empire there has ever been, embracing many nations from Austria to Java, and the literature on the Mongols and Mongolia is equally large and diverse. The Dictionary concentrates on twentieth-century Mongolia, particularly the recent period, and although the bibliography does likewise, books about Mongolia surely must begin with the *Secret History of the Mongols*. This exciting mixture of legend and record is essential reading for an understanding of Mongol life in the time of Genghis Khan. Thereafter Morgan's *The Mongols* provides a scholarly and amusing introduction to the rise and fall of the Mongol Empire. For its perceptive survey of the Manchu and early communist periods of Mongolian history, Bawden's *The Modern History of Mongolia* is unsurpassed. Rupen's *Mongols of the Twentieth Century,* with its focus on Soviet influence and the Stalinist purges in Mongolia, is another classic.

Heissig and Müller's *Die Mongolen* is a big and beautiful collection of contributions by leading Mongolists who share with us their personal insight into many aspects of Mongol history and culture. Heissig, who "rediscovered" the "lost" Mongols well before the latecomers to the scene, is the author of *The Religions of Mongolia* and a history of Mongolian literature in German, and the editor of a series of Mongol epics.

Hangin's basic and intermediate textbooks of Mongol have been reprinted, but would-be students of the language face a narrow choice. German-speakers might try to find textbooks and dictionaries by Vietze. Some textbooks of Mongol have been published in Russian in the USSR and in Mongolia (Lhagva, Luvsanjav). The *Textbook of Colloquial Mongolian* by Vacek and Luvsandorj, with its excellent drills and models, was published in Prague in Czech. Hangin's *Modern Mongolian-English Dictionary* is the best available, if rather expensive. The English-Mongolian dictionaries by Hangin and Altangerel are more useful to Mongols learning English than English-speakers trying to express themselves in Mongol. All these are in the Cyrillic script. Poppe's *Grammar of Written Mongolian* was reprinted for the fourth time in 1991.

The first and so far the only guidebook entirely devoted to Mongolia is Robert Storey's *Mongolia: A Travel Survival Kit*. He gets full marks for exploring and describing some of the remotest attractions of Mongolia today, but the "kit" is marred by historical and linguistic errors. The recent travel books about Mongolia include Severin's *In Search of Genghis Khan* and Becker's *The Lost Country: Mongolia Revealed.* With the help of fine color photos, the former describes a horseback expedition in central Mongolia; the latter is about rediscovering the Mongol nation's roots in both Mongolia and adjacent areas. Some of the amusing and frustrating aspects of Mongolian life depicted in Middleton's *The Last Disco in Outer Mongolia* have changed little in the 30 years since MacColl's *The Land of Genghis Khan.* For a short, clear view of the Mongols and Mongolia, the *Encyclopaedia Britannica* entries should not be overlooked.

The Pergamon Press's *Information Mongolia,* prepared by the Mongolian Academy of Sciences as the definitive "official" handbook, was overtaken by events. For all its many color photos, intricate detail and massive size (and cost), it is a splendid obituary for the MPR. Worden and Savada's *Mongolia: A Country Study* is without the former's propaganda and is recommended for its clear analysis of the Mongolian political and economic situation as the transition to democracy was about to begin; it also has a good bibliography. The contributions to Akiner's *Mongolia Today* were originally papers for a London conference in 1987, describing features of the old "socialist" MPR, and don't form a real link with the new democratic Mongolia, whose birth still awaits its first full-length description.

Similarly the tide of change has turned William Butler's *The Mongolian Legal System* from a reference book into a history book. The development of constitutional law in Mongolia has been an important feature of the recent period. The 1992 Constitution (see Appendix 4) has generated a diverse range of new legislation appropriate to a democracy building a market economy. Dozens of new laws have been adopted affecting many facets of social and economic life, including the conditions for foreign investment in Mongolia (see Appendix 5), but outside Mongolia they are scarcely known, let alone understood.

Little of lasting value was written about the economy of "socialist" Mongolia. Outside the country only a few specialists had the skills to produce a good analysis of the often untrustworthy official statistical data, of which there was plenty, and sometimes the conclusions in retrospect were still wrong. International interest now focuses closely on exploring and mapping the country's mineral resources. The economy is essentially in the hands of the International Monetary Fund, the Asian Development Bank, and the regular Tokyo donors' conferences, whose financial experts produce charts, diagrams, and projections in their arcane language.

The appearance last year of Judith Nordby's annotated bibliography of Mongolia, a very useful guide to some 500 mostly English books and articles about Mongolia, prompted me to select some entries from the Mongolian and Russian literature on Mongolia. During the period of Soviet domination in Mongolia, books for foreign consumption were largely limited to glowing political and economic success stories. Behind this facade, however, some serious academic works were being published, mostly in Mongol but some in Russian. Of course, the authors could not contradict the "party line" on a wide range of important issues from Genghis Khan to birth control. The censorship prevented the airing of many matters concerning the country's political and social life and distorted the Mongols' view of the outside world. Life was especially difficult for historians. As one said: "Only the future was certain. The past was changing all the time."

Over the years the Mongolian Terminological Commission has produced many useful short dictionaries and glossaries, in which Russian was usually the key to discovering facets of Mongolian life as varied as aircraft engineering and epizootic disease. The publications of the Mongolian Academy of Sciences have grown into a large fund of valuable research materials in several series, on Mongolian language, archaeology, botany, zoology, etc. Rinchen's *Ethnological and Linguistic Atlas of the MPR* is outstanding. Rinchen was in and out of prison at various times during his long academic career, yet the charges of "bourgeois nationalism" against him were no deterrent to the fulfillment of his task of creating for posterity cultural, archaeological and linguistic records of the Mongols—and much of what communism had destroyed.

The *National Atlas of the MPR,* published jointly by the Mongolian and Soviet Academies of Sciences, was a big undertaking—literally, it measures 18 inches by 23. Its 276 color plates illustrate the political and physical geography, climate, geology, soils, flora and fauna, etc., yet only the contents are in English. It was an act of folly to produce such a monumental work with the text and map keys in Mongolian only.

Since the launching of a market economy, Mongolia's publishing industry has been facing many difficulties in its newfound freedom—the end of subsidies, the lack of foreign exchange, and the shortage of paper. The emergence of new publishers in Mongolia and the appearance of their first books and pamphlets, on Genghis Khan and other subjects close to the Mongol's heart, is therefore very welcome. Fresh biographical material on Choybalsan and Danzan has been published, and the new political parties have produced booklets about themselves.

Mongolian studies are a long-established, distinguished, and diverse field of Russian academic life. Even during the Soviet regime, many useful academic publications about Mongolia appeared in Russian. In the recent period, the geography of Mongolia by Ovdiyeno was translated into English in the USA. Gol'man has written or coauthored several reference books, including documentation of Mongolian-Soviet agreements. Grayvoronskiy observed the development of Mongolian agriculture from the vantage point of the Soviet embassy in Ulan Bator. The ethnographical collections by Viktorova and Zhukovskaya are important and also very readable. Of course, Soviet Mongolists were required to serve the state's political purposes. Delegates to the sixth International Congress of Mongolists in Ulan Bator in 1992 listened with polite interest as the now ex-Soviet Russian Mongolists recanted apologetically.

Mongolia is a remote and still rather inaccessible country, and its publishing industry, tourism organization, and media are too small and weak to have much impact on the world at large. Thus foreign journalists have had an important role to play in telling the world what Mongolia is doing and thinking. Mostly they go to Ulan Bator only for brief visits, but in recent years a few, like Peter Hannam, writing for the *Far Eastern Economic Review,* have lived in Ulan Bator for months at a time and gained a real understanding of the country. Meanwhile, the US Foreign Broadcast Information Service and Joint Publications Research Service, and the BBC Monitoring Service, have for many years provided for government officials, commercial publishers, and researchers of every kind a steady flow of documentation from Mongolian and other sources about the country.

For almost the whole "socialist" period in Mongolia, official information was published in *Ünen,* the daily "Truth" (fortunately only four pages) of the MPRP Central Committee and Council of Ministers. Only a shadow of its former self, *Ünen* has been relegated to twice-weekly publication, its now unsubsidized circulation down from 67,500 to 9,000 copies. Since 1990 a great number of new newspapers and magazines have appeared (266 had been registered by the end of 1993), ranging from the publications of the new political parties to pornography. Some have already ceased publication, and many more with very small circulations will surely go under.

The essential reading for today is the newspaper *Ardyn Erh,* which publishes the speeches of the president and prime minister, accounts of proceedings in the Hural, and the texts of new laws, information about banks and companies, etc. Two English-language papers are published in Ulan Bator: the weekly *Mongol Messenger,* and the fortnightly *Mongolian Independent*. The problem is finding out how to subscribe and ensure a regular supply. Now that there is no State Publishing House to monopolize the book trade, there are also no publisher's catalogs. For the moment, the best way to find new Mongolian books is to shop in Ulan Bator.

Bibliography: Contents

1. General

Bibliography

Ewing, Thomas E. "Outer Mongolia, 1911-1940: A Bibliographical Review." *Zentralasiatische Studien,* Harrassowitz, Wiesbaden, Vol. 14, no. 2, 1980, pp. 205-219.

Hurlat, V. V. *Bibliografiya rabot po Mongolii: Ukazetel' knig i statey na russkom i drugikh yevropeyskikh yazykakh, postupivshikh v gosudarstvennuyu publichnuyu biblioteku po 1957 god vklyuchitel'no* (Bibliography of Works about Mongolia: Index of Books and Articles in Russian and other European Languages Received by the State Public Library up to 1957 Inclusive). MPR State Public Library, Ulan Bator, 1962.

Ishdorj, Ts., and Dorj, D. *Works by Mongolian Historians, Trudy mongol'skikh istorikov (1960-1974): Annotated Bibliography in English and Russian* (trans. Tsendsüren, Ts., ed. Bira, Sh.). MPR Academy of Sciences Press, Ulan Bator, 1975.

Nordby, Judith. *Mongolia.* World Bibliographical Series Volume 156, Clio Press, Oxford, Santa Barbara, Denver, 1993.

Rupen, Robert A. *Mongols of the Twentieth Century. Part II: Bibliography.* Indiana University Press, Bloomington, 1964. (For Part I see section 4. History, Communist Period).

Schwarz, Henry G. *Bibliotheca Mongolica: Works in English, French,*

228 • Bibliography

and German. Western Washington University Press, Bellingham, Washington, 1978.

————. *Mongolian Publications at Western Washington University*. Western Washington University Press, Bellingham, Washington, 1984.

Reference

Dariymaa, S. *Ulaanbaatar hot dah' alban bayguullaguudyn telefony jagsaalt* (Telephone Directory of Official Organizations in Ulan Bator). Ministry of Communications, Ulan Bator, 1987 (updated 1992).

Dupuy, Trevor, and Blanchard, Wendell. *Area Handbook for Mongolia*. American University, Washington, DC, 1970.

Gataullina, L. M. *Mongol'skaya Narodnaya Respublika - Spravochnik* (The Mongolian People's Republic - A Handbook). USSR Academy of Sciences, Nauka Press, Moscow, 1986.

Heissig, Walther, and Müller, Claudius C. *Die Mongolen* (The Mongols). Umschau Verlag, Frankfurt-am-Main, 1989.

Information Mongolia. MPR Academy of Sciences, Pergamon Press, Oxford and New York, 1990.

Jambaldorj, S. (ed.). *Hüühed-zaluuchuudyn nevterhiy tol'* (Encyclopedia for Children and Young People). Vol. I "Miniy Eh oron - Mongol" (My Homeland - Mongolia), State Publishing House, Ulan Bator, 1983; Vol. II "Augaa ih nayramdal" (Great Friendship), State Publishing House, Ulan Bator, and Progress Publishers, Moscow, 1986.

Radnaabazar, G. *Mongol shuudangiyn mark; Pochtovyye marki MNR* (Mongolian Stamp Catalog). State Publishing House, Ulan Bator, 1984.

Sanders, Alan J. K. *Mongolia: Politics, Economics and Society*. Frances Pinter, London, and Lynne Rienner, Colorado, 1987.

————. *The People's Republic of Mongolia: A General Reference Guide*. Oxford University Press, London and New York, 1968.

Worden, Robert L., and Savada, Andrea M. *Mongolia: A Country Study*. Library of Congress, Washington, DC, 1991.

Yearbooks

Heaton, William R. "Mongolia." *1991 Yearbook on International Communist Affairs* (ed. Staar, Grigory). Hoover Institution Press, Stanford, 1991.

Sanders, Alan J. K. "Mongolia." *The Annual Register 1992: A Record of World Events* (ed. Day, Alan J.). Longman, London, 1993, pp. 367-369 (and previous editions).

————. "Mongolia." *The Europa World Year Book* (Vol. II). Europa Publications, London, 1993, pp. 1968-1980 (and previous editions).

————. "Mongolia." *The Far East and Australasia 1993*. Europa Publications, London, 1993, pp. 551-568 (and previous editions).

————. "Mongolia." *World of Learning 1993*. Europa Publications, London, 1993, pp. 1025-1026 (and previous editions).

————. "Mongolia." *1993 Asia Yearbook* (ed. Malik, Michael). Far Eastern Economic Review, Hong Kong, 1993, pp. 168-170 (and previous editions.)

————. "Mongolia." *1993 Britannica Book of the Year* (ed. Daume, Daphne). Encyclopaedia Britannica, Chicago, 1993, pp. 401-402 (and previous editions).

————. "Mongolia." *1993 International Year Book* (ed. Famighetti, Robert). Collier, New York, 1992, pp. 334-335 (and previous editions).

Statistics

50 years of the MPR—Statistical Collection. Central Statistical Board under the Council of Ministers of the MPR, Ulan Bator, 1971.

National Economy of the MPR for 60 Years (1924-1984): Anniversary Statistical Collection. Central Statistical Board of the MPR, Ulan Bator, 1984 (and previous editions).

National Economy of the MPR for 65 Years: Anniversary Statistical Collection. Central Statistical Board, Ulan Bator, 1986.

National Economy of the MPR for 70 Years (1921-91): Anniversary Statistical Yearbook. State Statistical Office of the MPR, Ulan Bator, 1991.

Statisticheskiy yezhegodnik stran-chlenov Soveta Ekonomicheskoy Vzaimopomoshchi (Statistical Yearbook of the Member Countries of the Council for Mutual Economic Aid). Secretariat of the CMEA, Finansy i Statistika Press, Moscow, 1990 (and previous editions).

Travel and Description

Becker, Jasper. *The Lost Country: Mongolia Revealed*. Hodder and Stoughton, London, 1992.

Bisch, Jørgen. *Mongolia: Unknown Land* (trans. Spink, Reginald). Dutton, New York, and Allen and Unwin, London, 1963.

Expedition Mongolia 1990: The First Anglo-Mongolian Expedition in History. Expedition Mongolia Publications, London, 1990.

Latham, Ronald (trans.). *The Travels of Marco Polo*. Penguin Books, Harmondsworth, England, 1958.

MacColl, René M. *The Land of Genghis Khan: A Journey in Outer Mongolia*. Oldbourne, London, 1963.

Major, John S. *The Land and People of Mongolia*. Lippincott, New York, 1990.

Middleton, Nicholas J. *The Last Disco in Outer Mongolia*. Sinclair-Stevenson, London, 1992.

230 • Bibliography

Montagu, Ivor. *Land of the Blue Sky: A Portrait of Modern Mongolia.* Dobson, London, 1956.
Severin, Tim. *In Search of Genghis Khan.* Hutchinson, London and Sydney, 1991.
Stefoff, Rebecca. *Mongolia.* Chelsea House, Edgemont, 1986.
Thevenet, Jacqueline, *Les Mongols de Genghis-Khan et d'aujourd'hui* (The Mongols of Genghis Khan and of Today). Armand Colin, Paris, 1986.

Maps, Atlases, and Guides

Avirmed, E. (ed.). *BNMAU-yn ashigt maltmalyn zurag* (Map of the MPR's Useful Minerals 1:2 500 000. State Directorate of Geodesy and Cartography, Ulan Bator, 1983.
Baasanhüü, L. (ed.). *Arhangay aymgiyn atlas* (Atlas of Arhangay Province). State Directorate of Geodesy and Cartography, Ulan Bator, 1987.
Badamjav, D. *BNMAU-yn gazarzüyn atlas* (Geographical Atlas of the MPR). Ministry of Education, Ulan Bator, 1966.
Bügd Nayramdah Mongol Ard Uls: Ündesniy atlas (The Mongolian People's Republic: National Atlas). USSR and MPR Academies of Sciences, Ulan Bator and Moscow, 1990.
China World-Continent Map 1:4 Mio. GeoCenter International, RV Reise- und Verkehrsverlag, Berlin, 1992/93 (includes Mongolia and Russian republics and shows topography).
China & Mongolia World Travel Map. Bartholomew, Harper Collins, London, 1994. (1:6 000 000 showing political divisions, with index).
Damdinsüren, D., and Zogsohpürev, D. (ed.). *BNMAU* (Administrative Map of the MPR 1:2 500 000). State Directorate of Geodesy and Cartography, Ulan Bator, 1984.
Ethnological and Linguistic Atlas: see section 2. Culture, Language, and Script.
Ganbaatar, Z. (comp.). *Atlas: Zam Hariltsaa: Transport Network.* State Directorate of Geodesy and Cartography, Ulan Bator, 1991.
Jargalsayhan, D., and Eimon, Paul I. *Mineral Resources Map of Mongolia* (1:3 000 000), Minerals Evaluation Network, Commonwealth Int., Amarillo, Texas, 1993 (with 19-page legend).
Mönhtör, O. (ed.). *Hovd aymag—yörönhiy gazarzüyn zurag* (Hovd Province—A General Geographical Map 1:750 000). State Directorate of Geodesy and Cartography, Ulan Bator, 1986 (one of a set of the 18 provinces).
Oyuunchimeg. *BNMAU tsomog zurag* (MPR Map Set). State Directorate of Geodesy and Cartography, Ulan Bator, 1984.
Oyuungerel, J. (ed.). *BNMAU: Gazar dürsiyn zurag* (Geophysical Map

of the MPR 1:2 500 000). State Directorate of Geodesy and Cartography, Ulan Bator, 1985. ´

Sanders, Alan J. K. "Mongolia." *All-Asia Travel Guide* (ed. Malik, Michael). Far Eastern Economic Review, Hong Kong, 1993, pp. 326-333 (and previous editions).

———. "The Languages of Mongolia." *Atlas of the World's Languages* (ed. Moseley, Christopher, and Asher, R. E.). Routledge, London, 1993.

Saynbayar, A., and Sodnomvaanchig, G. (comp.). *Ediyn zasgiyn dornod muj, Ediyn zasgiyn örnöd muj* (Eastern Economic Zone, Western Economic Zone 1:1 500 000). State Directorate of Geodesy and Cartography, Ulan Bator, 1985.

———. *Ediyn zasgiyn töv muj* (Central Economic Zone 1:1 500 000). State Directorate of Geodesy and Cartography, Ulan Bator, 1985.

Storey, Robert. *Mongolia: A Travel Survival Kit.* Lonely Planet Publications, Hawthorn, Victoria, 1993.

Süh-Ochir, R. (comp.). *BNMAU atlas* (Atlas of the MPR). State Directorate of Geodesy and Cartography, Ulan Bator, 1990.

Tsend-Ochir, I., and Urtnasan, S. *Turistskiye marshruty Mongolii* (Mongolia's Tourist Routes). Juulchin, Ulan Bator, 1978.

Tserenbyambaa, Ts. *BNMAU-yn baygaliyn büs, büshüüriyn zurag* (Map of the MPR's Natural Zones). State Directorate of Cartography and Geodesy, Ulan Bator, 1979.

Ulaanbaatar City Map (1:20 000). Nüüdelchin Co Ltd, Ulan Bator, and BAKS Co Ltd Warsaw, 1992.

2. Culture

General

Bira, Sh. (ed.). *Olon ulsyn mongol erdemtniy V ih hural: Pyatyy mezhdunarodnyy kongress mongolovedov: Fifth International Congress of Mongolists* (1987). International Association for Mongol Studies, Ulan Bator, 1992 (summaries of congress papers; also previous editions).

Jagchid, Sechin, and Hyer, Paul. *Mongolia's Culture and Society.* Westview, Boulder, CO, and Dawson, Folkestone, England, 1979.

"Mongolia: Life and Culture of the Great Nomads." *Asian Pacific Culture,* Asian Cultural Center for UNESCO, Tokyo, 1992, no. 47.

Pringle, James. "Breaking silence - Genghis Khan is rehabilitated as a national hero." *Far Eastern Economic Review,* Hong Kong, August 24, 1989, p. 26.

Sanders, Alan. "Hordes of pride—Ulan Bator rehabilitates Genghis Khan." *Far Eastern Economic Review,* Hong Kong, February 23, 1989, p. 24.

232 • Bibliography

————. "Laying down the line—party warns against excessive nationalism." *Far Eastern Economic Review,* Hong Kong, June 1, 1989.
Viktorova, Lidiya Leonidova. *Mongoly—proiskhozhdeniye naroda i is-
toki kul'tury* (The Mongols—National Origins and Cultural Sources).
Nauka Press, Moscow, 1980.

Arts

Chabros, Krystyna. "The Decorative Art of Mongolia in Relation to
Other Aspects of Traditional Mongol Culture." *Zentralasiatische Stu-
dien,* Harrassowitz, Wiesbaden, Vol. 20, 1987, pp. 250-281.
————. "A Glossary of Mongolian Material Culture with Particular
Reference to Needlework." *Acta Orientalia,* Hungarian Academy of
Sciences, Budapest, Tom. XLVI, fasc. 1, 1992/93, pp. 31-50.
Forman, Werner, and Rinchen, Byambyn. *Lamaistische Tanzmasken:
der Erlik-Tsam in der Mongolei* (Lamaist Dance Masks: the Erlig
Tsam in Mongolia). Koehler and Amelang, Leipzig, 1967.
Trésors de Mongolie XVIIe-XIXe Siècles. Musée National des Arts Asi-
atiques—Guimet, Paris, 1993.
Tsültem, Nyam-Osoryn. *Dekorativno-prikladnoye iskusstvo Mongolii:
Mongolian Arts and Crafts.* State Publishing House, Ulan Bator,
1967.
————. *Mongol'skaya natsional'naya zhivopis' "Mongol Zurag": De-
velopment of the Mongolian National Style of Painting "Mongol
Zurag".* State Publishing House, Ulan Bator, 1986.
————. *Skul'ptura Mongolii: Mongolian Sculpture: La Sculpture de la
Mongolie: La Escultura de Mongolia.* State Publishing House, Ulan
Bator, 1989.
————. Vydayushchiysya mongol'skiy skul'ptor G. Zanabazar: The
Eminent Mongolian Sculptor—G. Zanabazar. State Publishing House,
Ulan Bator, 1982.
————. *Iskusstvo Mongolii s drevneyshikh vremen do nachala XX veka*
(Mongolian Art from Ancient Times to the Beginning of the 20th Cen-
tury). Izobrazitel'noye Iskusstvo Press, Moscow, 1984.

Language and Script

Abbreviations in the Mongolian Press: A Reference Aid. Joint Publications Research Service, Washington, DC, 1972.
Badan, G., and Battulga, D. *Mongol helniy dasgaltay unshih bichig:
Kniga dlya chteniya (Teksty i uprazhneniya dlya inostrantsev,
izuchayushchikh mongol'skiy yazyk: Mongolian Reader with Exercises for Foreign Learners).* Ministry of Education, Ulan Bator, 1987.
Bazilhaan, B. "Mongol'skiye zaimstvovaniya v Bayan-Ul'geyskom
govore kazakhskogo yazyka" (Mongolian Loanwords in the Bayan-
Ölgiy Dialect of the Kazakh Language). *Mongolyn Sudlal* (Mongolian

Studies), MPR Academy of Sciences, Ulan Bator, Tom. VI, Fasc. 11, 1966.

Beffa, Marie-Lise, and Hamayon, Roberte. "Les langues mongoles" (The Mongolian languages). *Etudes Mongoles et Sibériennes,* University of Paris, Nanterre, Vol. 14, 1983, pp. 121-169.

Bertagayev, Trofim Alekseyevich. *Sintaksis sovremennogo mongol'-skogo yazyka* (Syntax of Modern Mongolian). USSR Academy of Sciences, Nauka Press, Moscow, 1964.

Bold, L. *Orchin tsagiyn mongol helniy dagavar* (The Suffix in Modern Mongolian). State Publishing House, Ulan Bator, 1986.

Bosson, James E. *Modern Mongolian: A Primer and Reader.* Indiana University Press, Bloomington, 1964.

Chinggaltai. *A Grammar of the Mongol Language.* Frederick Ungar, New York, 1963 (classical script).

Dashdavaa, D., and Ravdan, E. *Ner tom"yoony tuhay (Oros-mongol ner tom"yoony zarim asuudal)* (On Terminology: Some Questions of Russian-Mongolian Terminology). State Publishing House, Ulan Bator, 1980.

Grønbech, Kaare, and Krueger, John R. *An Introduction to Classical (Literary) Mongolian.* Harrassowitz, Wiesbaden, 1976.

Hangin, John Gombojab. *Basic Course in Mongolian.* Indiana University Press, Bloomington, 1987.

———. *Intermediate Mongolian.* Indiana University Press, Bloomington, 1975.

The Languages of Mongolia: see section 1. General, Maps, Atlases and Guides.

Lhagva, L., and Luvsandorj, J. *Uchites' govorit' po-mongol'ski (Mongoloor yar'j surtsgaaya)* (Teach Yourself Mongolian). Mongolian State University, Ulan Bator, 1978.

Luvsanbaldan, H., and Shagdarsüren, Ts. *Mongolchuudyn üseg bichig, üg hellegiyn tüüh garlaas* (From the Historical Origins of the Mongols' Script and Speech). Ministry of Education, Ulan Bator, 1986.

Luvsanjav, Choy. *Mongol hel surah bichig (gadaadynhand zoriulav): Uchebnik mongol'skogo yazyka (dlya inostrantsev)* (Mongolian Language Textbook (for foreigners)). Committee for Higher, Special Secondary, and Technical-Vocational Education, Ulan Bator, 1976.

Montgomery, David C. *Mongolian Newspaper Reader: Selections from Ünen.* Indiana University Press, Bloomington, 1969.

Poppe, Nicholas N. "Introduction to Mongolian Comparative Studies." *Suomalais-Ugrilaisen Seuran Toimituksia: Mémoires de la Société Finno-Ougrienne no. 110, Helsinki, 1955.*

———. *The Mongolian Monuments in hP'ags-pa Script* (trans. Krueger, John R.). Harrassowitz, Wiesbaden, 1957.

———. *Mongolian Language Handbook.* Center for Applied Linguistics, Washington, DC, 1970.

————. *A Grammar of Written Mongolian*. Harrassowitz, Wiesbaden, 1974 (classical Mongolian).

Rinchen, B. *Mongol ard ulsyn ugsaatny sudlal, helniy shinjlehiyn atlas: Atlas ethnologique et linguistique de la République Populaire de Mongolie* (Ethnological and Linguistic Atlas of the Mongolian People's Republic). Academy of Sciences, Ulan Bator, 1976.

Sanzheyev, G. D. *The Modern Mongolian Language*. Nauka Press, Moscow, 1973.

Tsoloo, J. *Mongol Helniy aviany ögüülegdeh yos* (Phonetic Rules of Mongolian). Ministry of Education, Ulan Bator, 1967.

Vacek, Jaroslav, Luvsandordž, Dž. and Luvsandžav, Coj. *Učebnice Mongolštiny: Hovorový styl: Mongol hel surah bichig: Yariany hel* (Textbook of Colloquial Mongolian). Charles University, State Pedagogical Publishing House, Prague, 1979.

Literature

Aikman, David B. T. "Mongolian Poetry since the Revolution." *Mongolia Society Bulletin,* Bloomington, Vol. 5, 1966, pp. 11-21.

Akim, G. (ed.) *Bilgüün nomch Byambyn Rinchen* (The Talented Writer Byambyn Rinchen). Mongolian Literature Publishing House, Ulan Bator, 1990.

Altangerel, Damdinsürengiyn (ed.). *Modern Mongolian Poetry (1921-1986)* (trans. Khuushaan, L., Enkhbayar, N., and Gaunt, John). State Publishing House, Ulan Bator, 1989.

————. *(trans.). The Legend of Cuckoo Namjil: Folk Tales from Mongolia* (ed. Lattimore, Owen). State Publishing House, Ulan Bator, (no date).

————. (trans.). *How Did the Great Bear Originate? Folktales from Mongolia* (ed. Luvsanjav, Choi., and Travers, Robert). State Publishing House, Ulan Bator, 1988.

Batchuluun, Ch. *Mongolyn emegteychüüdiyn hevleliyn toym* (Review of Mongolian Women's Publications). State Publishing House, Ulan Bator, 1982.

Bawden, Charles R. "Mongolian Literature." *A Guide to Eastern Literatures* (ed. David M. Lang). Weidenfeld and Nicholson, London, 1971, pp. 343-357.

————. (trans.). *Mongolische Epen X: Eight North Mongolian Epic Poems*. Harrassowitz, Wiesbaden, 1982.

Gerasimovich, Lyudmilla K. *History of Modern Mongolian Literature (1921-1964)* (trans. Mongolia Society). Mongolia Society, Bloomington, 1970.

Hangin, John Gombojab. "Dashdorjiin Natsagdorj (1906-1937)." *Mongolia Society Bulletin,* Bloomington, Vol. 6, 1967, pp. 15-22.

————. *Köke Sudur. (The Blue Chronicle.) A Study of the First Mongolian Historical Novel by Injannasi.* Harrassowitz, Wiesbaden, 1973.

Heissig, Walther. *A Lost Civilization: The Mongols Rediscovered* (trans. Thomson, D. J. S.). Thames and Hudson, London, 1966.

————. *Geschichte der mongolischen Literatur* (History of Mongolian Literature). Harrassowitz, Wiesbaden, 1972 (two volumes).

Kara, György. *Knigi Mongol'skikh kochevnikov (sem' vekov mongol'-skoy pis'mennosti)* (Books of the Mongolian Nomads: Seven Centuries of the Mongol Script). Nauka Press, Moscow, 1972.

Mikhaylov, G. I. *Literaturnoye nasledstvo mongolov* (The Mongols' Literary Heritage). Nauka Press, Moscow, 1969.

Montgomery, David C. "Mongolian Heroic Literature." *Mongolia Society Bulletin,* Bloomington, Vol. 9, no. 1, 1970, pp. 30-36.

Oyuunhüü, J., and Shagdar, H. *Chingis Haany tuhay tüühen ülgerüüd* (Legends about Genghis Khan). Ulan Bator, 1992.

Poppe, Nicholas. *The Heroic Epic of the Khalkh Mongols* (trans. Krueger, J. et al). Mongolia Society, Bloomington, 1979.

Sanders, Alan. "The writer's role." *Far Eastern Economic Review,* Hong Kong, September 24, 1973, p. 32.

————. "Lock up your typewriters." *Far Eastern Economic Review,* Hong Kong, August 2, 1984, p. 30.

The Secret History of the Mongols: see section 4. History, the Mongol Empire.

Shüger, Ts. *Mongol modon baryn nom* (Mongolian Xylographs). "Soyombo" Publishing House, Ulan Bator, 1991.

Sodnom, B. (comp.). *D. Natsagdorj: Zohioluud* (Works of D. Natsagdorj). State Publishing House, Ulan Bator, 1961.

Vietze, Hans-Peter, and Lubsang, Gendeng. *Altan Tobči: Eine mongolische Chronik des XVII. Jahrhunderts von Blo bzaň bstan 'jin: Text und Index* (The Altan Tobči: A Mongolian Chronicle of the 17th Century). Institute for the Study of Languages and Cultures of Asia and Africa, Tokyo, 1992 (transcription from classical script, with disk).

Dictionaries and Glossaries

Akim, G. *Mongol övörmöts heltsiyn tovch taylbar tol': Kratkiy frazeologicheskiy slovar' mongol'skogo yazyka* (Short Phraseological Dictionary of the Mongolian Language). State Publishing House, Ulan Bator, 1982.

Altangerel, D. *A New English-Mongolian Dictionary: Shine angli-mongol tol'* (ed. Humphrey, Caroline). State Cartography Publishers Company, Ulan Bator, 1993.

Badamgarav, G., and Lhagva, L. *Mongol-oros tovch tol': Kratkiy mongolo-russkiy slovar'* (Shorter Mongolian-Russian Dictionary).

State Committee for Higher, Special Secondary, and Technical-Vocational Education, Ulan Bator, 1982.

Bat-Ireedüy, J., and Baasanbat, D. *Mongol bichgiyn tovch tol'* (Short Dictionary of the Mongolian Script). Seoul, 1993 (classical Mongol equivalents of Cyrillic entries)

Bazylhaan, B. *Kazaksha-Mongolsha Sözdik: Kazah-Mongol Tol'* (Kazakh-Mongolian Dictionary). Academy of Sciences, Ulan Bator, 1977.

————. *Mongol-Kazah Tol': Mongolsha-Kazaksha Sözdik* (Mongolian-Kazakh Dictionary). Academy of Sciences, Ulan Bator and Ölgiy, 1984.

Buck, Frederick H. *Glossary of Mongolian Technical Terms.* American Council of Learned Societies, New York, 1958.

Butler, William E., and Nathanson, Alynn J. *Mongolian-English-Russian Dictionary of Legal Terms and Concepts.* Nijhoff, The Hague and Boston, 1982.

Damdinsüren, Ts. *Oros-mongol tol'* (Russian-Mongolian Dictionary). MPR Academy of Sciences, Ulan Bator, 1969 (two volumes, including a Mongolian historical chronology for which it was banned).

Damdinsüren, Ts., and Osor, B. *Mongol üsgiyn dürmiyn tol'* (Mongolian Orthographical Dictionary). Ministry of Education, Ulan Bator, 1983.

Gongor, Dugarsürengiyn. *Gesprächsbuch Mongolisch-Deutsch: Mongol-German Yariany Devter* (Mongol-German Phrasebook). VEB Verlag Enzyklopädie, Leipzig, 1988.

Hangin, John Gombojab. *A Concise English-Mongolian Dictionary.* Inner Mongolian Autonomous Regional People's Publishing House, Höhhot, 1986 (classical Mongolian).

————. *A Modern Mongolian-English Dictionary* (with Krueger, John R., Buell, Paul D., Rozycki, William V., and Service, Robert G.). Indiana University Press, Bloomington, 1986.

————. *A Modern English-Mongolian Dictionary.* Indiana University Press, Bloomington. 1987.

Lessing, Ferdinand D. (ed.). *Mongolian English Dictionary* (comp. Haltod, Mattai, Hangin, John Gombojab, Kassatkin, Serge, and Lessing, Ferdinand D.) University of California Press, Berkeley, 1960.

Luvsanjav, Choy., Tsetsegmaa, L., and Erdenetsetseg, Ts. *Mongol angli yariany devter: Mongolian-English Phrase Book.* Ministry of Education, Ulan Bator, 1988.

Nyamsüren, S. *Angli-mongol tovch tol'* (Shorter English-Mongolian Dictionary). Mongolian State University, Ulan Bator, 1968.

Tömörtogoo, D., Ozawa, Shigeo, and Hazumi, Haruo. *A Modern Mongolian-English-Japanese Dictionary.* Kaimei Shoin, Tokyo, 1979.

Tsedendamba, Ts. *Mongol-oros-angli tol': Mongol'sko-russko-angliyskiy slovar': Mongolian-Russian-English Dictionary.* Ministry of Education, Ulan Bator, 1986.

Tsevel, Ya (comp.). *Mongol helniy tovch taylbar tol'* (Shorter Explanatory Dictionary of the Mongolian Language). State Committee for Publishing Affairs, Ulan Bator, 1966.

Tsogbadrah, J. *Mongol helniy ijil neriyn tol'* (Dictionary of Mongolian Synonyms). Ministry of Education, Ulan Bator, 1981.

Tsydenzhapov, Shirab-Nimbu Rinchinovich. *Buryaad-mongol-orod tobsho toli: Buriad-mongol-oros tovch tol': Kratkiy buryatsko-mongol'sko-russkiy slovar'* (Shorter Buryat-Mongolian-Russian Dictionary). Buryat Ministry of the Press and Mass Media, Ulan-Ude, 1987.

Vietze, Hans-Peter. *Wörterbuch Deutsch-Mongolisch* (German-Mongolian Dictionary) (with Nagy, Gabriele, Damdinsüren, Tsendiyn, and Luvsan, Gendegiyn). VEB Verlag Enzyklopädie, Leipzig, 1987.

————. *Wörterbuch Mongolisch-Deutsch* (Mongolian-German Dictionary) (with Koppe, Klaus, Nagy, Gabriele, and Dashtseden, Tümenbayaryn). VEB Verlag Enzyklopädie, Leipzig, 1988.

Zebek, Schalonow. *Mongolisch-Deutsches Wörterbuch* (Mongolian-German Dictionary). VEB Verlag Enzyklopädie, Leipzig, 1961.

3. Economy

General

Campi, Alicia. "An Insider's View of Recent Political and Economic Changes in Mongolia." *Mongolia*. US Mongolia Advisory Group Inc., Washington, New York, and Ulan Bator, 1992.

Gungaasdash, Baldangiyn. *BNMAU-yn niygem-ediyn zasgiyn gazarzüy* (Socio-Economic Geography of the MPR). State Publishing House, Ulan Bator, 1986.

Hannam, Peter. "Troubled transition—Mongolians feel the chill of a slumping economy." *Far Eastern Economic Review,* Hong Kong, February 6, 1992, pp. 49-50.

————. "Life on the brink— Mongolians wonder how long the power will last." February 18, 1993, p. 55.

Kaser, Michael. "Economic Developments." *Mongolia Today* (ed. Akiner, Shirin). Kegan Paul International, London and New York, 1991, pp. 94-122.

Lhaashid, Davaagiyn. "The Problem of Mongolian Economic Security and Industrialisation Policy." UNDP and Institute of Administration and Management Development, Ulan Bator, Oct. 1992.

Luvsandorj, P., and Kim, G. F. *BNMAU-yn sotsialist ediyn zasgiyn tüüh* (History of the MPR's Socialist Economy). MPR and USSR Academies of Sciences, State Publishing House, Ulan Bator, 1986.

"Medium-Term Sectoral Priorities in the Transformation of the Economy." World Bank and UNDP, Meeting of Donors, Tokyo, September 1993.

238 • Bibliography

Milne, Elizabeth. *The Mongolian People's Republic: Toward a Market Economy* (with Leimans, John, Rozwadowski, Franek, and Sukachevin, Padej). International Monetary Fund, Washington, DC, 1991.

Mongolia: A Centrally Planned Economy in Transition. Asian Development ment Bank, Oxford University Press, London, 1992.

Namjim, T. (ed.) *BNMAU-yn üyldverleh hüchniy högjil bayrshlyn asuudal* (The Question of the Development and Location of the MPR's Productive Forces). MPR Academy of Sciences, Ulan Bator, 1980.

Ovidyenko, Ivan Karitonovich. *Economic-Geographical Sketch of the Mongolian People's Republic* (trans. Dougherty, William, et al). Mongolia Society, Bloomington, 1965.

Sanders, Alan. "Economic realism." *Far Eastern Economic Review,* Hong Kong, December 10, 1987, pp. 41-42.

Sendenjav, N. *MNR i razvitiye sotrudnichestva v sovmestnoy planovoy deyatel'nosti* (The MPR and the Development of Cooperation in Joint Planning Activity). State Publishing House, Ulan Bator, 1981.

Tai Ming Cheung. "The cure hurts—Mongolia pursues a painful transition." *Far Eastern Economic Review,* Hong Kong, September 19, 1991, pp. 70-72.

"Towards Stabilisation and Economic Recovery—An Assessment of Recent Economic Developments." Meeting of Donors, Tokyo, Sep. 1993.

Agriculture

Baldorj, R. *Ayrag* (Koumiss). Academy of Sciences. Ulan Bator, 1967.

BNMA Ulsyn hödöö aj ahuyn negdliyn ülgerchilsen dürem (Model Statutes of MPR Agricultural Production Associations). State Publishing Combine, Ulan Bator, 1967.

Gonchigjav, Z., Javzmaa, R. et al. *Mal aj ahuy* (Livestock Raising). State Committee for Higher, Special Secondary and Technical-Vocational Education, Ulan Bator, (1980).

Grayvoronskiy, V. V. *Kooperirovannoye aratstvo MNR: Izmeneniya v urovne zhizni 1960-80* (The Cooperativized Herdsmen of the MPR: Changes in Living Standards). USSR Academy of Sciences, Nauka Press, Moscow, 1982.

Jähne, Günter. "Socialist Agriculture outside Europe: New Ways in Mongolian Agriculture?" *Communist Agriculture: Farming in the Far East and Cuba* (ed. Wädekin, Karl-Eugen). Routledge, London and New York, 1990.

Mijiddorj, Go., and Jigmedsüren, S. "Mal tejeevriyn ner tom"yoo" (Terminology of Domesticated Animals). *Ulsyn Ner Tom"yoony Komissyn Medee* (Bulletin of the State Commission for Terminology) no. 75, Academy of Sciences, Ulan Bator, 1968.

Rosenberg, Daniel. " 'Negdel' Development: A Socio-Cultural Perspective." *Mongolian Studies,* Bloomington, Vol. 1, 1974, pp. 62-75.
————. "Leaders and Leadership Roles in a Mongolian Collective: Two Cases." *Mongolian Studies,* Bloomington, Vol. 7, 1981-1982, pp. 17-51.
Sambuu, J. *Kak vesti skotovodcheskoye khozyaystvo* (Advice to Herdsmen) (trans. Ayurzhanayev, Ya. from *Malchdad ögöh sanamj*). Ulan Bator, 1945.
————. *Malchin ardyn am'dral ahuy, hev zanshlaas* (From the Life and Traditions of the Herdsmen). State Publishing House, Ulan Bator, 1971.
Sanders, Alan. "Mongolia turns to crops and mining." *Far Eastern Economic Review,* Hong Kong, May 21, 1976, pp. 54-56.
————. "Golden herds and 130 production targets." *Far Eastern Economic Review,* Hong Kong, November 19, 1982, pp. 38-39.
Shirendev, Bazaryn. "Some Aspects of the History of Land Rights in Mongolia." *Journal of the Anglo-Mongolian Society,* Cambridge, Vol. 3, no. 1, 1976, pp. 41-57.
Shirnen, G., and Bazargür, D. *BNMAU-yn hödöö aj ahuyn gazarzüy (ündsen asuudal)* (Agricultural Geography of the MPR—Basic Questions). Academy of Sciences, Ulan Bator, 1987.
Wädekin, Karl-Eugen. "Agrarian Policies in China, Vietnam, Mongolia and Cuba." *Communist Agriculture: Farming in the Far East and Cuba* (ed. Wädekin, Karl-Eugen), Routledge, London and New York, 1990.

Finance

Aleksandrov, A. M. and Dolgormaa, B. "Finances of the Mongolian People's Republic." *Translations on Mongolia* no. 267, US Joint Publications Research Service, Washington, DC, 1972.
Bathuyag, J., and Davaadorj, Tsen. *Biznesiyn onol* (Business Theory). Army Publishing House, Ulan Bator, 1991.
Dolgormaa, B. "Monetary-Credit System of MPR." *Translations on Mongolia* no. 306, US Joint Publications Research Service, Washington, DC, 1979.
Hannam, Peter. "Bankers, beware." *Far Eastern Economic Review,* Hong Kong, January 23, 1992, p. 46.
————. "The first steppe." *Far Eastern Economic Review,* Hong Kong, February 20, 1992, p. 46 (opening of the Ulan Bator stockmarket).
————. "Donors turned off—Mongolia's aid honeymoon is over." *Far Eastern Economic Review,* Hong Kong, October 29, 1992, pp. 71-72.
————. "Fossil in the making—Japan finances Mongolian steel mill." *Far Eastern Economic Review,* Hong Kong, December 17, 1992.
Holstrom, Leslie. "Mongolia: Fast Forward." *Euromoney* (supplement), Euromoney Publications, London, 1991.
Sanders, Alan. "Shackled to the past—Soviet debt stymies development

of a market economy." *Far Eastern Economic Review,* Hong Kong, January 3, 1991, pp. 23-23.

Mining and Minerals

Barkov, Mikhail. "Tsvetmetpromeksport's Cooperation with Mongolian Coal and Mining Enterprises." *Foreign Trade,* Moscow, no. 7, 1985.

Byamba, J., and Gündsambuu, Ts. *Mongol orny erdes tüühiy ed* (Mongolia's Minerals and Raw Materials). State Publishing House, Ulan Bator, 1979

Dorian, James P. "Minerals: The Key to Mongolia's Economic Future." *AsiaPacific Briefing Paper* no. 8, East-West Center, Honolulu, 1991.

Hannam, Peter. "Beneath the steppes—Mongolia has trouble developing its mineral wealth." *Far Eastern Economic Review,* Hong Kong, May 13, 1993, pp. 60-61.

Hosbayar, P. (comp.) "Erdes, erdniyn chuluuny ner tom"yoo" (Terminology of Minerals and Precious Stones). *Ulsyn Ner Tom"yoony Komissyn Medee* (Bulletin of the State Commission for Terminology) no. 72-73, Academy of Sciences, Ulan Bator, 1968.

Knot, Terry. "Mongolia." *Petroleum Review,* Institute of Petroleum, London, Vol. 46, no. 541, 1992, pp. 57-59.

Mineral Resources Map of Mongolia: see section 1. General; Maps, Atlases, and Guides.

Pentilla, William C. "Newly Democratic Mongolia Offering Exploration Contracts." *Oil and Gas Journal* (special issue) December 1992.

Sanders, Alan. "Precious cairn." *Far Eastern Economic Review,* Hong Kong, April 9, 1973, p. 24.

———. "Mongolia's mineral wealth." *Far Eastern Economic Review,* Hong Kong, May 6, 1974, pp. 88-89.

———. "Letter from Erdenet." *Far Eastern Economic Review,* Hong Kong, October 28, 1977, p. 58.

———. "Enter the future with a deafening roar." *Far Eastern Economic Review,* Hong Kong, November 19, 1982, pp. 43-44.

———. "The glow of glasnost—Mongolia discloses existence of uranium mine." *Far Eastern Economic Review,* Hong Kong, November 30, 1989, p. 73.

Tai Ming Cheung. "Splitting at the seams - Mongolia searches for accessible mineral deposits." *Far Eastern Economic Review,* Hong Kong, September 19, 1991, p. 73.

Yeremin, I. V. "Coal Resources of the MPR Described." *Mongolia Report,* US Joint Publications Research Service, 1982.

Industry

Batdelger, Ch., and Kondrat'yev, Yu. "Dinamika razvitiya promyshlennogo kompleksa MNR" (Dynamics of the Development of the

MPR's Industrial Complex). *Novosti Mongolii,* Montsame News Agency, Ulan Bator, January 8, 1985.

Kaser, M. "The Industrial Revolution in Mongolia." *The World Today,* Royal Institute of International Affairs, London, Vol. 38, no. 1, 1982.

Nikitin, Vitali. "Soviet Assistance in Building Power-Generating Projects in Mongolia." *Foreign Trade,* Moscow, no. 7, 1985.

Transport

Bömbög, V. "Rail Transport in the Mongolian People's Republic." *Translations on Mongolia* no. 299, US Joint Publications Research Service, Washington, DC, 1978, pp. 19-26.

Dashbaldan, B. *BNMAU-yn agaaryn teevriyn högjilt* (Development of Air Transport in the MPR). State Publishing House, Ulan Bator, 1986.

Sanders, Alan. "Mongolia's modernisations." *Far Eastern Economic Review,* Hong Kong, May 29, 1986, pp. 109-100.

Sanders, Alan J. K. "Mongolia: The Development of Transport." *Focus,* The American Geographical Society, Vol. XX, no. 5, 1970, pp. 8-11.

Tserendorj, S., and Luvsanjav, Choy. (comp.). "Niseh ongotsny ner tom"yoo: Aviatsionnaya terminologiya" (Terminology of Aviation). *Ulsyn Ner Tom"yoony Komissyn Medee* (Bulletin of the State Commission for Terminology) no. 101-102, Academy of Sciences, Ulan Bator, 1975.

Foreign Trade and Aid

Barkmann, Udo B. (comp.). *Mongolische Republik: Aufstellung der Joint Venture, Staatsbetriebe sowie der Betriebe und Einrichtungen mit dem Recht auf Aussenhandel* (Mongolian Republic: List of Joint Ventures, State Enterprises, and Enterprises and Institutions with the Right to Engage in Foreign Trade as of September 1992). Ostasiatische Verein: German-Asia-Pacific Business Association, Hamburg, 1993.

Bavrin, Ye.P., and Meshcheryakov, M. V. *MNR: Ekonomika i vneshnyaya torgovlya* (The MPR: The Economy and Foreign Trade). Vneshtorgizdat, Moscow, 1961.

Dulmaa, J. "Vneshnyaya torgovlya—vazhnyy faktor razvitiya" (Foreign Trade—An Important Factor in Development). *Novosti Mongolii,* Montsame News Agency, Ulan Bator, July 3, 1984.

Hannam, Peter. "Must do better—Mongolia faces fresh scrutiny from donors." *Far Eastern Economic Review,* Hong Kong, April 9, 1992, pp. 60 and 62.

Jambaldorj, D. "Ekonomicheskoye i tekhnicheskoye sotrudnichestvo MNR i SSSR" (Economic and Technical Cooperation between the MPR and USSR). *Vneshnyaya Torgovlya,* Moscow, no. 11, 1984.

Mongolian Law on Foreign Investment: see section 5. Politics, Law.
Ochir, Yondongiin. "MPR-Soviet Foreign Trade History." *Mongolia Report* no. 316, US Joint Publications Research Service, Washington, DC, 1979, pp. 16-24.
———. "MPR Trade with CEMA Countries Examined." *Mongolia Report,* US Joint Publications Research Service, Washington, DC, 1982, pp. 47-51.
Sanders, Alan. "More help from the Kremlin." *Far Eastern Economic Review,* Hong Kong, October 31, 1980, p. 47.
Tai Ming Cheung. "Road to recovery." *Far Eastern Economic Review,* Hong Kong, September 19, 1991, pp.72-73.

4. History

General

Amar, A. *Mongolyn tovch tüüh* (Short History of Mongolia). State Publishing House, Ulan Bator, 1989.
Bai Shouyi. *An Outline History of China.* Foreign Languages Press, Peking, 1982.
Bawden, Charles R. *The Modern History of Mongolia.* Kegan Paul International, London, and Routledge, Chapman and Hall, New York, 1989.
Bira, Sh. *Mongol'skaya istoriografiya (XIII-XVIIvv.)* (Mongolian Historiography of the 13th to 17th Centuries). USSR Academy of Sciences, Nauka Press, Moscow, 1978.
Damba, Sanjaajavyn. *Mongolyn ertniy ulsuud* (The Ancient States of Mongolia). (No publisher's name), Ulan Bator, 1992. (school history of Mongolia from the old stone age to the Kidan state)
Demberel, S. (comp.) and Pürev, O. (ed.). *BNMAU-yn tüühiyn zarim ner tom"yoo, on tsagiyn taylbar tol'* (Dictionary of Terminology and Chronology of MPR History). State Publishing House, Ulan Bator, 1991.
Dügersüren, L. *Ulaanbaatar hotyn tüühes* (From the History of Ulan Bator). State Publishing House, Ulan Bator, 1956.
Gol'man, M. I. *Izucheniye Mongolii na zapade XIII-seredine XX v.* (The Study of Mongolia in the West from the 13th Century to the mid-20th Century). USSR Academy of Sciences, Nauka Press, Moscow, 1988.
Grousset, Réné. *The Empire of the Steppes: a History of Central Asia* (Trans. Walford, Naomi). Rutgers University Press, New Brunswick, New Jersey, 1970.
Rossabi, Morris. *China and Inner Asia from 1368 to the Present Day.* Thames and Hudson, London, 1975.
Shirendev, B., and Natsagdorj, Sh. *BNMAU-yn tüüh* (History of the MPR). State Publishing Committee, Ulan Bator, 1966 (Vol. I, Ancient Times to XVIIth Century), 1968 (Vol. II, 1604-1917) and 1969

(Vol. III, The Modern Period). (see Communist Period, Onon and Brown)

Sinor, Denis (ed). *The Cambridge History of Early Inner Asia*. Cambridge University Press, Cambridge and New York, 1990.

Sühbaatar, Günjiyn. *Mongol Nirun Uls (330 orchim - 550 on)* (The Mongol Nirun State from around 330 to 555). Academy of Sciences, Ulan Bator, 1992. (the Nirun, also called Joujan, were predecessors of the Turks)

Mongol Empire

Ar"yaasüren, Ch., Chingel,G. et al. *Chingis Haany tuhay tovch taylbar tol'* (Short Explanatory Dictionary about Genghis Khan). "Süülenhüü" Children's Publishing House, Ulan Bator, 1992.

Bawden, Charles R. *The Mongol Chronicle Altan* Tobči*: Text, Translation, and Critical Notes*. Harrassowitz, Wiesbaden, 1955.

Cleaves, Francis Woodman (trans., ed.). *The Secret History of the Mongols: For the First Time Done into English out of the Original Tongue and Provided with an Exegetical Commentary*. Harvard University Press, Cambridge, MA, and London, 1982.

Dalay, Chuluuny. *Mongolyn tüüh 1260-1388* (Mongolian History). Academy of Sciences, Erdem Publishing Company, Ulan Bator, 1992.

Gumilev, Lev Nikolayevich. *Searches for an Imaginary Kingdom—The Legend of the Kingdom of Prester John* (trans. Smith, R. E. F.). Cambridge University Press, Cambridge, 1987.

Halperin, C. J. *Russia and the Golden Horde: The Mongol Impact on Medieval Russian History*. Bloomington, 1985, and Tauris, London, 1987.

Juvaini, Ala-ad-Din Ata-Malik. *The History of the World Conqueror* (trans. Boyle, John A.). Manchester University Press, Manchester, 1958.

Jügder, Ch. *Chingisiyn töriyn üzel, tsergiyn urlag* (The Statesmanship and Military Art of Genghis). Believers' Society Publishers, Ulan Bator, 1990.

Kahn, Paul. *The Secret History of the Mongols—The Origin of Chingis Khan*. North Point Press, San Francisco, 1984.

Marshall, Robert. *Storm from the East: From Genghis Khan to Khubilai Khan*. BBC Books, London, 1993 (book of BBC/NHK television series).

Morgan, David. "The 'Great Yasa of Chingiz Khan' and Mongol Law in the Ilkhanate." *Bulletin of the School of Oriental and African Studies*, London, Vol. 49, no. 1, 1986, pp. 163-176.

———. *The Mongols*. Basil Blackwell, Oxford, and Cambridge, MA, 1987.

Munkuyev, N. Ts. *Kitayskiy istochnik o pervykh mongol'skikh khanakh* (A Chinese Source on the First Mongol Khans). Nauka Press, Moscow, 1965.

Natsagdorj, Sh. *Chingis haany tsadig* (Biography of Genghis Khan). "Soyombo" Publishing Co., Ulan Bator, 1991.

Onon, Urgunge. *The History and the Life of Chinggis Khan*. Brill, Leiden and New York, 1990 (translation of the Secret History of the Mongols).

Poucha, Pavel. *Die Geheime Geschichte der Mongolen als Geschichtsquelle und Literaturdenkmal: Ein Beitrag zu Ihrer Erklärung* (The Secret History of the Mongols as a Historical Source and a Literary Monument: A Contribution to its Elucidation). Czechoslovak Academy of Sciences Press, Prague, 1956.

de Rachewiltz, I. *Papal Envoys to the Great Khans*. Faber, London, 1971.

Ratchnevsky, Paul. *Genghis Khan: His Life and Legacy* (trans. Haining, Thomas N.). Basil Blackwell, Oxford and Cambridge, MA, 1992.

Rossabi, Morris. *Khubilai Khan: His Life and Times*. University of California Press, Berkeley, 1988.

Saunders, John J. *The History of the Mongol Conquests*. Routledge and Kegan Paul, London, and Barnes and Noble, New York, 1971.

Spuler, Bertold. *The Mongols in History* (trans. Wheeler, Geoffrey). Pall Mall Press, London, 1971.

———. *History of the Mongols* (trans. Drummond, Helga and Stuart). Dorset Press, New York, 1988.

Tsydenzhapov, Shirab-Nimbu. *Tayna Chingiskhana* (Genghis Khan's Secret). Buryat Book Publishing House, Ulan-Ude, 1992.

Vernadsky, George. *The Mongols and Russia*. Yale University Press, New Haven, CT, 1953.

Yegorov, Vadim Leonidovich. *Istoricheskaya geografiya Zolotoy Ordy v XIII-XIV vv* (Historical Geography of the Golden Horde in the 13th-14th Centuries). USSR Academy of Sciences, Nauka Press, Moscow, 1985.

Ming and Qing Period

Bawden, Charles R. "The Mongol Rebellion of 1756-1757." *Journal of Asian History*, Vol. 2, no. 1, 1968, pp. 1-31.

Cheney, George A. "The Pre-Revolutionary Culture of Outer Mongolia." *Occasional Paper* no. 5, Mongolia Society, Bloomington, 1968.

Chimitdorzhiyev, Shirap Bodiyevich. *Rossiya i Mongoliya* (Russia and Mongolia). USSR Academy of Sciences, Nauka Press, Moscow, 1987.

Miasnikov, Vladimir S. *The Ch'ing Empire and the Russian State in the 17th Century* (trans. Schneierson, Vic). Progress Publishers, Moscow, 1980.

Natsagdorj, Sh. *Halhyn tüüh 1691-1911* (History of Khalkha). State Committee for Press Affairs, Ulan Bator, 1963.

Sanjdorj, M. (trans. Onon, Urgunge). *Manchu Chinese Colonial Rule in Northern Mongolia*. Hurst, London, and St. Martins, New York, 1980.

Serruys, Henry. *Sino-Mongolian Relations During the Ming*. Institut Belge des Hautes Etudes Chinoises, Brussels, (three vols.) 1959, 1967, 1975.

Autonomous Period

Aalto, Pentti. "G. J. Ramstedt and the Mongolian Independence Movement." *Suomalais-Ugrilaisen Seuran Aikakauskirjasta: Journal de la Société Finno-Ougrienne* no. 72, Helsinki, 1973, pp. 21-32.

Bawden, Charles R. "A Contemporary Mongolian Account of the Period of Autonomy." *Mongolia Society Bulletin,* Bloomington, Vol. 9, no. 1, 1970, pp. 8-29.

Ewing, Thomas E. *Between the Hammer and the Anvil? Chinese and Russian Policies in Outer Mongolia 1911-1921*. Research Institute for Inner Asian Studies, Bloomington, 1980.

Gaunt, John. "Mongolia's Renegade Monk: The Career of Dambiijantsan." *Journal of the Anglo-Mongolian Society,* Cambridge, Vol. 10, no. 1, 1987, pp. 27-41.

Isono, Fujiko. "Ungern, le 'Baron Fou' de la Révolution Mongole" (Ungern, the Mongolian Revolution's "Mad Baron"). *L'Histoire* no. 49, 1982, pp. 62-70.

Onon, Urgunge, and Pritchatt, Derrick. *Asia's First Modern Revolution: Mongolia Proclaims Its Independence*. Brill, Leiden and New York, 1989.

Sanjmyatav, Bazaryn. *Tüühen ünen: Gurvan ulsyn Hiagtyn gereeniy tuhay* (The Historical Truth: Concerning the Three-Nation Treaty of Kyakhta). Army Publishing House, Ulan Bator, 1991.

Shirendyb, B. *Mongoliya na rubezhe XIX-XX vekov* (Mongolia on the Boundary between the 19th and 20th Centuries). Committee for Press Affairs, Ulan Bator, 1963.

———. *By-passing Capitalism*. MPR State Publishers, Ulan Bator, 1968.

Underdown, Michael R. "Aspects of Mongolian History. 1901-1915." *Zentral-asiatische Studien,* Harrassowitz, Wiesbaden, Vol. 15, 1981, pp. 151-240.

Ungern-Sternberg, Nils Freiherr (Baron) von. *De Hungaria. Ungern-Sternberg zu Pürkel: Ein Geschlecht im Wandel der Zeiten* (De Hungaria. The Ungern-Sternbergs of Pürkel: A Noble Family Through the Ages). Aku-Fotodruck, Bamberg, 1979.

Communist Period

Agvaan, Sh. *H. Choybalsan ba Dotood yavdlyn yaam* (H. Choybalsan and the Ministry of Internal Affairs). Chief Directorate of State Security, Ulan Bator, 1991.

Akiner, Shirin (ed). *Mongolia Today*. Kegan Paul International, London and New York, 1991.

Balhaajav, Ts., Gürbadam, Ts. et al. *Sotsialisticheskaya Mongoliya* (Socialist Mongolia). State Publishing House, Ulan Bator, 1981.

Barkmann, Udo B. "Erste Anmerkungen zu einem traurigen Kapitel mongolischer Geschichte—die dreissiger Jahre: First Remarks on a Painful Chapter of Mongolian History—the 1930s." *Asien, Afrika, Lateinamerika,* Harwood Academic Publishers, Vol. XX, no. 6, 1993, pp. 1043-1062.

Bira, Sh., and Okladnikov, A. P. *Istoriya Mongol'skoy Narodnoy Respubliki* (History of the Mongolian People's Republic). Nauka Press, Moscow, 1983.

Dash, D. *Tüühen biye hün. Uls Töriyn hörög: Soliyn Danzan* (A Historical Personality. Political Portrait: Soliyn Danzan). Research Center of the MPRP Central Committee, Ulan Bator, 1990.

Dashdavaa, G. (ed). *The Mongolian People's Republic.* Union of Journalists, Ulan Bator, 1981.

Heaton, William R. "Mongolia in 1986: New Plan, New Situation." *Asian Survey,* University of California Press, Berkeley, Vol. XXVII, no. 1, 1987, pp. 75-80.

Knutson, Jeanne Nickell. *Outer Mongolia: A Study in Soviet Colonialism.* Union Research Institute, Hong Kong, 1967.

Lattimore, Owen. *Nomads and Commissars: Mongolia Revisited.* Oxford University Press, New York, 1962.

Lattimore, Owen, and Onon, Urgunge. *Nationalism and Revolution in Mongolia, with a Translation from the Mongol of Sh. Nachukdorji's Life of Sukhebator.* Oxford University Press, New York, 1955.

Murphy, George G. S. *Soviet Mongolia: A Study of the Oldest Political Satellite.* University of California Press, Berkeley, and Cambridge University Press, Cambridge, 1966.

Namsray, Ts. (ed). *Yu. Tsedenbalyn udirdsan negen bügd hural (Mash nuuts barimt)* (A Plenum Chaired by Yu. Tsedenbal: Top Secret Account). State Publishing Combine, Ulan Bator, 1990. (the MPRP Central Committee plenum of March 1959 which expelled Damba)

Nordby, Judith. "The Mongolian People's Republic in the 1980s: Continuity and Change." *Communism and Reform in East Asia* (ed. Goodman, David S. G.). Cass, London, and Totowa, NJ, 1988, pp. 113-131.

Onon, Urgunge (ed). *Mongol Heroes of the Twentieth Century.* AMS Press, New York, 1976.

Onon, Urgunge, and Brown, William A. *History of the Mongolian People's Republic.* Harvard University, Cambridge, MA, and London, 1976 (translation of Vol. III of Bira. Sh., History of the MPR).

Puntsagnorov, T. *50 Years of People's Mongolia—Half a Century of Heroic Endeavour.* State Publishing House, Ulan Bator, 1971.

Rupen, Robert A. *Mongols of the Twentieth Century. Part I.* Indiana University Press, Bloomington, 1964 (for Part II see section 1. General, Bibliography).

Sanders, Alan. "Glasnost gathers support." *Far Eastern Economic Review,* Hong Kong, December 10, 1987, pp. 40-41.

————. "Studying stagnation." *Far Eastern Economic Review,* Hong Kong, June 30, 1988. p. 27.

————. "Rewriting history—Batmonh blames his predecessor for economic decline." *Far Eastern Economic Review,* Hong Kong, January 19, 1989, p. 21.

Sanders, Alan J. K. "Mongolia in 1975: 'One crew in battle, one brigade in labour' with the USSR." *Asian Survey,* University of California Press, Berkeley, Vol. XVI, no. 1, 1976, pp. 66-71.

————. "Mongolia 1976: Drawing together frankly with the Soviet Union." *Asian Survey,* University of California Press, Berkeley, Vol. XVII, no. 1, 1977, pp. 27-33.

————. "Mongolia 1977: Directive No 14." *Asian Survey,* University of California Press, Berkeley, Vol. XVIII, no. 1, 1978, pp. 29-35.

———— "Mongolia: Nation in the Middle." *Asiaweek,* Hong Kong, February 29, 1980, pp. 29-34.

————. "Mongolia in 1988: Year of Renewal." *Asian Survey,* University of California Press, Berkeley, Vol. XXIX, no. 1, 1989, pp. 46-53.

————. "Afterword." (Bawden, Charles R.) *The Modern History of Mongolia.* Kegan Paul International, London, and Routledge, Chapman and Hall, New York, 1989, pp. 425-437.

————. "Mongolia in 1989: Year of Adjustment." *Asian Survey,* University of California Press, Berkeley, Vol. XXX, no. 1, 1990, pp. 59-66.

————. "'Restructuring' and 'Openness'." *Mongolia Today* (ed. Akiner, Shirin). Kegan Paul International, London and New York, 1991, pp. 57-75.

Post-Communist Period

Campi, Alicia. "The Rise of Nationalism in the MPR as Reflected in Language Reform, Religion and the Cult of Chinggis Khan." *Mongolia.* US Mongolia Advisory Group Inc, Washington, New York, and Ulan Bator, 1992.

Chuluunjav, D. *Yu. Tsedenbalyg hen zayluulsan be? (1984-90 on)* (Who Removed Yu. Tsedenbal?). (no publisher), Ulan Bator, 1990.

Milivojević, Marko. *The Mongolian Revolution of 1990: Stability or Conflict in Inner Asia?* Research Institute for the Study of Conflict and Terrorism, London, 1990.

"Mongolia." *China, Mongolia Country Report,* Economist Intelligence Unit, London, 1/93, pp. 30-37 (and subsequent editions).

Sanders, Alan J. K. "Mongolia 1990: A New Dawn?". *Asian Affairs,* Royal Society for Asian Affairs, London, Vol. 22, no. 2, 1991, pp. 158-166.

——. "Mongolia: Stepping Up the Pace." *The World Today,* Royal Institute of International Affairs, London, Vol. 49, no. 5, 1993, pp. 83-85.

——. "Mongolia: Striking a Balance," *The World Today,* Royal Institute of International Affairs, London, Vol. 50, no. 6, 1994, pp. 104-105.

5. Politics

Parties

Damdinsüren, S. (ed.). *MAHN ba Kommunist Internatsional* (The MPRP and the Comintern). State Publishing House, Ulan Bator, 1979.

Dashjamts, D. "Nachalo rasprostraneniya idey Marksizma-Leninizma v Mongolii 1917-1921" (The Beginning of the Dissemination of Marxist-Leninist Ideas in Mongolia). *Problemy Dal'nego Vastoka,* Institute of the Far East, Moscow, no.1, 1977.

Delfs, Robert, and Sanders, Alan. "Runaway reforms—communists agree to give up monopoly of power." *Far Eastern Economic Review,* Hong Kong, March 22, 1990, pp. 10-11.

——. "Pre-emptive purge—communist reformers could upstage the opposition." *Far Eastern Economic Review,* Hong Kong, March 29, 1990.

Enhee, Ch. *Mongolyn Ardchilsan Holboo, Mongolyn Ardchilsan Namyn tuhay bodol, evgetsüülel* (Thoughts and Ideas about the Mongolian Democratic Association and Mongolian Democratic Party). State Standards and Prices Publishers, Ulan Bator, 1991.

Kartunova, A. I., and Shakhnazarova, E. N. "Komintern i MNRP" (The Comintern and the MPRP). *Problemy Dal'nego Vostoka,* Institute of the Far East, Moscow, 1974.

Kaye, Lincoln. "After the banquet—communists face problems after landslide victory." *Far Eastern Economic Review,* Hong Kong, July 16, 1992, p. 13.

MUD Namyn anhdugaar ih hural (The First Congress of the Mongolian National Progress Party). Ministry of Environmental Protection Publishers, Ulan Bator, 1990.

"The Program of the Mongolian People's Revolutionary Party." *Translations on Mongolia* no. 124, US Joint Publications Research Service, Washington, DC, 1966.

Rupen, Robert A. *How Mongolia Is Really Ruled: A Political History of the Mongolian People's Republic.* Hoover Institution Press, Stanford, CA, 1979.

Sanders, Alan. "A bypass to communism." *Far Eastern Economic Review*, Hong Kong, December 13, 1974, pp. 33-36.

————. "Mongolia: Bypassing socialism?" *Far Eastern Economic Review*, Hong Kong, August 13, 1976, p. 38.

————. "New faces at the top." *Far Eastern Economic Review*, Hong Kong, June 19, 1981, pp. 10-11.

————. "Filling up the party ranks." *Far Eastern Economic Review*, Hong Kong, July 17, 1981, pp. 16-17.

————. "Big Brother is watching." *Far Eastern Economic Review*, Hong Kong, February 19, 1982, p. 28.

————. "Rooting out the weeds." *Far Eastern Economic Review*, Hong Kong, April 2, 1982, p. 35.

————. "Revenge of the 'weeds'." *Far Eastern Economic Review*, Hong Kong, September 6, 1984, pp. 16-17.

————. "Ill winds of anarchy—party organ warns against misuse of democratisation." *Far Eastern Economic Review*, Hong Kong, March 16, 1989, pp. 21-22.

————. "Stirring the hotpot—a new political group presses for reforms." *Far Eastern Economic Review*, Hong Kong, February 1, 1990, pp. 21-22.

————. "Hural for the party—oppositionists claim government is stalling on reform." *Far Eastern Economic Review*, Hong Kong, April 5, 1990, p. 29.

————. "Fair promise—communists announce multi-party polls." *Far Eastern Economic Review*, Hong Kong, April 24, 1990, p. 25.

————. "Too little, too late—congress fails to convince opposition on reforms." *Far Eastern Economic Review*, Hong Kong, May 17, 1990, p. 20.

————. "Democracy demands—direct elections and multi-party system introduced." *Far Eastern Economic Review*, Hong Kong, May 31, 1990, pp. 27-28.

————. "Break with the past—elections launch multi-party rule." *Far Eastern Economic Review*, Hong Kong, August 16, 1990, pp. 16-27.

————. "Dogma and deadwood." *Far Eastern Economic Review*, Hong Kong, March 28, 1991, pp. 16-17.

Sanders, Alan J. K. "Mongolia." *Revolutionary and Dissident Movements: An International Guide*. Longman, London, 1991, pp. 216-217.

————. "Mongolia." *The Oxford Companion to Politics of the World*. Oxford University Press, 1993, pp. 600-602.

"Short History of the Mongolian People's Revolutionary Party." *Translations on Mongolia*, US Joint Publications Research Service, Washington, DC, published in three parts: (1917-40) 1964, (1940-61) 1965, and (1961-66) 1967.

Tüdev, B. *Formirovaniye i razvitiye rabochego klassa MNR* (Formation and Development of the MPR's Working Class). Nauka Press, Moscow, 1968.

————. *Nekapitalisticheskiy put' razvitiya MNR i rabochiy klass* (The MPR's Non-Capitalist Road of Development and the Working Class). Academy of Sciences, Ulan Bator, 1981.

Government

Dojoodorj, D. *Arvan haluun ödör (BNMAU-yn Ardyn Ih Hurlyn anhdugaar huraldaanaas survaljilsan zohiolchiyn temdeglel)* (Ten Hot Days: The Author's Notes Reporting from the First Session of the MPR People's Great Hural). Hödölmör Newspaper Publishers, Ulan Bator, 1990. (Mongolia's first multiparty national assembly)

————. *Daaj yadsan achaatay dalan zurgaan ödör (BNMAU-yn Ardyn Ih Hurlyn hoyordugaar huraldaany tanhimaas survaljilsan zohiolchiyn temdegleliyn negdügeer devter)* (Seventy-six Unbearable Days: Book One of the Author's Notes Reporting from the Second Session of the MPR People's Great Hural). (no publisher), Ulan Bator, 1992. (debate over the new Constitution)

Hannam, Peter. "Toppling Goliath—President switches parties to win reelection." *Far Eastern Economic Review,* Hong Kong, June 17, 1993, p. 13.

Hatanbaatar, Davaasambuugiyn. *Yörönhiy saydyn örgöönd* (In the Prime Minister's Palace). "Shuvuun Saaral" Army Publishing Company, Ulan Bator, 1992.

"Members of the Mongolian Great Hural." *CMS Occasional Papers,* Centre for Mongolian Studies, School of Oriental and African Studies, London, Aug. 1992.

"Mongolia's Cabinet." *CMS Occasional Papers,* Centre for Mongolian Studies, School of Oriental and African Studies, London, Sep. 1992.

Sanders, Alan. "Wanted: Mr. Culture." *Far Eastern Economic Review,* Hong Kong, September 17, 1973, pp. 29-30.

————. "Merger mania." *Far Eastern Economic Review,* Hong Kong, February 11, 1988.

————. "Rural clout—assembly session appoints non-communist to key post." *Far Eastern Economic Review,* Hong Kong, September 27, 1990, p. 16.

Sanders, Alan J. K. "Mongolia: From Sambuu to Tsedenbal." *Asian Survey,* University of California Press, Berkeley, Vol. 14, no. 11, 1974, pp. 971-984.

————. "Mongolia in 1984: From Tsedenbal to Batmönh." *Asian Survey,* University of California Press, Berkeley, Vol. 25, no. 1, 1985, pp. 122-130.

Sanjdorj, M. "BNMAU-yn Ih, Baga hurluud ba Ardyn Ih hurlyn udaa daraagiyn songuuliyn chuulganuudyn tuhay tovch medee" (Brief In-

formation on the MPR Great and Little Hurals and Sessions of the
People's Great Hural of All Convocations). *Studia Historica,* MPR
Academy of Sciences, Ulan Bator, Tom. 9, fasc. 12, 1971.

Law

Butler, William E. (ed.). *The Mongolian Legal System: Contemporary
Legislation and Documentation.* Nijhoff, Boston, MA, 1982.
BNMAU-yn An agnuuryn huul', Hunting Law of the MPR. State Pub-
lishing House, Ulan Bator, 1974.
"The Constitution of Mongolia" (1992 text). *CMS Occasional Papers,*
Centre for Mongolian Studies, School of Oriental and African Stud-
ies, London, September 1992.
Damdinsüren, Ts., and Myagmarsüren, D. *Alban hereg, arhivyn ner
tom"yoony tol' bichig: Terminologicheskiy slovar' deloproizvodstva
i arkhiva MNR* (Russian-Mongolian Terminological Dictionary of
Administration and Archives). Directorate of State Archives, Acad-
emy of Sciences, Ulan Bator, 1976.
Grazhdanskiy Kodeks MNR (Civil Code of the MPR). Legal Affairs
Committee of the MPR Council of Ministers, Ulan Bator, 1967.
Mongol Ulsyn Undsen huul' (The Constitution of Mongolia) (text of
1992 Constitution in Cyrillic and Classical Scripts). "Shuvuun Saaral"
Army Publishing House, Ulan Bator, 1992.
Mongolian-English-Russian Dictionary of Legal Terms; see section 2.
Culture, Dictionaries.
"Mongolian Law on Foreign Investment" (1993 text). *CMS Occasional
Papers,* Centre for Mongolian Studies, School of Oriental and African
Studies, London, June 1993.
Sanders, Alan. "Defining the letter of the law." *Far Eastern Economic
Review,* Hong Kong, June 13, 1975, pp. 31-32.
Sanders, Alan J. K. "Mongolia's New Constitution: Blueprint for
Democracy." *Asian Survey,* University of California Press, Berkeley,
Vol. 32, no. 6, 1992, pp. 506-520.
Sangidanzan, D. *Courts of the Mongolian People's Republic (Historical
Notes)* (trans. Nathanson, Alynn J.). University College Faculty of
Laws, London, 1980.
Simons, William B. (ed.). *The Constitutions of the Communist World.*
Nijhoff, The Hague, and Lancaster, Boston, 1984 (including Mongo-
lian Constitution of 1960 as amended to 1979).
Triska, Jan F. (ed.). *Constitutions of the Communist Party-States.*
Hoover Institution, Stanford, CA, 1969 (including Mongolian Consti-
tutions of 1924, 1940, and 1960).
Tuyaa, O. (comp.). *BNMAU-yn hödölmöriyn huuliyg heregjüülehtey
holbogdson togtool, shiydver, asuult-hariult* (Decrees, Resolutions,
Questions, and Answers in Connection with Implementation of the
MPR Labor Law). Ministry of Labor, Ulan Bator, 1991.

Defense

Coox, Alvin D. *Nomonkhan: Japan against Russia, 1939.* Stanford University Press, Stanford, CA, 1985.

Gavaa, Ts. "Tsereg-tehnikiyn ner tom"yoo" (Military Technical Terminology) *Ulsyn Ner Tom"yoony Komissyn Medee* (Bulletin of the State Terminological Commission) no. 53, Academy of Sciences, Ulan Bator, 1965.

Milivojević, Marko. "The Mongolian People's Army." *Armed Forces,* Vol. 6, no. 12, 1987, pp. 562-565.

———. "The Mongolian People's Army: Military Auxiliary and Political Guardian." *Mongolia Today* (ed. Akiner, Shirin), Kegan Paul International, London and New York, 1991, pp. 136-153.

Moses, Larry W. "Soviet-Japanese Confrontation in Outer Mongolia: The Battle of Nomonkhan-Khalkhin Gol." *Journal of Asian History,* Vol. 1, 1967, pp. 64-85.

Rupen, Robert A. "The Mongolian Army." *Communist Armies in Politics* (ed. Adelman, Jonathan R.). Westview, Boulder, CO, and Bowker, Epping, England, 1982, pp. 167-183.

Samdangeleg, Ts. *Zövlölt-mongolyn armiud Halh Gold yapony türemgiychüüdiyg but tsohison n'* (How the Soviet and Mongolian Armies Defeated the Japanese Aggressors at Halhyn Gol). State Publishing House, Ulan Bator, 1981.

Foreign Relations: General

Bor, Jügderiyn. *Mongolyn uls töriyn gadaad bodlogo, diplomatyn ulamjlalyn zarim asuudal (Ert, dundad ba shine üye)* (Some Matters Concerning the Foreign Policy of the Mongolian State and Diplomatic Tradition: Ancient, Medieval, and Modern Periods). State Publishing House, Ulan Bator, 1988.

Cagnat, Réné, and Jan, Michel. *Le Milieu des Empires (Entre Chine, URSS et Islam) ou le Destin de l'Asie Centrale* (The Imperial Environment or the Destiny of Central Asia—Between China, the USSR and Islam). Editions Robert Laffont, Paris, 1981.

Sanders, Alan. "Looking beyond the steppe." *Far Eastern Economic Review,* Hong Kong, December 10, 1987, pp. 39-40.

Stolypine, Arcady. *La Mongolie entre Moscou et Pékin* (Mongolia between Moscow and Peking). Editions Stock, Paris, 1971.

Foreign Relations: China

Bawden, C. R. "Some Remarks on the Relationship between China and Mongolia." *China Society Occasional Papers* no. 17, The China Society, London, 1974.

Chuluun, O. "The Two Phases in Mongolian-Chinese Relations (1949-1972)." *Far Eastern Affairs,* Moscow, no. 1, 1974, pp. 24-32.

Hannam, Peter. "Dragon's breath—Mongolia fears China's economic clout." *Far Eastern Economic Review,* Hong Kong, June 17, 1993, p. 52.

Kaye, Lincoln. "Faltering steppes—China looms large in ethnic upsurge among Mongols." *Far Eastern Economic Review,* Hong Kong, April 9, 1992, pp. 16-18.

Sanders, Alan. "Poetry of dissent." *Far Eastern Economic Review,* Hong Kong, October 1, 1973, pp. 31-32 (literary journal's attack on China).

———. "China: The view from across the Gobi." *China News Analysis,* Hong Kong, August 1974, no. 969.

———. "Pointing a finger of suspicion at China." *Far Eastern Economic Review,* Hong Kong, February 7, 1975, p. 37.

———. "The border dispute: Chinese, Russian and Mongolian views." *China News Analysis,* Hong Kong, May 9, 1975, no. 999.

———. "China relations hit a low note." *Far Eastern Economic Review,* Hong Kong, May 5, 1978, p. 28.

———. "Defining the limits—Sino-Mongolian treaty signals improved ties." *Far Eastern Economic Review,* Hong Kong, December 22, 1988, p. 18.

"Sino-Mongolian Border Protocol" (text from Chunghua Jenmin Kunghokuo T'iaoyuehchi, Peking, 1964). *Translations on Communist China* no. 131, US Joint Publications Research Service, Washington, DC, 1971, pp. 1-178.

Foreign Relations: Russia/USSR

"Dogovor mezhdu pravitel'stvom SSSR i pravitel'stvom MNR o rezhime sovetsko-mongol'skoy gosudarstvennoy granitsy, sotrudnichestve i vzaimnoy pomoshchi po pogranichnym voprosam" (Treaty between the USSR Government and MPR Government on the Regime of the Soviet-Mongolian State Border and on Cooperation and Mutual Aid in Border Matters). *Vedomosti Verkhovnogo Soveta SSSR,* no. 30, Moscow, 1981, pp. 711-730.

Dolgikh, F. I., and Tserendorj, G. *Sovetsko-mongol'skiye otnosheniya 1921-1974* (Soviet-Mongolian Relations). International Relations Press, Moscow, 1979.

Gol'man, M. I., and Slesarchuk, G. I. (eds.). *Sovetsko-mongol'skiye otnosheniya 1921-66* (Soviet-Mongolian Relations). Nauka Press, Moscow, 1966.

Hyer, Paul V. "The Reevaluation of Chinggis Khan: Its Role in the Sino-Soviet Dispute." *Asian Survey,* University of California, Berkeley, Vol. 6, 1966, pp. 696-705.

Milivojević, Marko. "The Soviet Armed Forces and Mongolia." *Jane's Intelligence Review,* London, Vol. 3. no. 7, 1991, pp. 306-310.

Pringle, James. "Room to breathe—nationalist upsurge as Soviets pull out." *Far Eastern Economic Review,* Hong Kong, August 24, 1989, pp. 24-25.

Sanders, Alan. "Shield against China's hordes." *Far Eastern Economic Review,* Hong Kong, October 31, 1980, pp. 47-48.

———. "The best ideological glue still comes from Moscow." *Far Eastern Economic Review,* Hong Kong, November 19, 1982, pp. 38-39.

———. "Avoiding extremes—controversy over Soviet role in the country continues." *Far Eastern Economic Review,* Hong Kong, July 6, 1989, pp. 29-30.

Sanders, Alan J. K. "Mongolia in 1975: 'One crew in battle, one brigade in labour'." *Asian Survey,* University of California Press, Berkeley, Vol. 16, 1976, no. 1, pp. 66-71.

———. "Mongolia 1976: Drawing together frankly with the Soviet Union." *Asian Survey,* University of California Press, Berkeley, Vol. 17, no. 1, 1977, pp. 27-33.

Sodnom, Dumaagiin. "Cooperation between MPR and other CEMA Countries Detailed." *Mongolia Report* no. 370, US Joint Publications Research Service, Washington, DC, 1983, pp. 1-5.

Tai Ming Cheung. "Neutral respect—as Soviets withdraw, planners seek good neighbours." *Far Eastern Economic Review,* Hong Kong, July 25, 1991, pp. 16-17.

Tang, Peter S. H. *Russian and Soviet Policy in Manchuria and Outer Mongolia 1911-1931.* Cambridge University Press, Cambridge, 1959.

6. Science and Technology

General

Akademiya Nauk MNR (MPR Academy of Sciences). MPR Academy of Sciences, Ulan Bator, 1982.

Badarch, D. *Komp'yuter gej yuu ve?* (What Is a Computer?). "Soyombo" Publishers, Ulan Bator, 1991.

Chadraa, B. *Kosmicheskiye issledovaniya v MNR* (Space Research in the MPR). State Publishing House, Ulan Bator, 1981.

Chimitdorzhiyev, Sh.B. "Sotrudnichestvo uchenykh SSSR i MNR" (Co-operation between Scientists from the USSR and MPR). *Problemy Dal'nego Voatoka,* Institute of the Far East, Moscow, no. 2, 1978.

Archaeology and Paleontology

Dorjsüren, Ts. "Chingis Haany törsön Deliün Boldog haana bayna" (Where Genghis Khan's Birthplace Deliün Boldog Is Situated). *Stu-*

dia Archaeologica, Committee of Sciences, Ulan Bator, Tom. 1, fasc. 2, 1960.

Hannam, Peter. "In search of Genghis Khan—hitech hunt uncovers emperor's 13th century capital." *Far Eastern Economic Review,* Hong Kong, September 2, 1993, pp. 30-31.

Kielan-Jaworowska, Zofia. *Hunting for Dinosaurs.* MIT Press, Cambridge, MA, and London, 1969.

Larichev, V. E. *Aziya dalekaya i tainstvennaya* (Remote and Mysterious Asia). Nauka Press, Novosibirsk, 1968.

———. *Paleolit severnoy, tsentral'noy i vostochnoy Azii* (The Paleolithic in Northern, Inner, and Eastern Asia). Nauka Press, Novosibirsk, 1969.

Maydar, D. *Pamyatniki istorii i kul'tury Mongolii* (Monuments of Mongolia's History and Culture). Mysl' Press, Moscow, 1981.

Rinchen, B. "Mongol nutag dah' hadny bichees gerelt höshööniy züyl: Les Dessins Pictographiques et les Inscriptions sur les Rochers et sur les Stèles en Mongolie" (Pictographs and Rock and Stele Inscriptions in Mongolia). *Corpus Scriptorum Mongolorum,* Ulan Bator, Tom. 16, fasc. 1, 1968.

Sanders, Alan. "162 BC and all that." *Far Eastern Economic Review,* Hong Kong, July 21, 1978.

Shackley, Myra. "Palaeolithic Archaeology in the Mongolian People's Republic." *Proceedings of the Prehistoric Society,* Vol. 50, 1984, pp. 23-24.

Architecture and Planning

Alexandre, Egly. "Erdeni-zuu, un Monastère de XVI siècle en Mongolie" (Erdene Zuu, a 16th-Century Monastery in Mongolia). *Etudes Mongoles,* University of Paris, Nanterre, Vol. 10, 1979, pp 7-33.

Lourie, John. "The House of Weddings." *Journal of the Anglo-Mongolian Society,* Cambridge, Vol. 4, no. 1, 1978, pp. 37-39.

Maydar, D., and Pyurveyev, D. *Ot kochevoy do mobil'noy arkhitektury* (From Nomadic to Mobile Architecture). Stroyizdat, Moscow, 1980.

Maydar, D., Turchin, P., and Sayn-Er, D. *Gradostroitel'stvo MNR* (Town Planning in the MPR). State Publishing House, Ulan Bator, 1983.

Nergüi, P. "Various Aspects of Regional Planning Clarified." *Translations on Mongolia,* US Joint Publications Research Service, Washington, DC, 1970, pp. 40-45.

Shchepetil'nikov, Nikolay Mikhaylovich. *Arkhitektura Mongolii* (Mongolia's Architecture). Construction, Architecture, and Building Materials Literature Publishing House, Moscow, 1960.

Tsültem, Nyam-Osoryn. *Mongol-un uran barilga: Arkhitektura Mongolii:*

Mongolian Architecture: Architecture de la Mongolie: La Arquitectura de Mongolia. State Publishing House, Ulan Bator, 1988.

Geography

Baasan, Tüdeviin. *Mongol orny els (salhin garalt els): Aeolian Sands of Mongolia.* "Soyombo" Publishers, Ulan Bator, 1991.

Dansran, Damdinsürengiyn, and Namnandorj, Ochiryn. *Gazarzüyn ner tom"yoony oros-mongol tol'* (Russian-Mongolian Dictionary of Geographical Terminology). Academy of Sciences, Ulan Bator, 1986.

Gungaadash, B. *Mongoliya segodnya* (Mongolia Today) (trans. Dubinin, A. B., and Rinchine, A. R.). Progress Publishers, Moscow, 1969.

Murzayev, E. M. *MNR: Fiziko-geograficheskoye opisaniye* (The MPR: A Physical Geography). OGIZ, Moscow, 1948.

Sanders, Alan. "The tainted waters." *Far Eastern Economic Review,* Hong Kong, October 20, 1988, p. 40 (and *Ünen,* August 5, 1989).

Geology

Baras, Z. (ed.) *Mongolian Geology.* State Publishing House, Ulan Bator, (1988).

Bespalov, N. D. *Soils of the Mongolian People's Republic.* Israel Program for Scientific Translations, Jerusalem, 1964.

Florensov, N. A. and Solonenko, V. P. *The Gobi-Altai Earthquake.* Israel Program for Scientific Translations, Jerusalem, 1965.

Marinov, N. A. "Materials on the Geology of the Mongolian People's Republic." *Translations on Mongolia* no. 136, US Joint Publications Research Service, Washington, DC, 1967.

Yerenhüü, T. (Russian-Mongolian-English Dictionary of Hydrology). *Ulsyn Ner Tom"yoony Komissyn Medee* no. 117-118, Academy of Sciences, Ulan Bator, 1982.

Zoology

Bataa, D., and Byambaa, D. *Udamt sayn hüleg mor'd* (Pedigree Horses). State Publishing House, Ulan Bator, 1991.

Bawden, Charles R. "The Mongolian 'Red Book'." *Journal of the Anglo-Mongolian Society,* Cambridge, Vol. 12, nos. 1-2, 1989, pp. 73-91.

Dashdondog, J., and Dar'süren, N. *Manay orny zarim shuvuud* (Some of Our Country's Birds). Ministry of Education, Ulan Bator, 1967.

Mallon, D. P. "The Mammals of the Mongolian People's Republic." *Mammal Review,* Vol. 15, no. 2, 1985, pp. 71-102.

Namnandorj, O. *Conservation and Wild Life in Mongolia* (ed. Field, Henry). Field Research Projects, Miami, FL, 1970.

————. *Goviyn ih darhan gazar* (The Great Gobi Reserve). State Publishing House, Ulan Bator, 1990.

Travers, Robert A. "Systematic Account of a Collection of Fishes from the Mongolian People's Republic, with a Review of the Hydrobiology of the Major Mongolian Drainage Basins." *Bulletin of the British Museum (Natural History), Zoology Series,* London, Vol. 55, no. 2, 1989, pp. 173-207.

7. Social

Anthropology

Badamhatan, S. (ed.). *BNMAU-yn ugsaatny züy: Halhyn ugsaatny züy* (MPR Ethnology: Ethnology of the Khalkha). State Publishing House, Ulan Bator, 1987.

Batnasan, G. *Mongolyn ardyn huvtsas* (Mongolian People's Costume). State Publishing House, Ulan Bator, 1989.

Ethnological and Linguistic Atlas: see section 2. Culture, Language and Script

Goldstein, Melvyn C., and Beall, Cynthia M. *The Changing World of Mongolia's Nomads.* The Guidebook Company, Hong Kong, 1994.

Hansen, Henny Harald. *Mongol Costumes.* Thames and Hudson, London, 1993.

Humphrey, Caroline. "Life in the Mongolian Gobi." *Geographical Magazine,* Vol. 43, 1971, pp. 616-623.

Moses, Larry W. "Nomadism and Revolution." *Mongolia Society Bulletin,* Bloomington, Vol. 10, no. 2, 1971, pp. 35-41.

Nyambuu, H. *Mongolyn belegdel* (Mongolian Symbols). State Publishing House, Ulan Bator, 1979.

————. *Ovöögiyn ögüülsen tüüh* (Historical Heritage). State Publishing House, Ulan Bator, 1990.

————. *Hamgiyn erhem yoson* (The Best Traditions). "Süülenhüü" Children's Publishers, Ulan Bator, 1991.

————. *Hündlehiyn deed höh mongolyn törityn yoslol Chingisiyn tahilga* (Genghis's Sacrifice, the Blue Mongols' Supreme Ceremony). "Altan Usegt" Publishing Co, Ondörhaan, 1992.

————. *Olnoo örgögdsön bogd haant Mongol ulsyn töriyn yos, yoslol* (The Traditions and Ceremonial of Bogd Khan Mongolia). "Shuvuun Saaral" Publishers, Ulan Bator, 1993.

Nyambuu, H., and Natsagdorj, Ts. *Mongolchuudyn tseerleh yosny huraangüy tol'* (Short Dictionary of the Mongols' Taboos). "Shuvuun Saaral" Army Publishing Co, Ulan Bator, 1993.

Pavlović, Srđa M. *Mongolski Piktogram* (Mongolian Pictogram). Naučna Knjiga, Belgrade, 1989.

258 • Bibliography

Sanders, Alan J. K. "The Turkic Peoples of Mongolia." *The Turkic Peoples of the World* (ed. Bainbridge, Margaret). Kegan Paul International, London, and Routledge, Chapman and Hall, New York, 1933, pp. 179-200.

Serjee, J. *Mongol hüniy neriyn lavlah tol'* (A Guide to Mongolian Personal Names). "Asral" Group, Institute of Education, Ulan Bator, 1991 (personal names in Cyrillic with their Tibetan derivation and equivalents in the classical Mongolian script).

Sühbaatar, O. "BNMAU-yn hün amyn shiljih hödölgööniy tuhay zarim medee" (Some Information about Population Mobility in the MPR). *Mongol Orny Gazarzüyn Asuudal* (Questions of Mongolian Geography), MPR Academy of Sciences, Ulan Bator, no. 8, 1968.

Vanjil, B. *Mongol ulamjlalt ahuy am'dralyn tovch tol'* (Dictionary of the Mongolian Traditional Way of Life) (Cyrillicized by Jumdaan, Sh.). "Yösön Erdene" Publishing Cooperative, Ulan Bator, 1992.

Vreeland, Herbert H. III. *Mongol Community and Kinship Structure.* Greenwood, Westport, CT, 1973.

Whitaker, Ian. "Tuvan Reindeer Husbandry in the Early 20th Century." *Polar Record,* Vol. 20, no. 127, 1981, pp. 337-351.

Zhukovskaya, Natal'ya L'vovna. *Kategorii i simvolika traditsionnoy kul'-tury mongolov* (Categories and Symbolism in the Mongols' Traditional Culture). USSR Academy of Sciences, Nauka Press, Moscow, 1988.

———. *Sud'ba kochevoy kul'tury* (Fate of a Nomadic Culture). USSR Academy of Sciences, Nauka Press, Moscow, 1990.

Education

Pritchatt, Derek. "Education in the Mongol People's Republic." *Asian Affairs,* Royal Society for Asian Affairs, London, Vol. 61, 1974, pp. 32-40.

———. "The Development of Education in Mongolia." *Mongolia Today* (ed. Akiner, Shirin). Kegan Paul International, London and New York, 1991, pp. 206-215.

Sengee, O. "Development of the People's Education in the MPR: A Statistical Compilation." *Translations on Mongolia* no. 300, US Joint Publications Research Service, Washington, DC, 1978.

Wolff, Serge M. "Mongol Delegations in Western Europe 1925-29." *Royal Central Asian Journal,* London, Vol. 33, 1946, pt. 1.

———. "Mongolian Educational Venture in Western Europe (1926-1929)." *Zentralasiatische Studien,* Harrassowitz, Wiesbaden, Vol. 5, 1971, pp. 247-320.

Health

Hatanbaatar, Jambalyn (ed.). *Otoch manla burhny zarligaar (Mongol emchilgeeniy argazüyn tovch).* (A Short Methodology of Mongolian Traditional Medicine). "Soyombo" Publishers, Ulan Bator, 1991.

Nyam-Osor, Dar'sürengiyn. "Public Health Development Reviewed." *Mongolia Report* no. 340, US Joint Publications Research Service, Washington, DC, 1982.

Oktyabr', J. *Nogoogoor hiyh amtat hool* (Making Tasty Food with Vegetables). State Publishing House, Ulan Bator, 1987.

Ongoodoy, Ch. *Mongolyn ideen tovchoo* (Data on Mongolian Food). Academy of Sciences, Erdem Publishing Co, Ulan Bator, 1991.

Püüshil, B. *Mongol-oros helniy yariany devter (emnelgiyn)* (Mongolian-Russian Phrase Book—Medical). Ministry of Education, Ulan Bator, 1987.

Radnaabazar, J. *Ner tom"yoony tsuvral bichig (hüühdiyn övchin sudlal)* (Russian-Latin-Mongolian Dictionary of Pediatric Terminology). Academy of Sciences, Ulan Bator, 1967.

Religion

Bawden, Charles R. *The Jebtsundamba Khutuktus of Urga: Text, Translation and Notes*. Harrassowitz, Wiesbaden, 1961.

———. *Shamans, Lamas and Evangelicals: The English Missionaries in Siberia*. Routledge and Kegan Paul, London and Boston, 1985.

Buddhism in Mongolia (Historical Survey). Section of Studies, Gandanthekchenling Monastery, Ulan Bator, 1981.

Cleaves, Francis W. *Manual of Mongolian Astrology and Divination*. Harvard University Press, Cambridge, MA, 1969.

Even, Marie-Dominique. "The Shamanism of the Mongols." *Mongolia Today* (ed. Akiner, Shirin). Kegan Paul International, London and New York, 1991, pp. 183-205.

Heissig, Walther. *The Religions of Mongolia* (trans. Samuel, Geoffrey). University of California Press, Berkeley, 1980.

Humphrey, Caroline. "Notes on Shamanism in Ar-Xangai Aimag." *Journal of the Anglo-Mongolian Society,* Cambridge, Vol. 6, no. 2, 1980, pp. 95-99.

Hyer, Paul V., and Jagchid, Sechen. *A Mongolian Living Buddha: Biography of the Kanjurwa Khutughtu*. State University of New York Press, Albany, 1983.

Jügder, Ch. "Certain Questions of Atheistic Propaganda." *Translations on Mongolia* no. 105, US Joint Publications Research Service, Washington, DC, 1966

Lamaist Dance Masks: see section 2. Culture, Arts.

Lattimore, Owen, and Isono, Fujiko. *The Diluv Khutagt: Memoirs and Autobiography of a Mongol Reincarnation in Religion and Revolution*. Harrassowitz, Wiesbaden, 1982.

Luvsantseren, G. "Buddologicheskiye issledovaniya v MNR" (Buddhological Research in the MPR). *Narody Azii i Afriki* (Peoples of Asia and Africa), Moscow, no. 6, 1984.

Moses, Larry W. *The Political Role of Mongol Buddhism.* Indiana University Press, Bloomington, 1977.
Sanders, Alan. "Marx versus God." *Far Eastern Economic Review,* Hong Kong, November 11, 1972, pp. 17-18.
———. "The lamps of enlightenment still flicker in the yurts." *Far Eastern Economic Review,* Hong Kong, November 19, 1982, p. 42.
———. "Mongolia warns against Christianity." *Far Eastern Economic Review,* Hong Kong, March 8, 1984.
———. "Guardians of culture—Buddhist renaissance helps rebuild national identity." *Far Eastern Economic Review,* Hong Kong, January 3, 1991, pp. 20-21.
Shine Geree (New Testament). United International Bible Society, Hong Kong, 1990.
Siklos, Bulcsu. "Mongolian Buddhism: A Defensive Account." *Mongolia Today* (ed. Akiner, Shirin). Kegan Paul International, London and New York, 1991, pp. 155-182.
Tsevegmid, Kh. "A Need to Intensify Atheistic Propaganda." *Translations on Mongolia* no. 105, US Joint Publications Research Service, Washington, DC, 1964.
Welch, Holmes. "An Interview with the Hambo Lama." *Journal of the Royal Central Asian Society,* London, Vol. 49, no. 2, 1962, pp. 172-182.

8. Mongols and Mongolia's Neighbors

China

Altantsetseg, N. *'Vnutrennyaya Mongoliya' vo vtoroy polovine XIX-nachale XX vv* ('Inner Mongolia' in the Second Half of the 19th Century and at the Beginning of the 20th). Institute of Oriental Studies, Ulan Bator, 1981.
Andrews, P. A. "The Tents of Chinggis Qan at Ejen Qoriy-a and Their Authenticity." *Journal of the Anglo-Mongolian Society,* Cambridge, Vol. 7, 1981, no. 2.
Atwood, Christopher. "The East Mongolian Revolution and Chinese Communism." *Mongolian Studies,* The Mongolia Society, Bloomington, Vol. 15, 1992, pp. 7-83.
Atwood, Christopher, and Kaye, Lincoln. "The Han hordes—Inner Mongolians a minority in their own homeland." *Far Eastern Economic Review,* Hong Kong, April 9, 1992, pp. 18-19.
Aubin, Françoise. "La Mongolie Intérieure et les Mongols de Chine: Elements de Bibliographie" (Inner Mongolia and China's Mongols: A Select Bibliography). *Etudes Mongoles,* University of Paris, Nanterre, Vol. 3, 1972, pp. 1-158.

China's Inner Mongolia. Inner Mongolian Association of Foreign Cultural Exchange, Inner Mongolian People's Publishing House, Höhhot, 1987.

Halkovic, Stephen A., Jr. *The Mongols of the West.* Indiana University, Bloomington, 1985.

Hyer, Paul V. "Ulanfu and Inner Mongolian Autonomy under the Chinese People's Republic." *Mongolia Society Bulletin,* Bloomington, Vol. 8, nos. 1-2, 1969, pp. 24-62.

Jagchid, Sechin. "Inner Mongolia under Japanese Occupation." *Zentralasiatische Studien,* Harrassowitz, Wiesbaden, Vol. 20, 1987, pp. 140-172.

Lattimore, Owen. Studies in Frontier History: Collected Papers 1929-58. Oxford University Press, London, 1962.

————. "Return to China's Northern Frontier." *The Geographical Journal,* London, Vol. 139, part 2, 1973.

————. "Inner Mongolian Nationalism and the Pan-Mongolian Idea: Recollections and Reflections." *Journal of the Anglo-Mongolian Society,* Cambridge, Vol. 6, no. 1, 1980.

Ma Yin (ed.). "The Mongolians", "The Daurs", "The Dongxiangs", "The Bonans" and "The Yugurs." *China's Minority Nationalities.* Foreign Languages Press, Peking, 1989, pp. 63-78, 109-112, 124-135.

Onon, Urgunge. *My Childhood in Mongolia.* Oxford University Press, London, 1972.

Ölziy, J. (ed. Ishjamts, N.). *Ovör Mongolyn Oörtöö Zasah Orny zarim ündesten, yastny garal üüsel, zanshil* (The Origins and Customs of Various Nationalities and Tribes of the Inner Mongolia Autonomous Region). State Publishing House, Ulan Bator, 1990.

Sanders, Alan. "Ulanfu's comeback." *Far Eastern Economic Review,* Hong Kong, October 22, 1973, p. 26.

————. "The framing of Ulanfu." *Far Eastern Economic Review,* Hong Kong, October 20, 1978, pp. 12-13.

Sanders, Alan J. K. "Inner Mongolia: Aftermath of the Cultural Revolution." *Journal of the Anglo-Mongolian Society,* Cambridge, Vol. 6, no. 1, 1980, pp. 42-49.

Underdown, Michael R. "De Wang's Independent Mongolian Republic." *Papers in Far Eastern History,* Canberra, no. 40, 1989, pp. 123-132.

Xiaolin. "The Mausoleum of Genghis Khan." *China Tourism Pictorial,* Hong Kong, 1980, no. 6.

Russia/USSR

Alatalu, Toomas. "Tuva—a State Reawakens." *Soviet Studies,* University of Glasgow, Vol. 44, no. 5, 1992, pp. 881-895.

Humphrey, Caroline. *Karl Marx Collective—Economy, Society and Religion in a Siberian Collective Farm.* Cambridge University Press, Cambridge, 1983 (at Barguzin in the Buryat Republic).

————. "Buryats." *The Nationalities Question in the Soviet Union* (ed. Smith, Graham). Longman, London and New York, 1990, pp. 290-303.

Khodarkovsky, Michael. "Of Russian Governors and Kalmyk Chiefs, or the Politics of the Steppe Frontier in the 1720s-1730s." *Central Asian Survey,* Society for Central Asian Studies, Vol. 11, no. 2, 1992, pp. 1-26.

Mongush, Mergen. "Remote and forlorn—tiny Tuva faces renewed hardship." *Far Eastern Economic Review,* Hong Kong, January 30, 1992, pp. 25-26.

Ramstedt, Gustav John. *Seven Journeys Eastward 1898-1912: Among the Cheremis, Kalmyks, Mongols and in Turkestan and to Afghanistan* (trans. Krueger, John R.). Mongolia Society Occasional Paper no. 9, Bloomington, 1978.

Sanders, Alan. "Siberian shakeout—Russians flee as Tuvans press for sovereignty." September 13, 1990, p. 30.

Vyatkina, Kapitolina Vasil'evna. *Ocherki kul'tury i byta buryat* (Sketches from Buryat Culture and Life). USSR Academy of Sciences, Nauka Press, Leningrad, 1969.

Zhukovskaya, N. L. "Buddhism and Problems of National and Cultural Resurrection of the Buryat Nation." *Central Asian Survey,* Society for Central Asian Studies, Vol. 11, no. 2, 1992, pp. 27-41.

Appendix 1
Mongolian Great Hural

(Members elected in 1992: For biographical details see individual entries.)

Adilbish, Yondonpuntsagiyn, MPRP, constituency 6 (Dornogov')

Algaa, Jam"yangiyn, MPRP, constituency 26 (Ulan Bator)

Bagabandi, Natsagiyn, MPRP, constituency 9 (Zavhan)

Batbaatar, Daadanhüügiyn, MPRP, constituency 22 (Ulan Bator)

Batbayar, Shiylegiyn, MPRP, constituency 10 (Övörhangay)

Batmönh, Osorhüügiyn, MPRP, constituency 10 (Övörhangay)

Batmönh, Sodnomyn, MPRP, constituency 8 (Dundgov')

Batsuur', Jam"yangiyn, MPRP, constituency 10 (Övörhangay)

Bayanjargal, Chültemsürengiyn, MPRP, constituency 19 (Darhan)

Bayartsayhan, Nadmidiyn, MPRP, constituency 15 (Uvs)

Bazarhüü, Ayuurzanyn, MPRP, constituency 5 (Gov'-Altay)

Bazarsad, Dashbalbaryn, MPRP, constituency 7 (Dornod)

Bolat, Ajhany, MPRP, constituency 2 (Bayan-Ölgiy)

Boldbaatar, Jigjidiyn, MPRP, constituency 4 (Bulgan)

Byambadorj, Jamsrangiyn, MPRP, constituency 16 (Hovd)

Byambajav, Janlavyn, (f) MPRP, constituency 22 (Ulan Bator)

Byambasüren, Dashiyn, MPRP, constituency 18 (Hentiy), (resigned December 1992)

Chimid, Byaraagiyn, MPRP, constituency 17 (Hövsgöl)

Chuluunbaatar, Samdangiyn, MPRP, constituency 21 (Ulan Bator)

Chunag, Sharavyn, MPRP, constituency 20 (Erdenet)

Dagvasüren, Dogdomyn, MPRP, constituency 7 (Dornod)

Dalayhüü, Minjüüriyn, MPRP, constituency 1 (Arhangay)

Danzan, Dariyn, MPRP, constituency 17 (Hövsgöl)

Dashdemberel, Chovdrongiyn, MPRP, constituency 14 (Töv)

Dashtseden, Dashdondogiyn, MPRP, constituency 3 (Bayanhongor)

Delgertsetseg, Jügderiyn, MPRP, constituency 20 (Erdenet)

Demberel, Bazaryn, MPRP, constituency 13 (Selenge)

Demberel, Damdingiyn, MPRP, constituency 16 (Hovd)

Elbegdorj, Tsahiagiyn, indept. (MDP/MNDP), constituency 17 (Hövsgöl), (resigned 1994)

Enebish, Lhamsürengiyn, MPRP, constituency 25 (Ulan Bator)
Enhbayar, Nambaryn, MPRP, constituency 23 (Ulan Bator)
Enhsayhan, Mendsayhany, MDP/MNDP, constituency 26 (Ulan Bator), (resigned July 1993)
Erdenebileg, Tömör-Ochiryn, MNDP, constituency 19 (Darhan), (since October 1993)
Ganbaatar, Ar"yaagiyn, MSDP, constituency 26 (Ulan Bator), (since July 1993)
Ganbat, Tserensodnomyn, MPRP, constituency 24 (Ulan Bator)
Ganbold, Baasanjavyn, MPRP, constituency 26 (Ulan Bator)
Ganbold, Davaadorjiyn, MNPP/MNDP, constituency 18 (Hentiy)
Ganbold, Gaanjuuryn, MPRP, constituency 23 (Ulan Bator)
Ganbyamba, Navaansamdangiyn, MPRP, constituency 18 (Hentiy)
Gandi, Tögsjargalyn, (f) indept. MPRP, constituency 25 (Ulan Bator)
Gan-Ölziy, Chimedtserengiyn, MPRP, constituency 18 (Hentiy), (since December 1992)
Gombo, Byambadorjiyn, MPRP, constituency 3 (Bayanhongor)
Gombojav, Jambyn, MPRP, constituency 12 (Sühbaatar)
Gombosüren, Tserenpiliyn, MPRP, constituency 25 (Ulan Bator)
Gonchigdorj, Radnaasümbereliyn, MPRP, constituency 1 (Arhangay)
Gündenbal, Sodnomtserengiyn, MPRP, constituency 4 (Bulgan)
Hurts, Choynjingiyn, MPRP, constituency 12 (Sühbaatar)
Idevhten, Doloonjingiyn, MPRP, constituency 11 (Ömnögov')
Jadambaa, Jam"yangiyn, MPRP, constituency 19 (Darhan)
Jalbajav, Nanzaddorjiyn, MPRP, constituency 22 (Ulan Bator)
Jantsannorov, Natsagiyn, MPRP, constituency 19 (Darhan) (resigned October 1993)
Jasray, Puntsagiyn, MPRP, constituency 26 (Ulan Bator)
Lhagvasüren, Bavuugiyn, MPRP, constituency 14 (Töv)
Lündeejantsan, Danzangiyn, MPRP, constituency 10 (Övörhangay)
Mendbileg, Mondoony, MPRP, constituency 14 (Töv)
Mönhöö, Dorjiyn, (f) MPRP, constituency 13 (Selenge)
Namhaynyambuu, Tserendashiyn, MPRP, constituency 9 (Zavhan)
Narangerel, Sodovsürengiyn, MPRP, constituency 25 (Ulan Bator)
Norovsambuu, Jambalyn, MPRP, constituency 16 (Hovd)
Nyamdorj, Tsendiyn, MPRP, constituency 21 (Ulan Bator)
Nyamzagd, Sühragchaagiyn, MPRP, constituency 9 (Zavhan)
Ochirhüü, Tüvdengiyn, MPRP, constituency 22 (Ulan Bator)
Pürevdorj, Choyjilsürengiyn, MPRP, constituency 1 (Arhangay)
Shaaluu, Oonoygiyn, MPRP, constituency 15 (Uvs)
Sharavdorj, Tserenhüügiyn, MPRP, constituency 6 (Dornogov')
Sultan, Taukeyn, MPRP, constituency 2 (Bayan-Ölgiy)
Togtoh, Norjmoogiyn, MPRP, constituency 8 (Dundgov')
Tovuusüren, Tsedeviyn, MPRP, constituency 24 (Ulan Bator)

Tömör, Sorogjoogiyn, MPRP, constituency 15 (Uvs)
Törmandah, Tsogbadrahyn, MPRP, constituency 7 (Dornod)
Törtogtoh, Gendengiyn, MPRP, constituency 17 (Hövsgöl)
Tsagaanhüü, Ravdangiyn, MPRP, constituency 11 (Ömnögov')
Tsedendagva, Gürjavyn, MPRP, constituency 3 (Bayanhongor)
Urtnasan, Jambaldorjiyn, MPRP, constituency 24 (Ulan Bator)
Volodya, Hambaryn, MPRP, constituency 2 (Bayan-Ölgiy)
Zenee, Mendiyn, MPRP, constituency 14 (Töv)
Zorig, Sanjaasürengiyn, UP/MNDP, constituency 23 (Ulan Bator)
Zorigtbaatar, Chuluuny, MPRP, constituency 13 (Selenge)
Zuunay, Gendensambuugiyn, MPRP, constituency 5 (Gov'-Altay), (died 1994)

Appendix 2
State Little Hural, 1990-1992

Altangerel, Erdenetogtohyn, (f) MPRP, b 1945, PGH deputy
Ayuurdzana, Chültemiyn, MPRP, b 1943, PGH deputy
Baldan-Ochir, Dogsomjavyn, MRYL, b 1963, PGH deputy
Batchuluun, Sarigiyn, MPRP, b 1954
Batsüh, Damdinsürengiyn, MNPA, b 1952
Battulga, Dashjamtsyn, MDP, b 1961, PGH deputy
Bayar, Sanjaagiyn, MPRP, b 1956, PGH deputy
Bayartsengel, Dashtserengiyn, MDA, b 1964, PGH deputy
Bayartsogt, Sangajavyn, MRYL, b 1967, PGH deputy
Bolat, Ajhany, MPRP, b 1945, PGH deputy (q.v.)
Bold, Luvsanvandangiyn, nonparty, b 1961, PGH deputy
Byambajav, Janlavyn, (f) MPRP, b 1953 (q.v.)
Byambatseren, Pandiyn, MPRP, b 1952.
Chilhaajav, Dambadarjaagiyn, MDP, b 1952, PGH deputy
Chimid, Byaraagiyn (Secretary), MPRP, b 1934, PGH deputy (q.v.)
Chuluunbaatar, Samdangiyn, MPRP, b 1941, PGH deputy (q.v.)
Damdin, Densmaagiyn, Lt. Col., nonparty, b 1950, PGH deputy (ex 1991)
Elbegdorj, Tsahiagiyn, MDP, b 1963, PGH deputy (q.v.)
Enhbaatar, Damdinsürengiyn, MDP, b 1960, PGH deputy
Enhsayhan, Mendsayhany, nonparty, b 1955, PGH deputy (q.v.)
Galsandorj, Bünchingiyn, MDP, b 1958
Ganbayar, Nanzadyn, MPRP, b 1953 (q.v.)
Ganbold, Dogsomyn, MDP, b 1963, PGH deputy
Gonchigdorj, Radnaasümbereliyn (Chairman), MSDP, b 1954, PGH deputy (q.v.)
Hatanbaatar, Ravdangiyn, MSDP, b 1955, PGH deputy
Iskra, Baataryn, MPRP, b 1948, PGH deputy
Jantsan, Dovdongiyn, MPRP, b 1947, PGH deputy
Jantsan, Navaanperenleyn, MPRP, b 1948, PGH deputy
Lamjav, Dondovyn, MSDP, b 1940, PGH deputy
Lhagvajav, Gombodorjiyn, MPRP, b 1932, PGH deputy
Lhagvajav, Günchingiyn, nonparty, b 1957

Lündeejantsan, Danzangiyn, MPRP, b 1957, PGH deputy (q.v.)

Maam, Dügerjavyn, MPRP, b 1935

Orchirhüü, Tüvdengiyn, MPRP, b 1948, PGH deputy (q.v.)

Ochirjav, Ochiryn, MDP, b 1960, PGH deputy

Ööld, Tseveenjavyn, MPRP, b 1942, PGH deputy (q.v.)

Pürev, Dagdangiyn, MPRP, b 1941, PGH deputy

Pürevdagva, Hadyn, MPRP, b 1947, PGH deputy

Samat, Nasyruly (Nasyryn), MDP, b 1964, PGH deputy

Sampilnorov, Nyamdolgoryn, MPRP, b 1942, PGH deputy

Shagdarsüren, Sharyn, MNPP, b 1954, PGH deputy

Sühbaatar, Hüüheegiyn, MPRP, b 1947, PGH deputy

Tovuusüren, Tsedeviyn, MPRP, b 1947 (q.v.)

Tserendagva, Chuluuny, MPRP, b 1944, PGH deputy

Tsog, Logiyn, MPRP, b 1952, PGH deputy

Tsog-Ochir, Luvsangiyn, MPRP, b 1944, PGH deputy

Ulaanhüü, Puntsagiyn, MSDP, b 1958

Urtnasan, Jambaldorjiyn, MPRP, b 1942, PGH deputy (q.v.)

Yandag, Yadamsürengiyn, MPRP, b 1944, PGH deputy

Zardyhan, Kinayatyn (Deputy Chairman), MPRP, b 1940, PGH deputy (q.v.)

Zuunay, Gendensambuugiyn, MPRP, b 1944, PGH deputy (q.v.)

Appendix 3
Mongolian Academy of Sciences

Avday, Chilhaajavyn (technology): department of technology; former rector of Technical University

Baatar, Dumaajavyn (biology): geneticist, department of chemistry and biology; president of the Academy since February 25, 1991 (q.v.)

Baatar, Tseepeldorjiyn (physics): department of physics and mathematics; director, Institute of Applied Physics

Badgaa, Dagvyn (chemistry): department of chemistry and biology; director, Institute of Chemistry; vice president of the Academy 1988-1990

Baldoo, Badamtaryn (philosophy): department of social sciences; director, MPRP Institute of Party History in the 1970s; director, Institute of Social Sciences in the 1980s

Barsbold, Renchingiyn (geology and minerology); department of geology and geography; director, Institute of Geology since 1990

Batmönh, Sereeteriyn (technology): department of technology; director, Institute of Technological Processes in Production and Services

Bira, Shagdaryn (history): department of social sciences; director, Institute of Oriental Studies from the 1970s-1982; vice president of Academy from the 1970s to January 1982; secretary-general of the International Association for Mongol Studies

Chadraa, Baataryn: department of technology; vice president of the Academy until January 1982 and since June 1991

Chadraabal, Gendengiyn (agriculture): department of agriculture; worked at the Institute of Animal Husbandry

Dalay, Chuluuny: director, Center for Northeast Asian Studies

Dash, Mangaljavyn (agriculture): department of agriculture; minister of agriculture in the 1970s and 1980-1981; head of agricultural department and secretary of the MPRP Central Committee May 1981-May 1986

Dashjamts, Batyn (chemistry): department of chemistry and biology; director, Higher School for Teachers in the 1970s; elected corresponding member in 1982; former member of Academy Presidium

Dashzeveg, D. (geology and minerology): paleontologist

268

Davaajamts, Tsevegiyn (botany): department of chemistry and biology; elected corresponding member of the Academy in 1971

Demberel, Bazaryn (medicine): former minister of health; head of department of medicine until elected member of the Great Hural in 1992 (q.v.)

Dorj, D. (history)

Dorj, Lodongiyn (physics): department of physics and mathematics; Learned Secretary of the Academy from 1989-December 1991

Dulmaa, Ayuuryn (biology): department of chemistry and biology; elected corresponding member of the Academy in 1982

Gonchig, Dendeviyn (animal husbandry): department of agriculture; elected corresponding member of the Academy in 1982

Haydav, Tsendiyn (medicine): department of medicine; elected corresponding member June 1982; worked at Institute of Biology

Horloo, Püreviyn (philology): department of social sciences; director, Institute of Literature and Language in the 1970s; member of the Presidium of the Academy 1982

Ishjamts, Nyambuugiyn (history): department of social sciences; deputy director, Institute of Oriental Studies in the 1970s

Jügder, Ch. (philosophy)

Lhamsüren, Badamyn (history): department of social sciences; candidate member of Politburo, secretary of MPRP Central Committee 1981-1982; director, MPRP Institute of Social Studies until 1984 (q.v.)

Luvsandagva, E. (medicine): director, Mother and Child Research Institute

Luvsandanzan, Butachiyn (geology): department of geology and geography; director, Institute of Geology from the 1970s-1990

Luvsandendev, Amgaagiyn (philology): department of social sciences; director, Institute of Language and Literature in the 1980s

Luvsandorj, Puntsagdashiyn (economics): department of social sciences; director, Institute of Economics; member of Academy Presidium 1987-1988

Namjim, Tömöriyn (economics): department of social sciences; director, Institute for the Development and Location of Productive Forces until 1982; member of the Presidium of the Academy 1982; deputy, first deputy chairman, State Planning Commission to April 1990 (q.v.)

Namsray, Havtgayn (nuclear physics): department of physics and mathematics; worked at Institute of Applied Physics

Natsagdorj, Shagdarjavyn (history): department of social sciences; director, Institute of History from the 1970s-1991; member of Academy since 1961, vice president of the Academy February 1982 to July 1988

Norovsambuu, Sodnomjamtsyn (philosophy): department of social sciences; director, Institute of Philosophy, Sociology and Law; elected corresponding member June 1982; vice president July 1988 to June 1991

Nyamdavaa, Pagvajavyn (medicine): department of medicine; minister of health since 1992 (q.v.)

Perlee, H. (history): archaeologist

Puntsag, Tovuugiyn (biology): department of chemistry and biology; director, Institute of Biotechnology

Ragchaa, Byambajavyn (medicine): department of medicine; corresponding member 1971, member of the Academy since 1990

Sereeter, Chimediyn (economics): department of social sciences; Academy's Learned Secretary, chairman of Society for Dissemination of Knowledge, head of an MPRP Central Committee department in 1970s; chairman, State Committee for Higher and Special Secondary Education to December 1989

Shagdarsüren, Osoryn (biology): department of chemistry and biology; director, Institute of General and Experimental Biology 1970s-1980s; Academy's Learned Secretary February to December 1982; elected corresponding member June 1982; rector of State University 1982-1989

Shirendev, Bazaryn (history): department of social sciences; president of the Academy from 1961 until January 1982 (q.v.)

Sodnom, Namsrayn (nuclear physics): department of physics and mathematics; rector, Mongolian State University 1970-1982; vice president, Joint Nuclear Research Institute, Dubna; president of Academy July 1987 to February 1991

Toyvgoo, Tsevegiyn (biology): department of chemistry and biology; worked at Institute of Animal Husbandry

Tömörtogoo, Onongiyn (geology and minerology): department of geology and geography; Learned Secretary, Institute of Geology in the 1970s

Tsegmid, Shagdaryn (geography): department of geology and geography; director, Institute of Geology and Cryopedology from the 1970s-1992; vice president of the Academy from the 1970s to July 1988

Tseren, Choydogiyn (physics): department of physics and mathematics; Chief Learned Secretary of the Academy 1980 to February 1982; president of the Academy January 1982 to July 1987; member of the Academy from June 1982; deputy chairman of the People's Great Hural 1982-1990

Tserendorj, Damdinragchaagiyn (animal husbandry): department of agriculture; corresponding member until 1992

Tserendulam, Rentsengiyn (animal husbandry): department of agriculture: corresponding member from June 1982; member from February 1990

Tserev, Hishigiyn (biology): department of chemistry and biology; vice president of the Academy in the 1970s, member of the Presidium of the Academy in the 1980s

Members of the Academy now deceased:

Ayuushjav, Ganjaagiyn (physics): director, Institute of Physics 1970s
Baldandash, Luvsannyamyn (agriculture): head of an MPRP CC department 1970s
Batsuur', D. (physics and mathematics): vice rector, State University 1970s
Damdinsüren, Tsendiyn (philology): journalist, writer, linguist
Dash, Mönhdorjiyn (animal husbandry): department of agriculture
Davaa, Naniraagiyn: department of chemistry and biology
Dugar, D. (economics): director, Institute of Economics 1970s
Gungaadash, Baldangiyn (geography): department of geology and geography
Ichinhorloo, V. (medicine)
Jagvaral, Nyamyn (economics): State vice president, Politburo member 1980s
Jamsran, Jamtsyn (chemistry): director, Institute of Chemistry 1970s
Luvsanvandan, Shadavyn (philology): Institute of Language and Literature
Puntsagnorov, Tsevegjavyn (history): department of social sciences
Rinchen, Byambyn (philology): historian, writer, linguist, nationalist
Shagdar, E. (biology): selectionist
Tömörjav, Myatavyn (animal husbandry): department of agriculture
Tömör-Ochir, Daramyn (philosophy): MPRP politician (q.v.)
Tsedev, D. (agriculture): director, Institute of Pasture and Fodder 1970s
Tsevegmid, Dondogiyn (biology): rector, State University; deputy premier

Appendix 4
Constitution of Mongolia

We the people of Mongolia, strengthening the independence and sovereignty of our nation, cherishing human rights, freedoms, justice and national unity, inheriting the traditions of our statehood, history and culture and respecting the common heritage of mankind, aspire to develop a humane, civil and democratic society in our homeland. Therefore the Constitution of Mongolia is proclaimed.

CHAPTER ONE
The Sovereignty of Mongolia

1/1   Mongolia is an independent sovereign republic.

1/2   The supreme principles of the state are democracy, justice, freedom, equality, national unity and respect for the law.

2/1   In structure Mongolia is a unitary state.

2/2   The territory of Mongolia is divided only into administrative units.

3/1   In Mongolia all power is vested in the people. The people of Mongolia exercise it through their direct participation in state affairs and through organizations of representatives of state power elected by them.

3/2   The illegal seizure or attempted seizure of state power is prohibited.

4/1   The territorial integrity and borders of Mongolia are sacred and inviolable.

4/2   The borders of Mongolia are guaranteed by law.

4/3   Unless otherwise provided for by law, the stationing of foreign military forces on the territory of Mongolia and their passage through it and across the national borders are prohibited.

5/1   Mongolia has a multiform economy in keeping with the trends of world economic development and its own characteristics.

5/2   The state permits all forms of public and private ownership and ownership rights are protected by law.

5/3   Ownership rights may be limited only on the basis of the law.

5/4   The state coordinates the economy to ensure the security of the national economy and the long-term development of all economic structures as well as the social development of the population.

5/5   Livestock are the national wealth and are under state protection.

6/1   In Mongolia the land, its subsoil, forests, waters, fauna and flora and other natural resources belong to the people alone and are under state protection.

6/2   Land, except that owned by Mongolian citizens, the subsoil and its resources, forest and water resources and fauna are state property.

6/3   Land, except pasture and land in public or special state use, may be owned only by citizens of Mongolia. This does not apply to ownership of its subsoil. Citizens are prohibited from transferring land they own to foreigners or stateless persons by selling, bartering, donating or pledging it, and from transferring it to others for use without permission from the competent state organizations.

6/4   The state has the right to hold landowners accountable for the manner in which land is used, to exchange or appropriate it with compensation if the state's special interests require this, or to confiscate the land if its exploitation and use are harmful to the population's health or contrary to the interests of environmental protection or national security.

6/5   The state may allow foreign citizens and legal entities or stateless persons to rent or lease land for fixed terms or use it under other conditions provided for by law.

7/1   The historical, cultural, scientific and intellectual heritage of the people of Mongolia is under state protection.

7/2   Intellectual property created by citizens belongs to its authors and is the national wealth of Mongolia.

8/1   The official language of the state is Mongolian.

8/2   The right of the population's national minorities speaking other languages to use their mother tongue in education, communication and cultural, artistic and scientific activity is not affected by paragraph 1 of this article.

9/1   In Mongolia the state respects religion and religion honors the state.

9/2   State organizations may not engage in religious activity and monasteries may not engage in political activity.

9/3   Relations between the state and monasteries are regulated by law.

10/1   In conformity with international law, agreements and principles Mongolia pursues a peaceful foreign policy.

10/2   Mongolia fulfills in good faith the obligations entered into under international treaties.

10/3   On ratification or accession Mongolia's international treaties have the force of domestic law.

10/4   Mongolia will not be bound by any international treaty or other instrument incompatible with its Constitution.

11/1   It is the state's duty to defend the homeland's independence and ensure national security and public order.

11/2   Mongolia has armed forces for self-defense. The structure and organization of the armed forces and service regulations are determined by law.

12/1   The symbols of the independence and sovereignty of Mongolia are the state emblem, banner, flag, seal and anthem.

12/2   The state emblem, banner, flag and anthem symbolize the historical traditions, aspirations, unity, justice and spirit of the people of Mongolia.

12/3   The state emblem is circular in shape with a white lotus as the base and a continuous swastika pattern forming its outer frame. The background is blue, signifying the eternal sky. A combination of the "precious steed" and "golden *soyombo*" is depicted in the center of the emblem as a symbol of the independence, sovereignty and spirit of Mongolia. At the top of the emblem the "triple gem" symbolizes the past, present and future. At the bottom of the emblem, against the background of a hill pattern conveying the idea of "mother earth", a wheel symbolizing prosperity and happiness is entwined with a silk scarf.

12/4   The traditional great white banner of the united Mongolian state is the symbol of state honor of Mongolia.

12/5   The state flag is red, blue and red. The center third of the flag is blue, the color of the eternal sky, and the two sides red, the symbol of prosperity. A "golden *soyombo*" is depicted on the red field at the hoist. The ratio of width to length is 1:2.

12/6   The state seal is square with the state emblem at the center and the word "Mongolia" inscribed on each side, and has a handle in the form of a lion. The President is the keeper of the state seal.

12/7   The procedure for the solemn use of state symbols and the words and music of the state anthem are confirmed by law.

13/1   The permanent seat of Mongolia's supreme state bodies is the country's capital. The capital of Mongolia is the town of Ulan Bator.

13/2   The legal status of the capital of Mongolia is defined by law.

CHAPTER TWO

Human Rights and Freedoms

14/1   All lawful residents of Mongolia are equal before the law and courts.

14/2   No one may be discriminated against on the basis of nationality, language, color, age, race, sex, social origin and status, property, occupation, rank, religion, beliefs or education. Everyone is a legal entity.

15/1 The grounds and procedure for granting or withdrawing the citizenship of citizens of Mongolia are defined only by law.

15/2 Deprivation of citizenship, expulsion and extradition of citizens of Mongolia are prohibited.

16/1 Citizens of Mongolia are guaranteed the enjoyment of the following basic rights and freedoms:

1) The right to life. Deprivation of human life is prohibited unless capital punishment is imposed by due judgement of the court for the most serious crimes under the Criminal Code of Mongolia.

2) The right to a healthy and safe environment, and the right to be free from environmental pollution and ecological imbalance.

3) The right to honest acquisition, possession and inheritance of movable and immovable property. Illegal seizure or confiscation of citizens' private property is prohibited. If the needs of society oblige the state or its competent organizations to confiscate private property, this property must be compensated and paid for.

4) The right to free choice of occupation, to conditions and remuneration commensurate with the work done, to rest, and to manage a private business. No one may be forced to work illegally.

5) The right to material and monetary assistance in old age, in case of disability, the birth and care of children and in other circumstances provided for by law.

6) The right to protection of health and medical care. The procedure and conditions for citizens' free medical aid are defined by law.

7) The right to education. The state provides free general public education. Citizens may establish and run private schools which meet the state's requirements.

8) The right to engage in cultural, artistic and scientific activities and creative work and to receive benefit from them. Copyright and patents are protected by law.

9) The right to participate in the conduct of state affairs directly or through representative organizations. The right to elect or to be elected to state organizations. The right to elect is enjoyed from the age of 18. The age of eligibility for election is defined by law according to the requirements of specific state organizations and posts.

10) The right to form parties or other public organizations and to unite voluntarily in associations in keeping with social or other interests or beliefs. All parties and other public organizations uphold public and state security and abide by the law. Discrimination or persecution for joining a party or other public organization or being a member is prohibited. The party membership of some categories of state employees may be suspended.

11) The equal rights of men and women in the political, economic, social and cultural fields and family matters. Marriage is based on equality and mutual consent of men and women who have attained the age of consent defined by law. The state protects the interests of the family, motherhood and children.

12) The right to submit a petition or complaint to state organizations and officials. State organizations and officials are obliged to deal with citizens' petitions or complaints in accordance with the law.

13) The right to inviolability and freedom. No one may be searched, arrested, detained or investigated, nor may one's freedom be restricted other than in accordance with the procedures and grounds defined by law. No one may be subjected to torture, inhuman, cruel or degrading treatment. In the event of arrest for committing a crime, within the period of time established by law the accused and the family and counsel of the accused shall be notified of the reasons and grounds for arrest. Citizens' personal privacy, the privacy of the family and correspondence and the inviolability of the home are protected by law.

14) The right to approach the courts to protect one's rights if one considers that rights or freedoms defined by Mongolian law or international treaties have been violated, to receive compensation for damage caused illegally by others, not to testify against oneself, one's family, parents or children, to self-defense, to receive legal advice, to examine evidence, to a fair trial, to be tried in one's presence, to appeal against a court judgement and to seek pardon. No one may be required or forced to testify against himself or to give evidence. The accused shall be presumed innocent until proven guilty by a court according to law. The bringing of charges against the family and relatives of the accused is prohibited.

15) The freedom to worship and not to worship.

16) The freedom of conscience, free expression of opinion, speech, the press, peaceful demonstration and assembly. Procedures for demonstrations and assemblies are defined by law.

17) The right to seek and receive information except that especially protected as a secret by the state and its organizations according to the law. To protect human rights, dignity and reputation and ensure state defense, national security and public order, secrets of the state, organizations or individuals not subject to disclosure are defined and protected by law.

18) The freedom of movement within the country and the freedom to choose one's place of residence, the right to travel or reside abroad, and to return to the home country. The right to travel and reside abroad may be limited only by law to ensure the security of the nation and population.

17/1 Citizens of Mongolia while respecting justice and humanity strictly perform the following duties:

1) respect and observe the Constitution and other laws;

2) respect the dignity, reputation, rights and legal interests of others;

3) pay taxies levied by law;

4) defend the homeland and perform military service according to law.

17/2 It is all citizens' noble duty to work, protect their health, raise and educate their children and protect nature and the environment.

18/1 The rights and duties of foreign citizens on the territory of Mongolia are regulated by Mongolian law and treaties concluded with the countries of the persons concerned.

18/2 Mongolia adheres to the principle of reciprocity in defining foreign citizens' rights and duties in keeping with international treaties.

18/3 The rights and duties of stateless persons on the territory of Mongolia are defined by its law.

18/4 Foreign citizens or stateless persons persecuted for their beliefs or their political or other just activities may be granted the right of asylum in Mongolia on the basis of their request.

18/5 In allowing foreign citizens and stateless persons in this country to exercise the basic rights and freedoms provided for citizens of Mongolia by Article 16 of the Constitution, with a view to ensuring the security of the nation and population the state may establish certain legal restrictions on other rights except inalienable rights enshrined in international conventions that Mongolia has joined.

19/1 The state is responsible to its citizens for creating the economic, social, legal and other guarantees for ensuring human rights and freedoms, for opposing violations of human rights and freedoms and for restoring rights that have been infringed.

19/2 In the event of a state of emergency or war occurring, human rights and freedoms defined by the Constitution or other laws are subject to restriction only by law. Such legal restriction does not affect the right to life, freedom of conscience and to worship or not to worship, or freedom from torture, inhuman treatment or cruel punishment.

19/3 The exercise of rights and freedoms may not infringe upon national security or the human rights and freedoms of others or violate public order.

CHAPTER THREE

Mongolia's State Structure

I. The Mongolian Great Hural

20 The Mongolian Great Hural (assembly) is the supreme organ of state power and supreme legislative power is vested only in the National Great Hural.

21/1 The National Great Hural has one chamber and 76 members.

21/2 The members of the National Great Hural are elected for a four-year term by universal, free and direct suffrage and secret ballot of citizens of Mongolia having the right to vote.

21/3 Citizens of Mongolia who have reached the age of 25 and have the right to vote may be elected members of the National Great Hural.

21/4 The procedure for election to the National Great Hural is defined by law.

22/1 If regular elections to the National Great Hural cannot take place because of a sudden danger, state of war, public disturbance or other special conditions in all or part of the country the National Great Hural retains its powers until these special conditions change and the newly elected members of the National Great Hural are sworn in.

22/2 The National Great Hural may decide on its dissolution if at least two-thirds of the members consider the National Great Hural unable to exercise its powers, or at the proposal of the President in consultation with the Chairman of the National Great Hural. After the decision on dissolution is taken, the National Great Hural retains its powers until the newly elected members are sworn in.

23/1 A member of the National Great Hural is an envoy of the people and represents and is guided by the interests of all citizens and the nation.

23/2 The term of office of a member of the National Great Hural begins with the oath taken before the state emblem and ends when the newly elected members of the National Great Hural are sworn in.

24/1 The Chairman and Vice-Chairman of the National Great Hural are nominated from among the members of the National Great Hural and elected by secret ballot.

24/2 The term of office of the Chairman and Vice-Chairman of the National Great Hural is four years, but on grounds defined by law they may be relieved of their duties or dismissed before the term expires.

25/1 The National Great Hural may consider any state domestic or foreign policy matters at its own initiative but retains the following matters within its exclusive competence:

1) enacting, supplementing and amending laws;

2) defining the basis of the state's domestic and foreign policy;

3) deciding and announcing the date of election of the President and the National Great Hural and its members;

4) determining and changing the structure and composition of the National Great Hural's standing committees, the Government and as prescribed by law other organizations directly accountable to the National Great Hural;

5) passing a law recognizing the powers of the President upon his election and relieving him of his duties or dismissing him;

6) appointing, changing or dismissing the Prime Minister and members of the Government and as prescribed by law members of other organizations responsible and accountable to the National Great Hural;

7) defining the state's financial, credit, tax and monetary policy, laying down the basic guidelines of the nation's economic and social development and approving the government's program, the national budget and the report on its implementation;

8) supervising the observance and implementation of laws and other decisions of the National Great Hural;

9) determining the nation's borders;

10) determining the composition, structure and powers of the National Security Council;

11) as proposed by the Government approving and changing territorial administrative divisions;

12) defining the legal basis of the system, structure and activities of the local bodies of self-government and administration;

13) instituting national honors, orders, medals and senior military ranks and deciding on the rank of posts in some special branches of state service;

14) declaring amnesties;

15) as proposed by the Government ratifying or denouncing international agreements that Mongolia has joined and establishing or severing diplomatic relations with foreign nations;

16) holding referendums, validating the results of referendums in which the majority of citizens with the right to vote took part, and declaring as decided the issue for which the majority voted;

17) if the independence and sovereignty of Mongolia are threatened or in the event of armed intervention by another nation declaring a state of war and annulling it;

18) in an emergency situation as defined in paragraphs 2 and 3 of this Article declaring a state of emergency or state of war in all or part of the nation's territory, or approving or rejecting the President's decree to that effect.

25/2   If the following emergency situation arises a state of emergency may be declared to eliminate the consequences and restore the life of the population and society:

1) the occurrence of a natural disaster or other sudden danger which threatens or might threaten directly the population's life, health, well-being and public security in all or part of the nation's territory;

2) the inability of state organizations to deal within their competence with a public disturbance caused by organized, violent or illegal activities of any organization or group of people threatening the constitutional order, the legal system or society's foundations.

25/3   If a public disturbance leads to armed conflict or the real danger of armed conflict is imminent in all or part of the nation's territory of if armed aggression by another nation is committed or is imminent a state of war may be declared.

25/4   The National Great Hural's other powers, organization and procedures are defined by law.

26/1   The President, members of the National Great Hural and the Government have the right to initiate laws.

26/2   Citizens and other organizations forward their proposals for draft laws to those entitled to initiate laws.

26/3   Laws of Mongolia are published officially by the National Great Hural and enter into force ten days after publication unless otherwise stated.

27/1   The National Great Hural exercises its powers through its sessions and other organizational forms.

27/2   Regular sessions of the National Great Hural are held once every half-year for not less than 75 working days.

27/3   An extraordinary session may be convened at the request of not less than one-third of the members of the National Great Hural, or at the initiative of the President or the Chairman of the National Great Hural.

27/4   The date of the first session of the National Great Hural is announced by the President within 30 days after the elections. Further sessions are decided upon and announced by the Chairman of the National Great Hural.

27/5   In the event of the President's declaration of a state of emergency or a state of war, an emergency session of the National Great Hural is convened within 72 hours without prior notice.

27/6   If not otherwise provided for by the Constitution and other laws, the presence of the majority of members of the National Great Hural is required for the session to be valid and decisions are taken by the majority of the members present and voting.

28/1   The National Great Hural has standing committees to deal with appropriate fields and directions of its activities.

28/2   The National Great Hural defines the powers, organization and activities of the standing committees.

29/1   The members of the National Great Hural receive remuneration from the national budget during their term of office. Members of the Mongolian Great Hural may not concurrently engage in other work or occupy another post not related to their duties as defined by law.

29/2   The immunity of members of the National Great Hural is protected by law.

29/3   If a member of the National Great Hural is accused of a crime, a session of the National Great Hural considers the matter and decides whether or not to suspend him. If the member's alleged offence is proven by a court, the National Great Hural revokes his membership.

II. The President of Mongolia

30/1   The President of Mongolia is the head of state and symbol of the Mongolian people's unity.

30/2   The President is elected for a four-year term from among indigenous citizens of Mongolia who have reached the age of 45 and have resided in the homeland continuously for at least the last five years.

31/1   The election of the President is conducted in two stages.

31/2   Each of the parties which have won seats in the National Great Hural individually or collectively nominates one person for President.

31/3   Citizens of Mongolia having the right to vote participate in primary elections by universal, free and direct suffrage and by secret ballot for presidential candidates.

31/4   The National Great Hural considers the candidate who has received the majority of votes cast by voters participating in the presidential primary elections to have been elected President and adopts a law recognizing the powers of the President.

31/5   If none of the presidential candidates wins a majority, the two candidates who have received the largest number of votes cast by voters participating in the elections submit themselves to election for a second time. The candidate who receives the majority of votes in the second ballot is considered by the National Great Hural to have been elected President and it adopts a law recognizing his powers.

31/6   If neither of the presidential candidates obtains a majority in the second ballot new elections are held.

31/7   The President may be re-elected only once.

31/8   The President may not be the Prime Minister, a member of the National Great Hural or the Government and may not concurrently engage in other work or occupy another post not related to his duties as defined by law. If the President holds another office or post he is relieved of it from the date on which he takes the oath.

32/1   The powers of the President begin with the oath and end when the oath is taken by the newly elected President.

32/2   Within 30 days after his election the President takes the following oath before the National Great Hural: "I swear that I will guard and defend the independence and sovereignty of Mongolia and the freedom and national unity of the people and that I will uphold and observe the Constitution and faithfully perform the duties of President."

33/1   The following basic powers are vested in the President:

   1) exercising the right of veto on all or part of laws and other decisions adopted by the National Great Hural. The laws or decisions remain in force if a two-thirds majority of members of the National Great Hural present and voting reject the President's veto;

   2) proposing to the National Great Hural the candidate for Prime Minister in consultation with the majority party in the National Great Hural or, if none of the parties obtains a majority, in consultation with the parties which have won seats, as well as proposing dismissal of the Government;

   3) directing the Government on matters within his own powers. If the President issues a decree to that effect it comes into force on being signed by the Prime Minister;

   4) representing the nation as plenipotentiary in foreign relations and with the consent of the National Great Hural concluding international treaties in Mongolia's name;

   5) with the consent of the National Great Hural appointing and

recalling heads of plenipotentiary representations of Mongolia in foreign nations;

6) receiving letters of credence or recall of heads of plenipotentiary representations of foreign nations in Mongolia;

7) conferring national honors and senior military ranks and awarding orders and medals;

8) granting pardon;

9) deciding matters relating to granting and withdrawing Mongolian citizenship and granting the right of asylum;

10) heading the Mongolian National Security Council;

11) declaring general or partial mobilization;

12) declaring a state of emergency or state of war in all or part of the nation's territory as well as issuing ordinances on the beginning of military operations in an emergency as described in paragraphs 2 and 3 of Article 25 of the Constitution when the National Great Hural is in recess and delay is impossible. Within seven days the President's decree on a state of emergency or state of war is considered by the National Great Hural which approves or rejects it. If the National Great Hural takes no decision on the matter the decree becomes invalid.

33/2 The President is commander-in-chief of the Mongolian armed forces.

33/3 The President may send messages to the National Great Hural or to the people, and he may at his own discretion attend sessions of the National Great Hural and provide information about the country's important domestic and foreign affairs and submit proposals.

33/4 Other specific powers may be vested in the President only by law.

34/1 The President within his powers issues decrees compatible with the law.

34/2 If a decree of the President is incompatible with the law the President himself or the National Great Hural invalidates it.

35/1 The President is responsible to the National Great Hural for his work.

35/2 If the President breaks his oath, violates the Constitution or exceeds his powers, proceeding from the findings of the Constitutional Court he may be dismissed by an absolute majority of votes of all members at a session of the National Great Hural held to discuss the matter.

36/1 The President's person, residence and means of transport are inviolable.

36/2 The President's dignity and immunity are protected by law.

37/1 In the temporary absence of the President his powers are exercised by the Chairman of the National Great Hural.

37/2   In the event of the resignation, death or voluntary retirement of the President his powers are exercised by the Chairman of the National Great Hural pending the swearing in of the newly elected President. In such a case the National Great Hural declares presidential elections and holds them within four months.

37/3   The procedure for the exercise of presidential duties by the Chairman of the National Great Hural is defined by law.

III. The Mongolian Government

38/1   The Mongolian Government is the highest executive body of the state.

38/2   In keeping with its duty to implement state laws and direct economic, social and cultural organizations the Government exercises the following basic powers:

1) organizing and supervising nationwide implementation of the Constitution and other laws;

2) working out an integrated scientific and technological policy and guidelines for national socio-economic development, drawing up the national budget, credit and fiscal plans, submitting them to the National Great Hural and implementing the decisions taken;

3) drawing up and implementing comprehensive measures regarding sector, intersector and regional development issues;

4) taking measures for the protection of the environment and the rational use and conservation of natural resources;

5) guiding the central organizations of state administration and directing the activities of local administrative organizations;

6) undertaking measures for strengthening national defense capacity and ensuring national security;

7) taking measures for the protection of human rights and freedoms, enforcing public order and fighting crime;

8) implementing the state's foreign policy;

9) with approval and subsequent ratification by the National Great Hural, concluding and implementing international treaties as well as concluding or denouncing inter-governmental treaties.

38/3   The regulations governing the specific powers, organization and activities of the Government are defined by law.

39/1   The Government comprises the Prime Minister and members.

39/2   The Mongolian Prime Minister submits his proposals on Government structure, composition or changes to the National Great Hural in consultation with the President.

39/3   The National Great Hural considers the Government members proposed by the Prime Minister one by one and decides on their appointment.

40/1 The Government's term of office is four years.

40/2 The Government's term of office begins on the day of the appointment of the Prime Minister by the National Great Hural and ends on the appointment of the new Prime Minister.

41/1 The Prime Minister is accountable to the National Great Hural for guiding the work of the Government and implementing state laws.

41/2 The Government is accountable for its activities to the National Great Hural.

42 The immunity of the person of the Prime Minister and members of the Government is protected by law.

43/1 The Prime Minister may submit his resignation to the National Great Hural before his term of office expires if he considers the Government unable to exercise its powers.

43/2 If the Prime Minister resigns or half the members of the Government resign at the same time, the whole Government resigns.

43/3 The National Great Hural, having taken the initiative to dismiss the Government, or on receiving the President's proposal or the Prime Minister's resignation, considers and decides on the Government's resignation within 15 days.

43/4 If not less than a quarter of the members of the National Great Hural formally propose the Government's resignation the National Great Hural decides on it.

44 If the Government submits a draft resolution requesting a vote of confidence, the National Great Hural decides on it according to the procedure prescribed in paragraph 3 of Article 43.

45/1 In conformity with laws and regulations the Government issues resolutions and ordinances signed by the Prime Minister and the minister concerned.

45/2 If the resolutions and ordinances are incompatible with the laws and regulations the Government itself or the National Great Hural invalidates them.

46/1 Ministries and other state institutions of Mongolia are organized in accordance with the law.

46/2 State employees of Mongolia are Mongolian citizens, strictly observe the Constitution and other laws and in order to serve their people work dutifully in the interests of the state.

46/3 The working conditions and remuneration of state employees are determined by law.

IV. The Judiciary

47/1 In Mongolia the power of the judiciary is vested in the courts alone.

47/2 The unlawful organization of a court and the exercise of judicial power by any other organization is prohibited whatever the circumstances.

47/3   Courts are organized only in accordance with the Constitution and other laws.

48/1   The basic judicial system consists of the National Supreme Court, courts of the provinces and capital, urban and rural district and interdistrict courts, and criminal, civil, administrative and other courts. The activities and judgements of special courts are under the supervision of the Supreme Court alone.

48/2   The organization of the courts and the legal status of their activities are defined by law.

48/3   The courts are financed from the national budget. The state ensures the economic means for the courts' activities.

49/1   The judiciary is independent and strictly guided by the law.

49/2   The President, Prime Minister, members of the National Great Hural or Government, officials of the state, political parties or other public organizations and citizens whoever they are may not interfere or intervene in the judges' exercise of their duties.

49/3   The function of the General Council of Courts is to ensure the integrity of the judges and independence of the courts.

49/4   Without interfering in the activities of the courts or judges the General Council of Courts deals with such matters as nominating judges, protecting their interests and ensuring the necessary conditions for the independence of the courts.

49/5   The organization and activities of the General Council of Courts are defined by law.

50/1   The Supreme Court of Mongolia is the supreme judicial organization and exercises the following powers:
1) reviewing and judging criminal cases and legal disputes assigned to it as a court of first instance by law;
2) examining decisions of courts of lower instance through appeal and review;
3) examining and judging matters relating to the protection of the law and human rights and freedoms embodied therein that have been passed to it by the Constitutional Court and the National Procurator General;
4) issuing official interpretations for correct application of all other laws except the Constitution;
5) making judgements on all other matters assigned by law.

50/2   Judgements of the National Supreme Court are the final decisions of the judiciary and are binding on all courts and other parties. If the National Supreme Court's judgement is incompatible with the law, the National Supreme Court itself invalidates it. If the

National Supreme Court's interpretation is incompatible with the law, the law takes precedence.

50/3 The National Supreme Court and other courts have no right to apply laws which are unconstitutional or have not been published officially.

51/1 The National Supreme Court comprises a Chief Justice and judges.

51/2 The President appoints the judges of the National Supreme Court presented to the National Great Hural by the General Council of Courts, and judges of other courts proposed by the General Council of Courts. The President appoints the Chief Justice proposed from among its members by the National Supreme Court for a term of six years.

51/3 Judges of the National Supreme Court must be Mongolian citizens, aged at least 35 with a higher education in law and not less than ten years' experience in legal practice, and judges of other courts must be Mongolian citizens, aged at least 25 with a higher education in law and at least three years' experience in legal practice.

51/4 The judge of a court of any instance may not be discharged except when relieved or dismissed on grounds provided for by the Constitution or court judgements in force or relieved at his own request.

52/1 Courts of all instances consider and judge cases and disputes on the basis of the principle of collectivity.

52/2 In bringing a collective judgement on cases and disputes courts of first instance allow citizens' representatives to participate in the proceedings according to the procedures prescribed by the law.

52/3 Judgements may be made by judges alone in certain cases specifically provided for by law.

53/1 Court proceedings are conducted in the Mongolian language.

53/2 Persons who do not know the Mongolian language are to be acquainted with all the documents of the case through an interpreter and are entitled to use their native language in court proceedings.

54 Court proceedings are open to the public except in cases specifically prescribed by law.

55/1 The accused has the right to defend himself.

55/2 In keeping with this right, the accused is to be given legal assistance at his own request or according to law.

56/1 Procurators supervise the registration of cases, their investigation and punishment and participate in court proceedings on behalf of the state.

56/2 The National Procurator General and his deputies are appointed by the President with the consent of the National Great Hural for a term of six years.

56/3 The legal basis of the system, organization and activities of the Mongolian National Procurator's organisation is defined by law.

CHAPTER FOUR

Mongolia's Territorial Administrative Units and Their Government

57/1 Mongolia's territory is divided administratively into provinces and the capital; the provinces are divided into rural districts and the rural districts into neighborhoods; the capital is divided into urban districts and the urban districts into wards.

57/2 The legal status of towns and settlements situated within territorial administrative units is defined by law.

57/3 The revision of territorial administrative units is decided by the National Great Hural on the basis of proposals from the local assembly and citizens, taking into account the structure of the economy and location of the population.

58/1 The provinces, capital and rural and urban districts are territorial administrative socio-economic complexes with their own functions and self-government as prescribed by law.

58/2 Definition of the boundaries of provinces, the capital and rural and urban districts is proposed by the Government and approved by the National Great Hural.

59/1 The government of Mongolian territorial administrative units is organized on the basis of the principle of local self-government combined with state government.

59/2 The body of local self-government in a province, the capital or a rural or urban district is the assembly of citizens' representatives of the territory, in a neighborhood or ward a general meeting of citizens, and between sessions of the assembly its presidium.

59/3 The assembly of representatives of a province or the capital is elected for a term of four years. The number of representatives comprising such an assembly or that of a rural or urban district and the procedure for their election are determined by law.

60/1 State government on the territory of a province, the capital, a rural or urban district, neighborhood or ward is exercised by the governor of the province, capital, rural or urban district, neighborhood or ward.

60/2 Candidates for the post of governor are nominated by the assembly of the province, capital, rural or urban district, neighborhood or ward; the governor of a province or of the capital is nominated by the Prime Minister, the governor of a rural or urban district by the governor of the province or the capital, and the governor of a neighborhood or ward by the governor of the rural or urban district respectively, for a four-year term.

60/3   If candidates are rejected by the Prime Minister or a governor of higher instance, new nominations are made in the manner described in the previous paragraph and pending the new nominations the previously appointed governor continues to exercise his powers.

61/1   While taking measures to carry out the decisions of his assembly, as a representative of the state a governor is accountable to the Government or the governor of higher instance for ensuring on his territory the observance of national laws and implementation of decisions of the Government and the administration of higher instance.

61/2   A governor has the right to veto a decision of the assembly of his province, the capital, rural or urban district, neighborhood or ward.

61/3   If the majority of representatives in an assembly rejects the veto, the governor may submit his resignation to the Prime Minister or to the governor of higher instance should he consider himself unable to implement the decision concerned.

61/4   The office of the governor of a province, the capital, rural or urban district is the seal office (secretariat). The Government determines its structure and staff individually or to a common standard.

62/1   A local self-government organization, besides taking independent decisions about matters concerning the socio-economic life of the province, capital, rural or urban district, neighborhood or ward, organizes the population's participation in the solution of problems of national scale or of higher units.

62/2   An organization of higher instance may not take decisions on matters within the jurisdiction of a local self-government organization. A local self-government organization takes decisions independently on specific matters relating to its territory in conformity with the Constitution unless otherwise provided for by laws and decisions of the respective higher state organization.

62/3   If the National Great Hural and the Government consider it necessary they may transfer some matters within their powers to the assembly or governor of a province or the capital for solution.

63/1   The assembly of a province, the capital, a rural or urban district, neighborhood or ward adopts resolutions within its competence and the governor issues ordinances.

63/2   An assembly's resolutions and a governor's ordinances must be in conformity with the law, presidential decrees and the decisions of the Government and organizations of higher instance and are binding within their territories.

63/3   Territorial administrative units, their powers, organization and activities are determined by law.

CHAPTER FIVE

The Constitutional Court of Mongolia

64/1   The Constitutional Court of Mongolia is the organization empowered to supervise implementation of the Constitution, make judgement on violation of its provisions and solve disputes, and it guarantees the strict observance of the Constitution.

64/2   The Constitutional Court and its members are guided by the Constitution alone in carrying out their duties and are independent of all organizations, officials and other persons.

64/3   The independence of the members of the Constitutional Court is protected by the Constitution and other laws.

65/1   The Constitutional Court consists of nine members. Three of them are nominated by the National Great Hural, three by the President and three by the National Supreme Court, and the National Great Hural appoints them for a six-year term.

65/2   Members of the Constitutional Court must be Mongolian citizens, at least 40 years old, with high legal and political qualifications.

65/3   The Chairman of the Constitutional Court is elected from among the nine members by a majority vote for a three-year term. He may be re-elected only once.

65/4   The Chairman of the Constitutional Court or a member who breaks the law may be withdrawn by the National Great Hural on the basis of a judgement of the Constitutional Court and the opinion of the organization which nominated him.

65/5   The President, members of the National Great Hural, the Prime Minister, members of the Government and the Chief Justice of the National Supreme Court may not be members of the Constitutional Court.

66/1   The Constitutional Court reviews and makes judgements on disputes arising from violations of the Constitution on the basis of petitions of citizens, on its own initiative, or at the request of the National Great Hural, the President, the Prime Minister, the National Supreme Court or the National Procurator General.

66/2   In accordance with paragraph 1 of this Article, the Constitutional Court makes and submits judgement to the National Great Hural on the following disputes:

     1) conformity with the Constitution of the laws, decrees, other decisions of the National Great Hural and President, as well as Government decisions and Mongolia's international treaties;

2) conformity with the Constitution of popular referendums and decisions of the central electoral organization on the election of the National Great Hural, its members and the President;

3) violation of the Constitution by the President, Chairman of the National Great Hural or its members, the Prime Minister, members of the Government, the Chief Justice of the National Supreme Court and the National Procurator General;

4) grounds for the dismissal of the President, Chairman of the National Great Hural, Prime Minister or the recall of National Great Hural members.

66/3   If a judgement submitted in accordance with clauses 1 or 2 of paragraph 2 of this Article is unacceptable to the National Great Hural, the Constitutional Court reexamines it and takes a final decision.

66/4   If the Constitutional Court decides that a law or decree or other decision of the National Great Hural or the President, a decision of the Government or an international treaty of Mongolia is unconstitutional, the said law, decree, ratification or decision is invalid.

67   Judgements of the Constitutional Court enter into force immediately.

CHAPTER SIX

Additions and Amendments to the Constitution of Mongolia

68/1   Organizations and officials entitled to initiate a law may propose additions or amendments to the Constitution and submit their proposals to the Constitutional Court or the National Great Hural.

68/2   A popular referendum may be held on additions or amendments to the Constitution on the proposal of not less than two-thirds of the members of the National Great Hural. The referendum is to be held in accordance with clause 16, paragraph 1, Article 25 of the Constitution.

69/1   An addition or amendment to the Constitution is adopted by not less than three-quarters of the votes of the National Great Hural members.

69/2   If after second consideration in the National Great Hural an addition or amendment to the Constitution does not receive three-quarters of the votes the draft may not be considered again until a new National Great Hural elected at regular elections begins work.

69/3   The National Great Hural may not make additions or amendments to the Constitution within six months of the next regular elections.

292 • Appendix Four

69/4   An addition or amendment when adopted has the same force as the Constitution.
70/1   Laws, decrees and other decisions of state organizations and the activities of all public organizations and citizens must be in full conformity with the Constitution.
70/2   The Constitution of Mongolia comes into force throughout the country from 12 o'clock on 12th February 1992, that is, from the horse hour, new ninth day of the lucky fine yellow horse, first spring month of the black tiger, water monkey year of the 17th 60-year cycle.

Know it and observe it!
The People's Great Hural of the Mongolian People's Republic
11:35 on January 13, 1992, Ulan Bator

Appendix 5
Mongolian Law on Foreign Investment

CHAPTER ONE
General Provisions

Article 1: Purpose of the law
The purpose of this law is to stimulate and promote foreign investment in Mongolia, protect the rights and assets of investors, and regulate the associated operations of business units with foreign investment.

Article 2: Legislation on foreign investment
1. Legislation on foreign investment comprises the Constitution, this law and other regulations and acts adopted in conformity with them.
2. If an international treaty to which Mongolia is a signatory provides other than this law, the international treaty prevails.

Article 3: Definitions of the law
1. "Foreign investment" means the investment of assets or intellectual property by a foreign investor in Mongolia by establishing a business unit on the territory of Mongolia or operating jointly with a Mongolian business unit.
2. "Foreign investor" means a foreign legal entity or individual (that is, a foreign citizen or stateless person not permanently resident in Mongolia, or a citizen of Mongolia permanently resident abroad) making an investment in Mongolia.
3. "Mongolian investor" means a Mongolian legal entity or individual (that is, a Mongolian citizen or a foreign citizen or stateless person permanently resident in Mongolia) who is making an investment.

Article 4: The range of foreign investment
1. Except where prohibited by Mongolian legislation, foreign investment may be in any area of production or services.
2. Except where prohibited by Mongolian legislation, foreign investment may be in any part of Mongolian territory.

Article 5: The forms of foreign investment
The foreign investor may invest as follows:
1) freely convertible currency, or revenue in tögrög from investment;
2) movable or immovable property with associated property rights;
3) intellectual or industrial property rights.

Article 6: Outline of implementation of foreign investment
Foreign investment in Mongolia may take the following forms:
1) the foreign investor simply establishes his business unit or branch and sets it to work;
2) the foreign investor establishes a joint business unit with a Mongolian investor;
3) the foreign investor invests directly with freely convertible currency or revenue in tögrög from his investments by buying stocks, shares or other securities of this country's business units, including stocks, shares or other securities of business units sold in accordance with the Mongolian Law on Privatization with investment vouchers.
4) by obtaining the right to exploit or process natural resources in accordance with regulations and contracts.

Article 7: Buying shares and other securities
A foreign investor may buy shares or other securities of business units engaging in operations on the territory of Mongolia in accordance with Mongolian legislation.

CHAPTER TWO

Protection of Foreign Investment

Article 8: Legal guarantees of foreign investment
1. Foreign investment is guaranteed legal protection on the territory of Mongolia by the Constitution, this law, and other legislative acts adopted in conformity with them, and by international treaties to which Mongolia is a signatory.
2. The nationalization or illegal seizure of foreign investment on the territory of Mongolia is prohibited.
3. Foreign investors' assets may be seized only for reasons of public interest and in accordance with legislation on the basis of non-discrimination and on condition of full compensation.
4. If not otherwise specified in international treaties to which Mongolia is a signatory, the scale of compensation for assets seized is defined according to their value at the time of seizure or of the seizure becoming known. Compensation is carried out without hindrance.
5. In the event of a state of emergency or war in Mongolia, the losses

suffered by foreign investors are decided on the same terms as those of Mongolian investors.

Article 9: Conditions for foreign investment
Mongolia provides for foreign investors no less advantageous and satisfactory conditions for ownership, operation, management and disposal of their investments than those provided for Mongolian investors.

Article 10: Rights and duties of foreign investors
1. Foreign investors have the following rights:
1) to own, operate and dispose of their assets, including the right to remit abroad assets invested in forming the capital of the business unit with foreign investment;
2) to manage or participate in the management of business units with foreign investment;
3) to transfer rights and duties to other parties in accordance with legislation;
4) to remit abroad without hindrance the following revenue or profit:
a) their private shareholder's revenue or profits from share allotment;
b) revenue from the sale of assets or securities, the transfer of assets to others or received from the business unit or allotted on liquidation;
5) other rights in accordance with legislation.
2. The following are foreign investors' duties:
1) to observe and carry out Mongolian legislation;
2) to carry out the duties envisaged by contracts and legislation concerning the establishment of business units with foreign investment;
3) to implement measures for the protection and restoration of the natural environment;
4) to respect the Mongolian people's national customs.

CHAPTER THREE

Operations of Business Units with Foreign Investment

Article 11: Business units with foreign investment
1. Business units with foreign investment are business units, established in accordance with Mongolian legislation, not less than 20 per cent of whose assets are foreign investors' private capital.
2. From the day of their registration business units with foreign investment become Mongolian legal entities and their operations are subject to Mongolian legislation.

Article 12: Approval of establishment of business units with foreign investment

1. Approval of the establishment of business units with foreign investment is granted by the state's central administrative organization implementing foreign investment policy (further "Ministry of Trade and Industry") on application from the investors.
2. Foreign investors' applications cover the following:
    1) the foreign investor's name, address and nationality;
    2) the type and scale of the investment;
    3) the form of business unit;
    4) the basic branch invested in and the production or service managed;
    5) the stages and duration of investment.
3. The application is to be accompanied by the following documents:
    1) copies of the investor's c.v. and certificate of incorporation;
    2) the contract for establishing the business unit with foreign investment;
    3) the rules of the business unit with foreign investment;
    4) the marketing, management, technological and other agreements in connection with the foreign investment;
    5) the technical and financial estimates;
    6) the servicing bank's confirmation of the investor's good standing;
    7) if a special permit is required for the purposes of engaging in production or services relating to the exploration, prospecting or processing of natural resources or the use of land, a permit from the competent Mongolian organization.
4. The application and attached documents shall be decided by the Minister of Trade and Industry within 60 days of receipt on the basis of specialist organizations' evaluation regarding the following:
    1) compliance with legislation;
    2) environmental impact;
    3) compatibility with health requirements;
    4) technological standard.
5. The evaluation under paragraph 4, sub-paragraphs 2 and 3 of this article is to be in accordance with international and Mongolian standards.
6. The evaluation under paragraph 4, sub-paragraph 4 is to be in accordance with the Mongolian government's enactments.
7. Approval for the establishment of business units with foreign investment is certified by the Ministry of Trade and Industry.
8. If the operations of business units with foreign investment are not compatible with Mongolian legislation or environmental, health or technological requirements as indicated in the evaluation, approval is refused.
9. The investor's application form and the certificate of approval for the establishment of business units with foreign investment indicated in this article shall be adopted by the Minister of Trade and Industry.

10. If additions or amendments are made to the capital, contract or rules of business units with foreign investment, the Ministry of Trade and Industry is to be informed within 30 days. The ruling on these additions or amendments is decided by the Ministry of Trade and Industry in accordance with this article within 30 days.

Article 13: Valuation of assets and intellectual property
1. The investors' contract values the assets or intellectual property invested by the investors in the capital of the business units with foreign investment in freely convertible currency or in tögrög on the basis of equality.
2. The tögrög is related to freely convertible currency at the rates fixed from time to time by Mongolbank.

Article 14: The right of the Ministry of Trade and Industry to implement foreign investment policy
The Ministry of Trade and Industry has the following rights concerning foreign investment policy:
   1) to supervise the drawing up of legislation on foreign investment;
   2) in accordance with Article 12, paragraph 4 of this law to organize evaluation work by specialist organizations in matters concerning the establishment of business units with foreign investment;
   3) to announce and examine tenders for foreign investment;
   4) to select foreign investors' projects proposed for implementation;
   5) to approve or reject the establishment of business units with foreign investment;
   6) to stop the operations of business units with foreign investment temporarily or permanently;
   7) other rights in accordance with legislation.

Article 15: Registration of business units with foreign investment
1. On the basis of a certificate provided by the Ministry of Trade and Industry, the National Taxation Directorate places business units with foreign investment on the register and makes this public.
2. On the basis of approval by the Ministry of Trade and Industry, additions or amendments to the assets, contract or rules of business units with foreign investment are registered by the National Taxation Directorate.

Article 16: Stopping the operations of business units with foreign investment
1. The operations of business units with foreign investment may be stopped on the basis of the Mongolian Law on Business Units.
2. If it is confirmed that the operations of a business unit with foreign

investment are not in accordance with any point of Article 12, paragraph 4 of this law, the Ministry of Trade and Industry may stop the operations of the given unit temporarily or permanently.

Article 17: Liquidation of business units with foreign investment
1. Business units with foreign investment which cease operations are to inform the Ministry of Trade and Industry within 14 days.
2. Business units with foreign investment being liquidated confirm to the Ministry of Trade Industry that the final accounts have been closed and that environmental restoration for which they are responsible according to Mongolian legislation has been implemented.
3. On the liquidation of a business unit with foreign investment the approval of the Ministry of Trade and Industry to establish the given unit becomes invalid and the National Taxation Directorate is informed of this.
4. On the basis of notification from the business unit with foreign investment, in accordance with paragraph 3 of this article the National Taxation Directorate removes it from the register and makes this public.
5. After the closure of the final accounts of the business unit with foreign investment, in accordance with Article 10, paragraph 4 of this law the foreign investor may remit his revenue and profits abroad.

Article 18: Tax liability
1. Business units with foreign investment are liable to pay tax under the Mongolian Taxation Law.
2. Foreign investors and business units with foreign investment, in accordance with the Mongolian Taxation Law and legislation, are granted extra favorable conditions under this law and legislation and other acts in conformity with it.

Article 19: Exemption from customs duty and sales tax
1. From the day the establishment of the business unit with foreign investment is approved by the Ministry of Trade and Industry, the technological equipment becoming part of the capital of the business unit with foreign investment is exempt from customs duty and sales tax.
2. From the day of the business unit's registration at the National Taxation Directorate the raw materials, components, equipment and spares intended for production in the business unit with foreign investment except for internal trade and catering are exempt from customs duty for five years.

Article 20: Reduction of corporation tax
1. Corporation tax reductions take effect from the day production begins in business units with foreign investment in the following branches:

1) heat and power stations and transmission lines, motor, rail and air transport, utilities construction and basic telecommunications networks are exempt for ten years with a 50 percent reduction for the next 5 years;

2) extraction and processing of minerals (other than precious metals), raw materials, oil and solid fuels, and the metallurgical, chemical, ferrous, engineering and electronics branches are exempt for five years with a 50 percent reduction for the next five years;

2. Business units with foreign investment organized in branches other than those in paragraph 1 which export more than 50 percent of their production are exempt from corporation tax for three years with a 50 percent reduction for the next three years.

3. Corporation tax may also be reduced for business units with foreign investment established in branches not included in this article. This is decided in each case by the National Great Hural on Government notification.

4. If the foreign investor reinvests his share of income in the given business unit, the unit's taxable income is reduced by this amount.

5. If the operations of a business unit with foreign investment under paragraph 1 of this article embrace several branches, the unit's reduction in corporation tax is determined according to the basic branch of operation.

6. Business units with foreign investment established through the purchase of stocks, shares or other securities of business units sold for investment vouchers in accordance with the Mongolian Law on Privatization do not qualify for reduction or exemption in accordance with paragraphs 1 and 2 of this article.

Article 21: Use of land by business units with foreign investment
1. Business units with foreign investment lease land in accordance with Mongolian land legislation and payment regulations.

2. The lease reflects the conditions of land use, duration, measures for environmental protection and restoration, payment for land use and the two parties' responsibilities.

3. Business units with foreign investment conclude land leases according to the following rules:

1. When a wholly-owned business unit is established in Mongolia by a foreign investor, a lease on state-owned land is drawn up between the Mongolian owner and the foreign investor, with the approval of the appropriate citizens' delegates' assembly and presidium;

2. When a Mongolian investor is participating in the business unit with foreign investment, a lease on state-owned land is drawn up between the Mongolian owner and the given business unit's management, with the approval of the appropriate citizens' delegates' assembly and presidium;

3. When a Mongolian investor is participating in the business unit with foreign investment, a lease on privately-owned land is drawn up between the given landowner and the management of the business unit with foreign investment, with the approval of the competent state organization.

4. In accordance with paragraph 3, sections 2 and 3, on the formation of the management of a business unit with foreign investment responsibilities arising from the lease on land are shared proportionately by the Mongolian investor and the foreign investor investing in the business unit.

5. The basic term of a land lease for a business unit with foreign investment is defined by the assigned period of operations of the given business unit. The initial term of a land lease is not greater than 60 years. The term of a contract for land use may be extended once for up to another 40 years under the original conditions of the lease.

6. If a business unit with foreign investment is liquidated within the term of the land lease, the term of the lease expires simultaneously.

7. Land may be exchanged or repossessed on the basis of the nation's special need. A decision on this can be taken only by the Government. Foreign investors are compensated for any losses without hindrance. Compensation is determined on the basis of valuation at the time of land exchange or repossession.

8. If the land use is incompatible with the population's health, environmental or national security conditions, the lease is annulled.

Article 22: Finance, credit, accounting, audit
1. The finance, tax, credit and hard currency operations of business units with foreign investment are carried out in accordance with Mongolian legislation.
2. The accounts and balances of business units with foreign investment are to be kept in accordance with Mongolian legislation.
3. The accounts and transactions of business units with foreign investment are audited in accordance with Mongolian legislation by national financial auditing organizations or independent qualified inspectors. In view of this requirement, independent foreign auditing organizations may be included.

Article 23: Insurance
Business units with foreign investment may be insured by Mongolian insurance organizations in accordance with Mongolian legislation.

Article 24: Labor and social security conditions
1. Business units with foreign investment primarily employ Mongolian citizens. When narrow speciality and high skill are required in the work,

people from abroad may be employed. This matter is decided in consultation with the Ministry of Demography and Labor.

2. Labor and social security conditions for Mongolian citizens working in business units with foreign investment are governed by Mongolian legislation on labor and social insurance.

3. People coming from abroad to work in business units with foreign investment have the right after taxation of their remuneration and other income to remit their remaining income abroad in accordance with Mongolian legislation.

CHAPTER FOUR

Other Articles

Article 25: Resolution of disputes

Disputes arising between foreign investors and Mongolian investors, likewise between foreign investors and Mongolian legal entities and individuals, in connection with foreign investment or the operations of business units with foreign investment, are resolved without discrimination by the Mongolian courts unless otherwise provided for in international treaties to which Mongolia is a signatory or the contract between the parties.

Article 26: The law's entry into force

This law comes into force on July 1, 1993.

Appendix 6
Administrative Gazetteer

List of *sum* (s—rural districts), former *horoo* (h—urban settlements) and towns (t) including provincial centers with their location within their provinces *(aymag)*, and (in capital letters) provinces (p) with the location within the country (n = north, s = south, e = east, w = west, c = center).

Rural district centers used to be given names different from the rural districts, but the *Ündesniy Atlas* (National Atlas 1990) indicated that this practice had lapsed. Urban districts (d) of Ulan Bator formed in 1992, including towns like Baganuur separate from the capital's territory, have been included. Darhan, Erdenet, and Choyr (qq.v.), previously "towns under national jurisdiction," were made the centers of three new provinces and the *horoo* were absorbed into neighboring *sum* in May 1994.

Key to some common words in place-names: bulag = spring; dalay = lake; davaa = pass; els = sands; gol = river; höndiy = valley; hudag = well; mörön = river; nuruu = mountains; nuur = lake; orgil = peak; ovoo = cairn and, by extension, mountain; tal = steppe; uul = mountain.

Adaatsag	s	Dundgov'	n
Alag-Erdene	s	Hövsgöl	c
Aldarhaan	s	Zavhan	s
Altanbulag	s	Selenge	n
Altanbulag	s	Töv	c
Altanshiree	s	Dornogov'	n
Altantsögts	s	Bayan-Ölgiy	n
Altay	s	Bayan-Ölgiy	w
Altay	s	Hovd	s
Altay	t	Gov'-Altay	(center) s
Arbulag	s	Hövsgöl	c
Argalant	s	Töv	c
ARHANGAY	p	Mongolia	(center Tsetserleg t) c
Arhust	h	Töv	s-e
Ar Saynshand	h	Dornogov'	(Saynshand s) c
Arvayheer	s	Övörhangay	c
Arvayheer	t	Övörhangay	(center) c
Asgat	s	Sühbaatar	c

Asgat	s	Zavhan	n
Ayrag	s	Dornogov'	n
Baatsagaan	s	Bayanhongor	e
Bagahangay	d	Töv (Ulan Bator)	(Bayan s) s-e
Baganuur	d	Töv (Ulan Bator)	(Bayandelger s) e
Baruunbayan-Ulaan	s	Övörhangay	s-w
Baruunbüren	s	Selenge	w
Baruunturuun	s	Uvs	n-e
Baruun-Urt	s	Sühbaatar	c
Baruun-Urt	t	Sühbaatar	(center) c
Batnorov	s	Hentiy	e
Bat-Ölziy	s	Övörhangay	n
Batshireet	s	Hentiy	n
Batsümber	s	Töv	n
Battsengel	s	Arhangay	c
Bayan	s	Töv	s-e
Bayan-Adraga	s	Hentiy	n-e
Bayan-Agt	s	Bulgan	w
Bayanbulag	s	Bayanhongor	n
Bayanchandman'	s	Töv	c
Bayandalay	s	Ömnögov'	s-w
Bayandelger	s	Sühbaatar	s-w
Bayandelger	s	Töv	e
Bayandun	s	Dornod	n
Bayangol	d	Ulan Bator	w suburb
Bayangol	s	Övörhangay	e
Bayangol	s	Selenge	s
Bayangov'	s	Bayanhongor	s
Bayanhangay	s	Töv	w
Bayanhayrhan	s	Zavhan	n
BAYANHONGOR	p	Mongolia	(center Bayanhongor t) s-w
Bayanhongor	s	Bayanhongor	n-e
Bayanhongor	t	Bayanhongor	(center) n-e
Bayanhutag	s	Hentiy	s
Bayanjargalan	s	Dundgov'	e
Bayanjargalan	s	Töv	s-e
Bayanlig	s	Bayanhongor	e
Bayanmönh	s	Hentiy	s
Bayannuur	s	Bayan-Ölgiy	e
Bayannuur	s	Bulgan	s-e
Bayan-Ovoo	s	Bayanhongor	c
Bayan-Ovoo	s	Hentiy	s-e
Bayan-Ovoo	s	Ömnögov'	s-e

BAYAN-ÖLGIY	p	Mongolia	(center Ölgiy t) w
Bayan-Öndör	s	Bayanhongor	s
Bayan-Öndör	s	Orhon	c
Bayan-Öndör	s	Övörhangay	n-e
Bayan-Önjüül	s	Töv	s
Bayantal	s	Gov'-Sümber	c
Bayanteeg	h	Övörhangay	(Nariynteel s) w
Bayantes	s	Zavhan	n
Bayantsagaan	s	Bayanhongor	c
Bayantsagaan	s	Töv	s
Bayantsogt	s	Töv	c
Bayantümen	s	Dornod	c
Bayan-Uul	s	Dornod	n-w
Bayan-Uul	s	Gov'-Altay	n
Bayanzürh	s	Hövsgöl	w
Bayanzürh-Uul	d	Ulan Bator	e suburb
Berh	t	Hentiy	(Batnorov s) c
Biger	s	Gov'-Altay	e
Binder	s	Hentiy	n
Bogd	s	Bayanhongor	e
Bogd	s	Övörhangay	s
Bornuur	s	Töv	n
Bor-Öndör	t	Hentiy	(Darhan s) s
Böhmörön	s	Uvs	w
Bömbögör	s	Bayanhongor	c
Bugat	s	Bayan-Ölgiy	c
Bugat	s	Bulgan	c
Bugat	s	Gov'-Altay	s-w
BULGAN	p	Mongolia	(center Bulgan t) n
Bulgan	s	Arhangay	s
Bulgan	s	Bayan-Ölgiy	s
Bulgan	s	Bulgan	c
Bulgan	s	Dornod	w
Bulgan	s	Hovd	s-w
Bulgan	s	Ömnögov'	n-w
Bulgan	t	Bulgan	(center) c
Bulnay	s	Zavhan	n-e
Buutsagaan	s	Bayanhongor	w
Buyant	s	Bayan-Ölgiy	c
Buyant	s	Hovd	c
Bürd	s	Övörhangay	n
Büreghangay	s	Bulgan	s
Büren	s	Töv	s-w
Bürenhaan	h	Hentiy	(Norovlin s) n-e

Bürentogtoh	s	Hövsgöl	s
Bürentsogt	h	Sühbaatar	(Mönhhaan s) n
Chandman'	s	Gov'-Altay	e
Chandman'	s	Hovd	n-e
Chandman'-Öndör	s	Hövsgöl	n
Chingeltey-Uul	d	Ulan Bator	n suburb
Choybalsan	s	Dornod	c
Choybalsan	t	Dornod	(center) c
Choyr	t	Gov'-Sümber	(center) c
Chuluunhoroot	s	Dornod	n
Chuluut	s	Arhangay	w
Dadal	s	Hentiy	n
Dalanjargalan	s	Dornogov'	n
Dalanzadgad	s	Ömnögov'	c
Dalanzadgad	t	Ömnögov'	(center) c
Darhan	s	Darhan-Uul	c
Darhan	s	Hentiy	s
Darhan	t	Darhan-Uul	(center) c
DARHAN-UUL	p	Mongolia	(center Darhan t) n
Darvi	s	Gov'-Altay	w
Darvi	s	Hovd	e
Dar'ganga	s	Sühbaatar	s
Dashbalbar	s	Dornod	n
Dashinchilen	s	Bulgan	s
Davst	s	Uvs	n
Delger	s	Gov'-Altay	n-e
Delgereh	s	Dornogov'	n
Delgerhaan	s	Hentiy	s-w
Delgerhaan	s	Töv	s-w
Delgerhangay	s	Dundgov'	w
Delgertsogt	s	Dundgov'	n
Delüün	s	Bayan-Ölgiy	s
Deren	s	Dundgov'	n
DORNOD	p	Mongolia	(center Choybalsan t) e
DORNOGOV'	p	Mongolia	(center Saynshand t) s-e
Dölgöön	h	Övörhangay	(Züünbayan-Ulaan s) c
Dörgön	s	Hovd	n
Dörvöljin	s	Zavhan	w
Dulaanhaan	h	Selenge	(Shaamar s) n
DUNDGOV'	p	Mongolia	(center Mandalgov') c

Duut	s	Hovd	w	
Erdene	s	Dorngov'	s-e	
Erdene	s	Gov'-Altay	s-e	
Erdene	s	Töv	c	
Erdenebulgan	s	Arhangay	c	
Erdenebulgan	s	Hövsgöl	n-e	
Erdenebüren	s	Hovd	n	
Erdenedalay	s	Dundgov'	w	
Erdenehayrhan	s	Zavhan	c	
Erdenemandal	s	Arhangay	n	
Erdenesant	s	Töv	s-w	
Erdenet	t	Orhon	(center), c	
Erdenetsagaan	s	Sühbaatar	e	
Erdenetsogt	s	Bayanhongor	n-e	
Ereen	h	Dornod	(Bayan-Uul s) n-w	
Gachuurt	d	Töv (Ulan Bator)	n-e of Ulan Bator	
Galshar	s	Hentiy	s	
Galt	s	Hövsgöl	s	
Galuut	s	Bayanhongor	n	
GOV'-ALTAY	p	Mongolia	(center Altay t) s-w	
GOV'-SÜMBER	p	Mongolia	(center Choyr t) c	
Gov'-Ugtaal	s	Dundgov'	n-e	
Guchin-Us	s	Övörhangay	c	
Gurvanbayan	s	Hentiy	c	
Gurvanbulag	s	Bayanhongor	n	
Gurvanbulag	s	Bulgan	s	
Gurvansayhan	s	Dundgov'	c	
Gurvantes	s	Ömnögov'	w	
Gurvanzagal	s	Dornod	n	
Guulin	h	Gov'-Altay	(Delger s) n-e	
Hajuu-Ulaan	h	Dornogov'	(Ihhet s) n	
Halhgol	s	Dornod	s-e	
Haliun	s	Gov'-Altay	c	
Halzan	s	Sühbaatar	c	
Hanbogd	s	Ömnögov'	c	
Hangal	s	Bulgan	e	
Hangay	s	Arhangay	n	
Hanh	h	Hövsgöl	(Hanh s) n	
Hanh	s	Hövsgöl	n	
Hanhongor	s	Ömnögov'	c	
Han-Uul	d	Ulan Bator	s suburb	
Harhiraa	s	Uvs	c	
Harhorin	t	Övörhangay	n	
Hashaat	s	Arhangay	e	

Hatanbulag	s	Dornogov'	s
Hatgal	t	Hövsgöl	(Alag Erdene s) c
Hayrhan	s	Arhangay	n
Hayrhandulaan	s	Övörhangay	w
HENTIY	p	Mongolia	(center Öndörhaan t) n-e
Herlen	t	Hentiy	(Darhan s) s
Herlen	s	Hentiy	c
Herlenbayan-Ulaan	h	Hentiy	(Delgerhaan s) s-w
Hishig-Öndör	s	Bulgan	c
Hongor	s	Darhan-Uul	c
Hotont	s	Arhangay	e
HOVD	p	Mongolia	(center Hovd t) w
Hovd	s	Hovd	n
Hovd	s	Uvs	s-w
Hovd	t	Hovd	(center) n
Höhmor't	s	Gov'-Altay	n
Hölönbuyr	s	Dornod	w
Hötöl	t	Selenge	(Sayhan s) c
HÖVSGÖL	p	Mongolia	(center Mörön t) n-w
Hövsgöl	s	Dornogov'	s
Hujirt	s	Övörhangay	n
Huld	s	Dundgov'	s
Hushaat	s	Selenge	w
Hutag-Öndör	s	Bulgan	n
Hüder	s	Selenge	n-e
Hüreemaral	s	Bayanhongor	n-w
Hürmen	s	Ömnögov'	s
Hyalganat	h	Bulgan	(Hangal s) n-w
Hyargas	s	Uvs	c
Ider	s	Zavhan	c
Ihhet	s	Dornogov'	n
Ihtamir	s	Arhangay	w
Ih-Uul	h	Övörhangay	(Arvayheer s) c
Ih-Uul	s	Zavhan	e
Ih-Uul	s	Hövsgöl	s-e
Jargalan	s	Gov'-Altay	n
Jargalant	d	Töv (Ulan Bator)	n of Ulan Bator
Jargalant	s	Arhangay	n
Jargalant	s	Bayanhongor	n
Jargalant	s	Hovd	c
Jargalant	s	Hövsgöl	s
Jargalant	s	Orhon	c

Jargalant	s	Töv	n
Jargalthaan	s	Hentiy	w
Javhlant	s	Selenge	c
Jinst	s	Bayanhongor	c
Luus	s	Dundgov'	c
Lün	s	Töv	w
Malchin	s	Uvs	c
Mandah	s	Dornogov'	w
Mandal	s	Selenge	s
Mandalgov'	s	Dundgov'	c
Mandalgov'	t	Dundgov'	(center) c
Mandal-Ovoo	s	Ömnögov'	n
Manhan	s	Hovd	c
Manlay	s	Ömnögov'	n-e
Matad	s	Dornod	s
Mogod	s	Bulgan	s
Möngönmor't	s	Töv	n-e
Mönhhaan	s	Sühbaatar	n
Mönhhayrhan	s	Hovd	w
Mörön	s	Hentiy	c
Mörön	s	Hövsgöl	c
Mörön	t	Hövsgöl	(center) c
Möst	s	Hovd	s
Myangad	s	Hovd	n
Nalayh	d	Töv (Ulan Bator)	s-e of Ulan Bator
Naran	s	Sühbaatar	s
Naranbulag	s	Uvs	c
Nariynteel	s	Övörhangay	w
Nogoonnuur	s	Bayan-Ölgiy	n
Nomgon	s	Ömnögov'	s
Norovlin	s	Hentiy	n-e
Noyon	s	Ömnögov'	w
Nömrög	s	Zavhan	n
Ongon	s	Sühbaatar	s
ORHON	p	Mongolia	(center Erdenet t) n
Orhon	s	Bulgan	c
Orhon	s	Darhan-Uul	c
Orhon	s	Selenge	s-w
Orhontuul	s	Selenge	s-w
Otgon	s	Zavhan	s-e
Ögiynuur	s	Arhangay	e
Ölgiy	s	Bayan-Ölgiy	n
Ölgiy	s	Uvs	s
Ölgiy	t	Bayan-Ölgiy	(center) n

Ölziyt	s	Arhangay	e
Ölziyt	s	Bayanhongor	e
Ölziyt	h	Bulgan	(Orhon s) c
Ölziyt	s	Dundgov'	s
Ölziyt	s	Hentiy	c
Ölziyt	s	Övörhangay	c
Ömnödelger	s	Hentiy	n-w
ÖMNÖGOV'	p	Mongolia	(center Dalanzadgad t) s
Ömnögov'	s	Uvs	s-w
Öndörhaan	s	Hentiy	c
Öndörhaan	t	Hentiy	(center) c
Öndörhangay	s	Uvs	e
Öndörshil	s	Dundgov'	e
Öndörshireet	s	Töv	w
Öndör-Ulaan	s	Arhangay	n
Örgön	s	Dornogov'	e
ÖVÖRHANGAY	p	Mongolia	(center Arvayheer t) c
Rashaant	s	Bulgan	s
Rashaant	s	Hövsgöl	s-e
Renchinlhümbe	s	Hövsgöl	n
Sagil	s	Uvs	n
Sagsay	s	Bayan-Ölgiy	c
Salhit	h	Darhan-Uul	(Hongor s) c
Sant	s	Övörhangay	e
Sant	s	Selenge	w
Santmargats	s	Zavhan	w
Sayhan	s	Bulgan	w
Sayhan	s	Selenge	c
Sayhandulaan	s	Dornogov'	w
Sayhan-Ovoo	s	Dundgov'	w
Saynshand	s	Dornogov'	c
Saynshand	t	Dornogov'	(center) c
Sayntsagaan	s	Dundgov'	c
SELENGE	p	Mongolia	(center Sühbaatar t) n
Selenge	s	Bulgan	n
Sergelen	s	Dornod	c
Sergelen	s	Töv	c
Sevrey	s	Ömnögov'	w
Shaamar	s	Selenge	n
Sharga	s	Gov'-Altay	c
Sharyn Gol	s	Darhan-Uul	e

Sharyn Gol	t	Darhan-Uul	e	
Shilüüstey	s	Zavhan	s	
Shine-Ider	s	Hövsgöl	s	
Shinejinst	s	Bayanhongor	s	
Shiveegov'	s	Gov'-Sümber	c	
Songino	s	Zavhan	w	
Songino-Hayrhan	d	Ulan Bator	n-w suburb	
Sühbaatar	d	Ulan Bator	c district	
SÜHBAATAR	p	Mongolia	(center Baruun-Urt t) e	
Sühbaatar	s	Selenge	c	
Sühbaatar	s	Sühbaatar	n	
Sühbaatar	t	Selenge	(center) n	
Sümber	s	Dornod	(joined with Halhgol s 1994)	
Sümber	s	Gov'-Sümber	c	
Sümber	s	Töv	n	
Taragt	s	Övörhangay	c	
Tarialan	s	Hövsgöl	e	
Tarialan	s	Uvs	c	
Tariat	s	Arhangay	n	
Tayshir	s	Gov'-Altay	n	
Telmen	s	Zavhan	c	
Tes	s	Uvs	n	
Tes	s	Zavhan	n	
Teshig	s	Bulgan	n	
Tolbo	s	Bayan-Ölgiy	c	
Tonhil	s	Gov'-Altay	w	
Tosontsengel	t	Zavhan	(Bulnay s) n-e	
Tosontsengel	s	Hövsgöl	s-e	
Tögrög	s	Gov'-Altay	c	
Tögrög	s	Övörhangay	s-e	
Tömörbulag	s	Hövsgöl	s	
TÖV	p	Mongolia	(center Zuunmod t) c	
Tsagaanchuluut	s	Zavhan	s	
Tsagaandelger	s	Dundgov'	n-e	
Tsagaanhayrhan	s	Uvs	s-e	
Tsagaanhayrhan	s	Zavhan	s	
Tsagaannuur	h	Bayan-Ölgiy	(Nogoonnuur s) n	
Tsagaannuur	s	Hövsgöl	n	
Tsagaannuur	s	Selenge	n-w	
Tsagaan-Ovoo	s	Dornod	w	
Tsagaan-Uul	s	Hövsgöl	s-w	

Tsagaan-Üür	s	Hövsgöl	n-e
Tseel	s	Gov'-Altay	c
Tseel	s	Töv	n-w
Tsengel	s	Bayan-Ölgiy	w
Tsenher	s	Arhangay	s
Tsenhermandal	s	Hentiy	w
Tsetseg	s	Hovd	s-e
Tsetsen-Uul	s	Zavhan	w
Tsetserleg	s	Arhangay	n
Tsetserleg	s	Hövsgöl	s-w
Tsetserleg	t	Arhangay	(center) c
Tsogt	s	Gov'-Altay	s
Tsogt-Ovoo	s	Ömnögov'	n
Tsogttsetsiy	s	Ömnögov'	n
Tuul	d	Ulan Bator	s-w suburb
Tüdevtey	s	Zavhan	n
Tümentsogt	s	Sühbaatar	n
Tünel	s	Hövsgöl	c
Tünhel	h	Selenge	(Mandal s) s
Türgen	s	Uvs	w
Tüshig	s	Selenge	n
Tüvshinshiree	s	Sühbaatar	w
Tüvshrüüleh	s	Arhangay	s
Ugtaaltsaydam	s	Töv	n-w
ULAN BATOR			
(ULAANBAATAR)		Töv	(national capital) c
Ulaanbadrah	s	Dornogov'	s
Ulaangom	s	Uvs	n
Ulaangom	t	Uvs	(center) n
Ulaanhus	s	Bayan-Ölgiy	w
Ulaan-Uul	s	Hövsgöl	n-w
Uliastay	s	Zavhan	s
Uliastay	t	Zavhan	(center) s
Urgamal	s	Zavhan	w
Uulbayan	s	Sühbaatar	w
UVS	p	Mongolia	(center Ulaangom t) w
Uyanga	s	Övörhangay	n-w
Uyench	s	Hovd	s
Yaruu	s	Zavhan	c
Yöröö	h	Selenge	(Yöröö s) e
Yöröö	s	Selenge	e
Yösönbulag	s	Gov'-Altay	s
Zaamar	s	Töv	n-w

Zag	s	Bayanhongor	n	
Zamyn-Üüd	s	Dornogov'	s-e	
Zamyn-Üüd	t	Dornogov'	s-e	
ZAVHAN	p	Mongolia	(center Uliastay t) n-w	
Zavhan	s	Uvs	s	
Zavhanmandal	s	Zavhan	w	
Zereg	s	Hovd	c	
Zuunmod	s	Töv	c	
Zuunmod	t	Töv	(center) c	
Züünbayan	h	Dornogov'	(Saynshand s) c	
Züünbayan-Ulaan	s	Övörhangay	c	
Züünbüren	s	Selenge	n	
Züüngov'	s	Uvs	n	
Züünhangay	s	Uvs	e	
Züünharaa	t	Selenge	(center of Mandal s) s	
Züyl	s	Övörhangay	n	

Addenda

Inevitably there have been changes since the *Dictionary* was written that could not be recorded in the text, despite some updating a year ago. In particular, data on the national economy and membership of the various Great Hural standing committees have proved impossible to update in detail. The text records the formation of three new provinces based on the towns of Erdenet, Darhan and Choyr, but it has not been possible to amend the text everywhere accordingly, although a second map, of central Mongolia, shows their location.

Mongolia has been passing through a period of relative stability, with few leadership changes as of the end of September 1995, and the *Dictionary* should provide an appropriate background to the Mongolian general elections of June 1996. However, some developments in Mongolia in the 1994-1995 period are worth recording for their intrinsic interest and importance, and they are listed here.

AMBASSADORS. Nadmidiyn Bavuu (1943-   ) was appointed ambassador to Russia in August 1994. He graduated from the All-Union Foreign Trade Academy in Moscow. Bavuu served as deputy minister and first deputy minister of foreign trade 1980-1988, minister of foreign economic relations and supply 1988-1990, and minister of trade and cooperation April-September 1990. He was a member of the MPRP Central Committee (q.v.) April 1990-February 1991.

Dagvyn Tsahilgaan (1941-   ) was appointed ambassador to China in August 1994. He graduated from the Mongolian State University and the Higher Party School and Academy of Social Sciences of the CPSU Central Committee. Tsahilgaan became deputy head of the MPRP's agitprop department in 1982 and chairman of both the Mongolian Peace Committee and the Mongolian Federation of Peace and Friendship Organizations 1986-1989. He was head of the MPRP's ideology department June 1989-April 1990, a member of the MPRP Central Committee and deputy of the People's Great Hural (*see* Hural, Great) 1986-1990.

CLASSICAL SCRIPT. A resolution of the Mongolian Great Hural in July 1994 canceled earlier plans for the introduction of the Mongolian classical script (*see* Script, Classical) for official use in 1994. President P. Ochirbat (q.v.) tried unsuccessfully to veto the resolution. The MGH found that the plans were unworkable because of lack of preparation and popular support, but the teaching of classical Mongolian in schools was expanded.

ECONOMY. Production figures for 1994 included (metric tons): gold, 1.9; copper concentrate, 343,300; fluorite, 383,200; coal, 5,000,000; cereals, 330,700; and potatoes, 54,000. Livestock totalled 26,796,700 head. The trade surplus was $105,632,000. Aid pledges to Mongolia for 1994-1995 were worth $210,000,000 (1993-1994 $250,000,000). The tögrög (q.v.) was worth 460=$1 in September 1995.

FOREIGN RELATIONS. Friendly relations with Russia and China are Mongolia's foremost objective, according to the Mongolian Foreign Policy Concept published in July 1994 by the MGH. It listed its other objectives as friendly relations with the "third neighbor," that is, the USA, Japan, Germany, and other advanced countries, as well as stronger ties with the Asia-Pacific region, deeper cooperation with the UN and international financial institutions, broader contacts with Eastern European and CIS countries, and better relations with developing and non-aligned countries.

GREAT HURAL. The ten standing committees of the MGH were reduced to six in January 1995. The new chairmen were: Ayuurzanyn Bazarhüü (q.v.), budget, finance, money and market policy; Minjüüriyn Dalayhüü (q.v.), rural policy and the environment (including food and agriculture); Jügderiyn Delgertsetseg (q.v.), economic policy (including infrastructure); Bazaryn Demberel (q.v.), social policy (combining population, health, labor, social security, education, science and culture); Danzangiyn Lündeejantsan (q.v.), state organization (combining security, foreign policy, internal affairs, local government and administration); and Tserenhüügiyn Sharavdorj (q.v.), law.

Following the death of MGH member G. Zuunay (q.v.), in October 1994 the MGH approved the membership of Vandangiyn Alzahgüy (1952-   ) to represent constituency 5. Alzahgüy was born in Sharga district of Gov'-Altay Province (q.v.) and received his basic and higher degrees from Moscow Higher School of the Komsomol (1976-1981 and 1987-1990). He was first secretary of Gov'-Altay MRYL Committee 1981-1987 and chairman of Gov'-Altay MPRP Committee (qq.v.) from February 1991.

LOCAL GOVERNMENT. Harhorin, Herlen (Bor-Öndör), Hötöl and Berh were accorded the status of provincial-level towns in July 1994. Dornod Province's Sümber district amalgamated with the province's Halh Gol district the same month. Ulan Bator's urban districts or *düüreg* were reduced from twelve to nine in January 1995 on amalgamation of Gachuurt with Bayanzürh-Uul, Jargalant with Songino-Hayrhan, and Tuul with Han-Uul (qq.v.).

NATIONAL SECURITY. The Mongolian National Security Concept, published in July 1994 by the MGH, declared that Mongolia upholds international law, supports the UN, and accords top priority to protecting its vital interests and maintaining a balanced but not equidistant relationship with Russia and China. The National Security Council is chaired by the Mongolian President and has two members, the prime minister and chairman of the MGH, and a secretary (Jargalsayhany Enhsayhan).

NEW MINISTERS. Erdeniyn Byambajav (1939-) was appointed minister of finance in January 1995, following the resignation of Dalrayn Davaasambuu (q.v.). He had been Mongolian ambassador to Kazakhstan since May 1992. Byambajav graduated from the Higher School of Finance and Economics in Irkutsk and served as first deputy minister, then from June 1979 as minister of finance until he was replaced in 1984 by Demchigjavyn Molomjamts, now director of Mongolbank (qq.v.). Chairman of the State Committee for Prices and Standards 1984-1988, Byambajav then became one of three first deputy chairmen of the new State Committee for Planning and the Economy until it was abolished in March 1990. He was a member of the MPRP Central Committee and deputy of the People's Great Hural 1981-1990, but is not a member of the Mongolian Great Hural (qq.v.).

Sanjbegziyn Tömör-Ochir (1950-) was appointed minister of science and education in May 1995, following the resignation of Nadmidiyn Ölziyhutag (q.v.). He had been director general of the ministry's vocational education department since October 1992. Tömör-Ochir graduated from Moscow State University in 1974 and taught mathematics at the State Higher Technical School 1974-1981. He was appointed director of studies at the Mongolian State University, then pro-rector 1981-1992. He is not a member of the Mongolian Great Hural (q.v.).

OTHER APPOINTMENTS. Dalhjavyn Sandag (1954-) was appointed head of the Mongolian Central Intelligence Directorate with the rank of major general in January 1994. Sandag trained at the Higher School of the USSR KGB and joined the Mongolian Ministry of Public Security. Later he entered the diplomatic service to Japan and the US. He also worked at the State Policy and Social Studies Center.

Janchiviyn Oyuungerel was appointed chairman of the board of directors of NIK Co., the Mongolian oil import concern, in August 1994. She remained director general, a post she had held since the formation of the Mongolian Oil Supply Co. in 1990 and its transformation into a "concern" in 1992. She had worked for the company since graduating from the Moscow V. Gubkin Higher School of the Oil, Chemical and Gas Industry.

Jigjidsürengiyn Yadamsüren (q.v.) was appointed chairman of the Mongolian Securities Committee on its formation in November 1994 to supervise share dealing.

Lhamsürengiyn Javzmaa (1945-   ) was appointed chairman of the State Auditing Committee on its establishment in June 1995. Trained as an agricultural economist, he had worked mostly in local government, including as deputy chairman of Ulan Bator People's Hural Executive Administration (see Hural, Great) and most recently governor of Bulgan Province (q.v.).

B. Bayarhüü replaced D. Sengee as director-general of the Mongol Gazryn Tos (q.v.) petroleum concern in July 1995. Bayarhüü was previously a geologist with the Ministry of Power, Geology and Mining.

PARTY DEVELOPMENTS. The Mongolian National Unity Party, chairman Namsrayn Nyam-Osor, was registered in August 1994. The Mongolian National Democratic Socialist Party, chairman G. Galma, was registered in April 1995. The Mongolian United Heritage (Conservative) Party (q.v.) elected Baasanjavyn Jamtsay its new chairman in February 1995. The Mongolian Workers' Party (registered in 1992), chairman H. Pürev, claimed a membership of 832 in June 1995.

About the Author

ALAN J. K. SANDERS (Fellow of the Institute of Linguists, London) is the Lecturer in Mongolian Studies at the School of Oriental and African Studies, University of London. Before he took up this appointment in 1991 he was the Editor of the *Summary of World Broadcasts* (Far East 1977-1981 and USSR 1981-1990), daily news digests published by the British Broadcasting Corporation's Monitoring Service. His first book, *The People's Republic of Mongolia: A General Reference Guide* (Oxford University Press, 1968), is a directory of institutions and personalities compiled from information published in the Mongolian press. It was followed by regular articles about Mongolia, supplemented by surveys of Soviet Central Asia, Siberia, and North Korea, for the Hong Kong *Far Eastern Economic Review* and a wide range of journals and yearbooks including *Asian Survey* and the *Annual Register*. His second book, *Mongolia: Politics, Economics and Society* (Marxist Regimes series, Pinter and Rienner, 1987), focuses on the formation and consolidation of communist power in Mongolia and analyzes its structures. Alan Sanders has visited Mongolia regularly, participating in the International Congresses of Mongolists and the Anglo-Mongolian Round Table Conferences. In 1992, he became a member of the Executive Committee of the International Association for Mongol Studies. He is a member of the Royal Society for Asian Affairs and the Royal Institute of International Affairs and has served as secretary and treasurer of the Anglo-Mongolian Society. His *Mongolian Phrasebook* was published by Lonely Planet in 1995.